Magical Girl Site

Magical Girl Site 6

Summary

Display Images

To unlock more of the mystery surrounding the Tempest, the girls needed to capture a Site Manager and question them... As Aya grew closer to her Magical Girl friends, her brother Kaname noticed the change in her mood. While keeping an eye on her, Kaname learned about Magical Girl Site and the wands.

Kaname used Anazawa Nijimi's crush on him against her to learn more information. He then stole Nijimi's wand and used it to control her.

Seeking to steal Aya and her friends' wands as well, Kaname raided the home of Ringa Sayuki. Using the power of Nijimi's wand, he subdued the Magical Girls and began to collect their wands.

When all hope appeared to be lost, Kiyoharu managed to overwrite Kaname's control over Nijimi. Nijimi then sacrificed herself in order to kill Kaname but ultimately failed to do so. As Kaname reached for Kosame's wand to heal himself, he was stopped by an unknown assailant, and then everyone lost consciousness.

The one who assailed Kaname was none other than Misumi Kiichiro. Under the orders of Site Manager Nana, he gathers and redistributes the wands of Magical Girls. Having taken a liking to Kaname, Misumi locked him up in the dungeon within the basement of his home, which also houses Misumi's huge collection of wands. Thus, Kaname's life of confinement began.

Then, in the wake of Anazawa Nijimi's death, someone appears while Aya is crying uncontrollably. Who has come to her in this time of weakness...?!

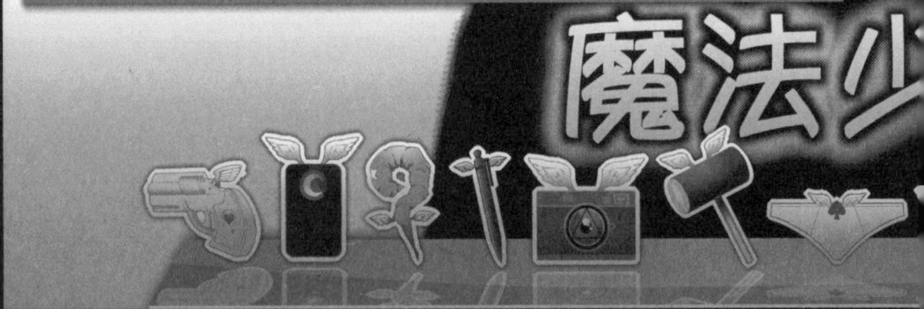
魔法少

SEVEN SEAS ENTERTAINMENT PRESENTS

MAGICAL GIRL SITE

story and art by KENTARO SATO

VOLUME 7

TRANSLATION
Wesley Bridges

ADAPTATION
Janet Houck

LETTERING AND LAYOUT
Meaghan Tucker

COVER DESIGN
Nicky Lim

PROOFREADER
Kurestin Armada

ASSISTANT EDITOR
Jenn Grunigen

PRODUCTION ASSISTANT
CK Russell

PRODUCTION MANAGER
Lissa Pattillo

EDITOR-IN-CHIEF
Adam Arnold

PUBLISHER
Jason DeAngelis

MAHO SYOJYO SITE Volume 7
© Kentaro Sato 2017
Originally published in Japan in 2017 by Akita Publishing Co., Ltd..
English translation rights arranged with Akita Publishing Co., Ltd. through
TOHAN CORPORATION, Tokyo.

Seven Seas books may be purchased in bulk for promotional, educational, or
business use. Please contact your local bookseller or the Macmillan Corporate
and Premium Sales Department at 1-800-221-7945, extension 5442, or by
e-mail at MacmillanSpecialMarkets@macmillan.com.

Seven Seas and the Seven Seas logo are trademarks of
Seven Seas Entertainment, LLC. All rights reserved.

ISBN: 978-1-626928-97-8

Printed in Canada

First Printing: September 2018

10 9 8 7 6 5 4 3 2 1

FOLLOW US ONLINE: *www.sevenseasentertainment.com*

READING DIRECTIONS

This book reads from *right to left*, Japanese style.
If this is your first time reading manga, you start
reading from the top right panel on each page and
take it from there. If you get lost, just follow the
numbered diagram here. It may seem backwards at
first, but you'll get the hang of it! Have fun!!

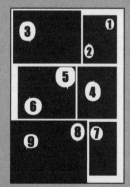

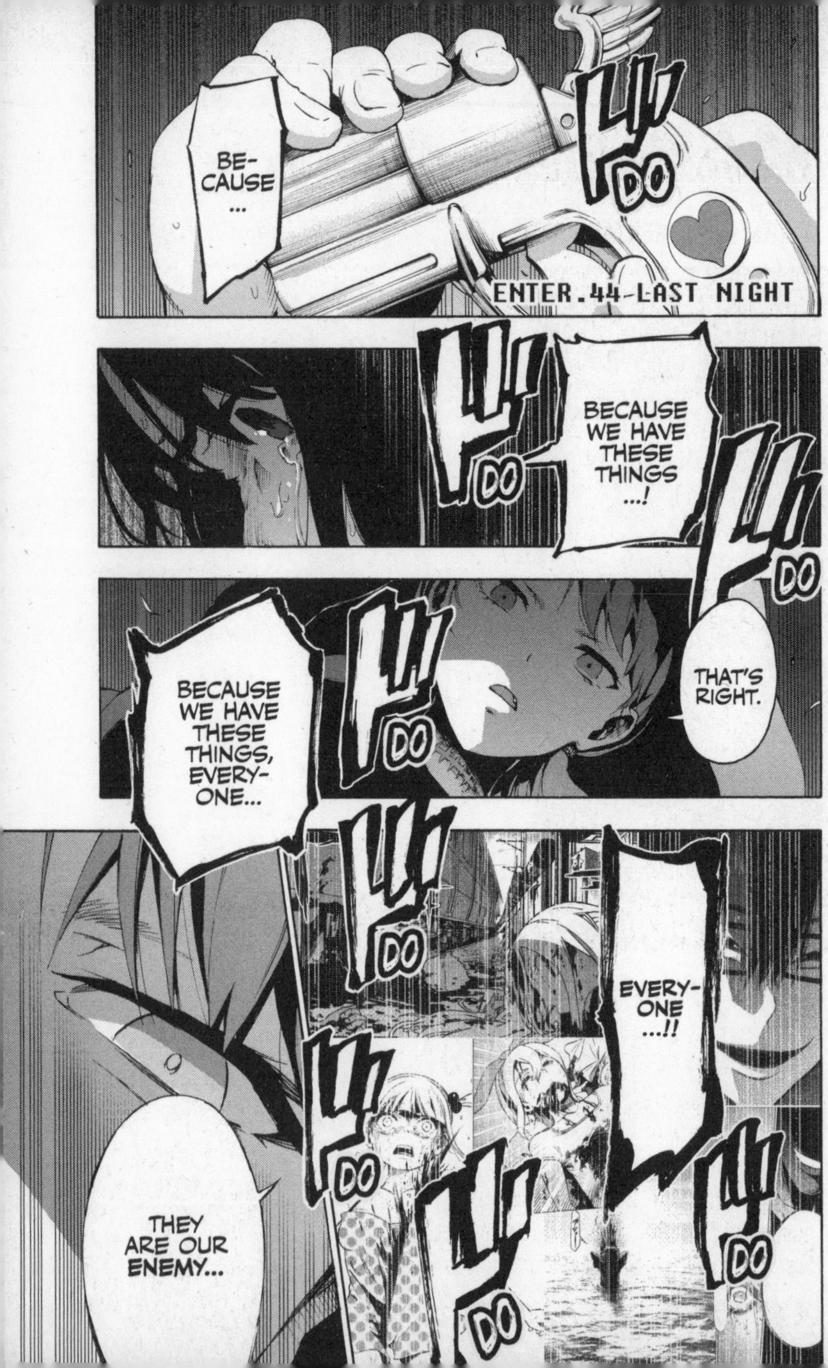
DO
BE-CAUSE ...
ENTER.44-LAST NIGHT
BECAUSE WE HAVE THESE THINGS ...!
DO
DO
THAT'S RIGHT.
DO
BECAUSE WE HAVE THESE THINGS, EVERY-ONE...
DO
EVERY-ONE ...!!
DO
DO
DO
THEY ARE OUR ENEMY...

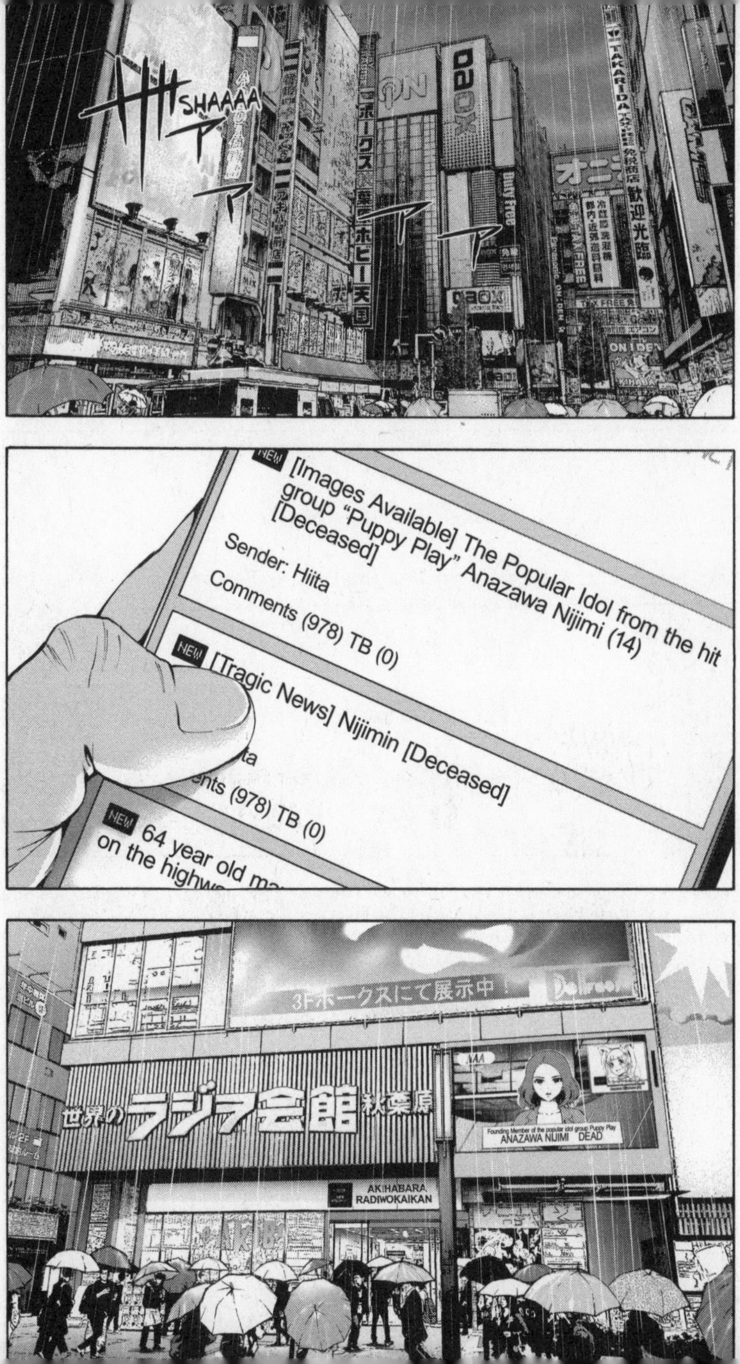
SHAAAA
TAKARIDA
TAX FREE
[Images Available] The Popular Idol from the hit group "Puppy Play" Anazawa Nijimi (14) [Deceased]
Sender: Hiita
Comments (978) TB (0)
[Tragic News] Nijimin [Deceased]
ta
ents (978) TB (0)
64 year old ma
on the highw
3Fホークスにて展示中！
世界のラジオ会館 秋葉原
AKIHABARA RADIWOKAIKAN
Founding Member of the popular idol group Puppy Play
ANAZAWA NIJIMI DEAD

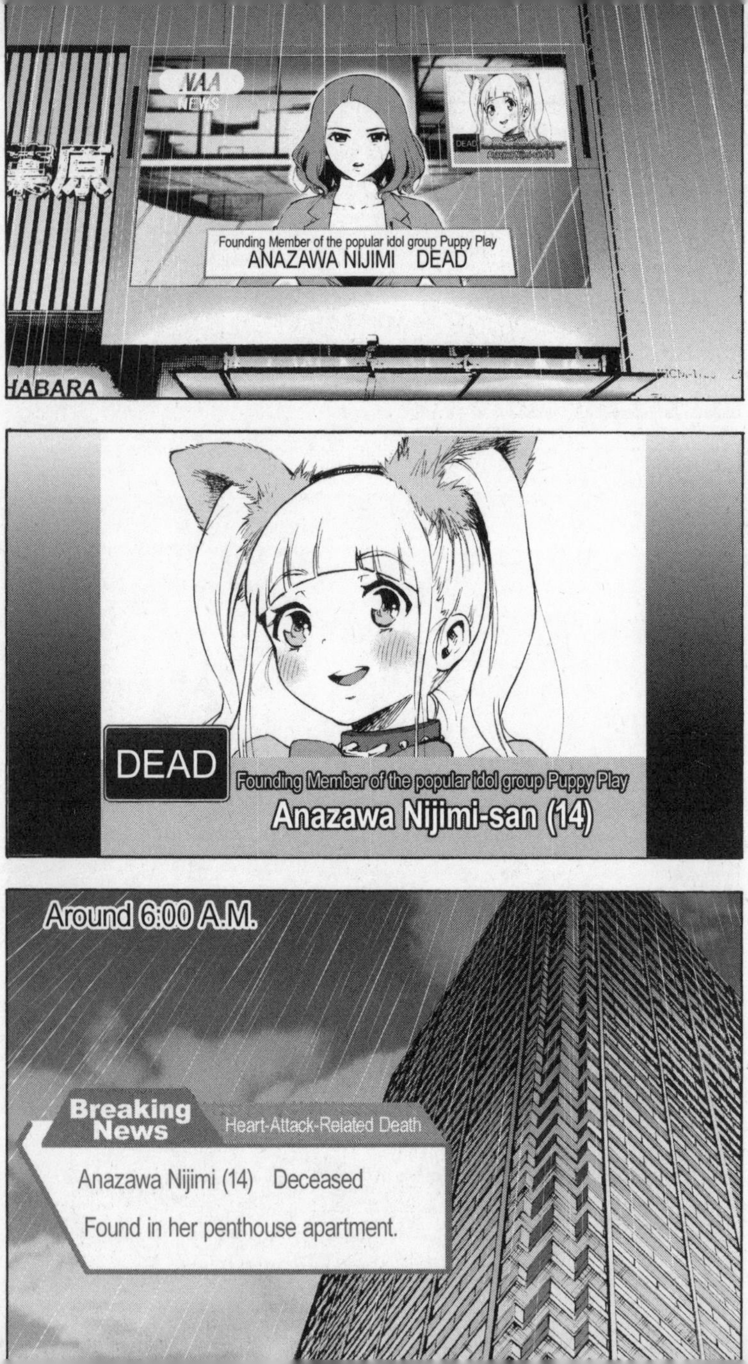
NAA
NEWS
Founding Member of the popular idol group Puppy Play
ANAZAWA NIJIMI DEAD
HABARA
DEAD
Founding Member of the popular idol group Puppy Play
Anazawa Nijimi-san (14)
Around 6:00 A.M.
Breaking News
Heart-Attack-Related Death
Anazawa Nijimi (14) Deceased
Found in her penthouse apartment.

SHAAAAA
アアアア

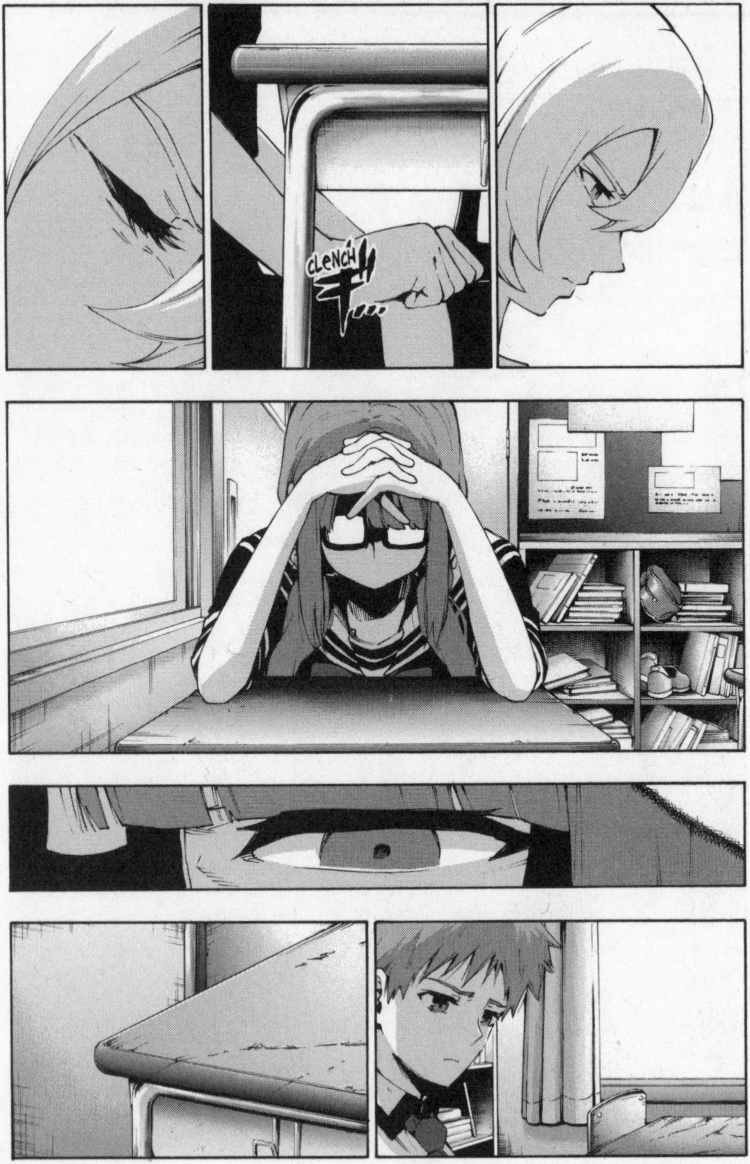
CLENCH

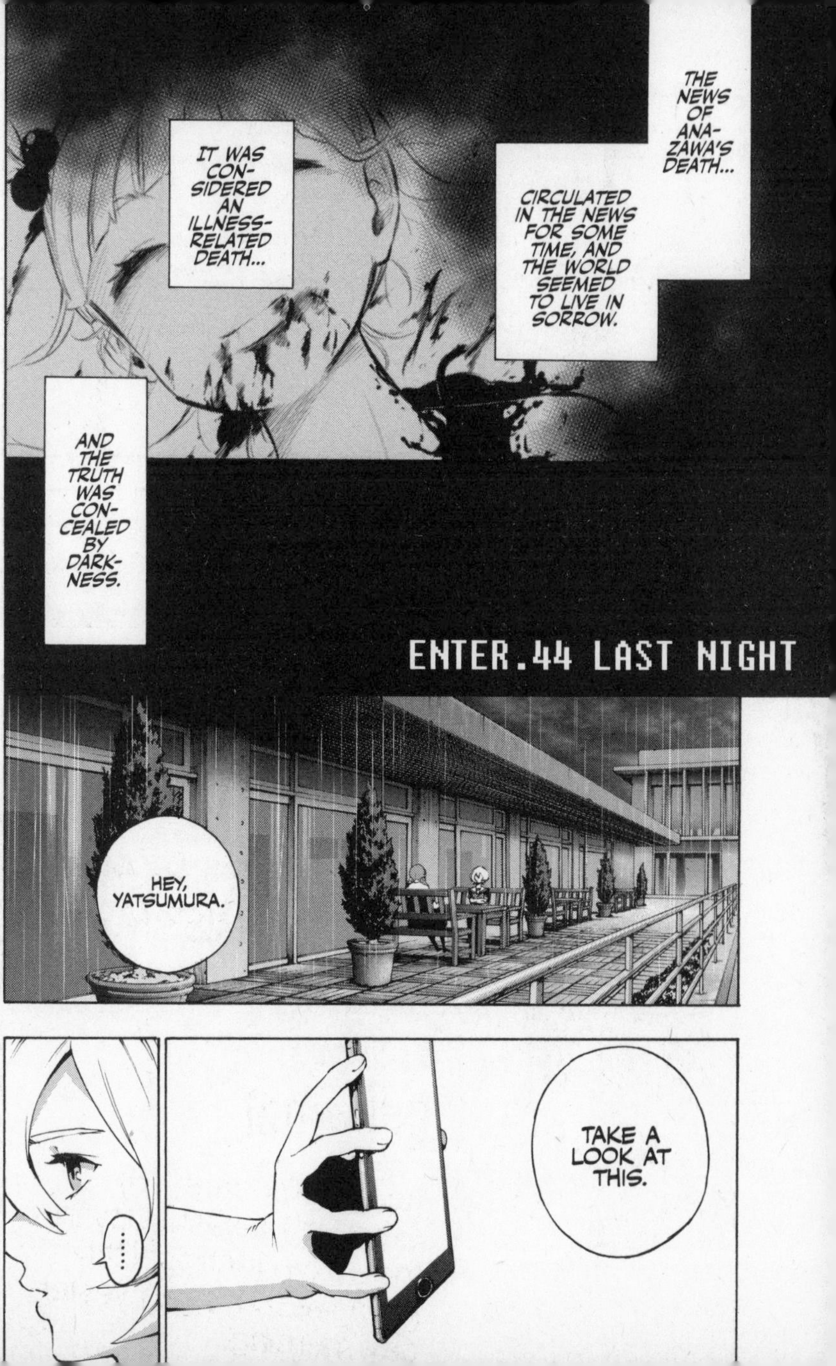
THE NEWS OF ANA-ZAWA'S DEATH...
CIRCULATED IN THE NEWS FOR SOME TIME, AND THE WORLD SEEMED TO LIVE IN SORROW.
IT WAS CON-SIDERED AN ILLNESS-RELATED DEATH...
AND THE TRUTH WAS CON-CEALED BY DARK-NESS.
ENTER.44 LAST NIGHT
HEY, YATSUMURA.
TAKE A LOOK AT THIS.
......

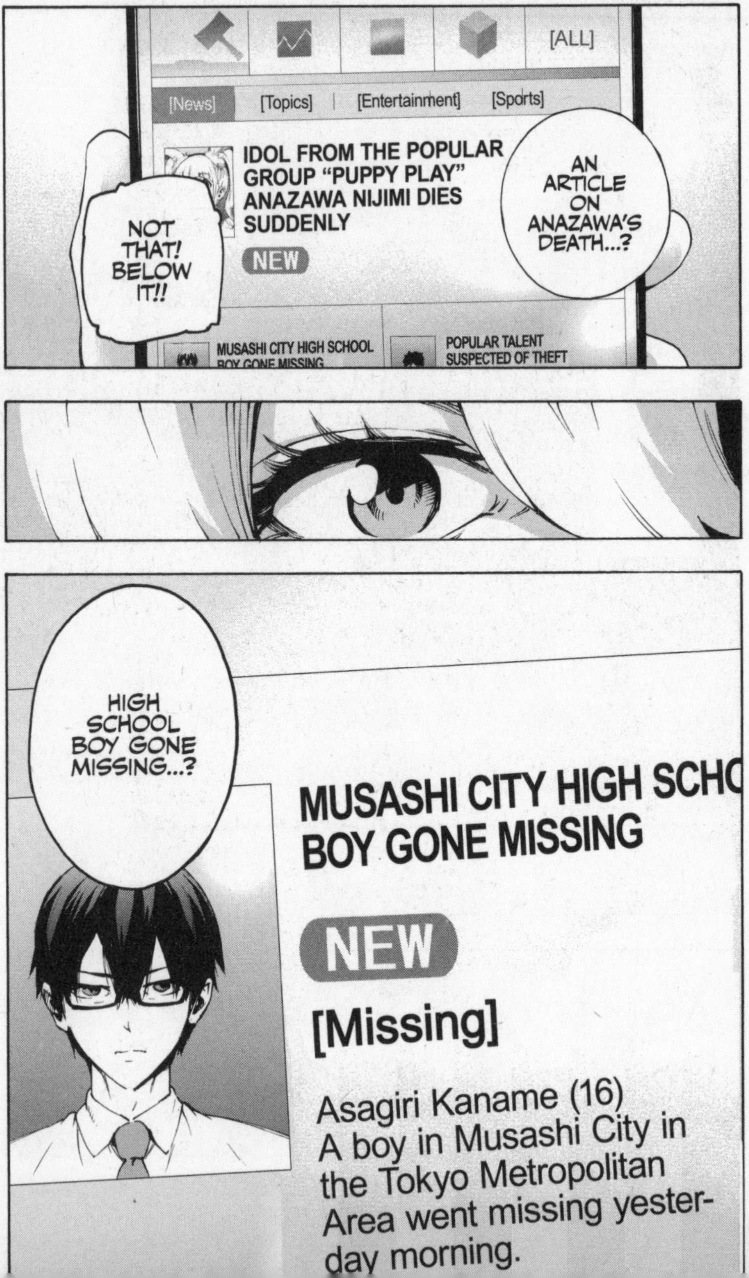
[ALL]
[News] [Topics] [Entertainment] [Sports]
IDOL FROM THE POPULAR GROUP "PUPPY PLAY" ANAZAWA NIJIMI DIES SUDDENLY
NEW
AN ARTICLE ON ANAZAWA'S DEATH...?
NOT THAT! BELOW IT!!
POPULAR TALENT SUSPECTED OF THEFT
MUSASHI CITY HIGH SCHOOL BOY GONE MISSING
HIGH SCHOOL BOY GONE MISSING...?
MUSASHI CITY HIGH SCHO
BOY GONE MISSING
NEW
[Missing]
Asagiri Kaname (16)
A boy in Musashi City in the Tokyo Metropolitan Area went missing yester-day morning.

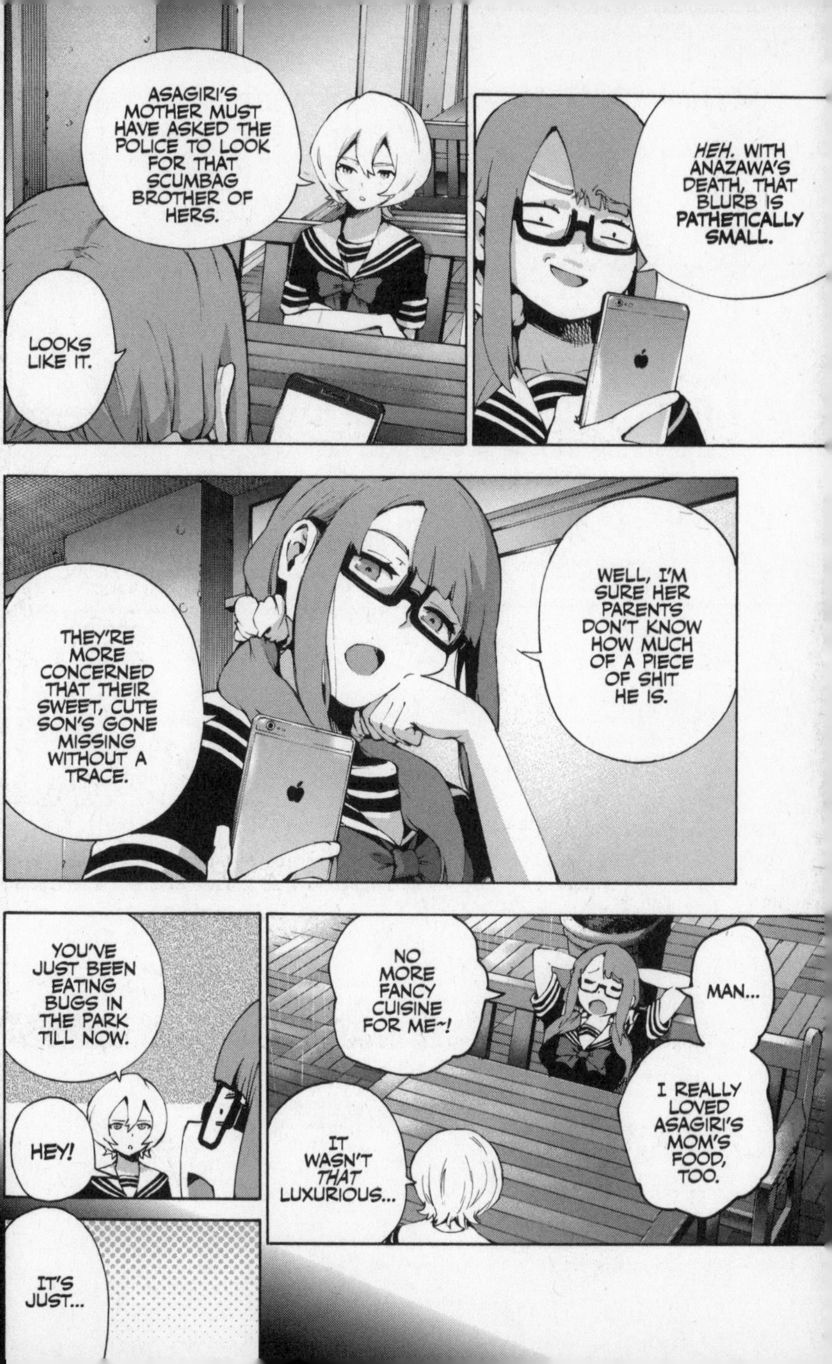
HEH. WITH ANAZAWA'S DEATH, THAT BLURB IS PATHETICALLY SMALL.
ASAGIRI'S MOTHER MUST HAVE ASKED THE POLICE TO LOOK FOR THAT SCUMBAG BROTHER OF HERS.
LOOKS LIKE IT.
WELL, I'M SURE HER PARENTS DON'T KNOW HOW MUCH OF A PIECE OF SHIT HE IS.
THEY'RE MORE CONCERNED THAT THEIR SWEET, CUTE SON'S GONE MISSING WITHOUT A TRACE.
MAN...
NO MORE FANCY CUISINE FOR ME~!
I REALLY LOVED ASAGIRI'S MOM'S FOOD, TOO.
IT WASN'T *THAT* LUXURIOUS...
YOU'VE JUST BEEN EATING BUGS IN THE PARK TILL NOW.
HEY!
IT'S JUST...

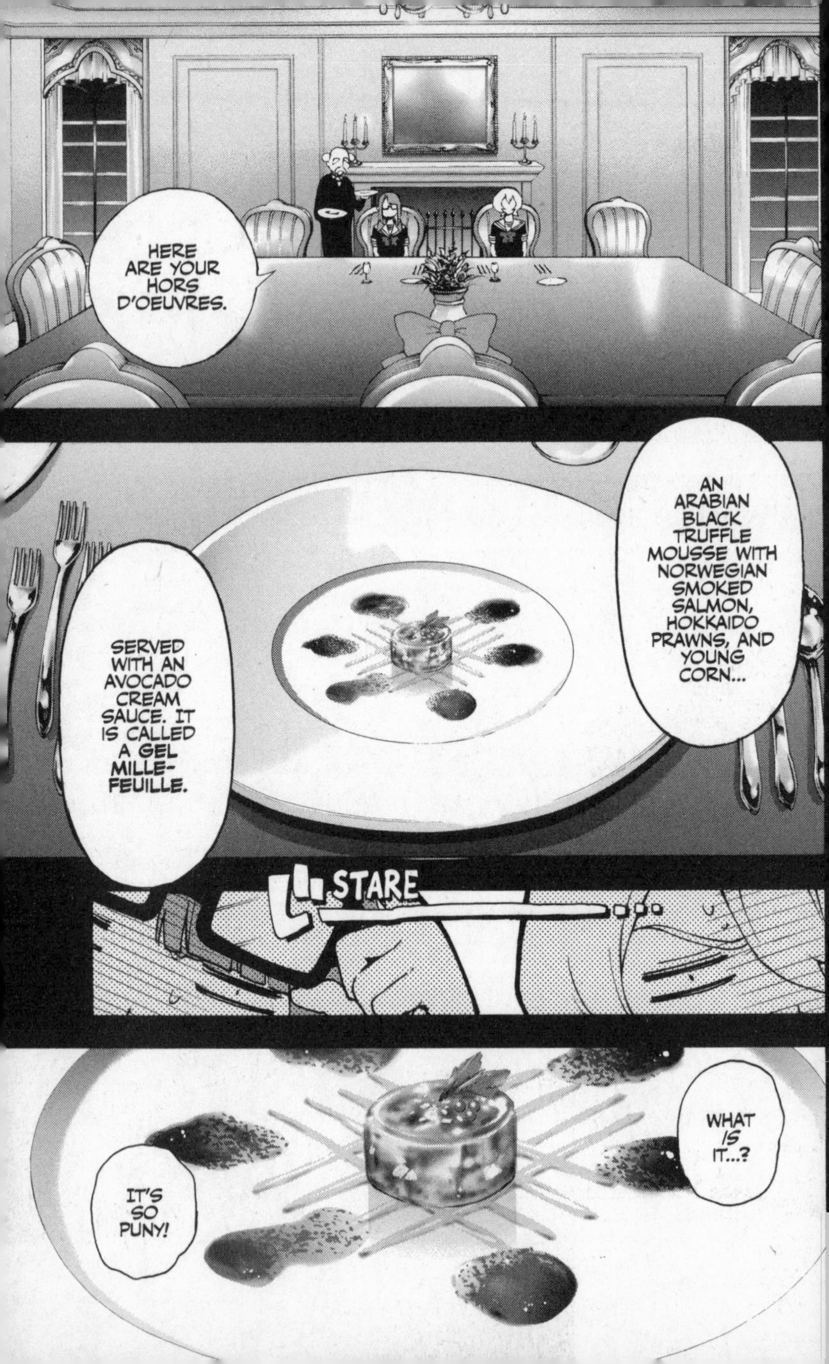
HERE ARE YOUR HORS D'OEUVRES.
AN ARABIAN BLACK TRUFFLE MOUSSE WITH NORWEGIAN SMOKED SALMON, HOKKAIDO PRAWNS, AND YOUNG CORN...
SERVED WITH AN AVOCADO CREAM SAUCE. IT IS CALLED A GEL MILLE-FEUILLE.
STARE
WHAT *IS* IT...?
IT'S SO PUNY!

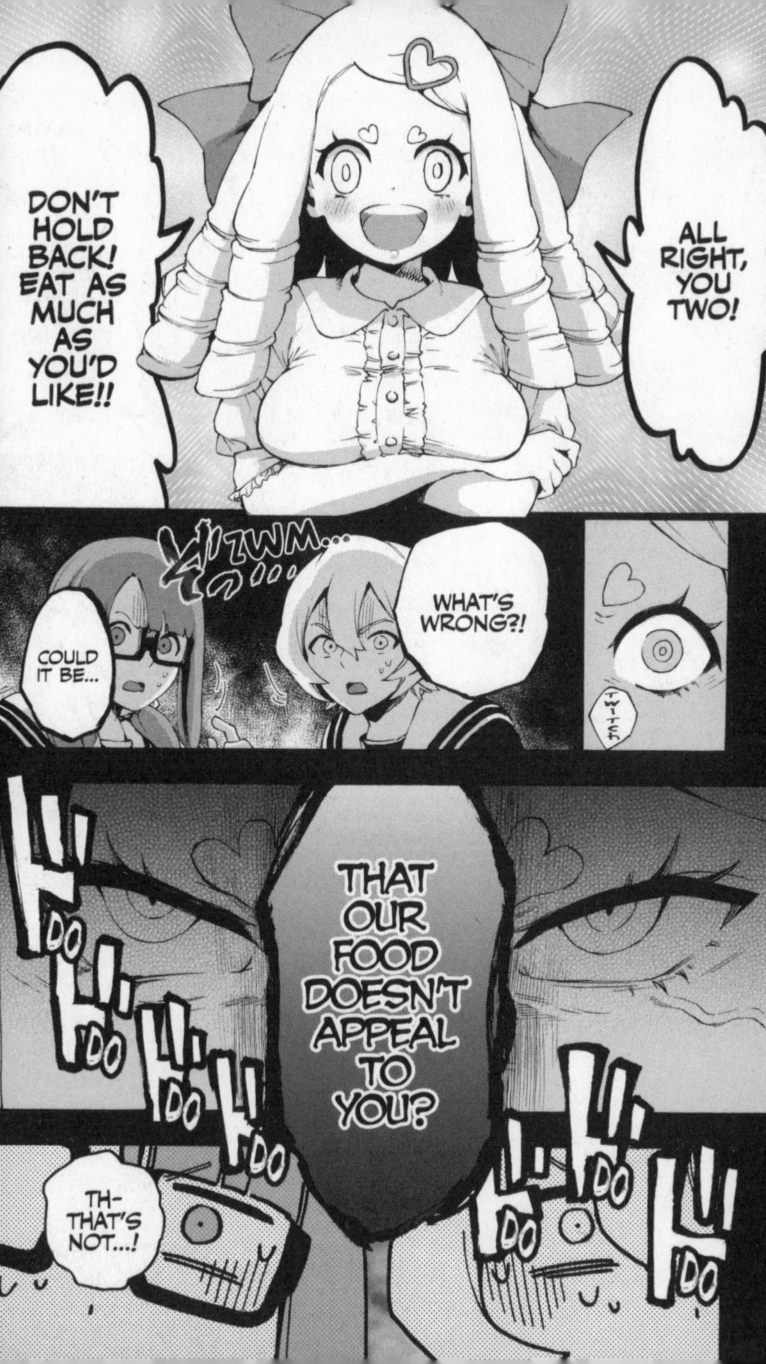
ALL RIGHT, YOU TWO!
DON'T HOLD BACK! EAT AS MUCH AS YOU'D LIKE!!
TWITCH
WHAT'S WRONG?!
ZWM...
COULD IT BE...
THAT OUR FOOD DOESN'T APPEAL TO YOU?
DO DO DO DO DO DO
DO DO DO
TH- THAT'S NOT...!

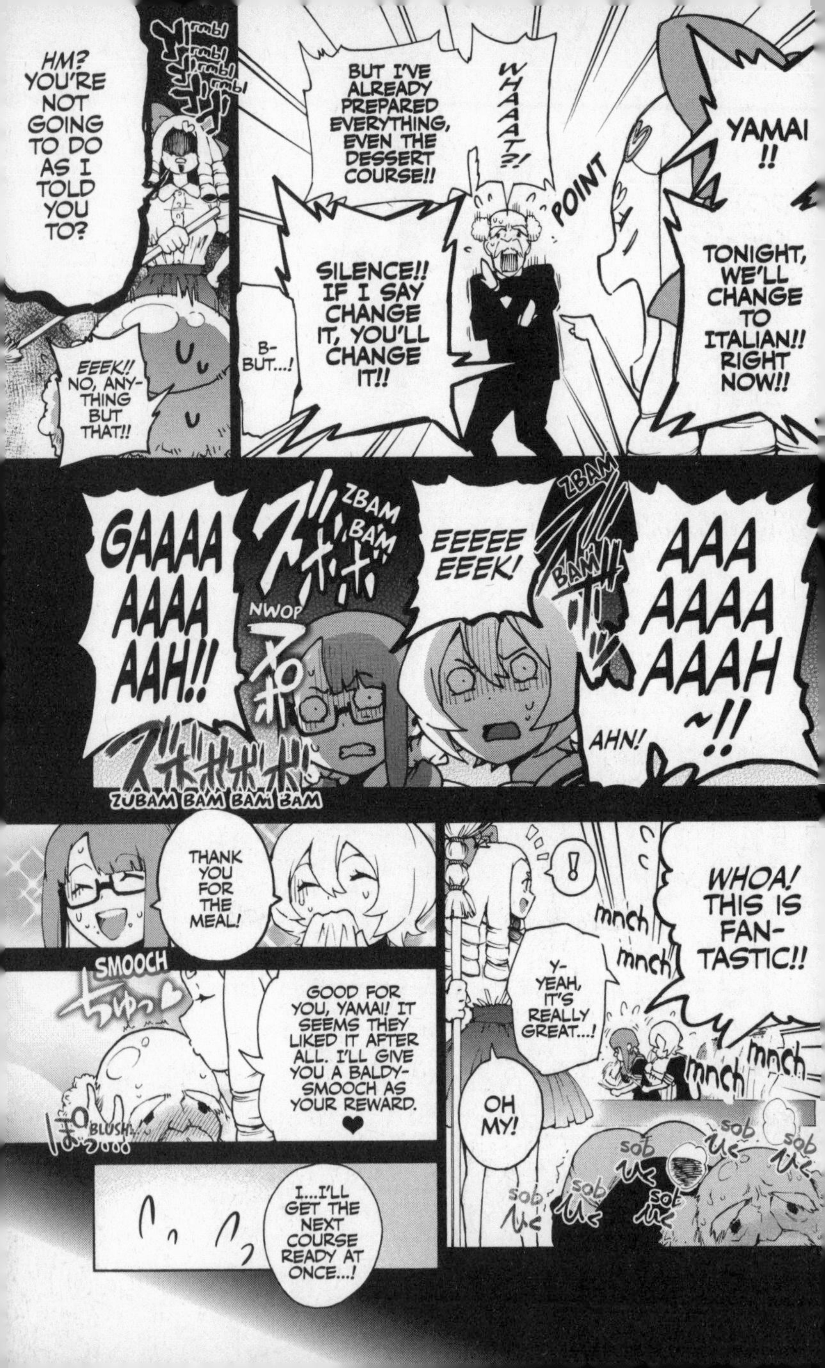
YAMAI!!
POINT
TONIGHT, WE'LL CHANGE TO ITALIAN!! RIGHT NOW!!
WHAAAAT?!
BUT I'VE ALREADY PREPARED EVERYTHING, EVEN THE DESSERT COURSE!!
B-BUT...!
SILENCE!! IF I SAY CHANGE IT, YOU'LL CHANGE IT!!
rmbl rmbl rmbl rmbl
HM? YOU'RE NOT GOING TO DO AS I TOLD YOU TO?
EEEK!! NO, ANYTHING BUT THAT!!
AAA AAAA AAAH~!!
AHN!
ZBAM
BAM
EEEEE EEEK!
ZBAM BAM BAM
NWOP
GAAAA AAAA AAH!!
ZUBAM BAM BAM BAM
WHOA! THIS IS FAN-TASTIC!!
mnch mnch
!
Y-YEAH, IT'S REALLY GREAT...!
mnch mnch
OH MY!
sob sob sob sob sob
THANK YOU FOR THE MEAL!
SMOOCH
ちゅっ♥
GOOD FOR YOU, YAMAI! IT SEEMS THEY LIKED IT AFTER ALL. I'LL GIVE YOU A BALDY-SMOOCH AS YOUR REWARD. ♥
BLUSH
I...I'LL GET THE NEXT COURSE READY AT ONCE...!

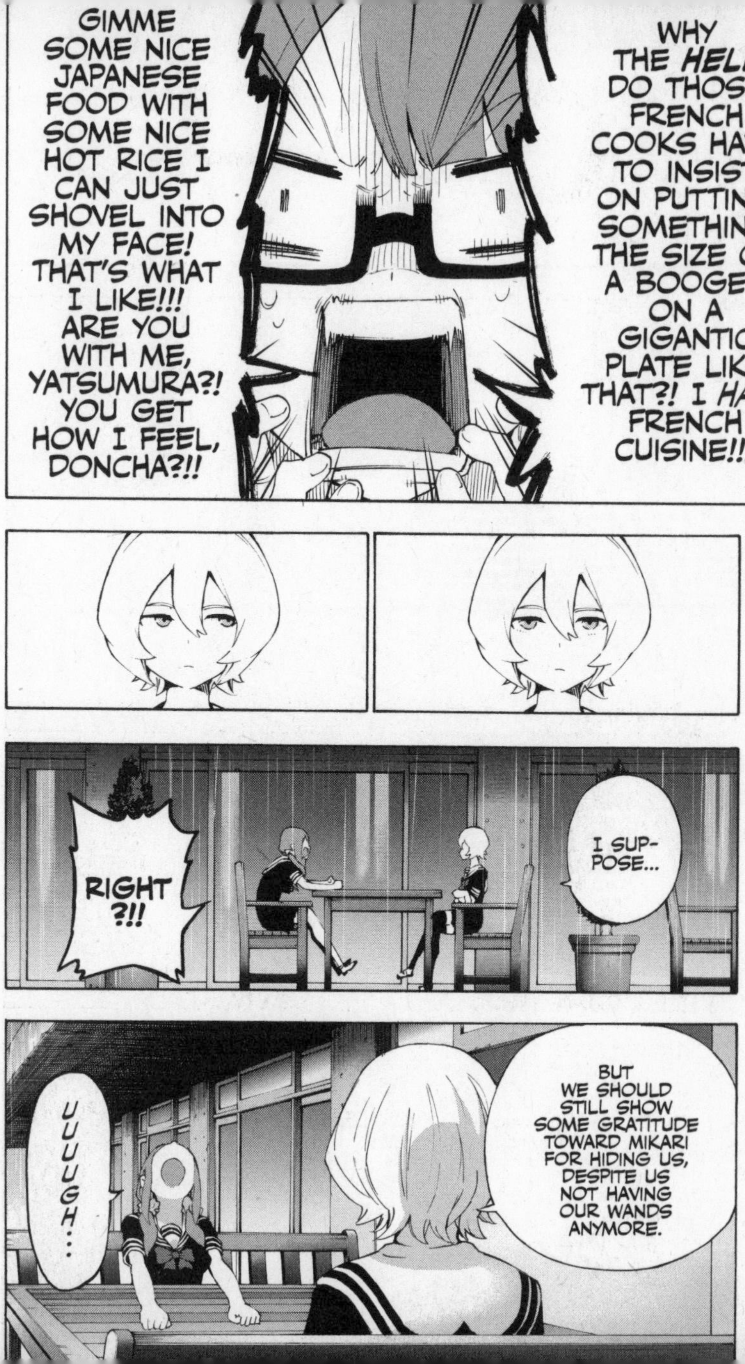
WHY THE *HELL* DO THOSE FRENCH COOKS HAVE TO INSIST ON PUTTING SOMETHING THE SIZE OF A BOOGER ON A GIGANTIC PLATE LIKE THAT?! I *HATE* FRENCH CUISINE!!!
GIMME SOME NICE JAPANESE FOOD WITH SOME NICE HOT RICE I CAN JUST SHOVEL INTO MY FACE! THAT'S WHAT I LIKE!!! ARE YOU WITH ME, YATSUMURA?! YOU GET HOW I FEEL, DONCHA?!!
I SUP-POSE...
RIGHT?!!
BUT WE SHOULD STILL SHOW SOME GRATITUDE TOWARD MIKARI FOR HIDING US, DESPITE US NOT HAVING OUR WANDS ANYMORE.
UUUUGH...

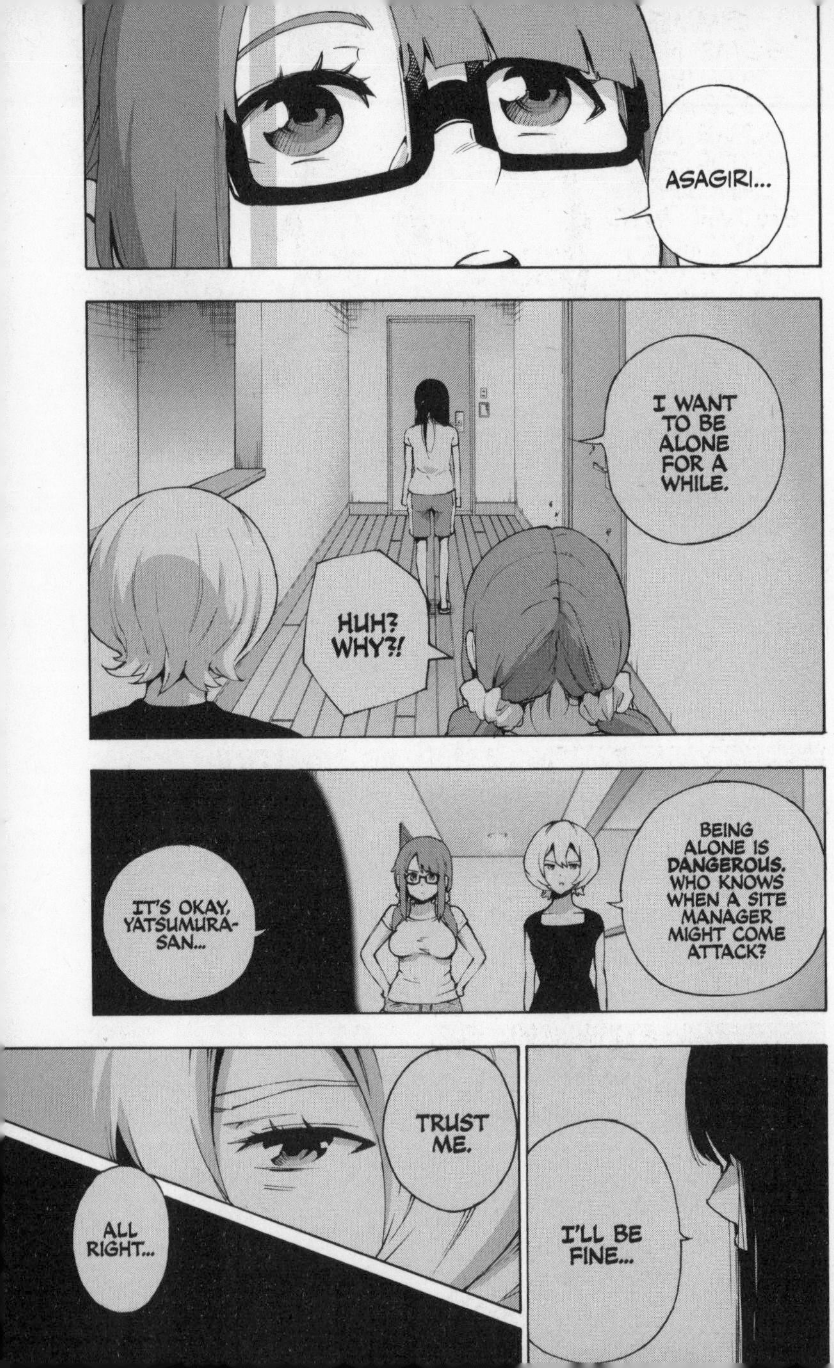
ASAGIRI...
I WANT TO BE ALONE FOR A WHILE.
HUH? WHY?!
BEING ALONE IS DANGEROUS. WHO KNOWS WHEN A SITE MANAGER MIGHT COME ATTACK?
IT'S OKAY, YATSUMURA-SAN...
I'LL BE FINE...
TRUST ME.
ALL RIGHT...

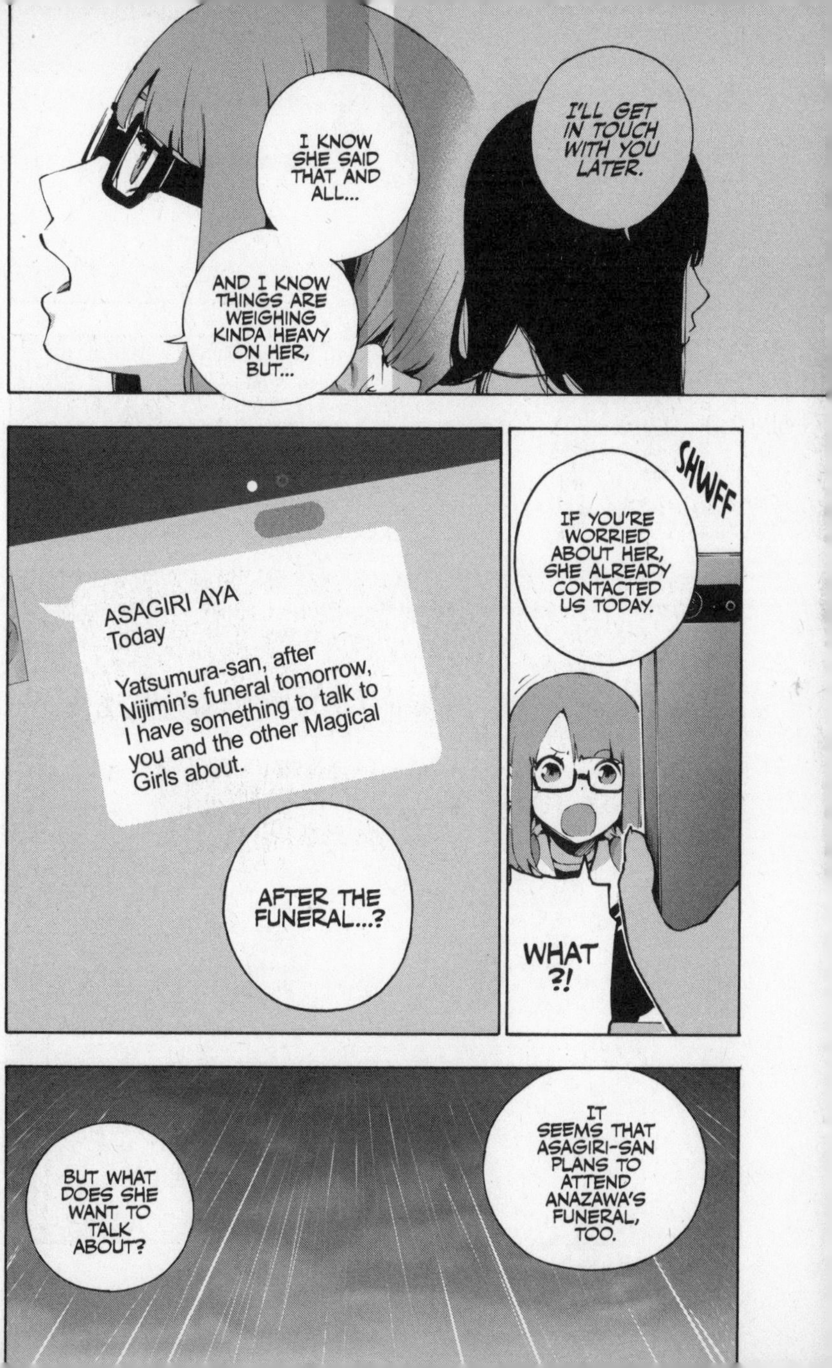
I'LL GET IN TOUCH WITH YOU LATER.
I KNOW SHE SAID THAT AND ALL...
AND I KNOW THINGS ARE WEIGHING KINDA HEAVY ON HER, BUT...
SHWFF
IF YOU'RE WORRIED ABOUT HER, SHE ALREADY CONTACTED US TODAY.
WHAT ?!
ASAGIRI AYA
Today
Yatsumura-san, after Nijimin's funeral tomorrow, I have something to talk to you and the other Magical Girls about.
AFTER THE FUNERAL...?
IT SEEMS THAT ASAGIRI-SAN PLANS TO ATTEND ANAZAWA'S FUNERAL, TOO.
BUT WHAT DOES SHE WANT TO TALK ABOUT?

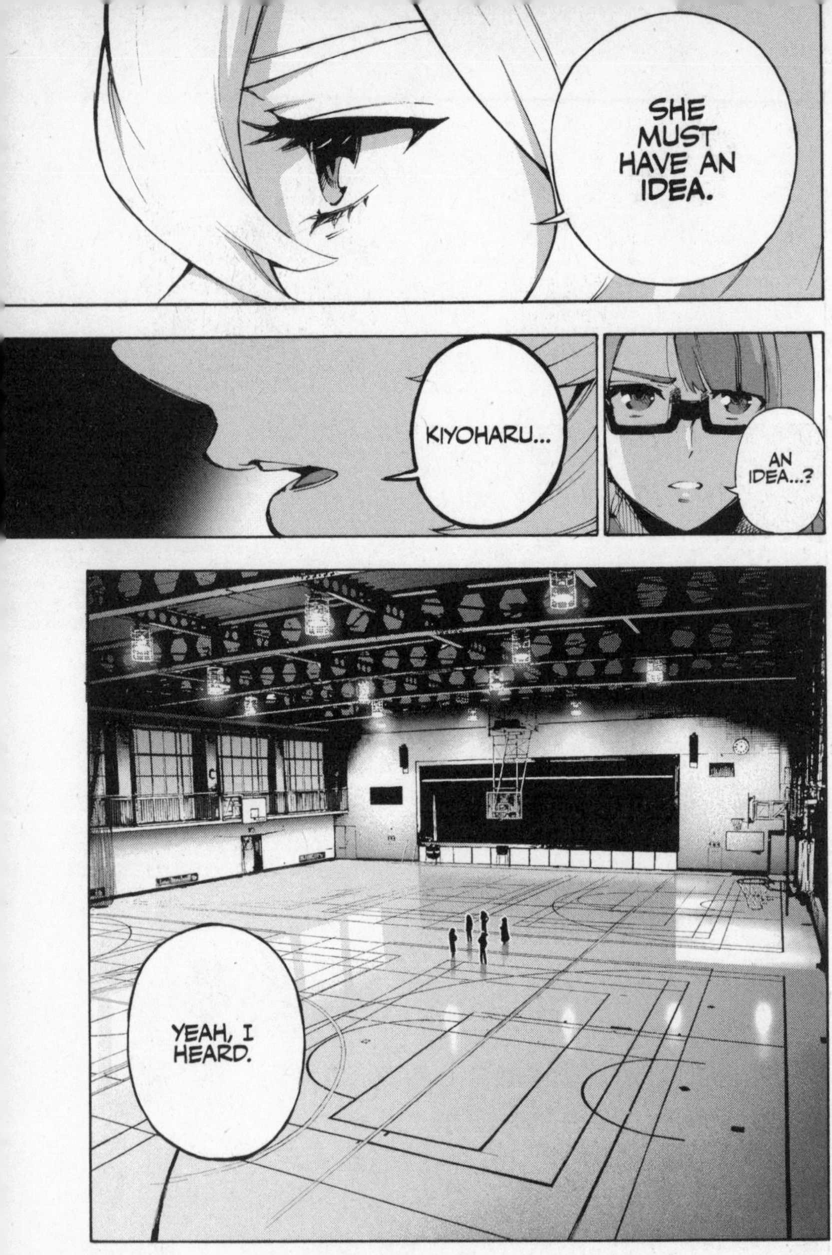
SHE MUST HAVE AN IDEA.
AN IDEA...?
KIYOHARU...
YEAH, I HEARD.

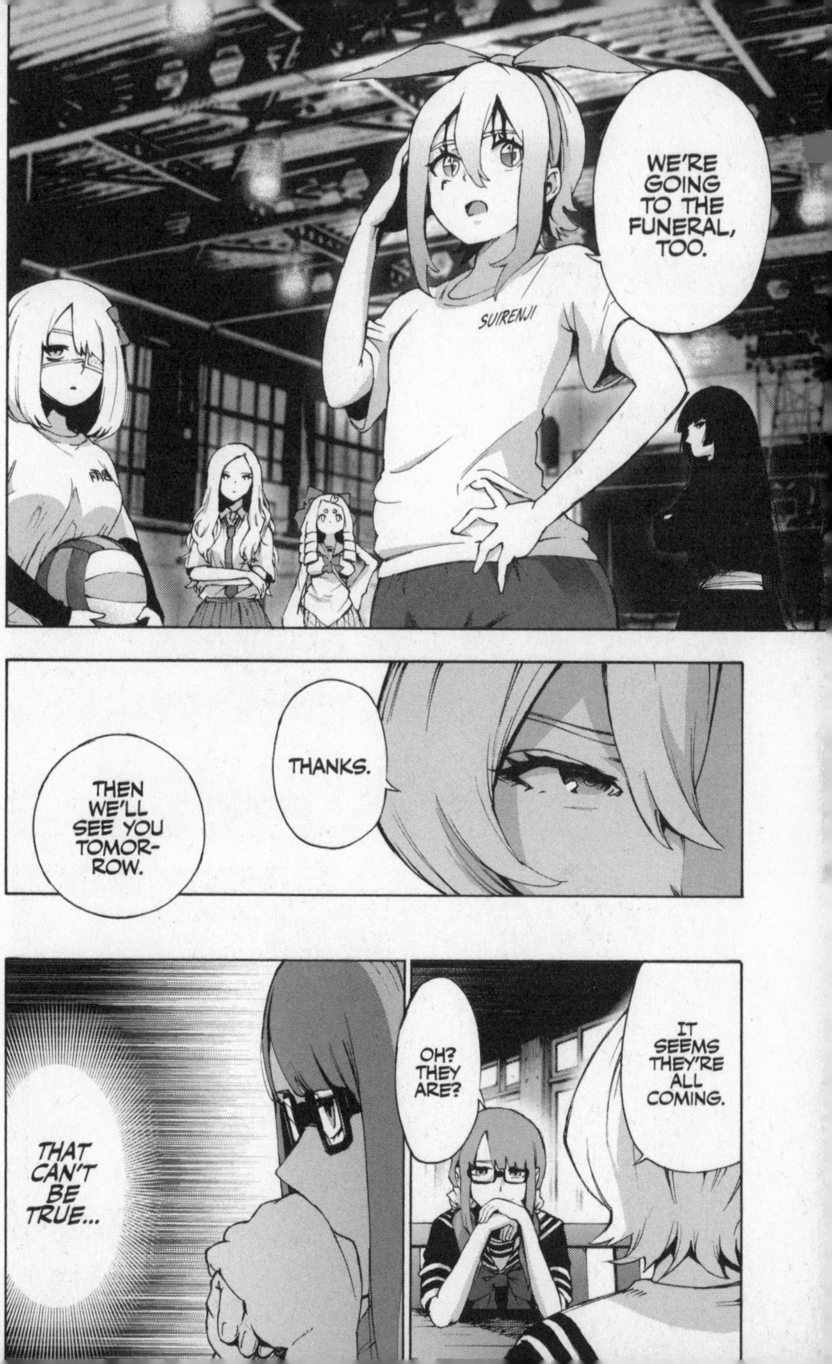
WE'RE GOING TO THE FUNERAL, TOO.
SUIRENJI
THANKS.
THEN WE'LL SEE YOU TOMOR-ROW.
IT SEEMS THEY'RE ALL COMING.
OH? THEY ARE?
THAT CAN'T BE TRUE...

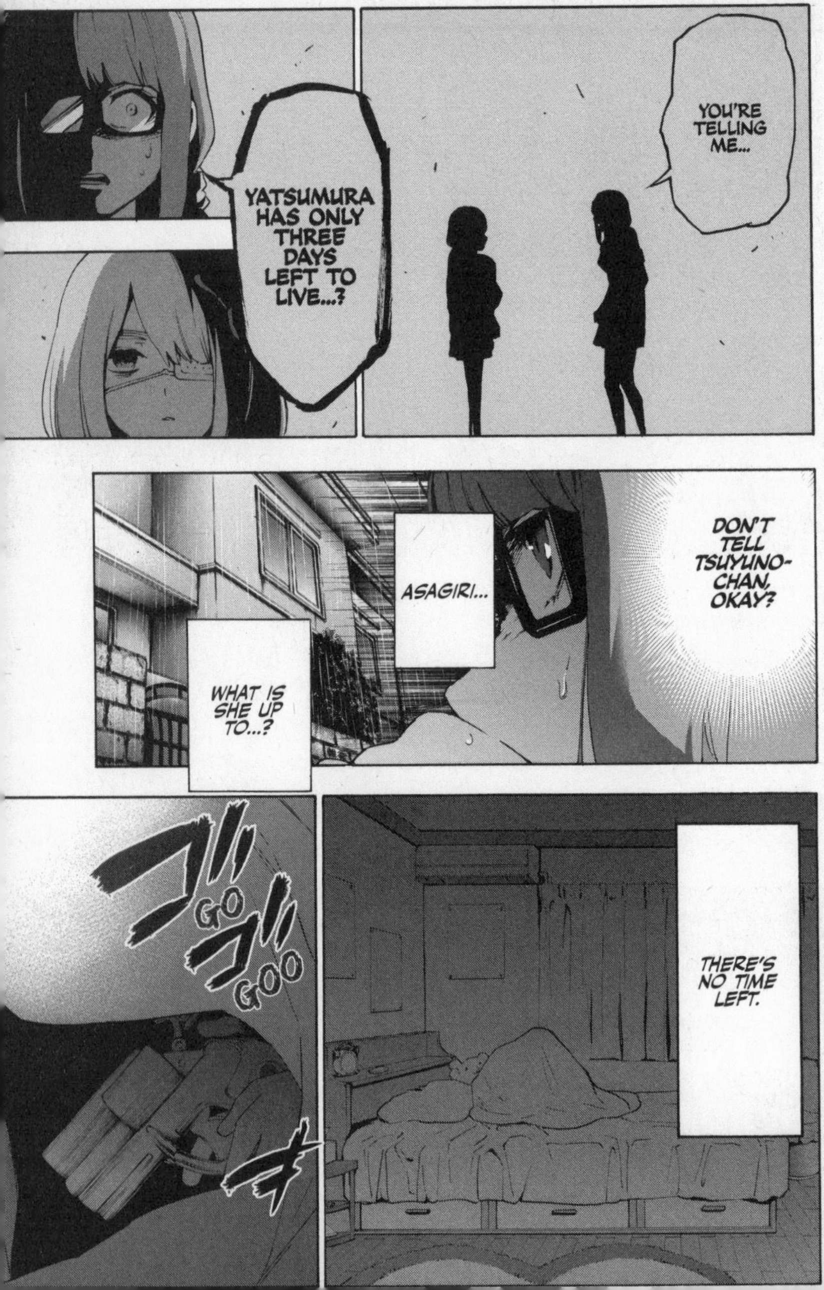
YOU'RE TELLING ME...
YATSUMURA HAS ONLY THREE DAYS LEFT TO LIVE...?
DON'T TELL TSUYUNO-CHAN, OKAY?
ASAGIRI...
WHAT IS SHE UP TO...?
THERE'S NO TIME LEFT.
GO
GOO

Misumi Kiichiro

Sex: Male
Age: 28
Date of Birth: August 10 (Leo)
Height: 181cm
Weight: 75kg
Blood Type: AB
Birthplace: Aichi Prefecture

Interests/Hobbies: Cooking, training (exercise, etc), bodybuilding, playing the piano

Strengths: Calm and collected; likes beautiful things

Dislikes/Weakness: Bugs, lowlife humans

Likes: Antiques, flowers, beautiful things

- He is always calm and collected, and it's rare for him to show emotion.
- He is incredibly intelligent, and his ability at sports (of all kinds) is second to none.
- There are times when he appears nervous.
- He holds many secrets, which cannot be revealed publicly right now.

Enter.45 Funeral Service

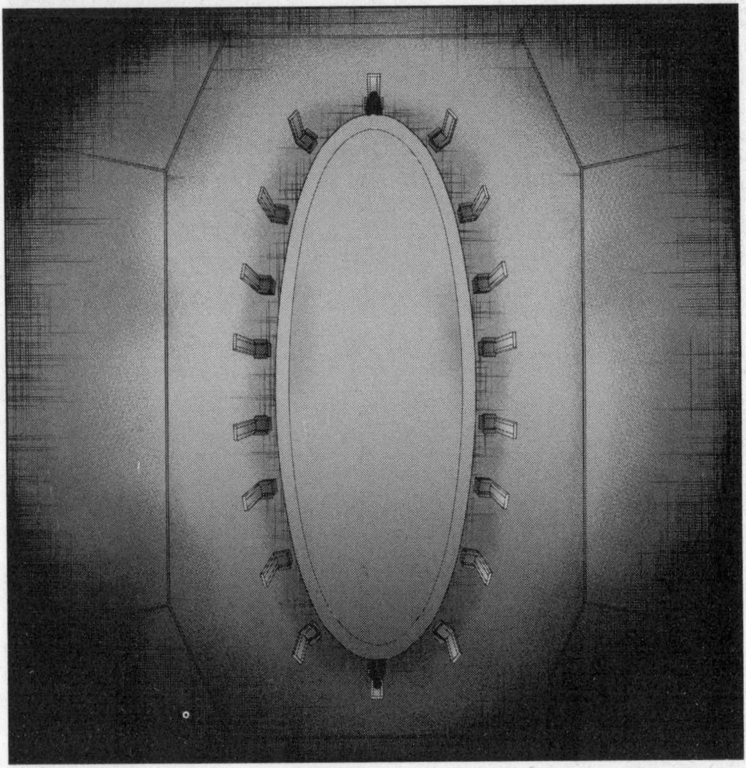

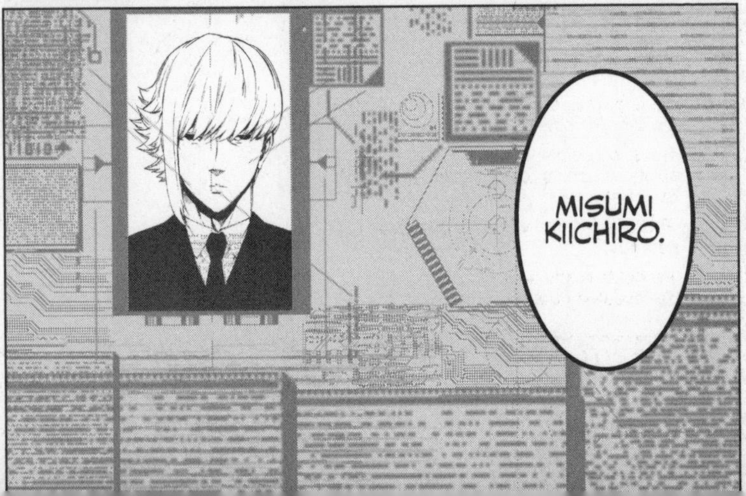
MISUMI KIICHIRO.

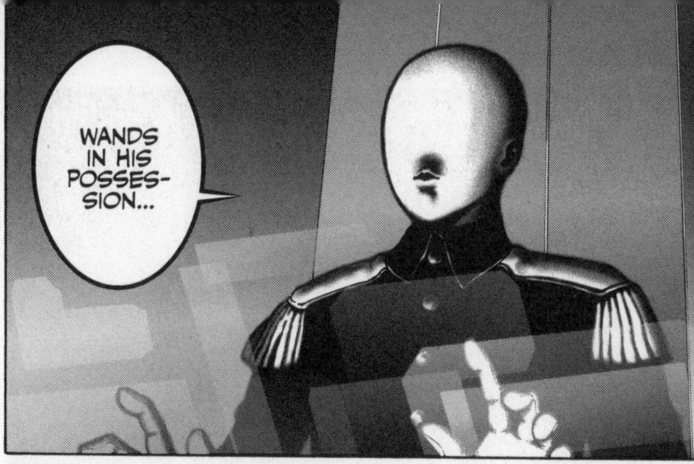
WANDS IN HIS POSSES-SION...

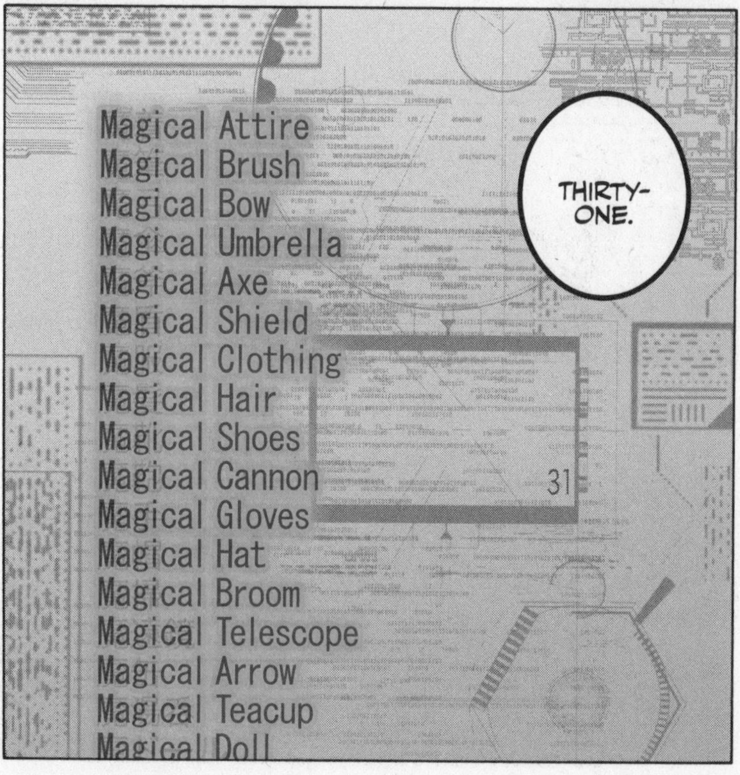
THIRTY-ONE.
Magical Attire
Magical Brush
Magical Bow
Magical Umbrella
Magical Axe
Magical Shield
Magical Clothing
Magical Hair
Magical Shoes
Magical Cannon
31
Magical Gloves
Magical Hat
Magical Broom
Magical Telescope
Magical Arrow
Magical Teacup
Magical Doll

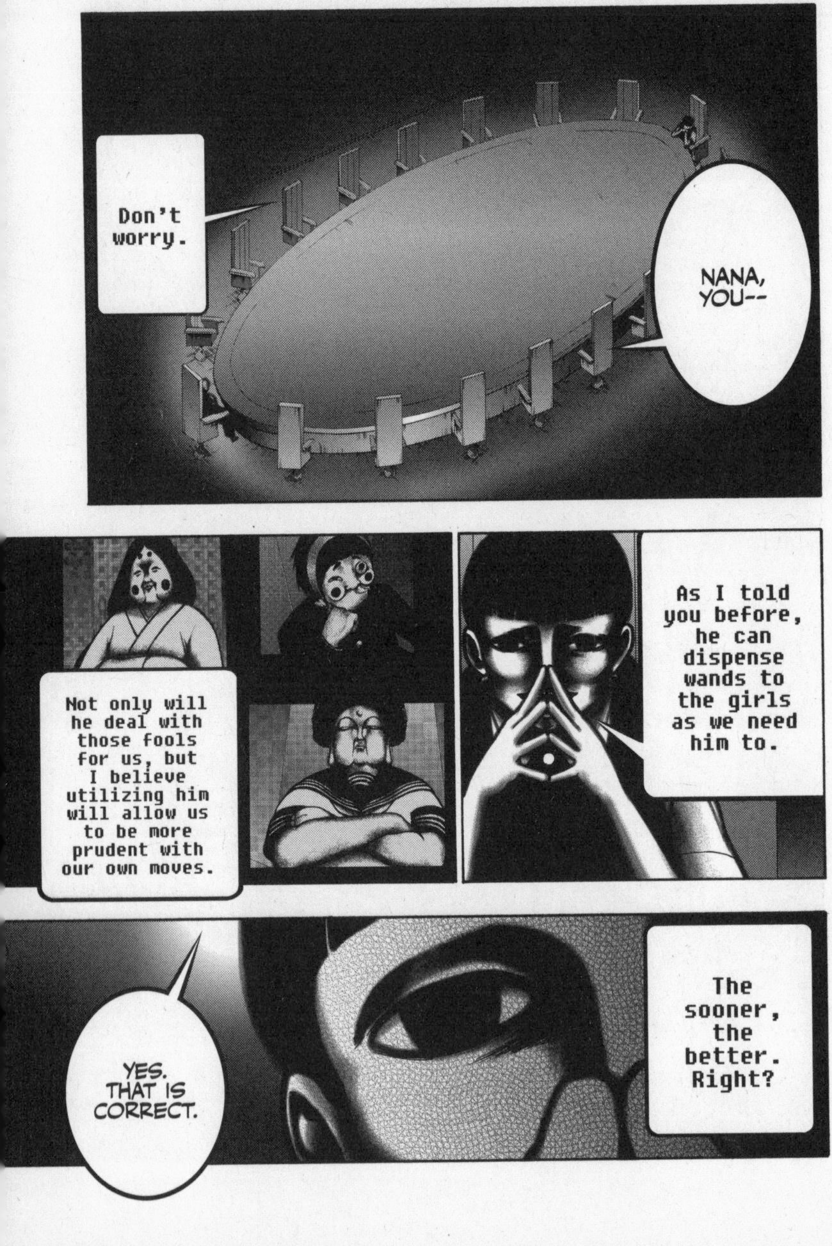
NANA, YOU--
Don't worry.
As I told you before, he can dispense wands to the girls as we need him to.
Not only will he deal with those fools for us, but I believe utilizing him will allow us to be more prudent with our own moves.
The sooner, the better. Right?
YES. THAT IS CORRECT.

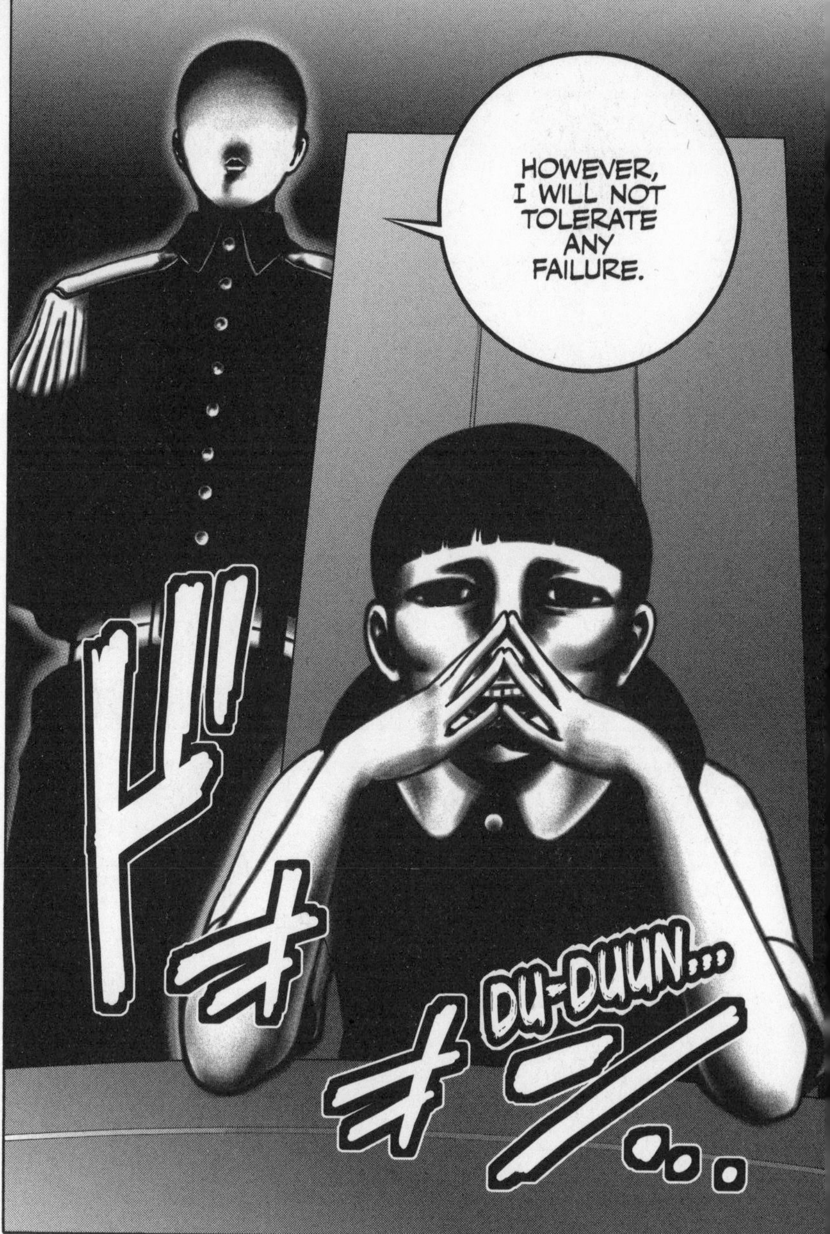
HOWEVER, I WILL NOT TOLERATE ANY FAILURE.
DU-DUUN...

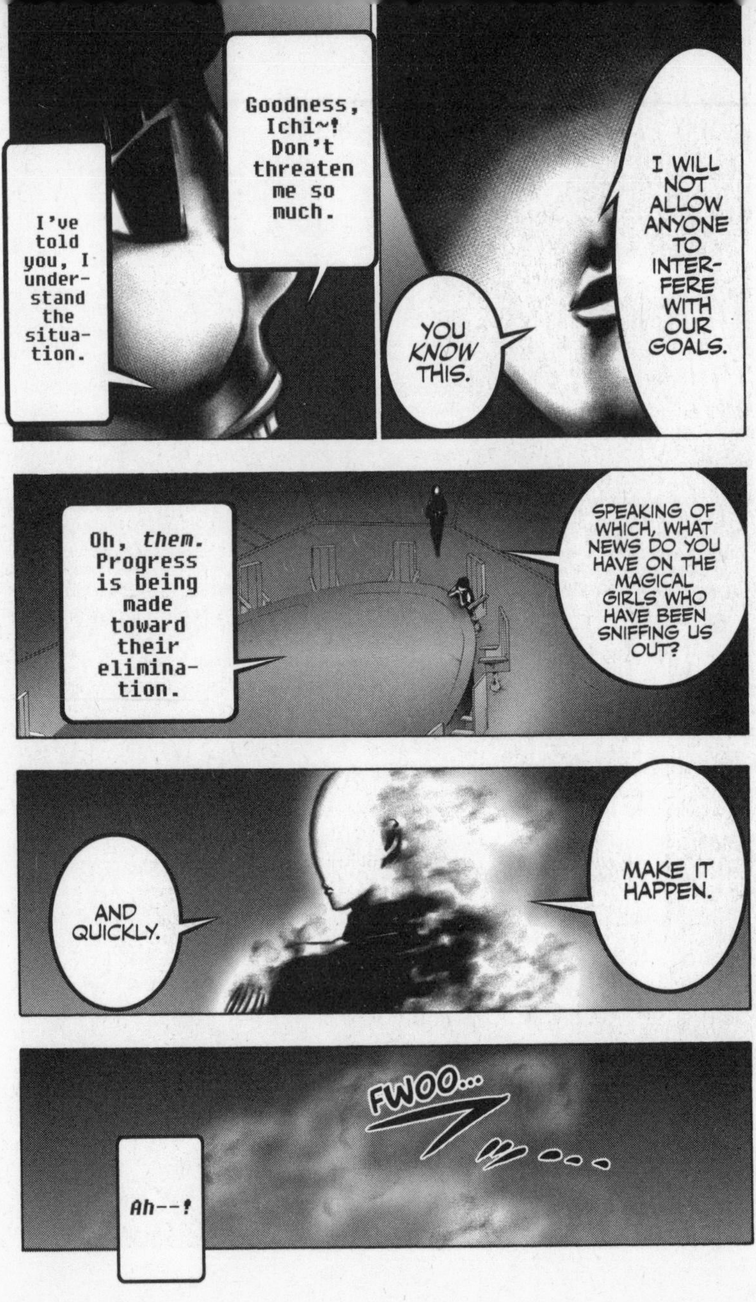
I WILL NOT ALLOW ANYONE TO INTERFERE WITH OUR GOALS.
YOU KNOW THIS.
Goodness, Ichi~! Don't threaten me so much.
I've told you, I understand the situation.
SPEAKING OF WHICH, WHAT NEWS DO YOU HAVE ON THE MAGICAL GIRLS WHO HAVE BEEN SNIFFING US OUT?
Oh, *them*. Progress is being made toward their elimination.
MAKE IT HAPPEN.
AND QUICKLY.
FWOO...
Ah--!

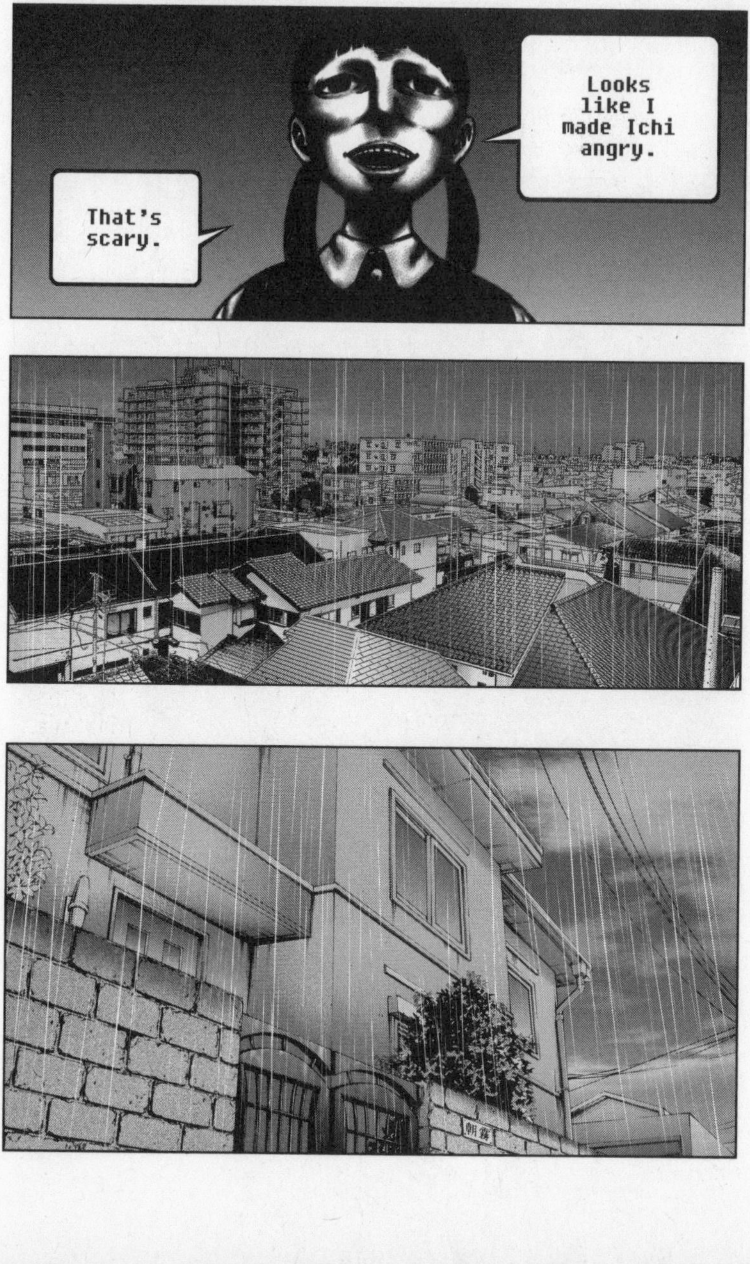
Looks like I made Ichi angry.
That's scary.
朝霧

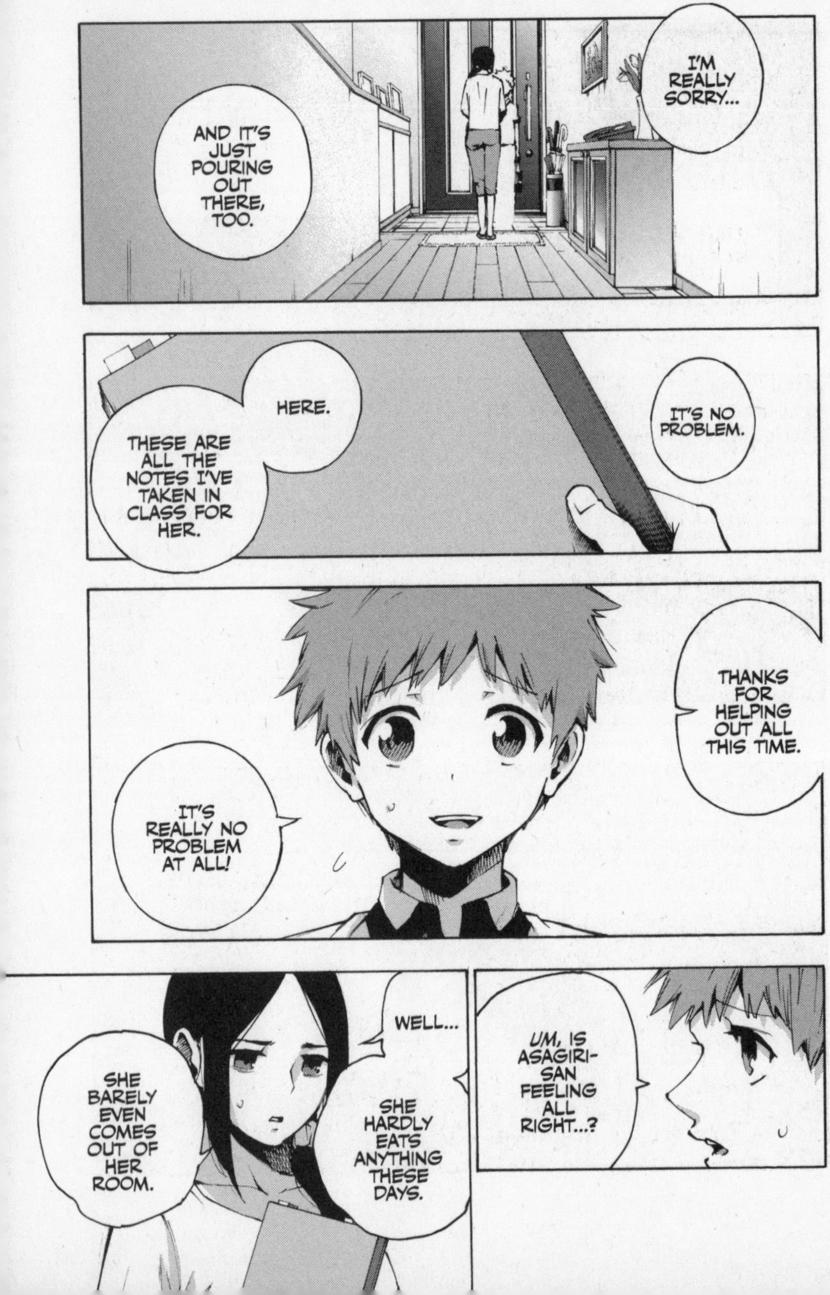
I'M REALLY SORRY...
AND IT'S JUST POURING OUT THERE, TOO.
IT'S NO PROBLEM.
HERE.
THESE ARE ALL THE NOTES I'VE TAKEN IN CLASS FOR HER.
THANKS FOR HELPING OUT ALL THIS TIME.
IT'S REALLY NO PROBLEM AT ALL!
UM, IS ASAGIRI-SAN FEELING ALL RIGHT...?
WELL...
SHE HARDLY EATS ANYTHING THESE DAYS.
SHE BARELY EVEN COMES OUT OF HER ROOM.

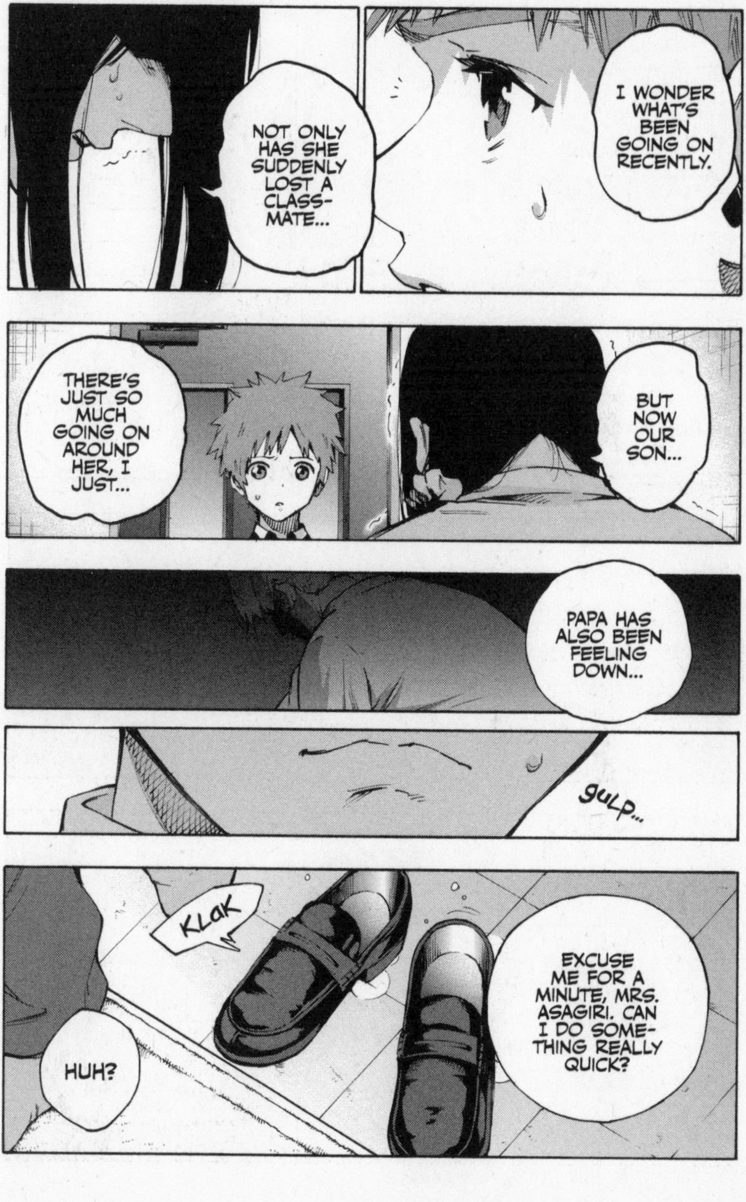
I WONDER WHAT'S BEEN GOING ON RECENTLY.
NOT ONLY HAS SHE SUDDENLY LOST A CLASS-MATE...
BUT NOW OUR SON...
THERE'S JUST SO MUCH GOING ON AROUND HER, I JUST...
PAPA HAS ALSO BEEN FEELING DOWN...
gulp...
EXCUSE ME FOR A MINUTE, MRS. ASAGIRI. CAN I DO SOME-THING REALLY QUICK?
KLAK
HUH?

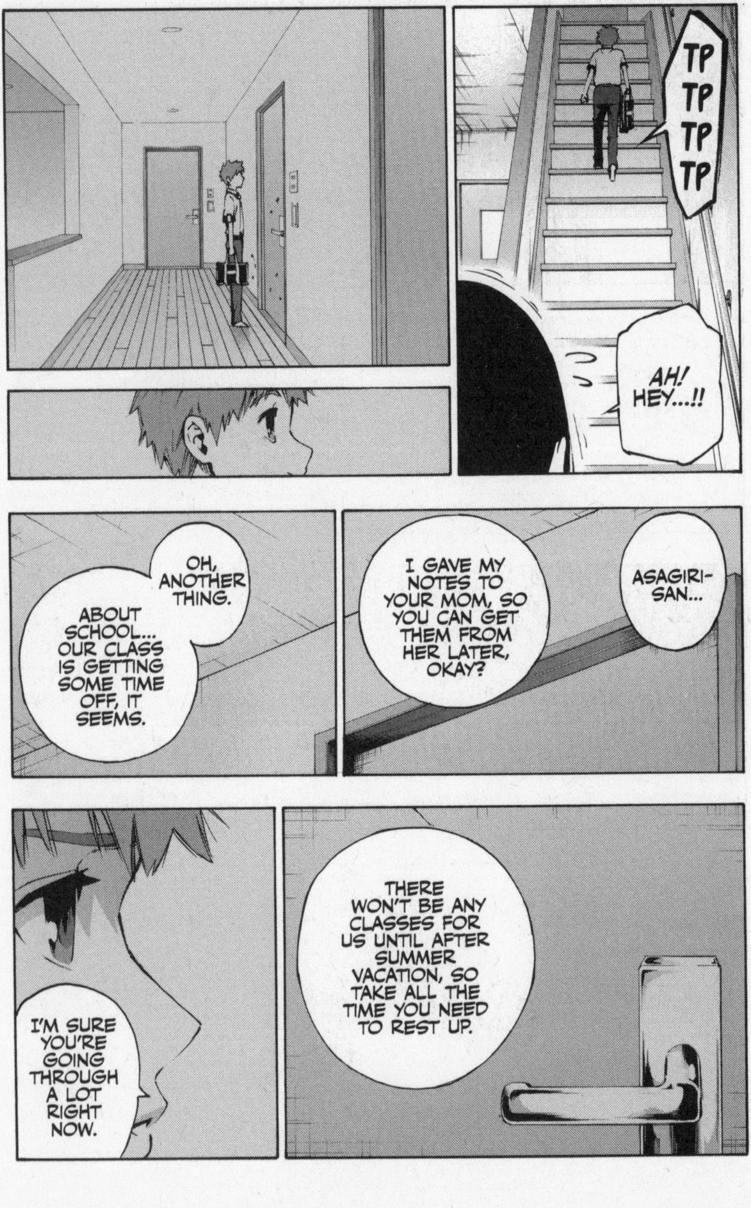
TP TP TP TP
AH! HEY...!!
ASAGIRI-SAN...
I GAVE MY NOTES TO YOUR MOM, SO YOU CAN GET THEM FROM HER LATER, OKAY?
OH, ANOTHER THING.
ABOUT SCHOOL... OUR CLASS IS GETTING SOME TIME OFF, IT SEEMS.
THERE WON'T BE ANY CLASSES FOR US UNTIL AFTER SUMMER VACATION, SO TAKE ALL THE TIME YOU NEED TO REST UP.
I'M SURE YOU'RE GOING THROUGH A LOT RIGHT NOW.

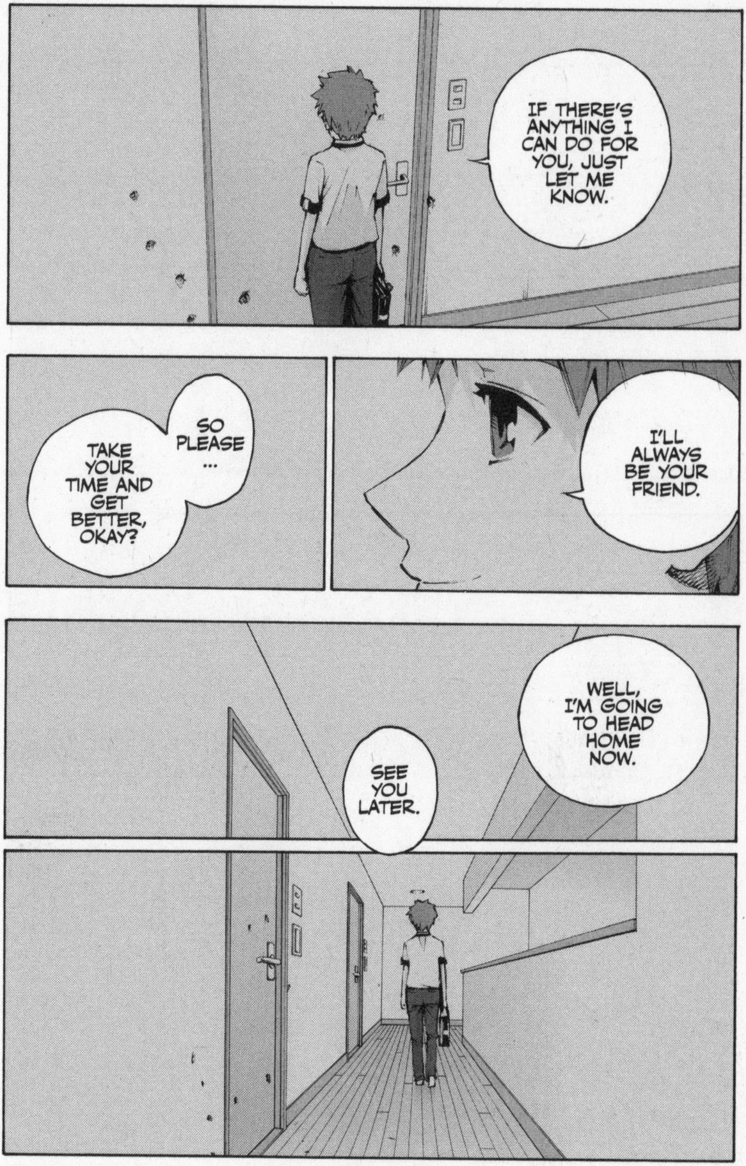
IF THERE'S ANYTHING I CAN DO FOR YOU, JUST LET ME KNOW.
I'LL ALWAYS BE YOUR FRIEND.
SO PLEASE ...
TAKE YOUR TIME AND GET BETTER, OKAY?
WELL, I'M GOING TO HEAD HOME NOW.
SEE YOU LATER.

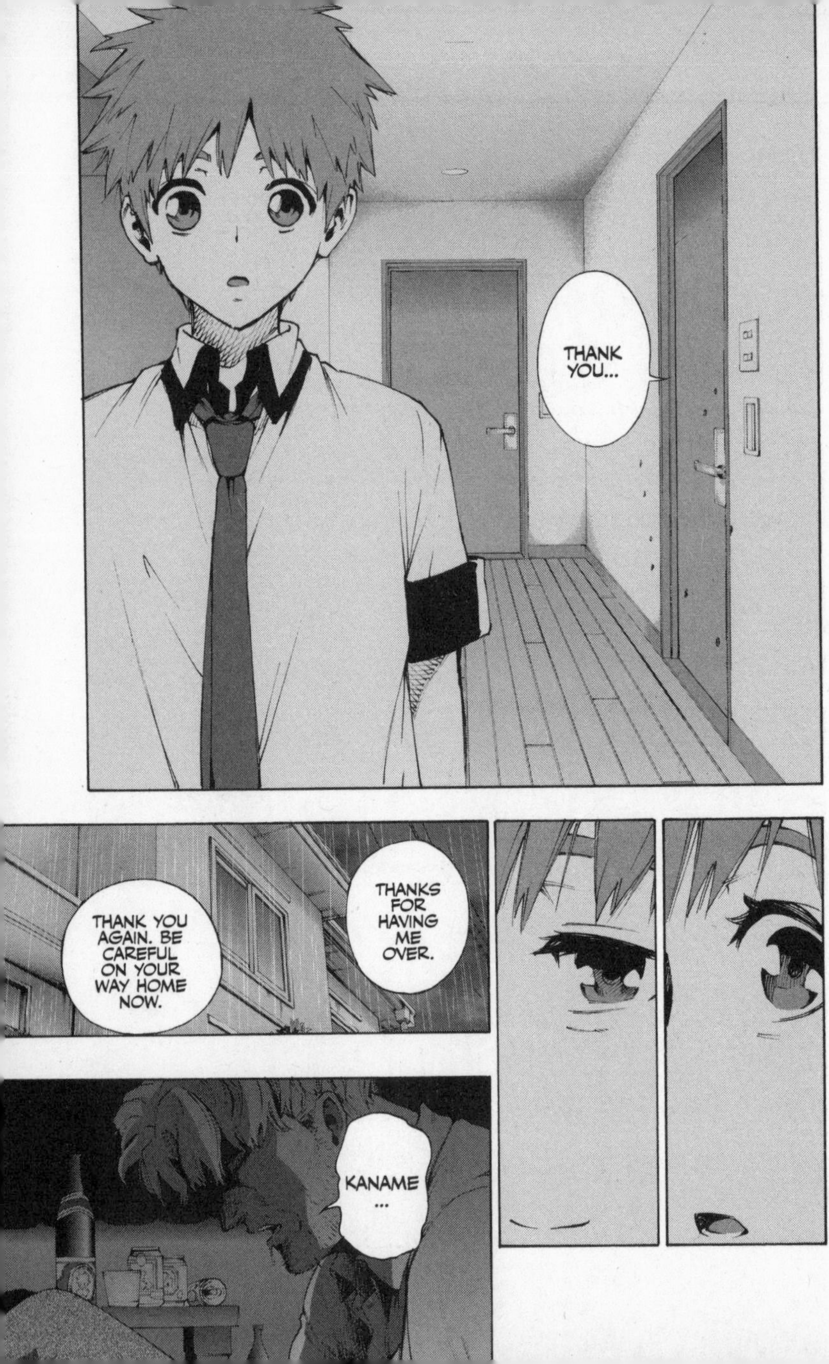
THANK YOU...
THANKS FOR HAVING ME OVER.
THANK YOU AGAIN. BE CAREFUL ON YOUR WAY HOME NOW.
KANAME ...

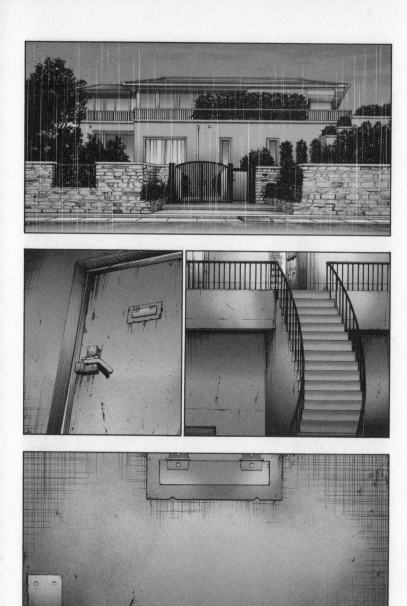

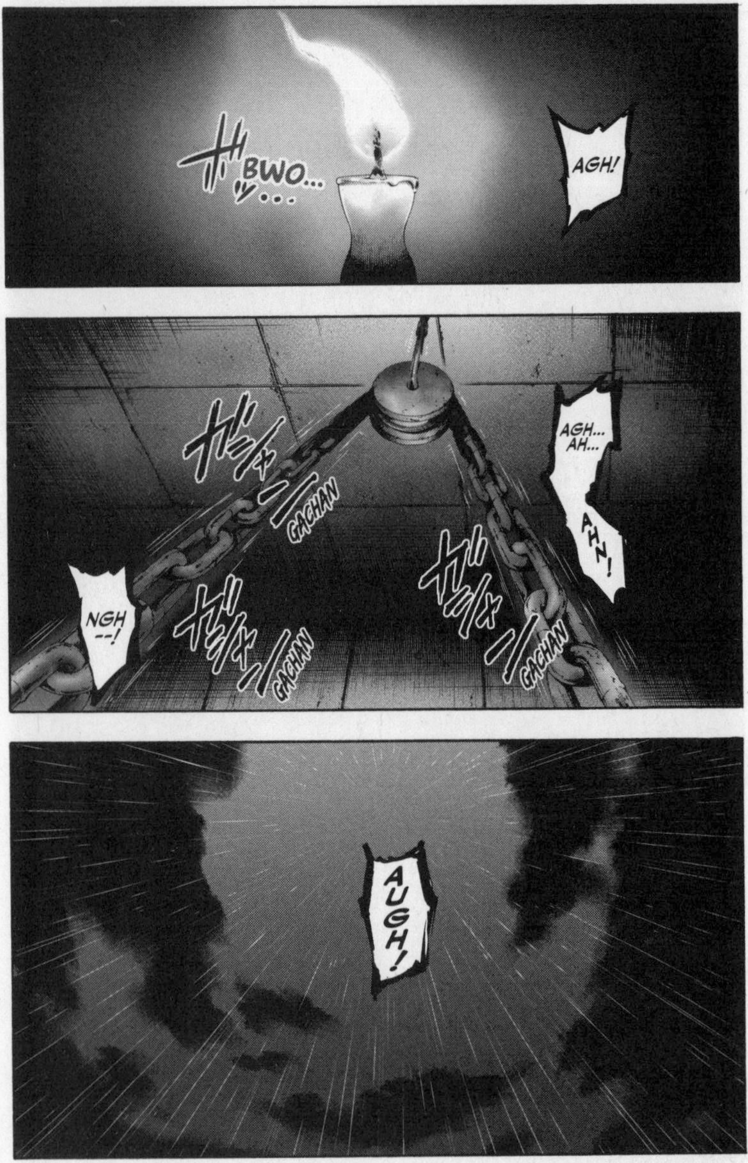
AGH!
BWO...
AGH... AH...
AHN!
GACHAN
GACHAN
GACHAN
NGH --!
AUGH!

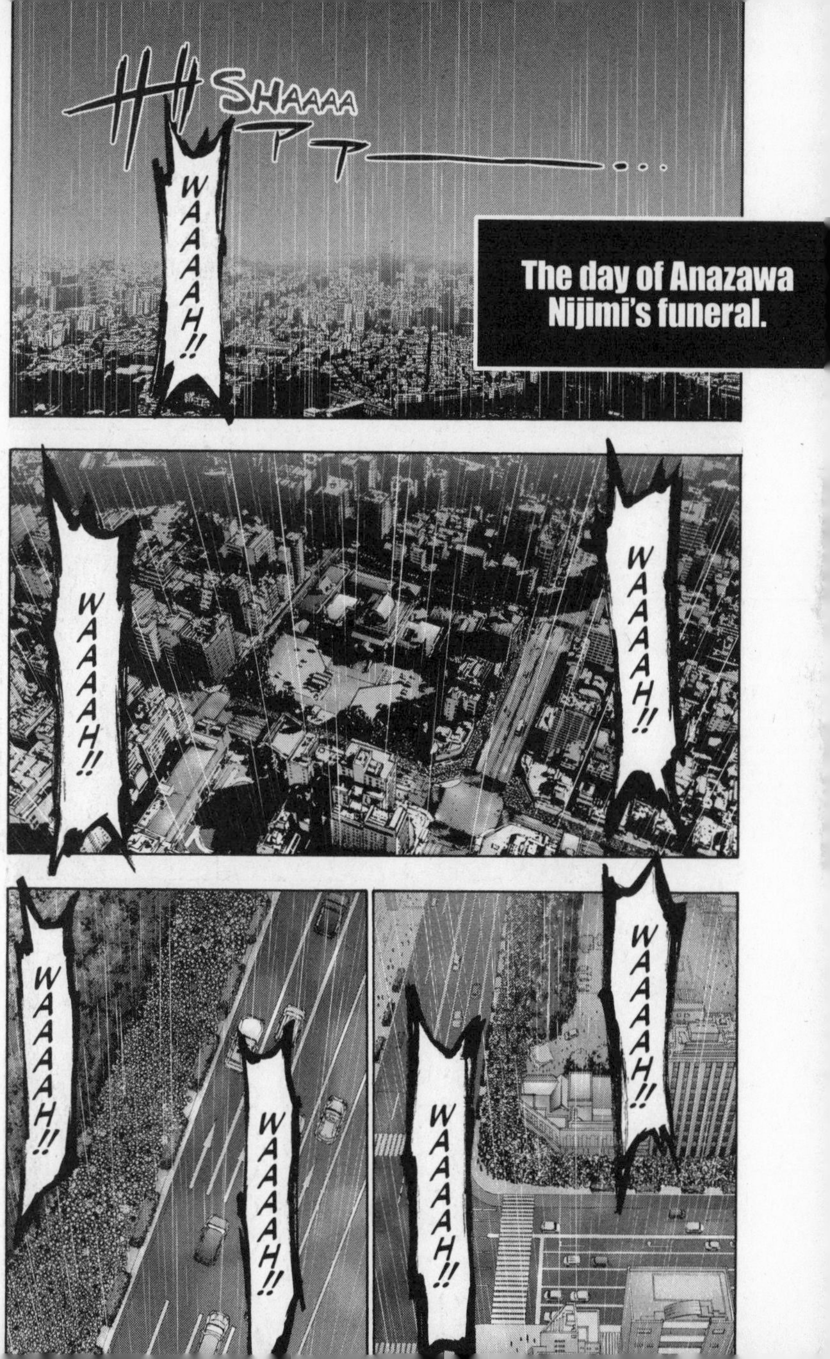
The day of Anazawa Nijimi's funeral.
SHAAAA...
WAAAAAH!!
WAAAAAH!!
WAAAAAH!!
WAAAAAH!!
WAAAAAH!!
WAAAAAH!!
WAAAAAH!!

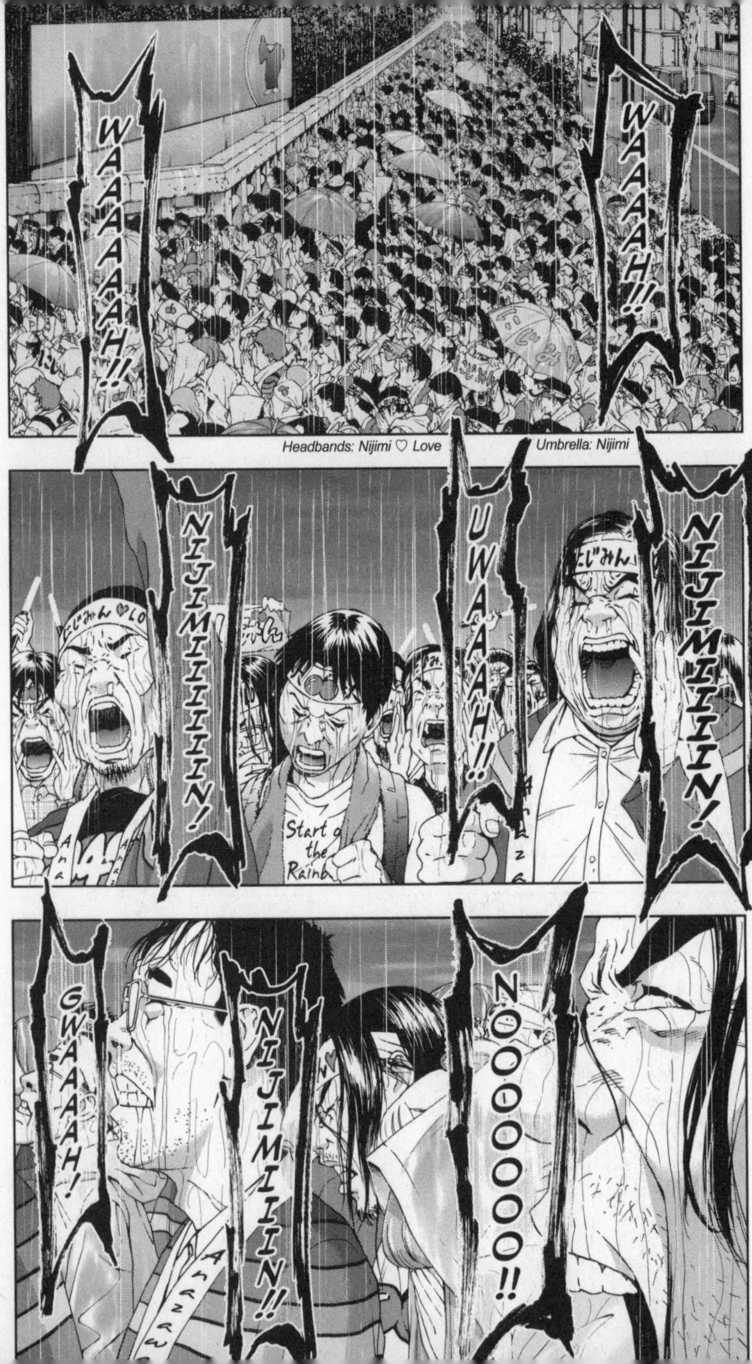
WAAAAAH!!
WAAAAAAH!!
Umbrella: Nijimi
Headbands: Nijimi ♡ Love
NIJIMIIIIIN!
UWAAAAAH!!
NIJIMIIIIIIIN!
Start of the Rainb
NOOOOOOO!!
NIJIMIIIN!!
GWAAAAH!

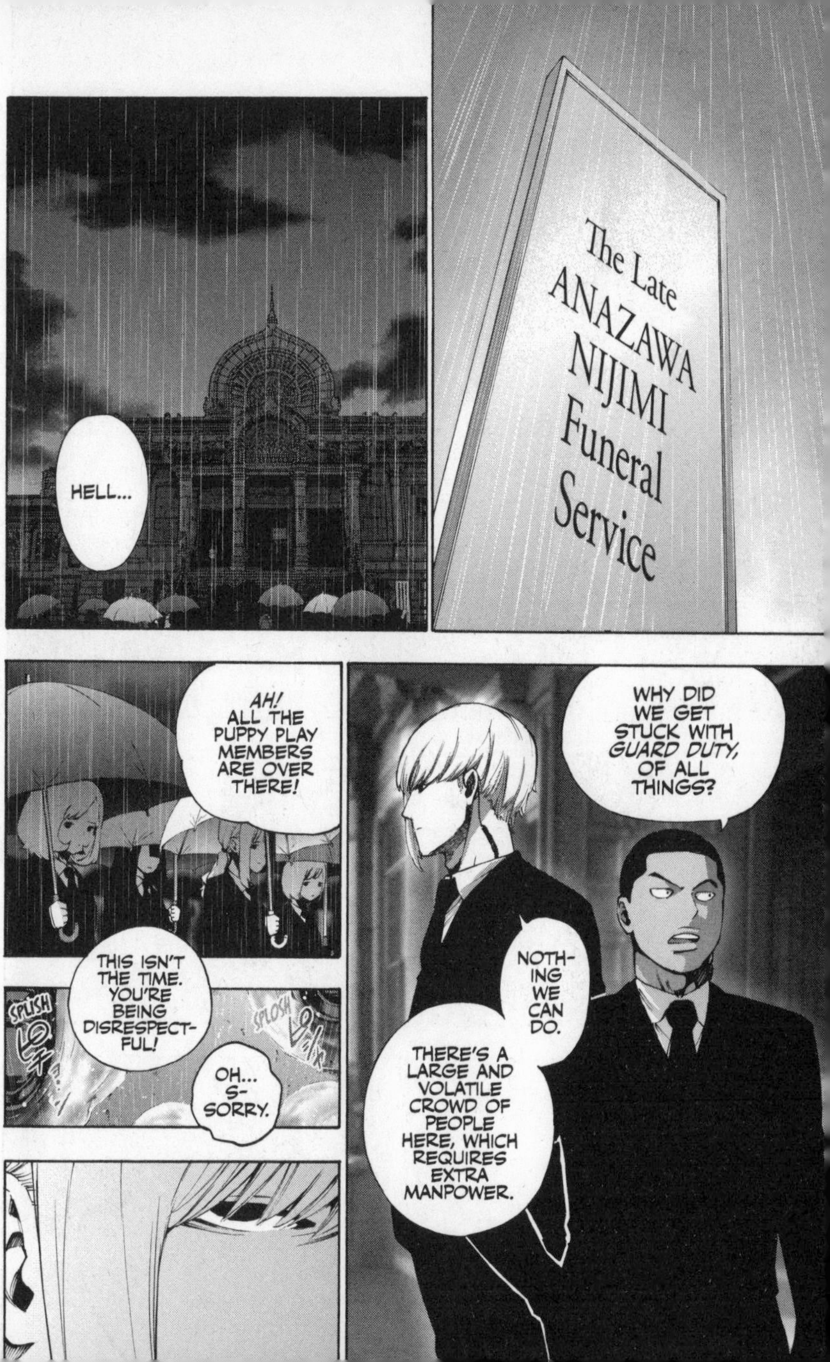
The Late ANAZAWA NIJIMI Funeral Service
HELL...
WHY DID WE GET STUCK WITH GUARD DUTY, OF ALL THINGS?
NOTH-ING WE CAN DO.
THERE'S A LARGE AND VOLATILE CROWD OF PEOPLE HERE, WHICH REQUIRES EXTRA MANPOWER.
AH! ALL THE PUPPY PLAY MEMBERS ARE OVER THERE!
THIS ISN'T THE TIME. YOU'RE BEING DISRESPECT-FUL!
SPLOSH
SPLISH
OH... S-SORRY.

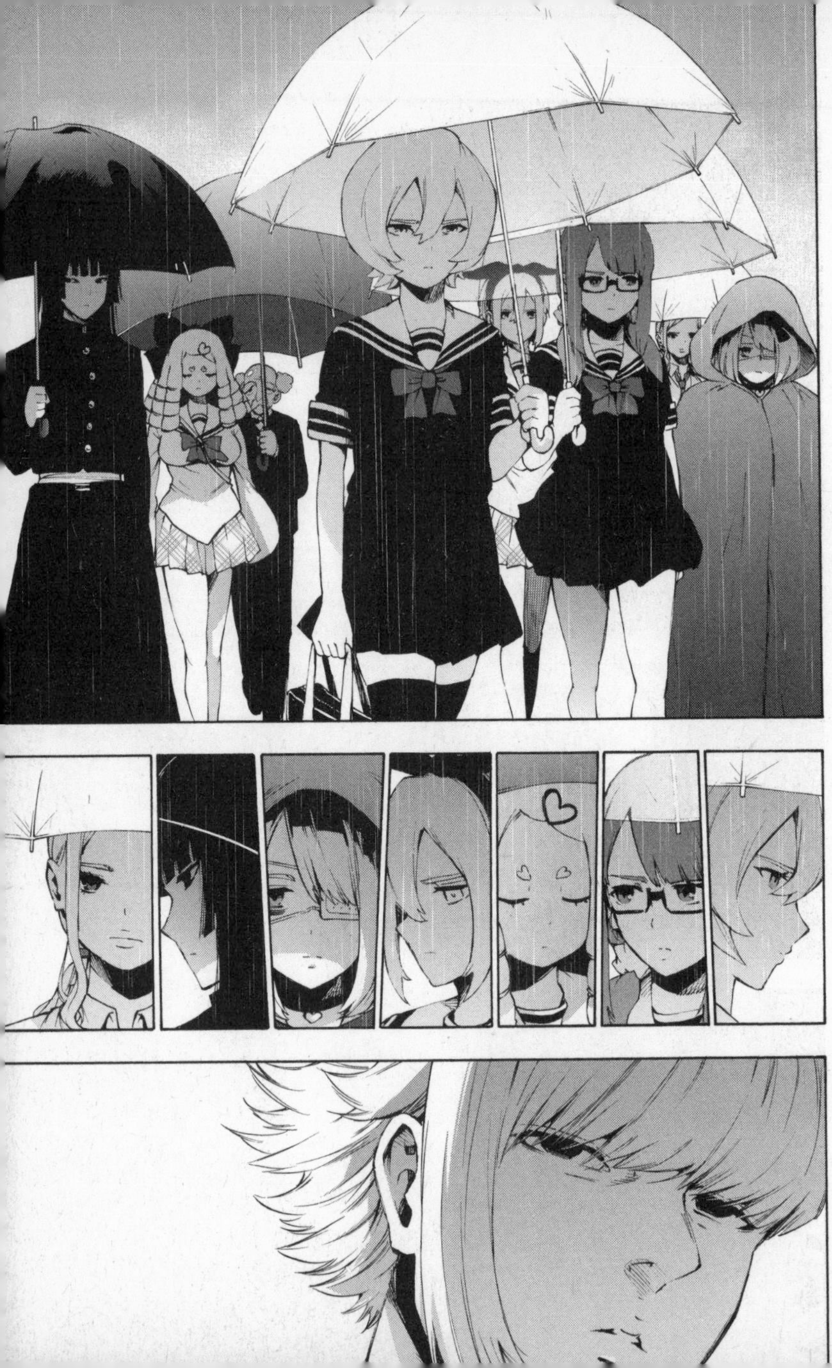

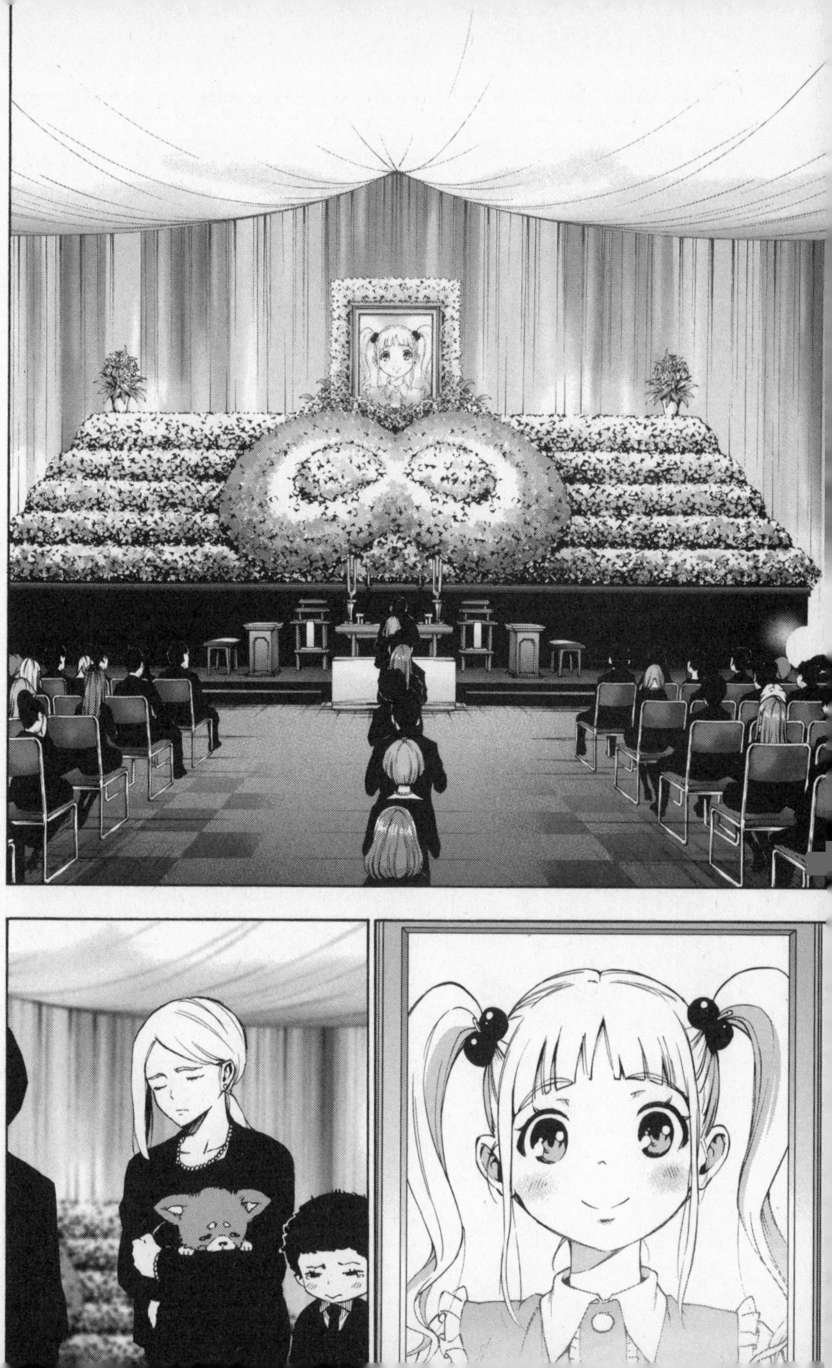

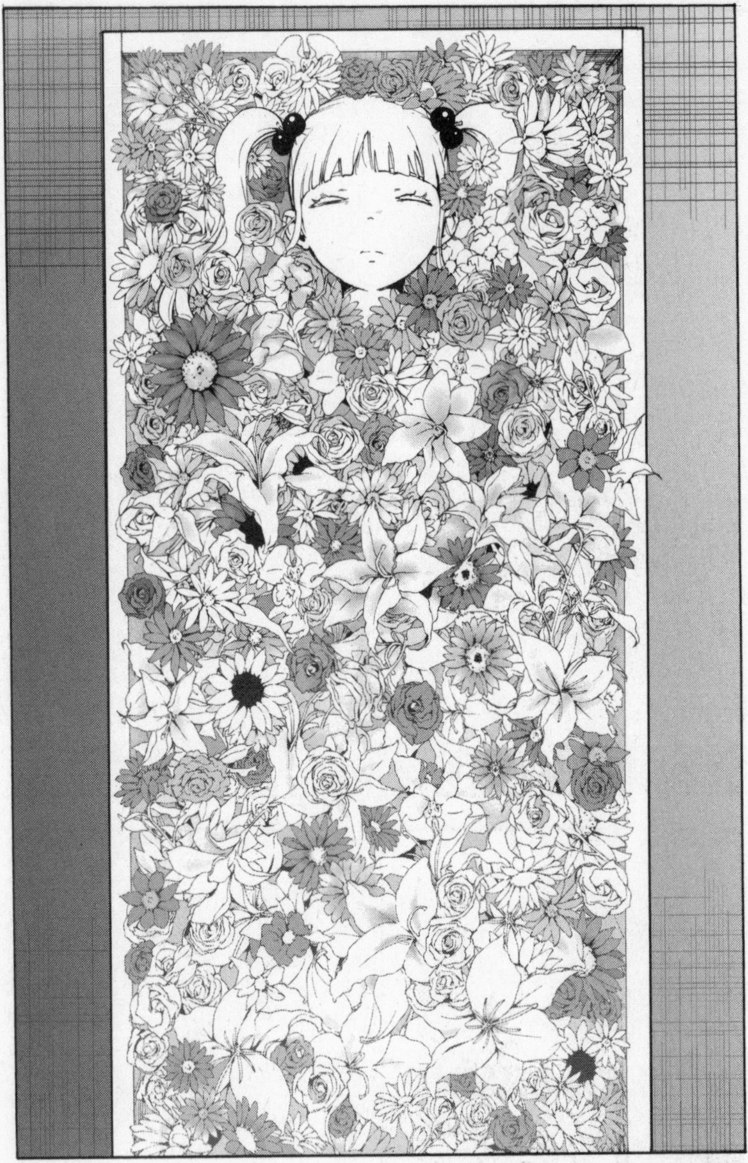

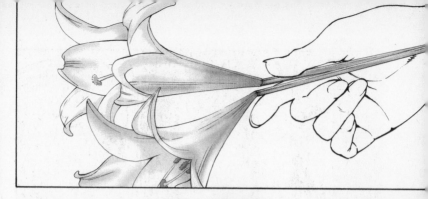

SHFF
す…っ

REST IN
PEACE.

ANAZAWA...

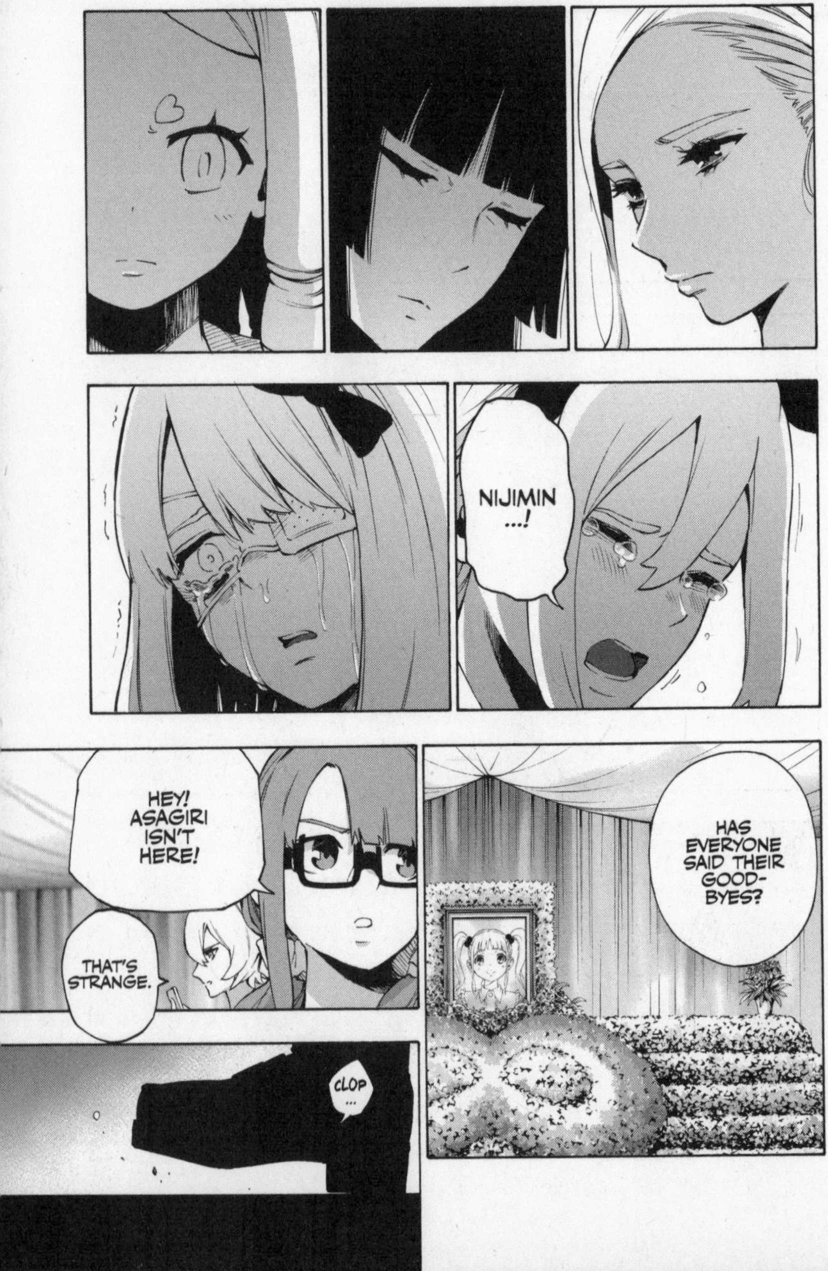
NIJIMIN ...!
HAS EVERYONE SAID THEIR GOOD-BYES?
HEY! ASAGIRI ISN'T HERE!
THAT'S STRANGE.
CLOP ...

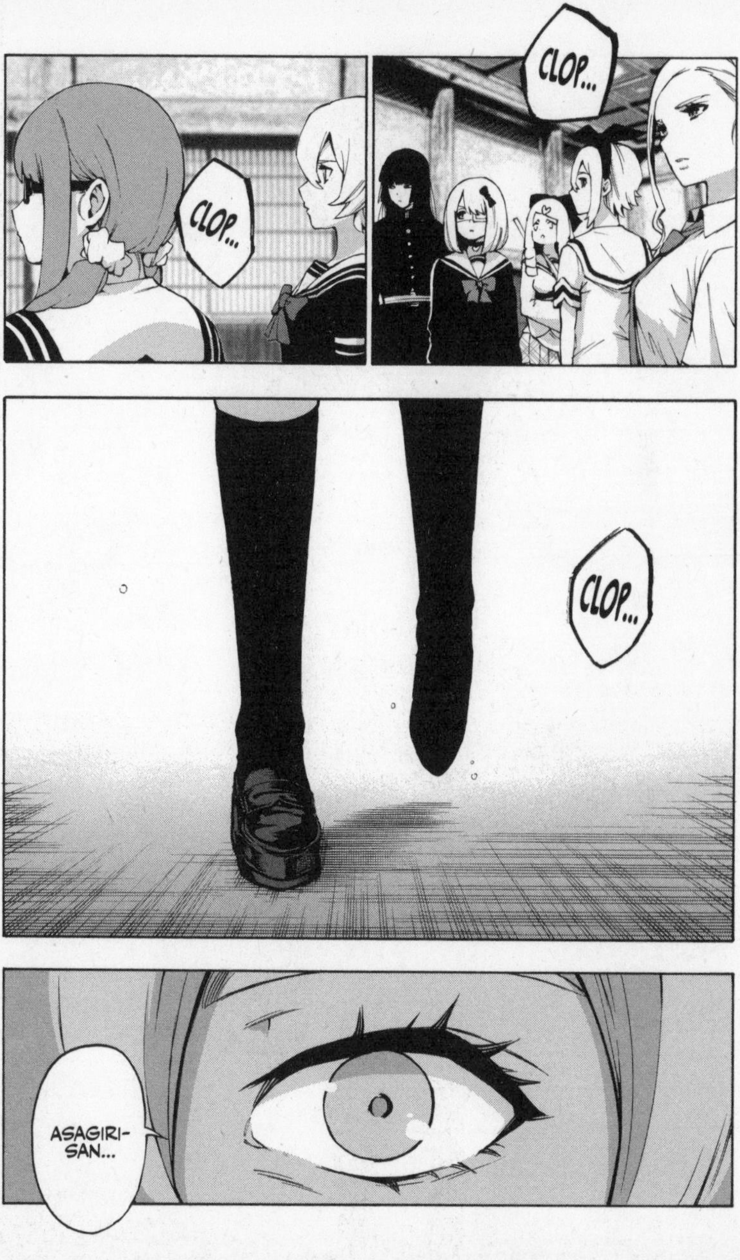
CLOP...
CLOP...
CLOP...
ASAGIRI-SAN...

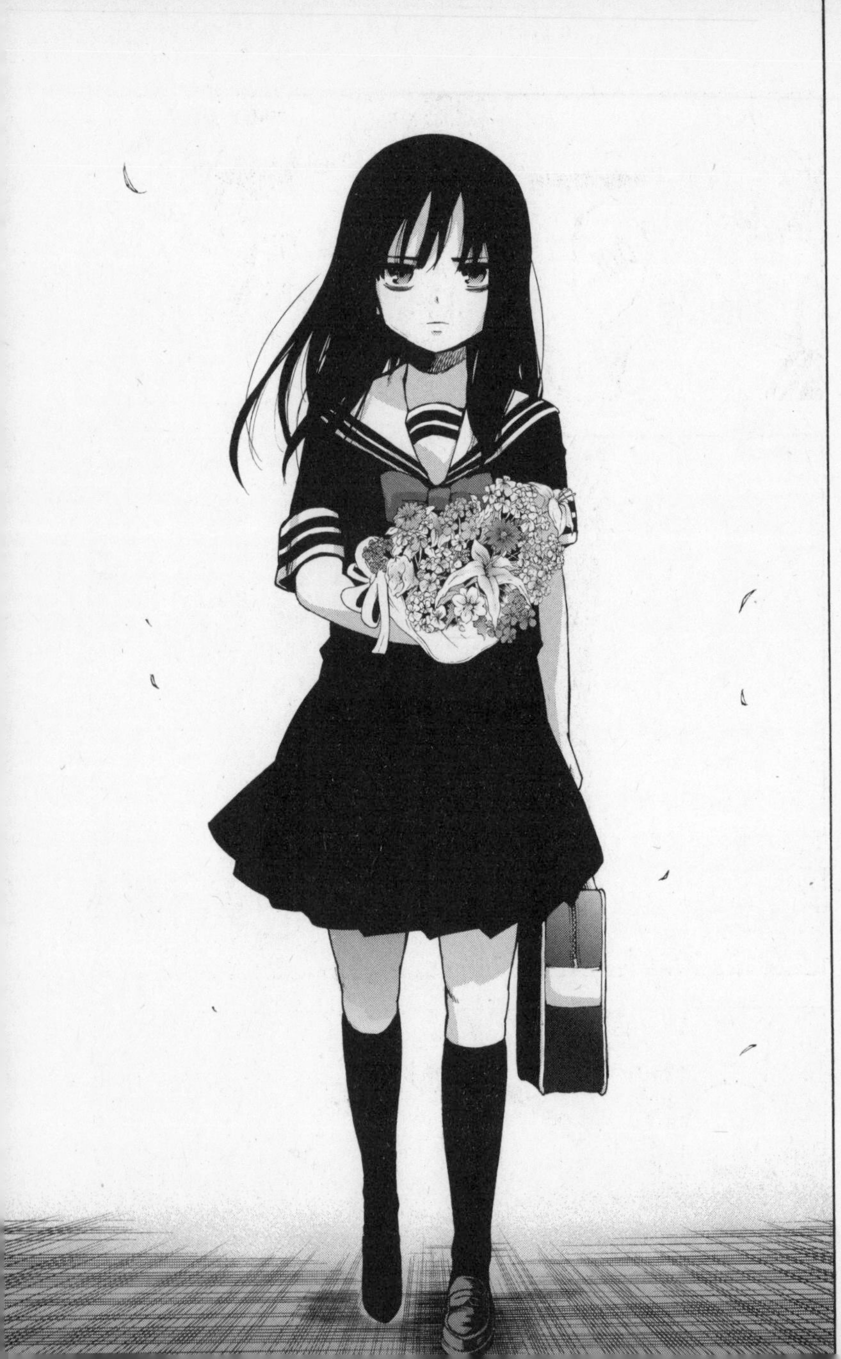

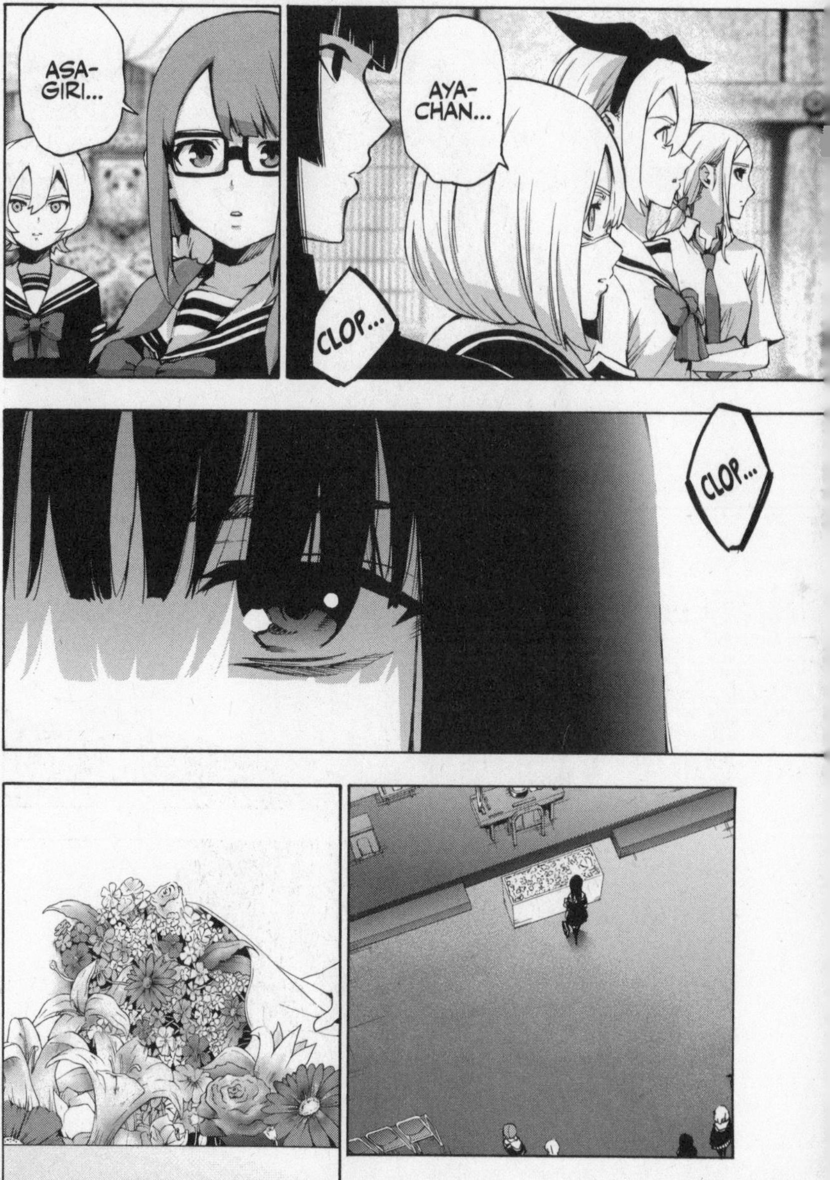
AYA-CHAN...
CLOP...
ASA-GIRI...
CLOP...

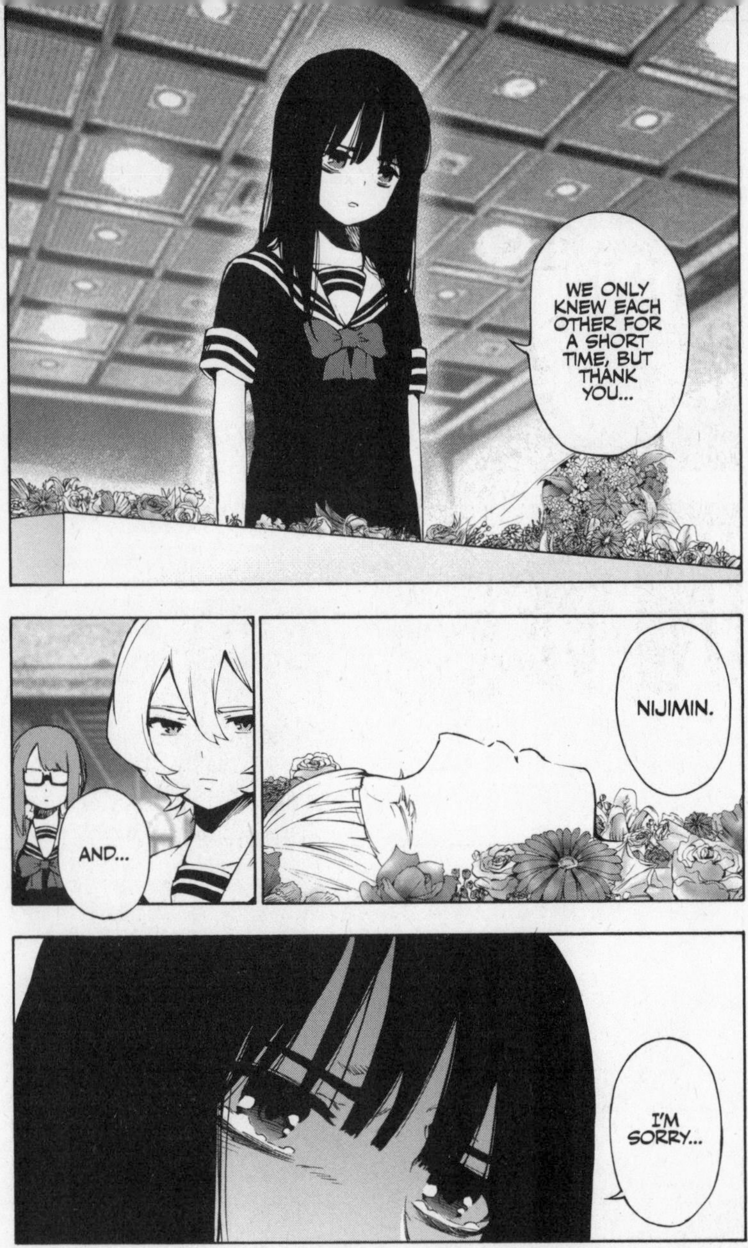
WE ONLY KNEW EACH OTHER FOR A SHORT TIME, BUT THANK YOU...
NIJIMIN.
AND...
I'M SORRY...

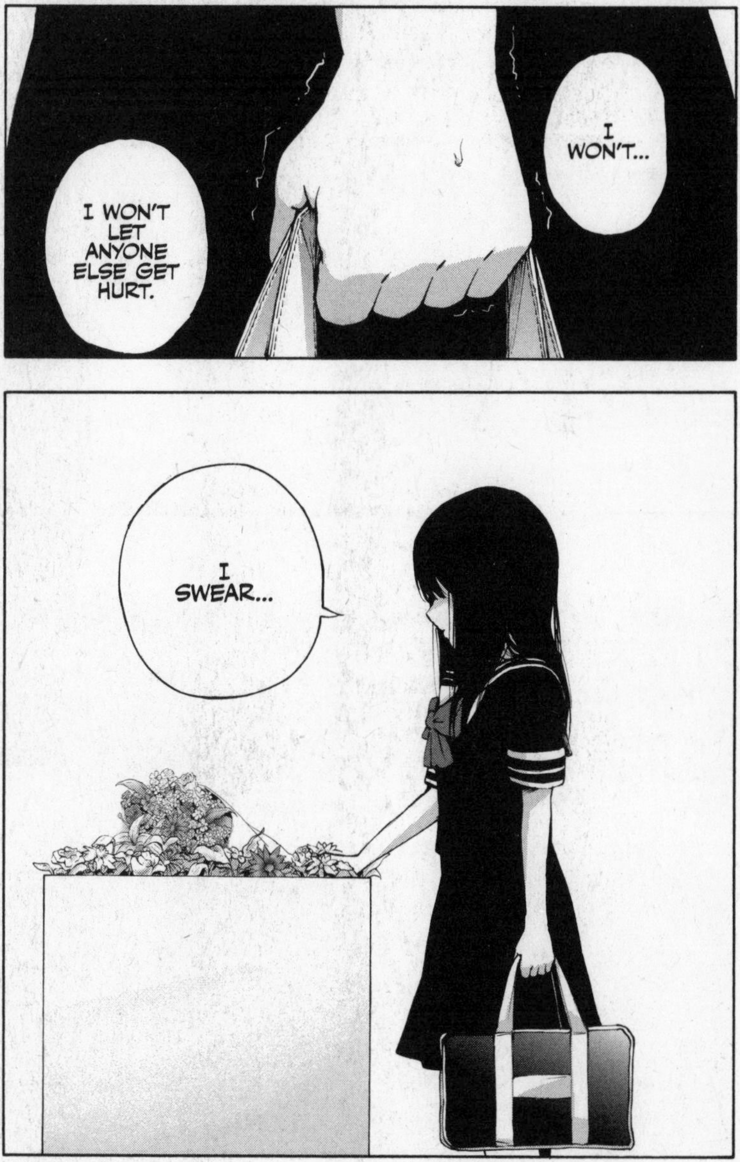
I WON'T...
I WON'T LET ANYONE ELSE GET HURT.
I SWEAR...

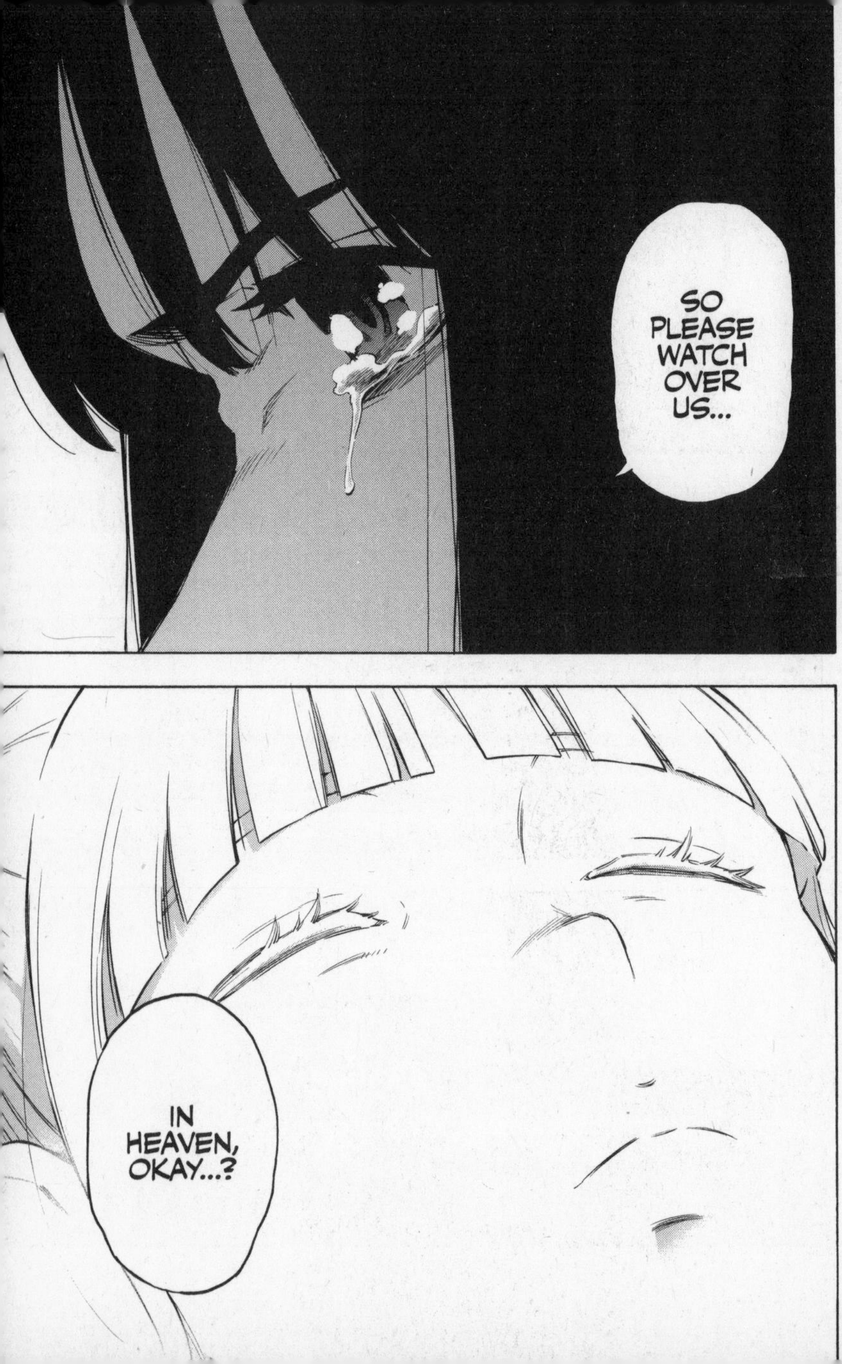
SO PLEASE WATCH OVER US...
IN HEAVEN, OKAY...?

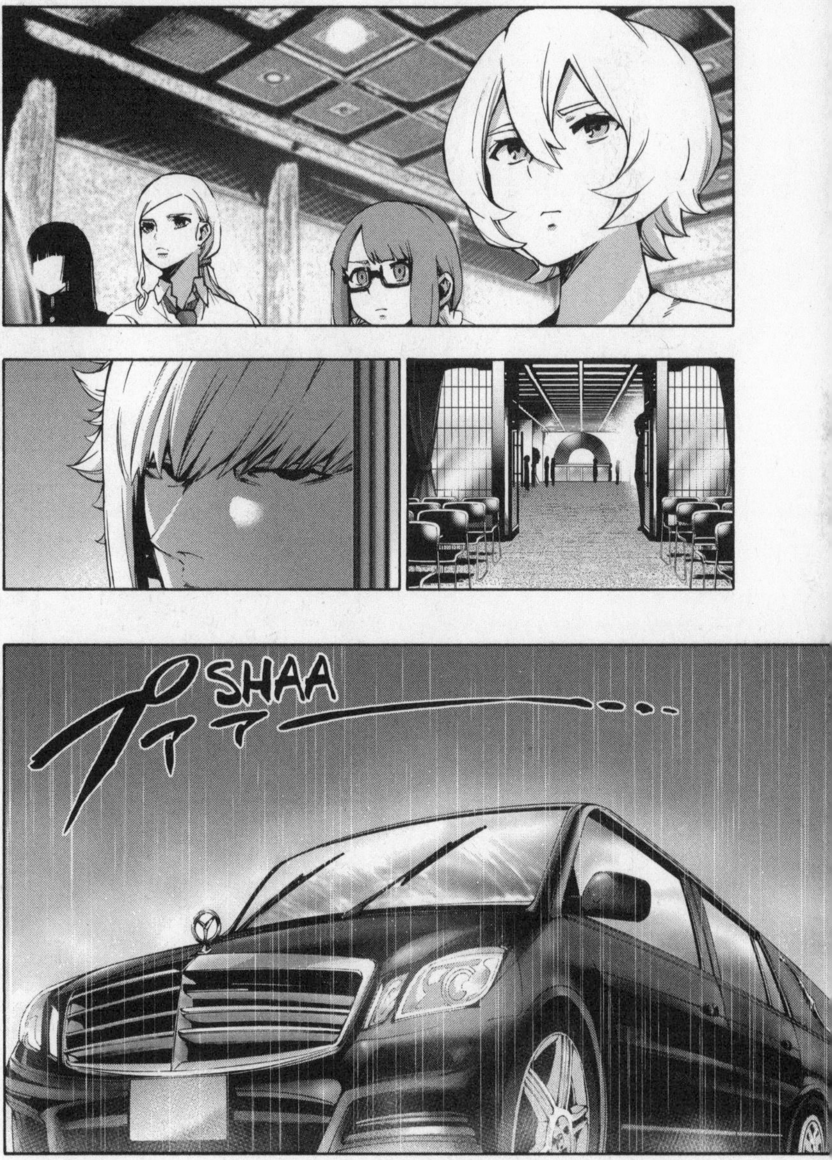
SHAA

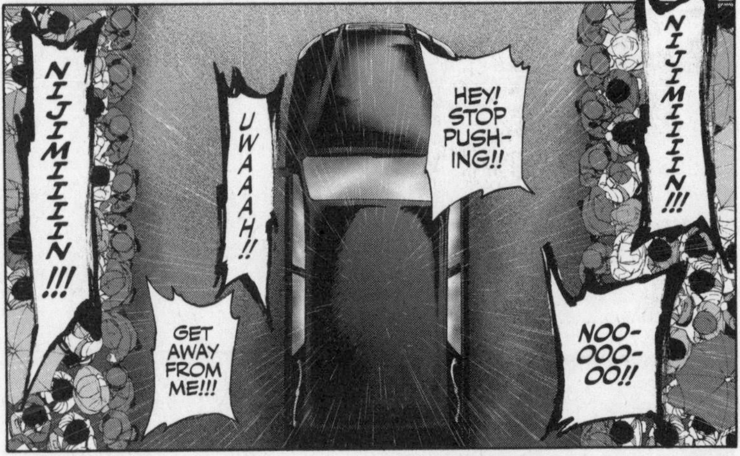
NIJIMIIIIN!!!
NOO-OOO-OO!!
HEY! STOP PUSH-ING!!
UWAAAAH!!
GET AWAY FROM ME!!!
NIJIMIIIIN!!!

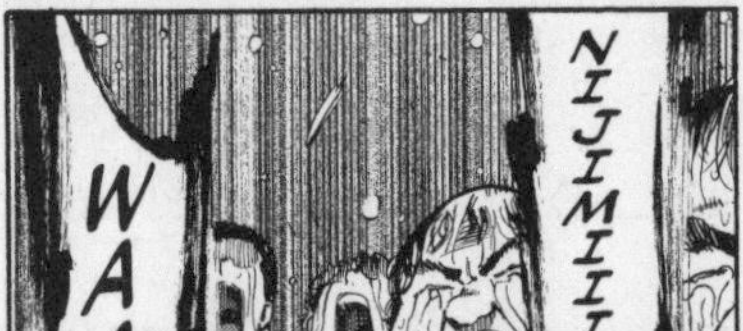
NIJIMIIIIN!!
WAAAAAH!

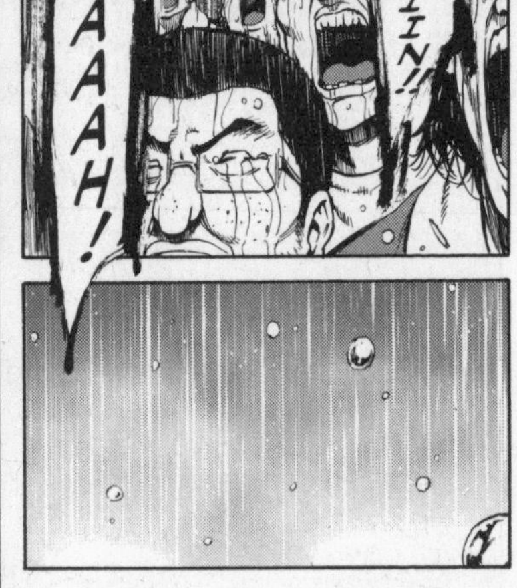

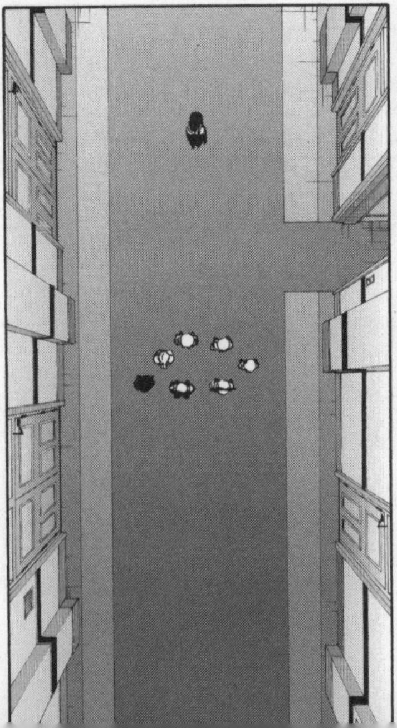

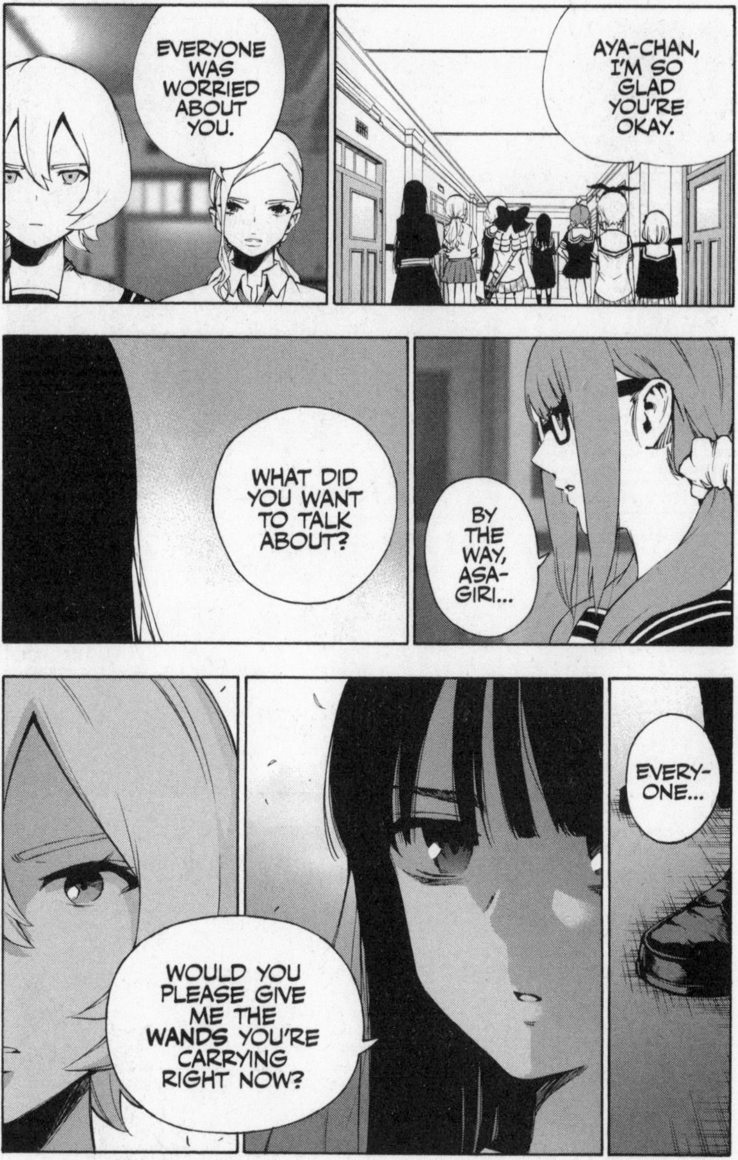
AYA-CHAN, I'M SO GLAD YOU'RE OKAY.
EVERYONE WAS WORRIED ABOUT YOU.
BY THE WAY, ASA-GIRI...
WHAT DID YOU WANT TO TALK ABOUT?
EVERY-ONE...
WOULD YOU PLEASE GIVE ME THE WANDS YOU'RE CARRYING RIGHT NOW?

ENTER.46 BOOM

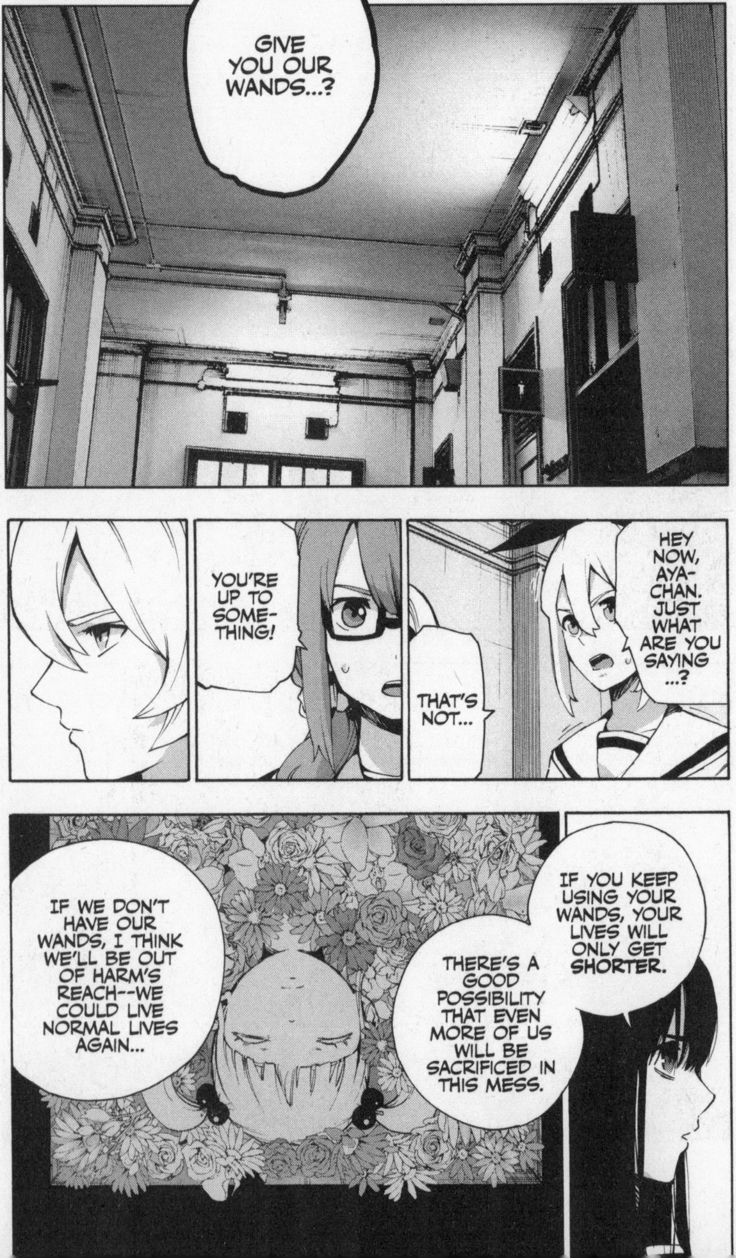
GIVE YOU OUR WANDS...?
HEY NOW, AYA-CHAN. JUST WHAT ARE YOU SAYING ...?
THAT'S NOT...
YOU'RE UP TO SOME-THING!
IF YOU KEEP USING YOUR WANDS, YOUR LIVES WILL ONLY GET **SHORTER.**
THERE'S A GOOD POSSIBILITY THAT EVEN MORE OF US WILL BE SACRIFICED IN THIS MESS.
IF WE DON'T HAVE OUR WANDS, I THINK WE'LL BE OUT OF HARM'S REACH--WE COULD LIVE NORMAL LIVES AGAIN...

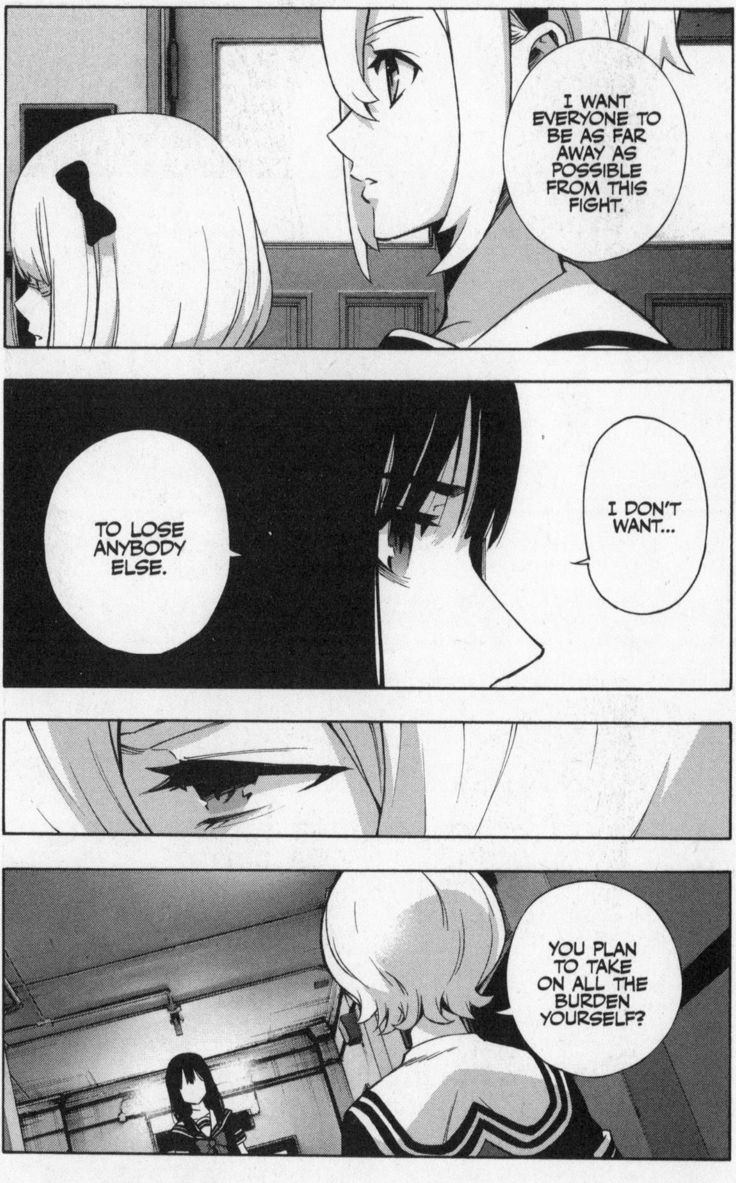
I WANT EVERYONE TO BE AS FAR AWAY AS POSSIBLE FROM THIS FIGHT.
I DON'T WANT...
TO LOSE ANYBODY ELSE.
YOU PLAN TO TAKE ON ALL THE BURDEN YOURSELF?

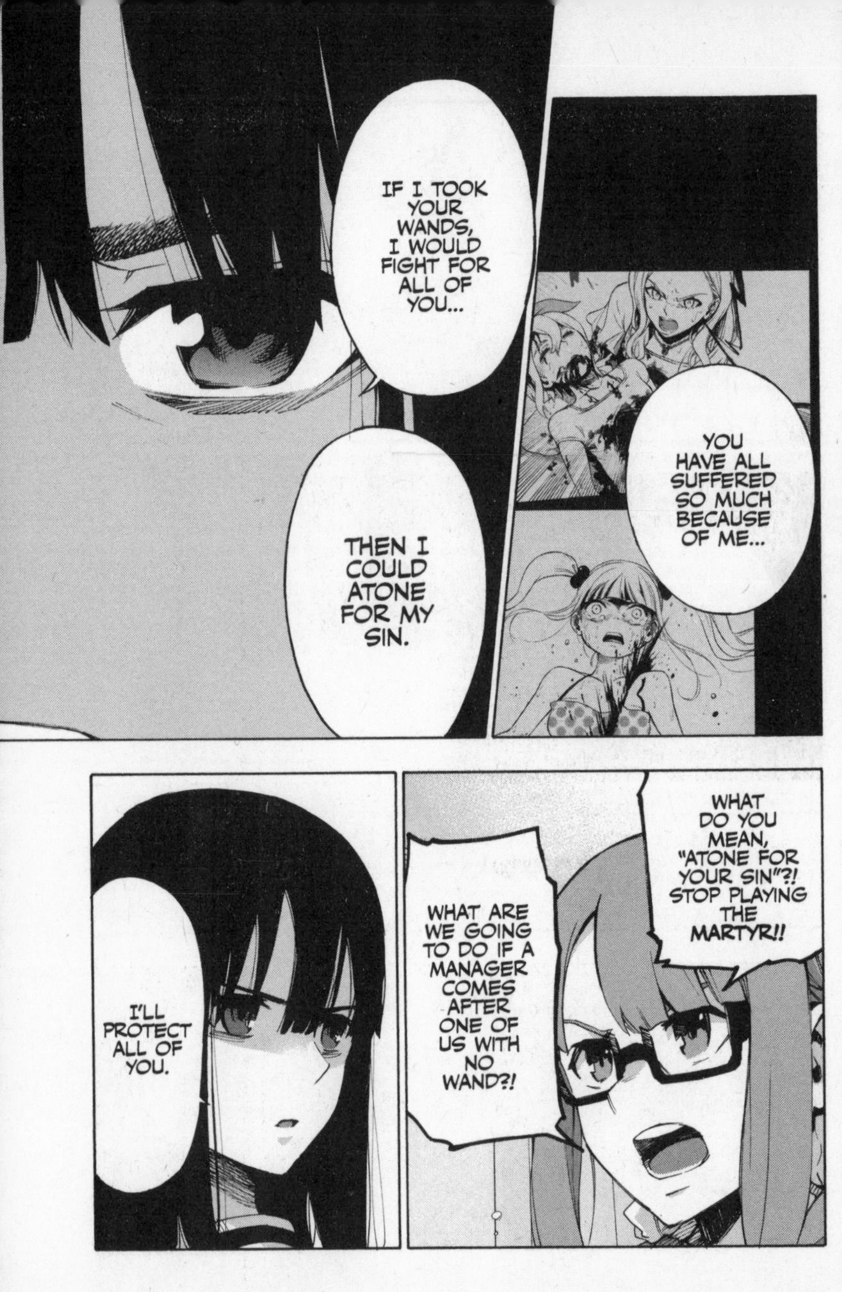
YOU HAVE ALL SUFFERED SO MUCH BECAUSE OF ME...
IF I TOOK YOUR WANDS, I WOULD FIGHT FOR ALL OF YOU...
THEN I COULD ATONE FOR MY SIN.
WHAT DO YOU MEAN, "ATONE FOR YOUR SIN"?! STOP PLAYING THE MARTYR!!
WHAT ARE WE GOING TO DO IF A MANAGER COMES AFTER ONE OF US WITH NO WAND?!
I'LL PROTECT ALL OF YOU.

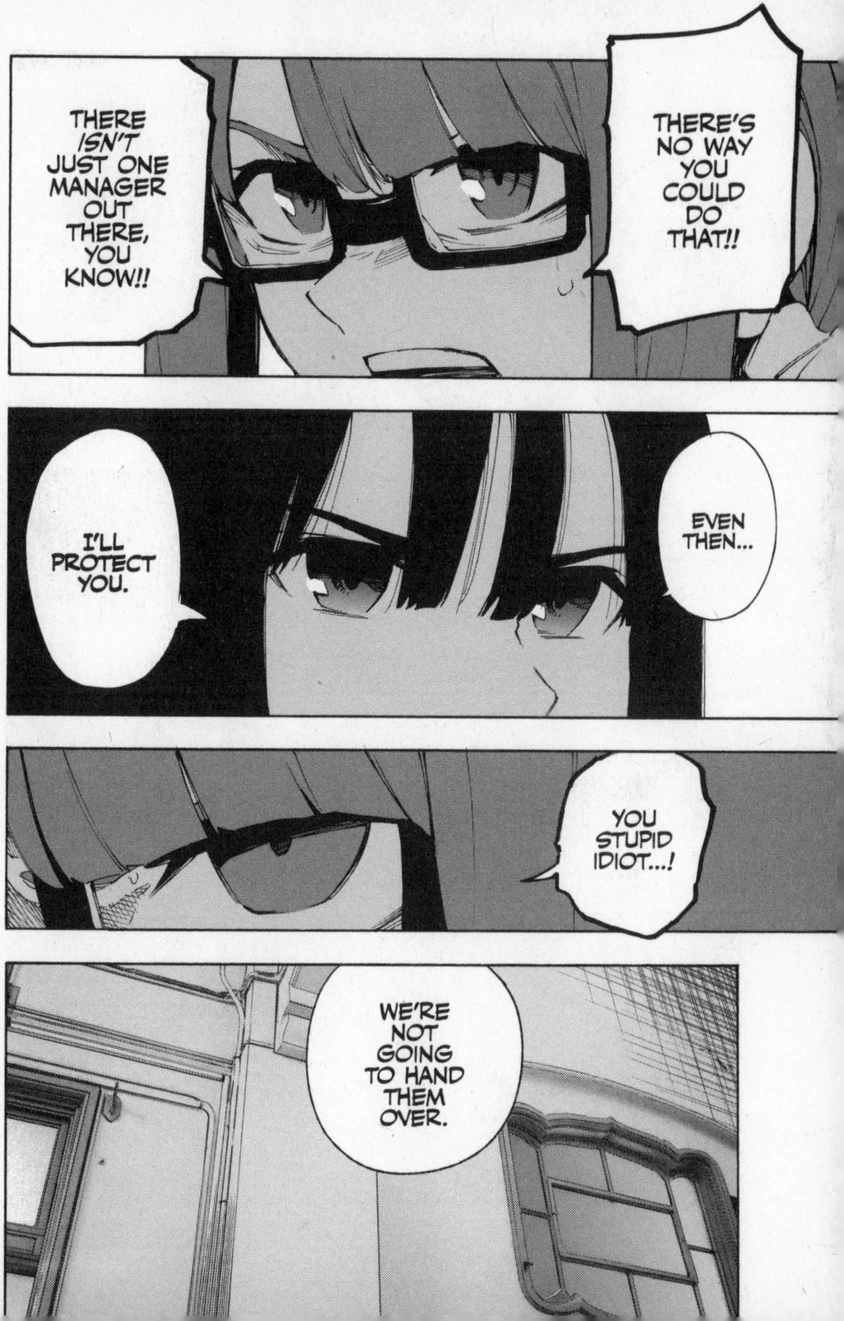
THERE'S NO WAY YOU COULD DO THAT!!
THERE *ISN'T* JUST ONE MANAGER OUT THERE, YOU KNOW!!
EVEN THEN...
I'LL PROTECT YOU.
YOU STUPID IDIOT...!
WE'RE NOT GOING TO HAND THEM OVER.

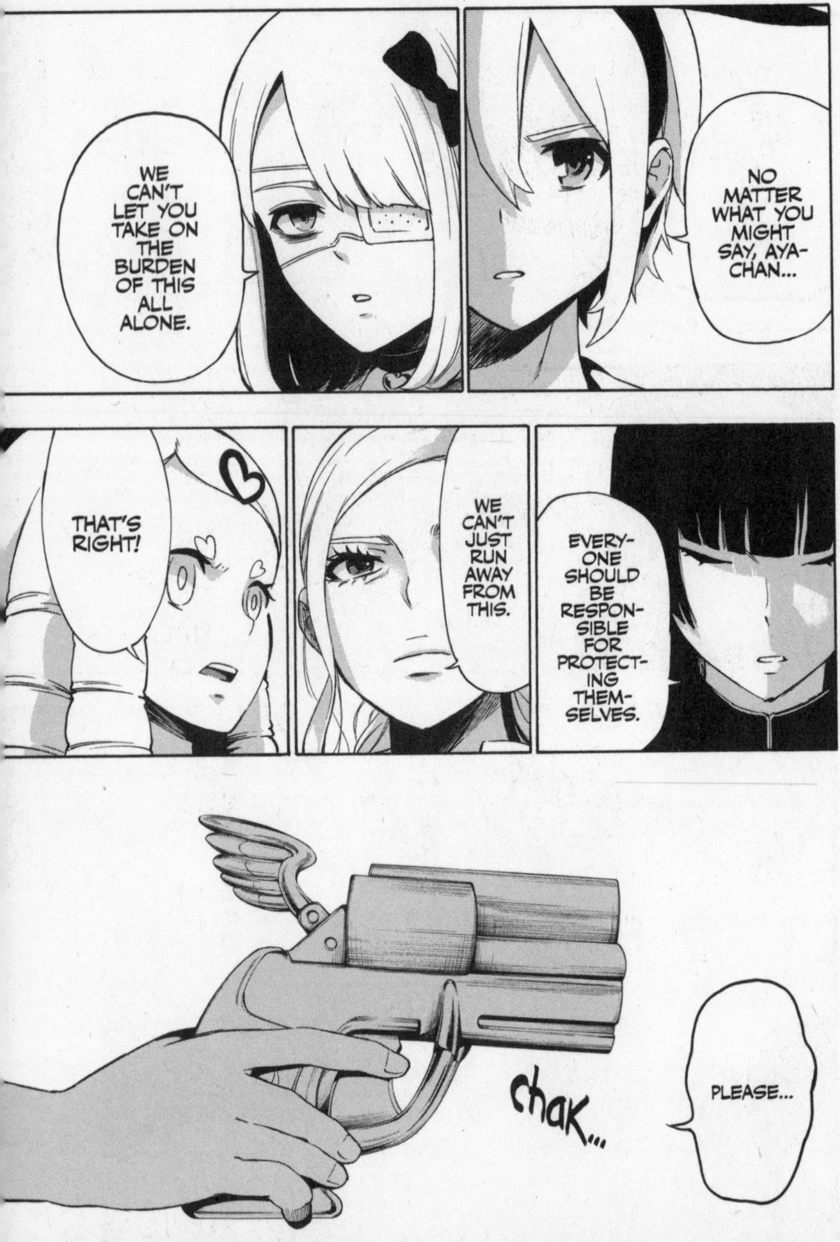
NO MATTER WHAT YOU MIGHT SAY, AYA-CHAN...
WE CAN'T LET YOU TAKE ON THE BURDEN OF THIS ALL ALONE.
EVERY-ONE SHOULD BE RESPON-SIBLE FOR PROTECT-ING THEM-SELVES.
WE CAN'T JUST RUN AWAY FROM THIS.
THAT'S RIGHT!
PLEASE...
chak...

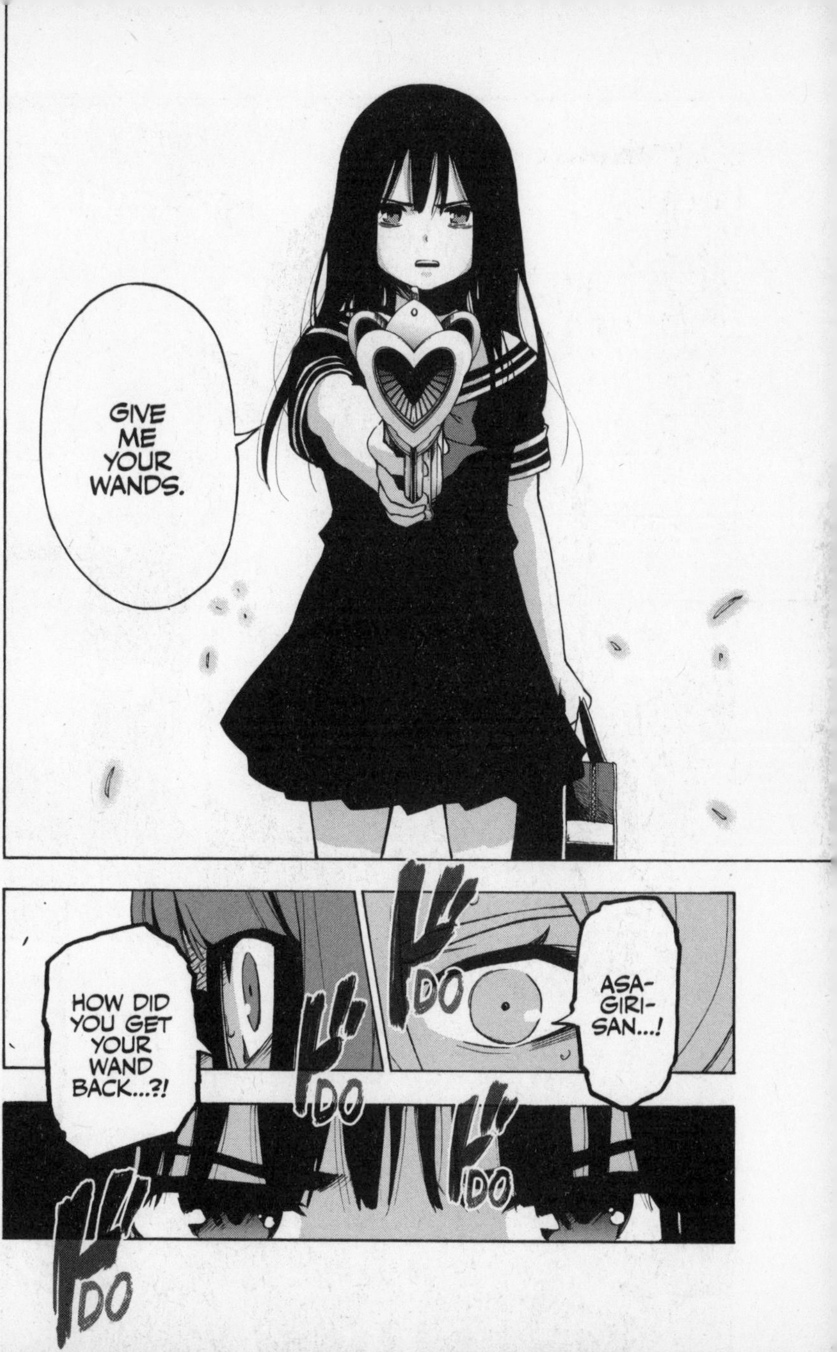
GIVE ME YOUR WANDS.
DO
ASA-GIRI-SAN...!
HOW DID YOU GET YOUR WAND BACK...?!
DO
DO
DO

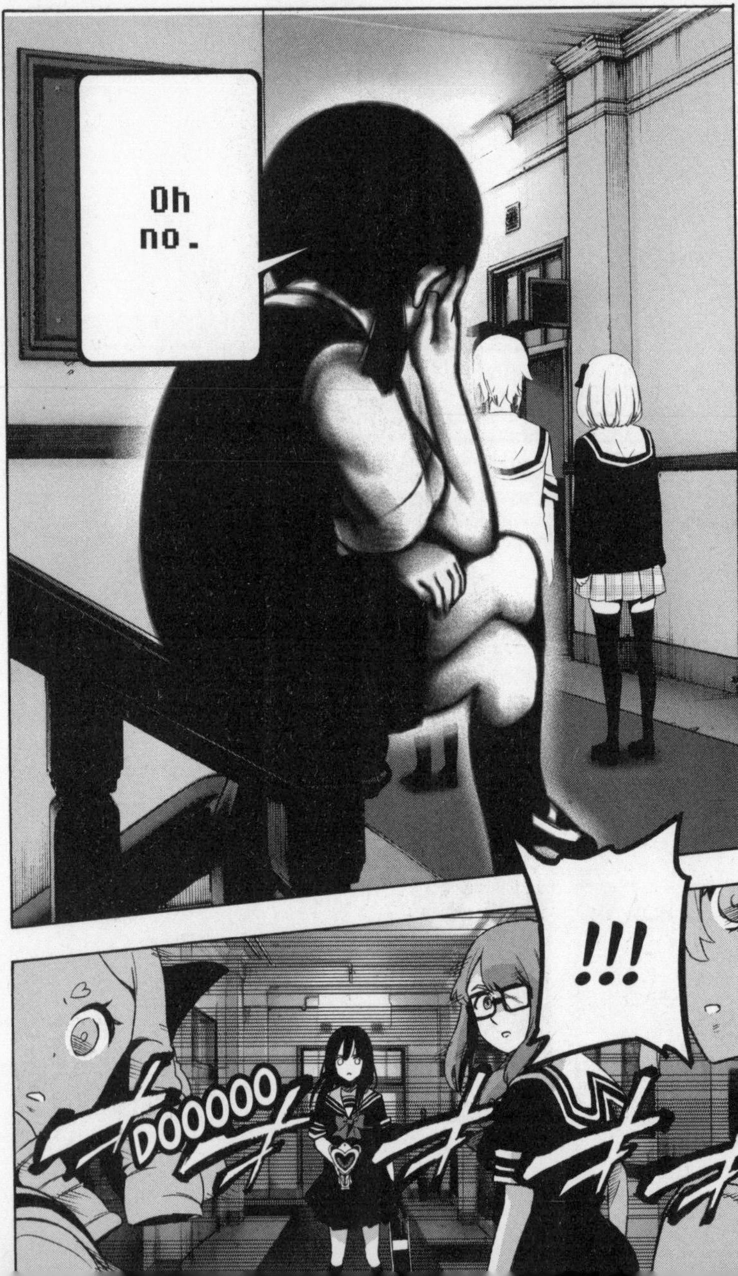
Oh no.
!!!
DOOOOO

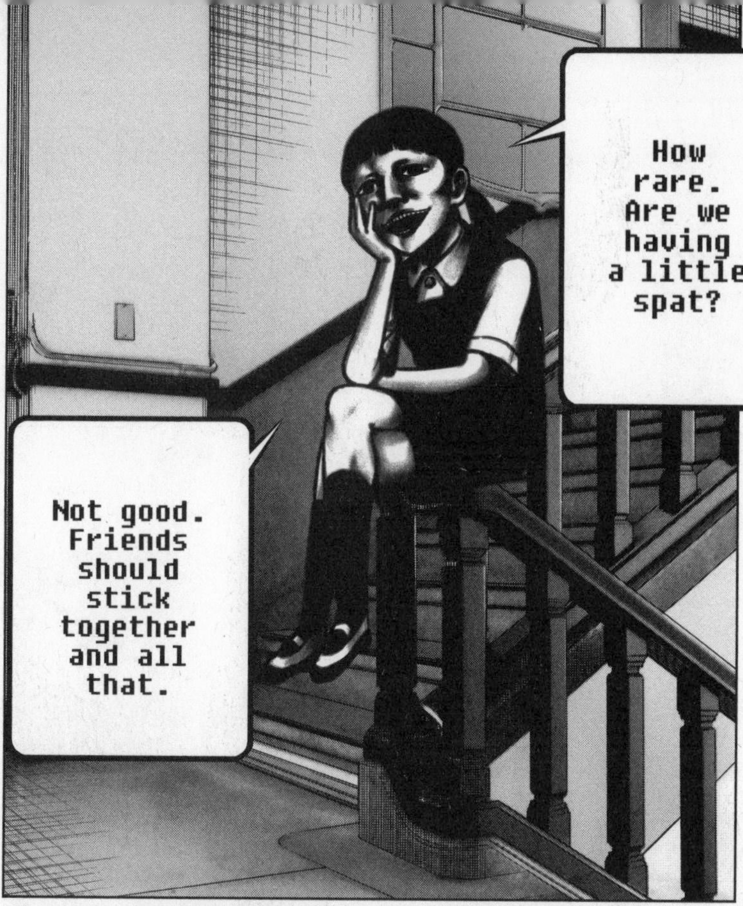
How rare. Are we having a little spat?
Not good. Friends should stick together and all that.
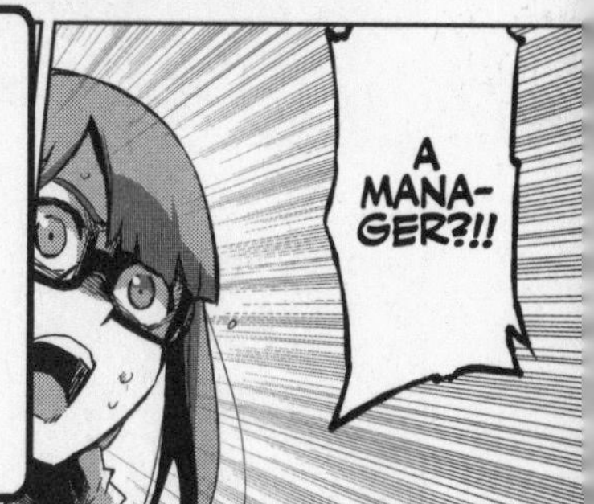
A MANA-GER?!!
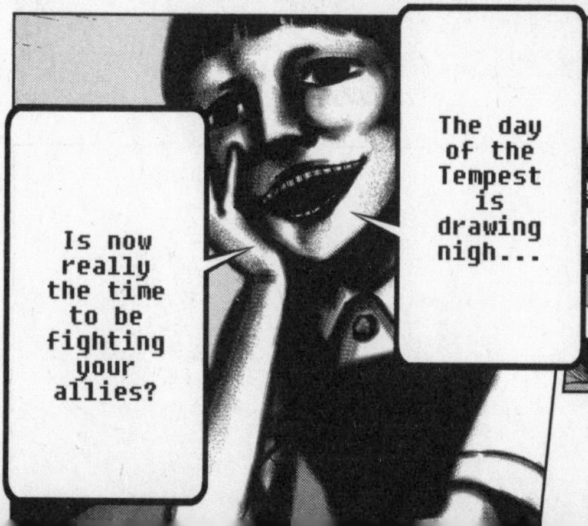
The day of the Tempest is drawing nigh...
Is now really the time to be fighting your allies?

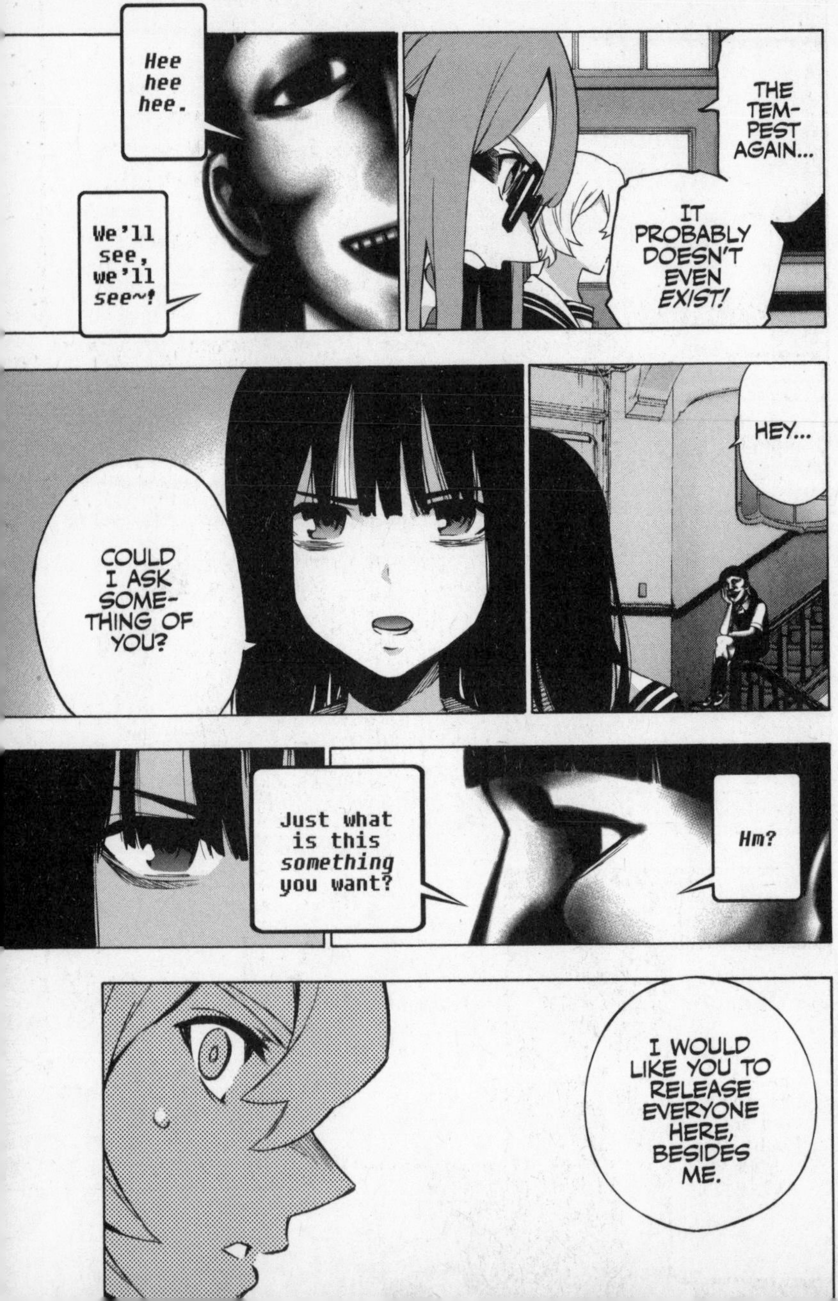
THE TEMPEST AGAIN...
IT PROBABLY DOESN'T EVEN *EXIST!*
Hee hee hee.
We'll see, we'll see~!
HEY...
COULD I ASK SOMETHING OF YOU?
Hm?
Just what is this *something* you want?
I WOULD LIKE YOU TO RELEASE EVERYONE HERE, BESIDES ME.

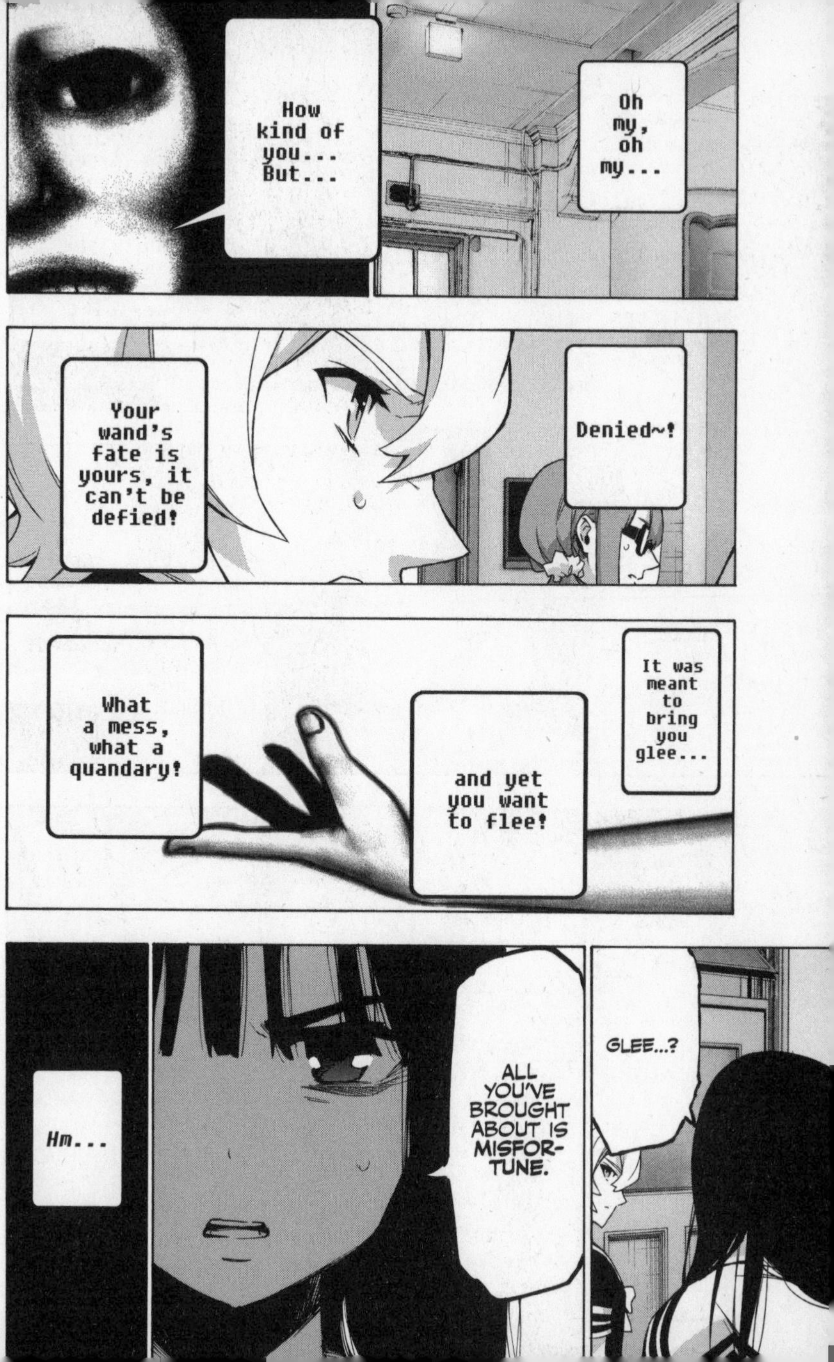
Oh my, oh my...
How kind of you... But...
Denied~!
Your wand's fate is yours, it can't be defied!
It was meant to bring you glee...
and yet you want to flee!
What a mess, what a quandary!
GLEE...?
ALL YOU'VE BROUGHT ABOUT IS MISFOR-TUNE.
Hm...

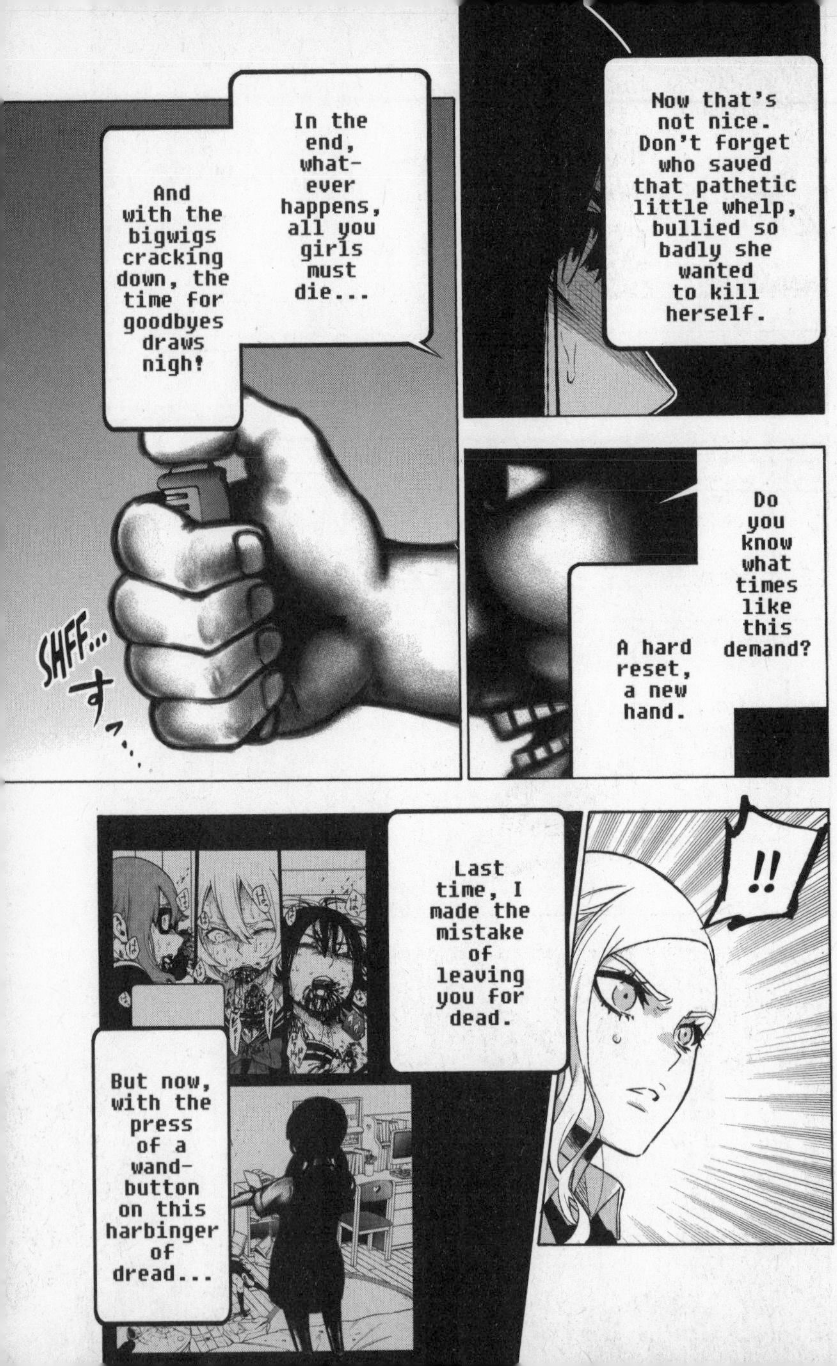

Now that's not nice. Don't forget who saved that pathetic little whelp, bullied so badly she wanted to kill herself.
Do you know what times like this demand?
A hard reset, a new hand.
In the end, what-ever happens, all you girls must die...
And with the bigwigs cracking down, the time for goodbyes draws nigh!
SHFF...
!!
Last time, I made the mistake of leaving you for dead.
But now, with the press of a wand-button on this harbinger of dread...

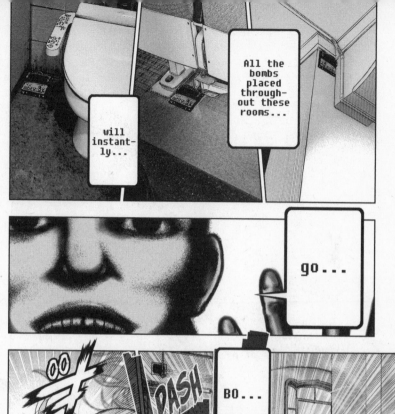

All the
bombs
placed
through-
out these
rooms...

will
instant-
ly...

go...

BO...

DASH

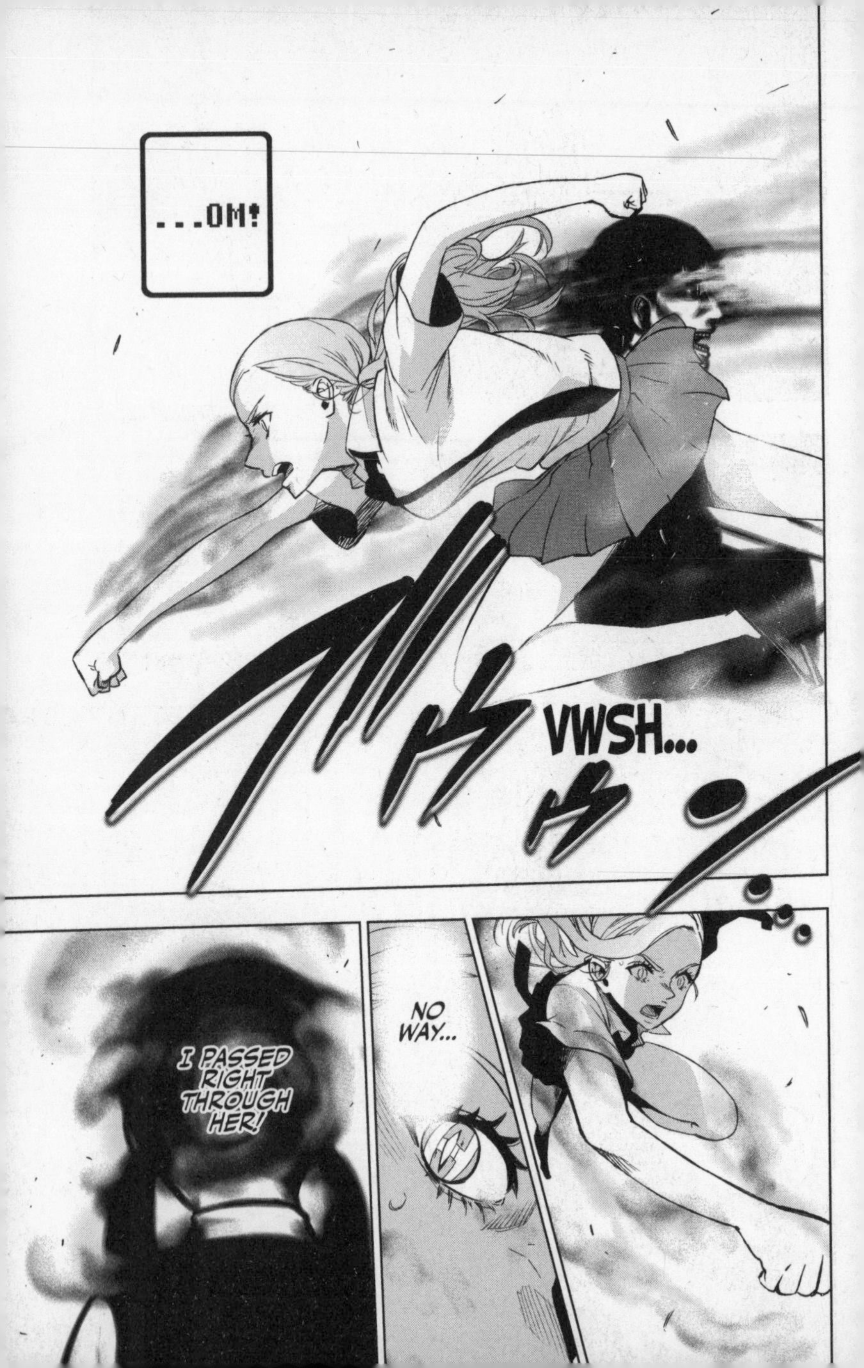
...OM!
VWSH...
NO WAY...
I PASSED RIGHT THROUGH HER!

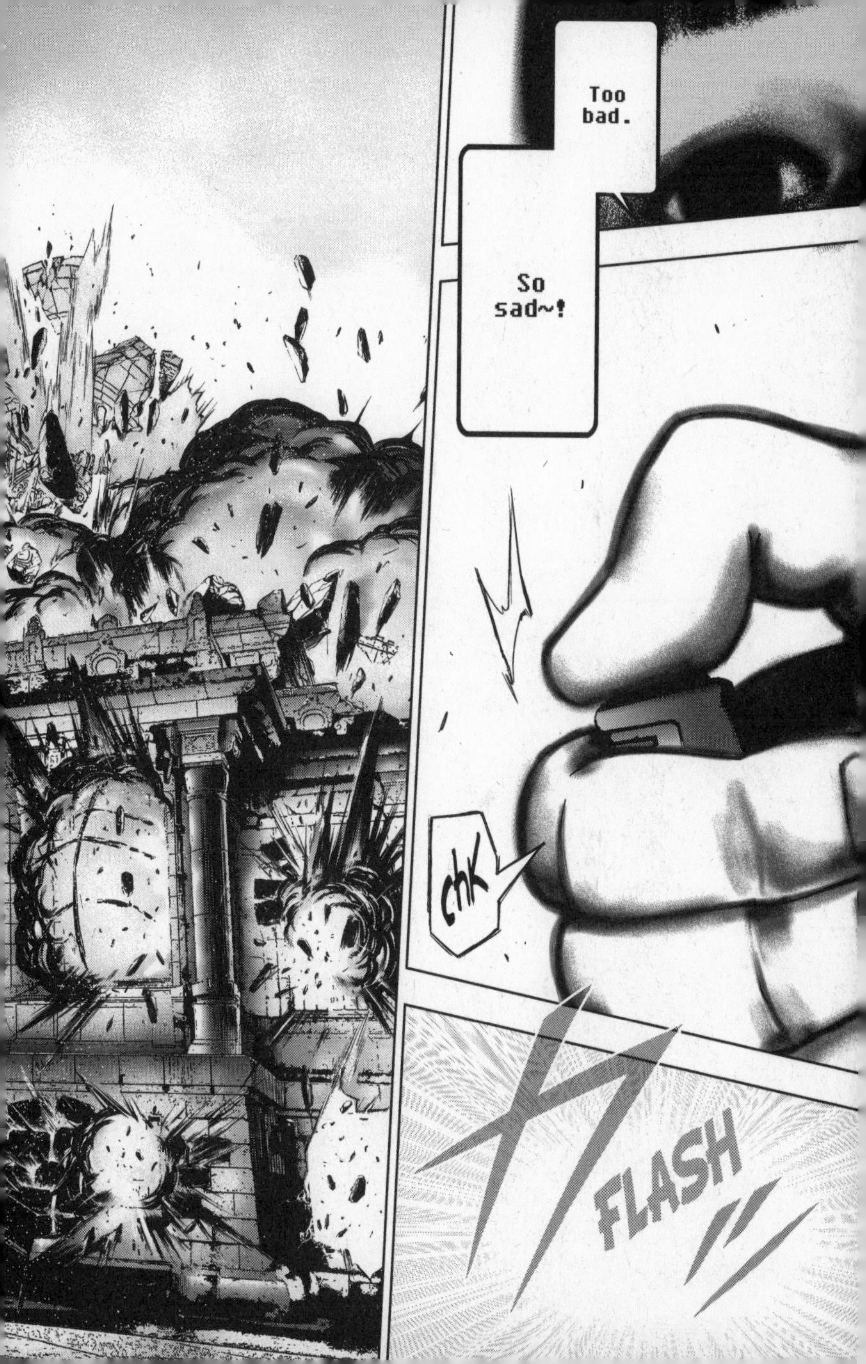
Too bad.
So sad~!
chk
FLASH

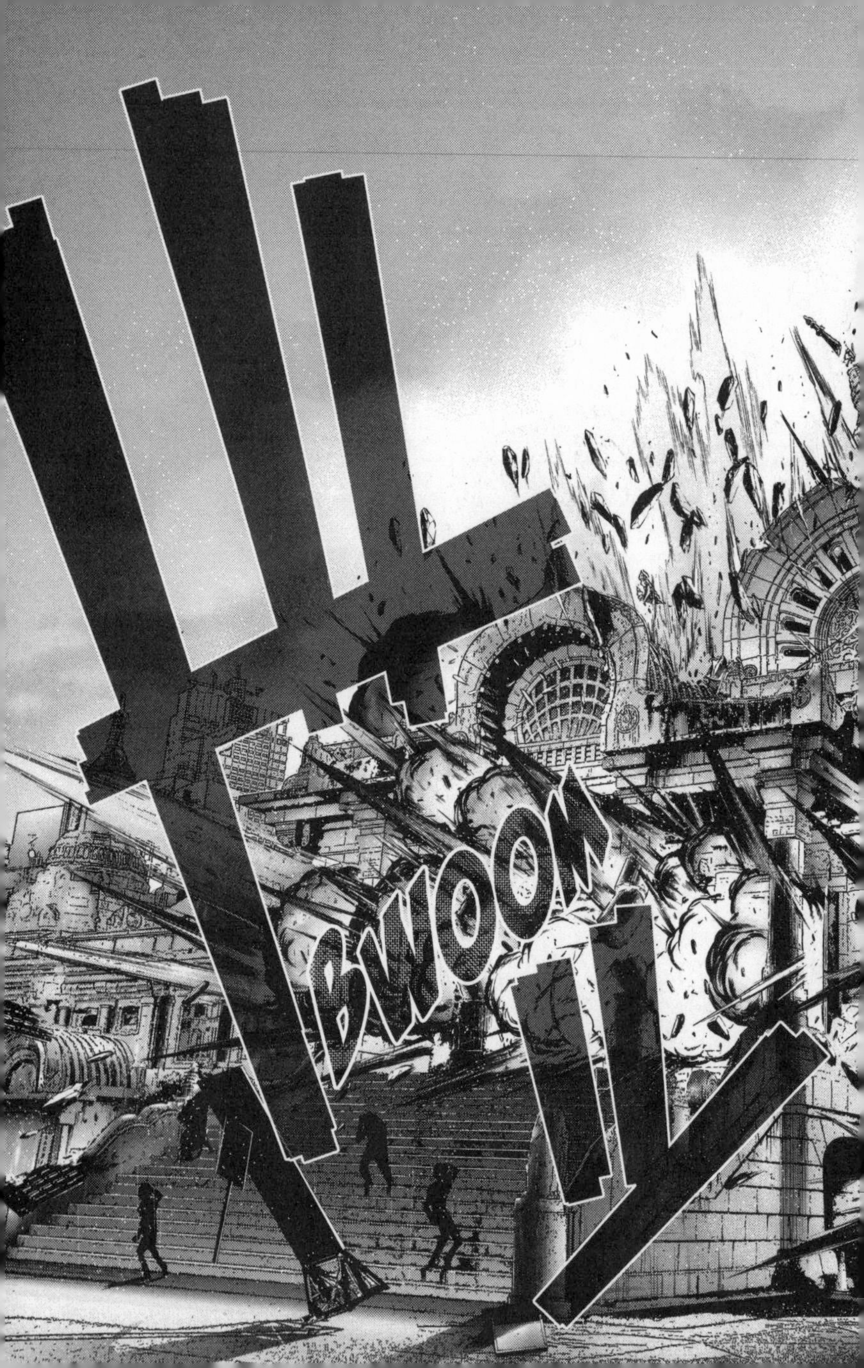
BWOOM

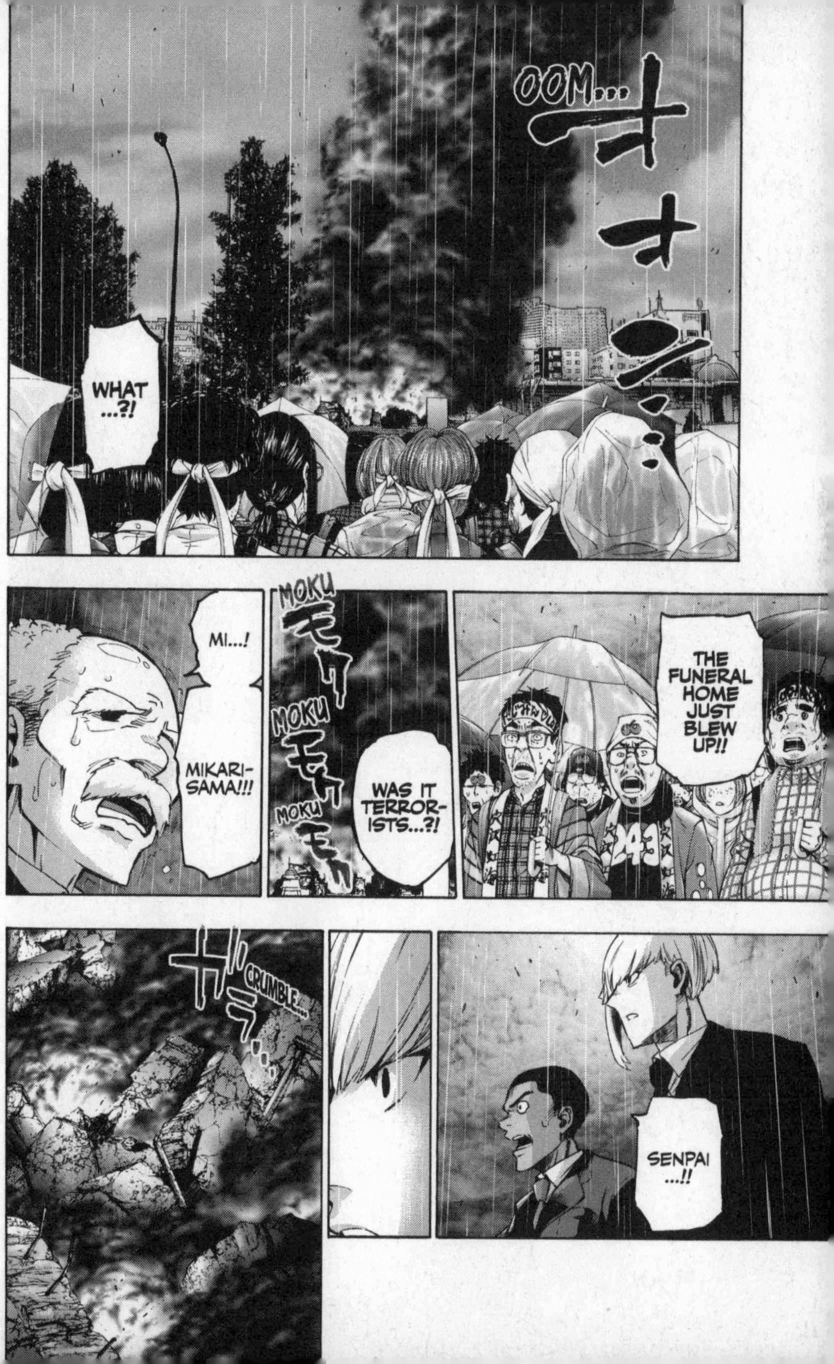
OOM...
WHAT ...?!
THE FUNERAL HOME JUST BLEW UP!!
WAS IT TERRORISTS...?!
MOKU
MOKU
MOKU
MI...!
MIKARI-SAMA!!!
SENPAI ...!!
CRUMBLE...

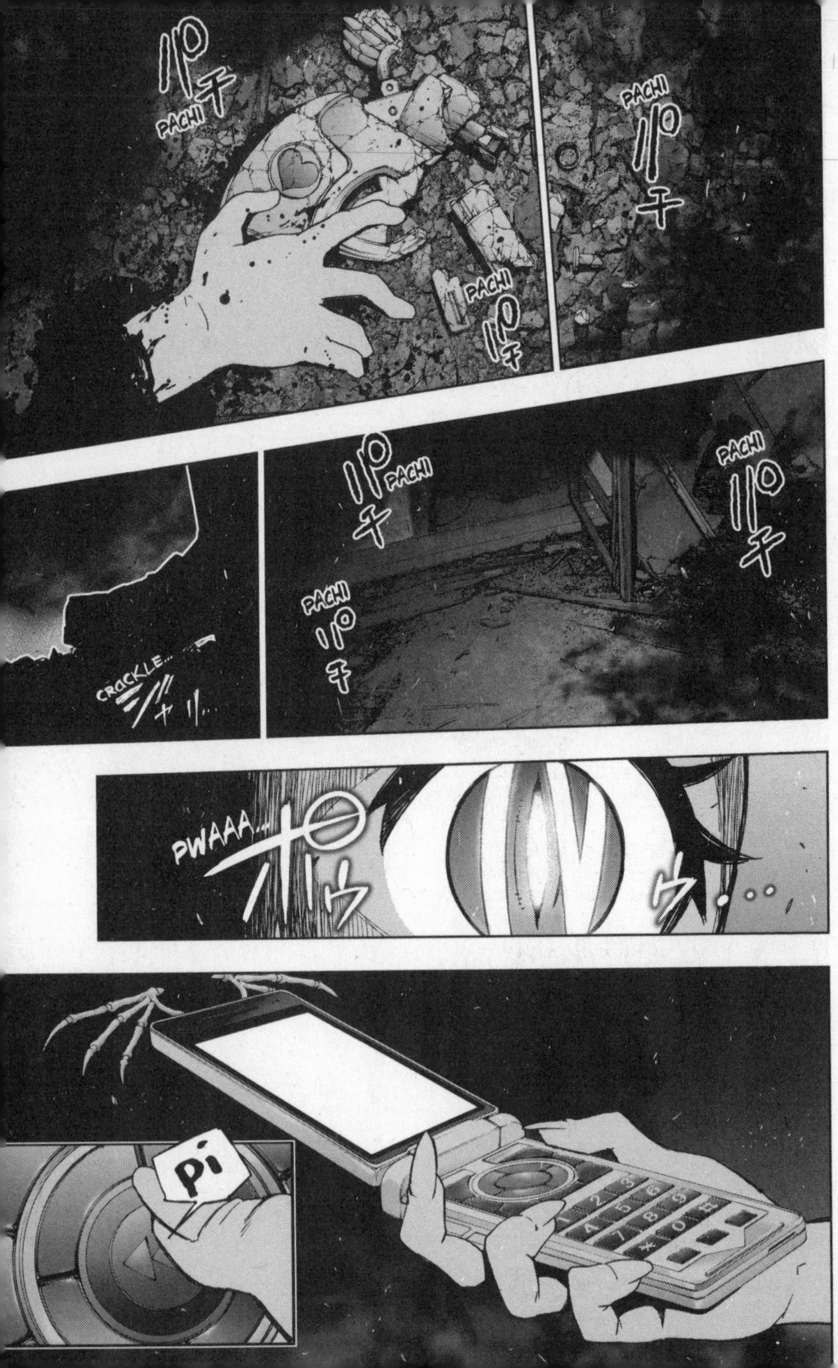
PACHI
パチ
パチ
PACHI
PACHI
パチ
PACHI
パチ
パチ
PACHI
PACHI
パチ
CRACKLE...
ジャリ...
PWAAA...
ポゥ
ゥ...
Pi

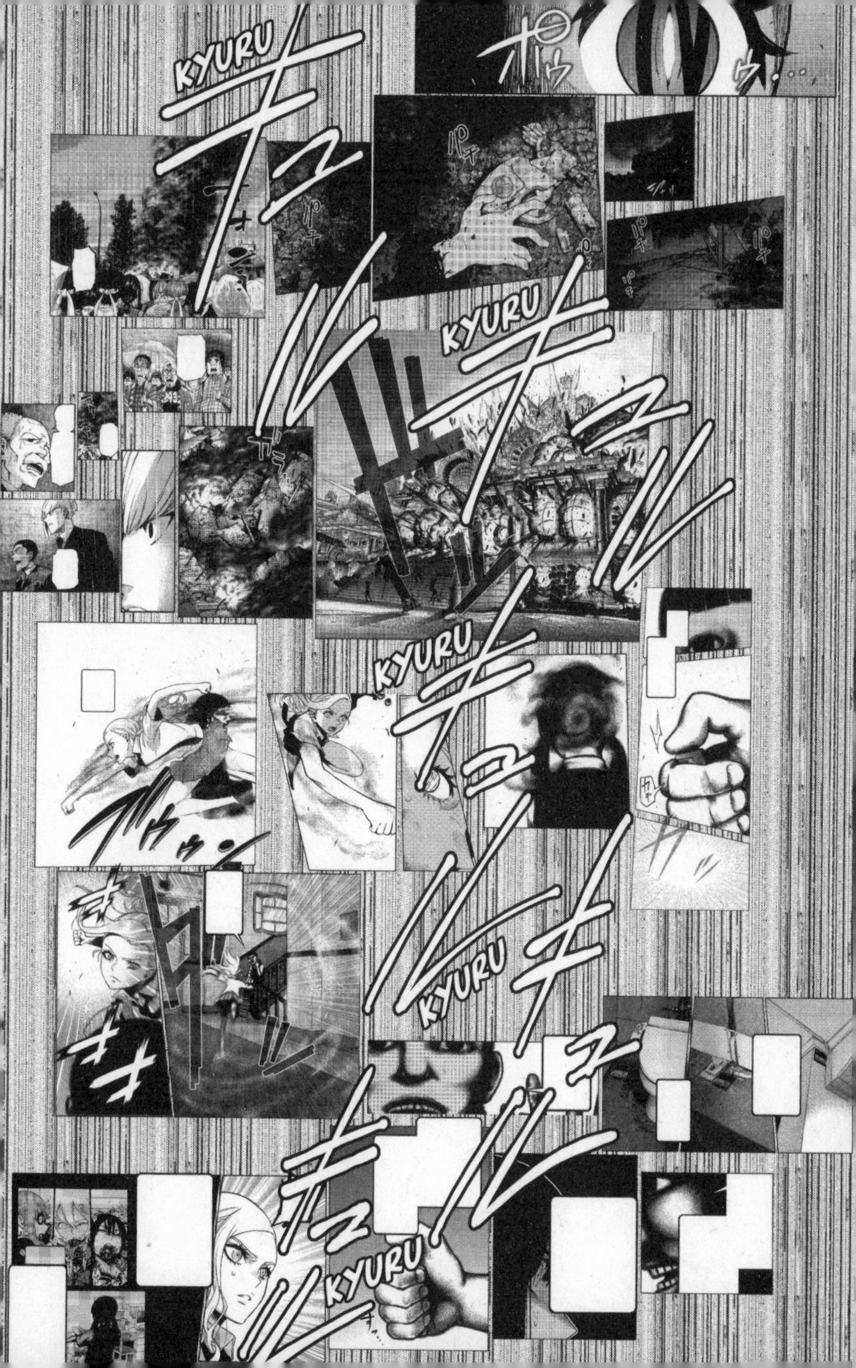
KYURU
KYURU
KYURU
KYURU
KYURU

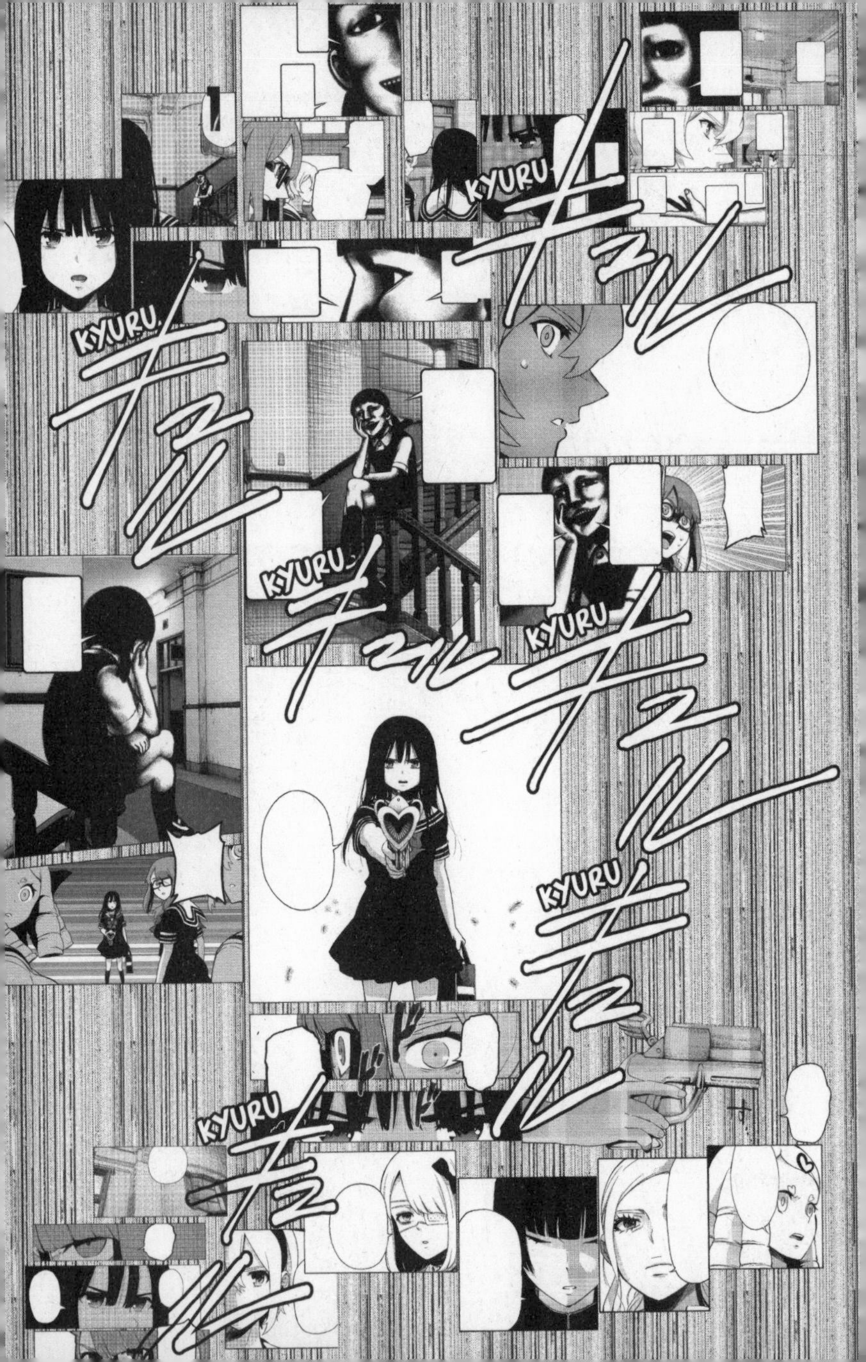
KYURU
KYURU
KYURU
KYURU
KYURU
KYURU

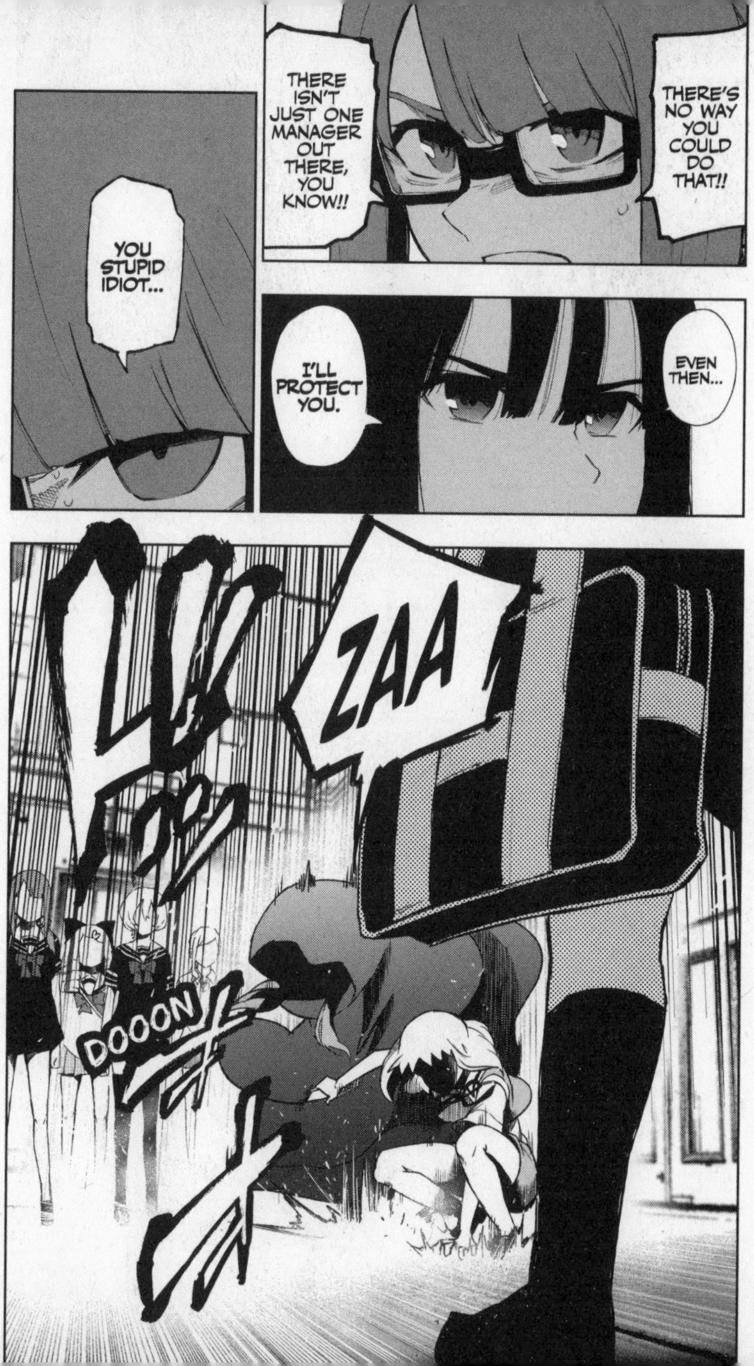
THERE'S NO WAY YOU COULD DO THAT!!
THERE ISN'T JUST ONE MANAGER OUT THERE, YOU KNOW!!
EVEN THEN...
I'LL PROTECT YOU.
YOU STUPID IDIOT...
ZAA
DOOON

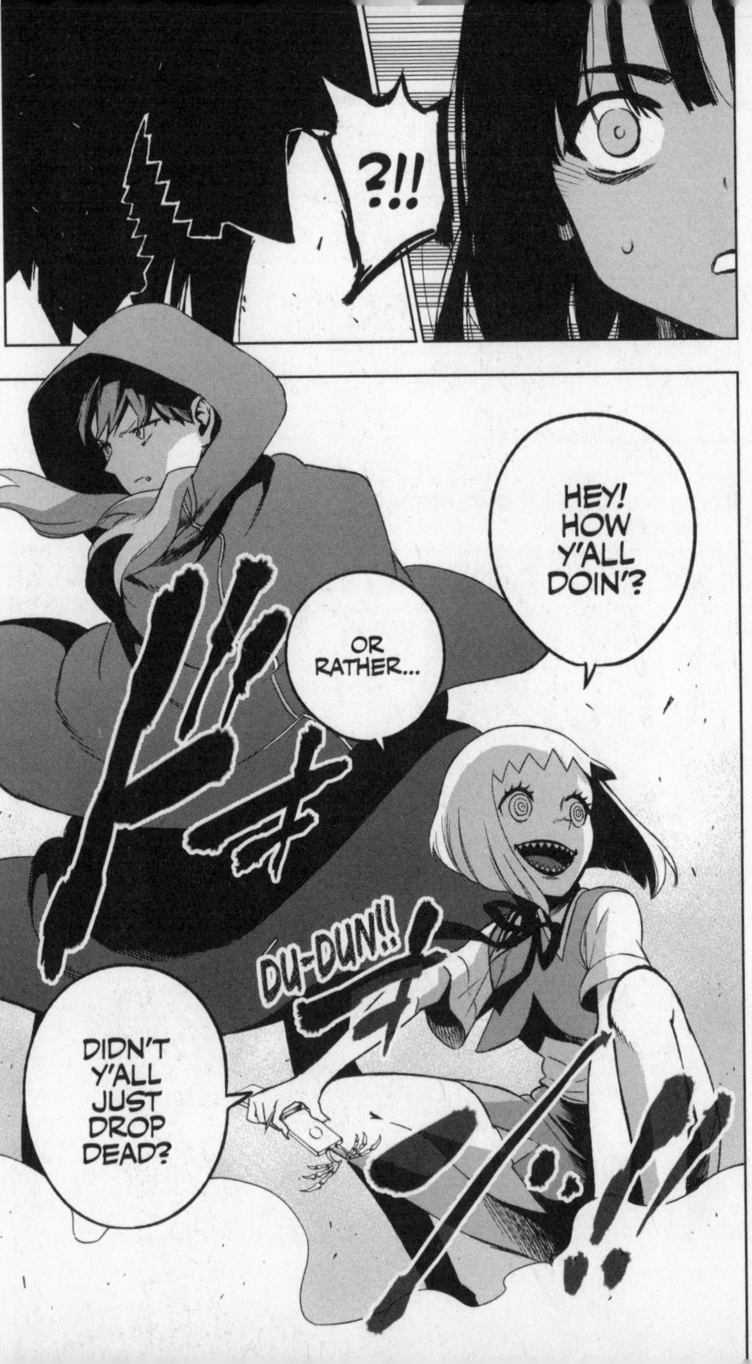
?!!
HEY! HOW Y'ALL DOIN'?
OR RATHER...
DU-DUN!!
DIDN'T Y'ALL JUST DROP DEAD?

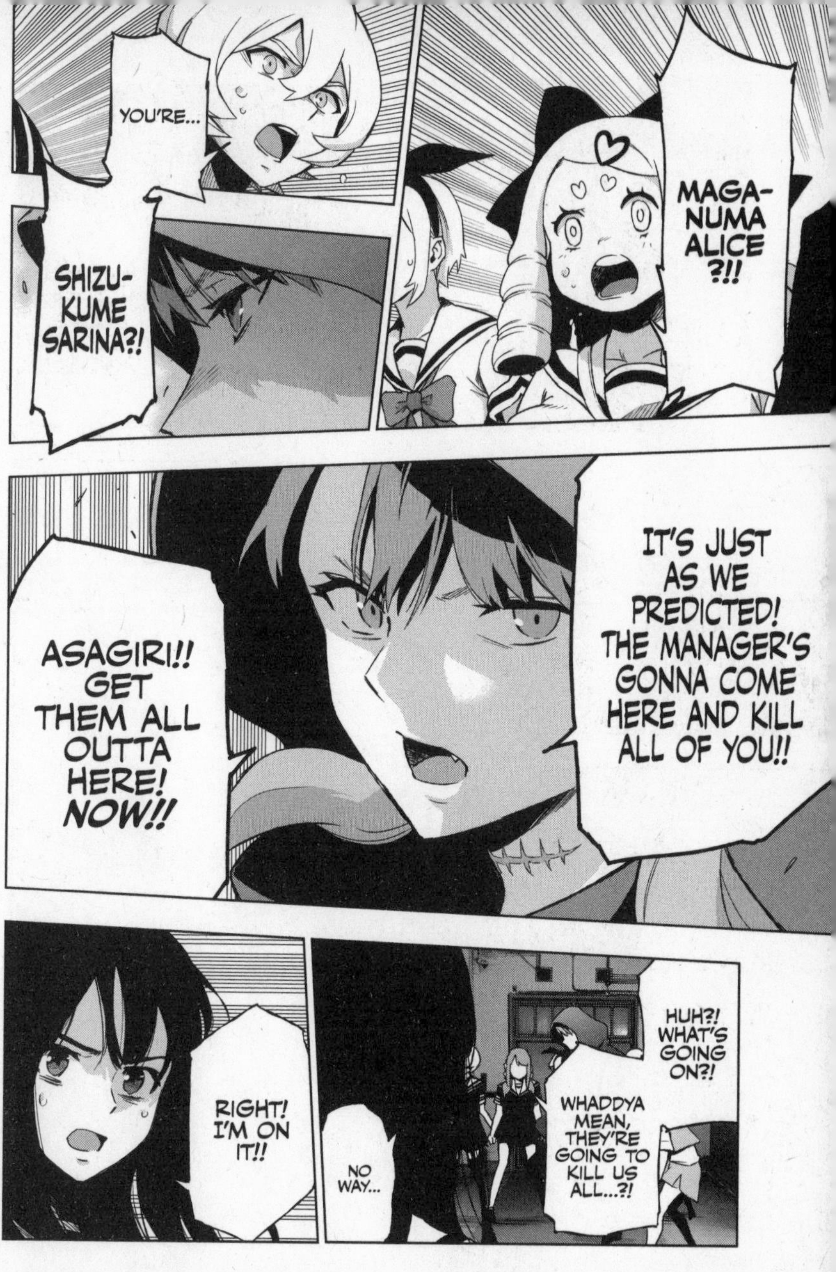
MAGA-NUMA ALICE ?!!
YOU'RE...
SHIZU-KUME SARINA?!
IT'S JUST AS WE PREDICTED! THE MANAGER'S GONNA COME HERE AND KILL ALL OF YOU!!
ASAGIRI!! GET THEM ALL OUTTA HERE! *NOW!!*
HUH?! WHAT'S GOING ON?!
WHADDYA MEAN, THEY'RE GOING TO KILL US ALL...?!
NO WAY...
RIGHT! I'M ON IT!!

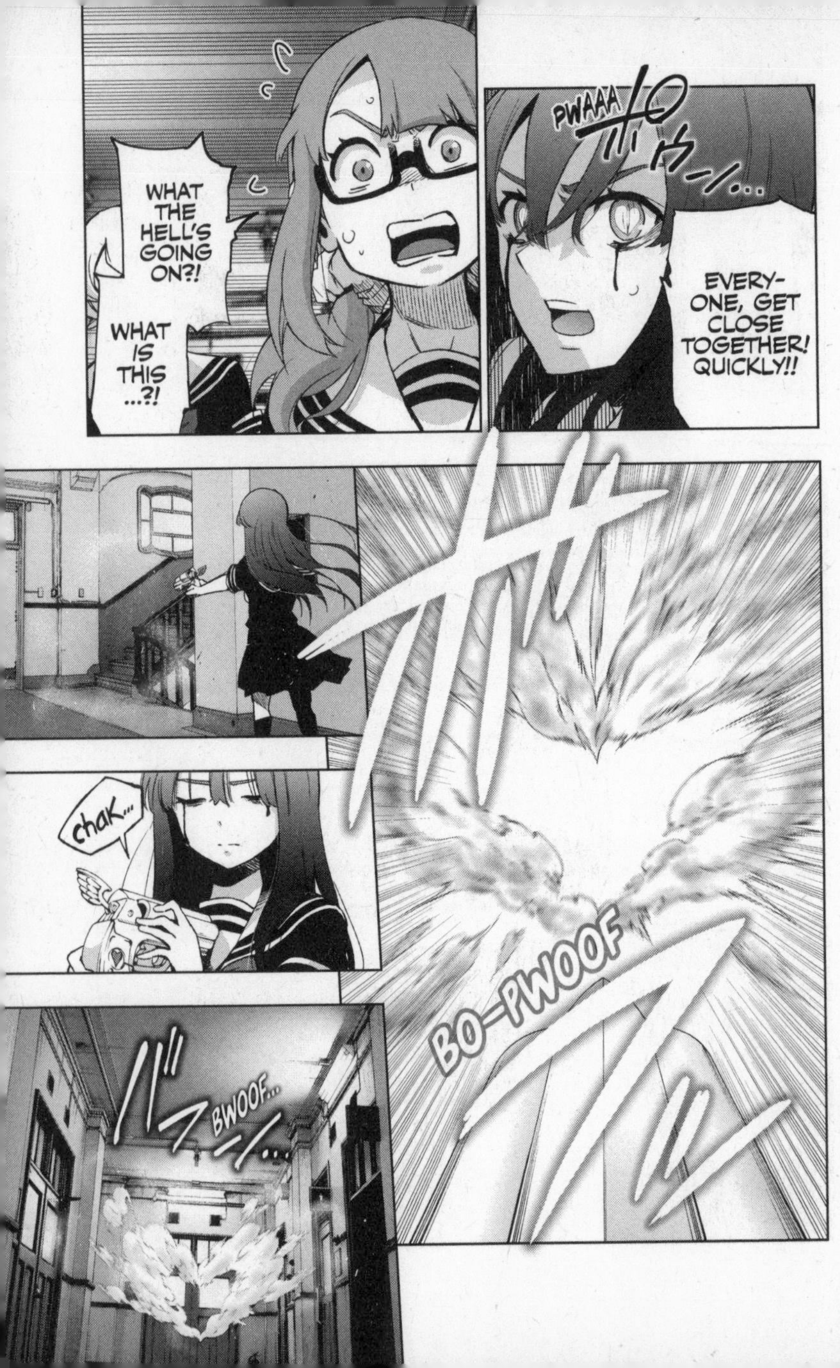
PWAAA
EVERY-ONE, GET CLOSE TOGETHER! QUICKLY!!
WHAT THE HELL'S GOING ON?!
WHAT IS THIS ...?!
BO-PWOOF
chak...
BWOOF...

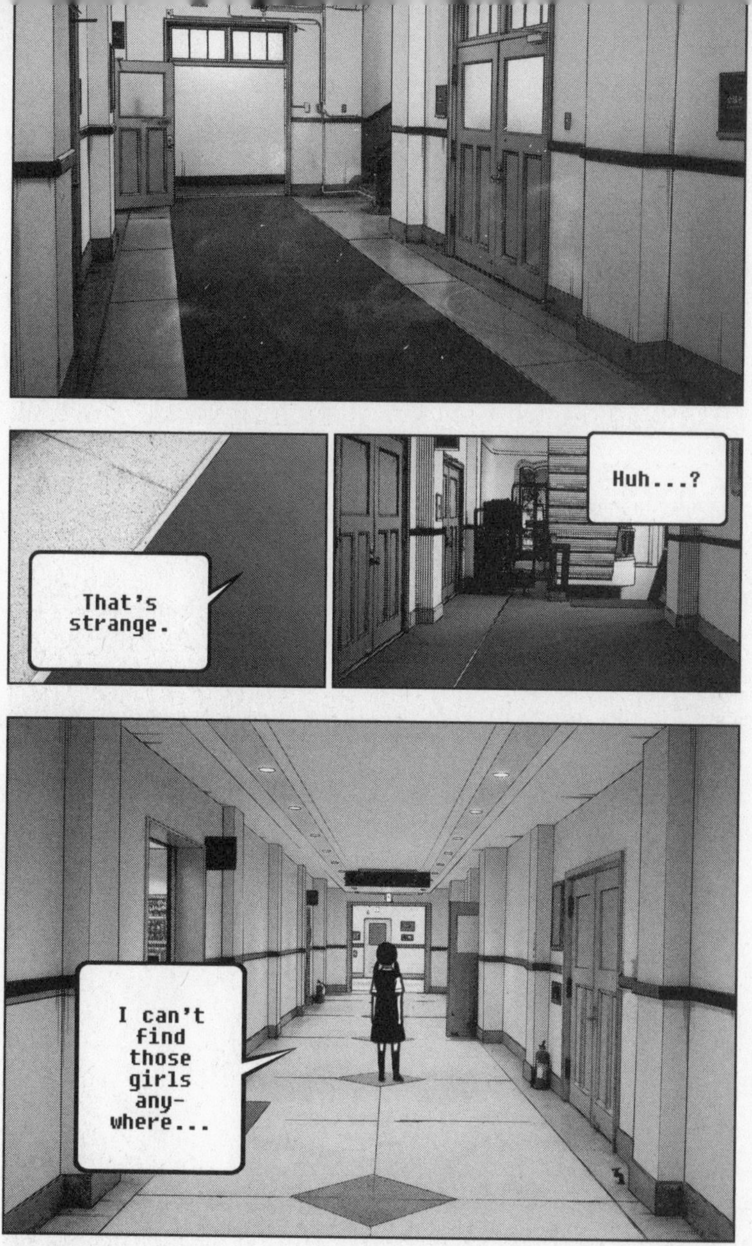
Huh...?
That's strange.
I can't find those girls any-where...

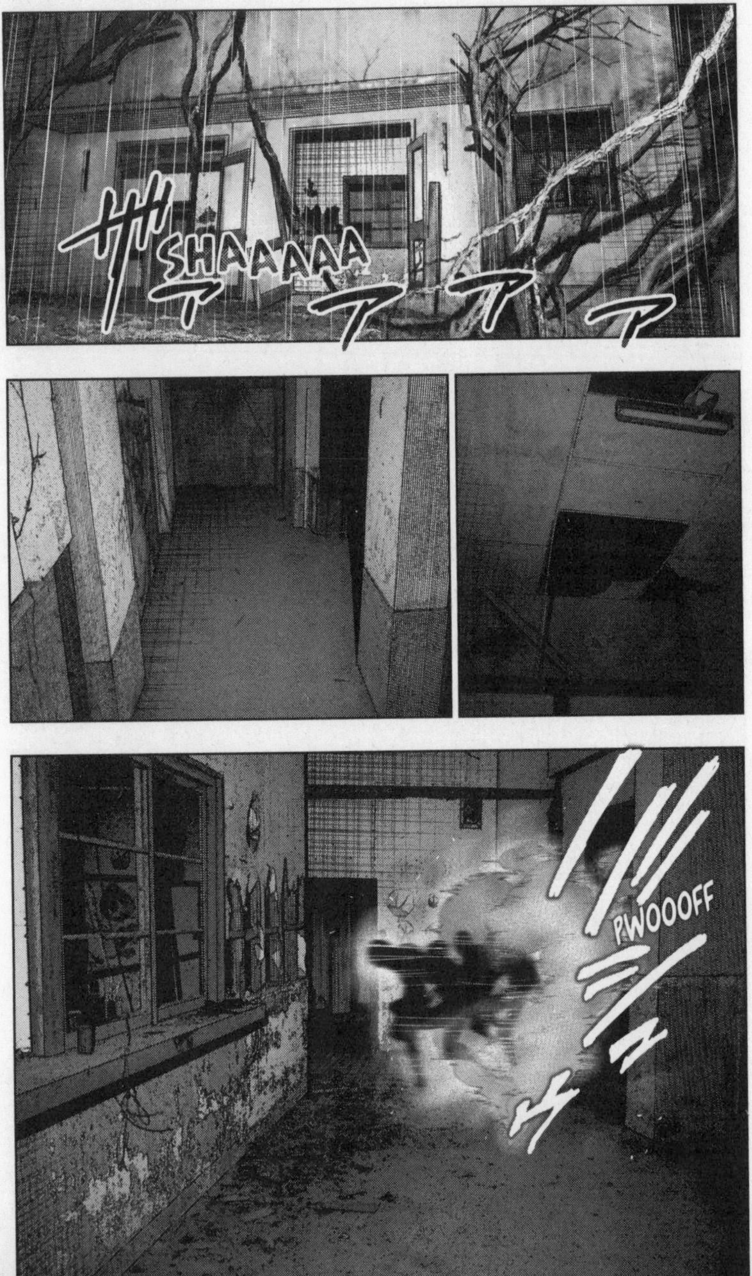
SHAAAAA
PWOOOFF

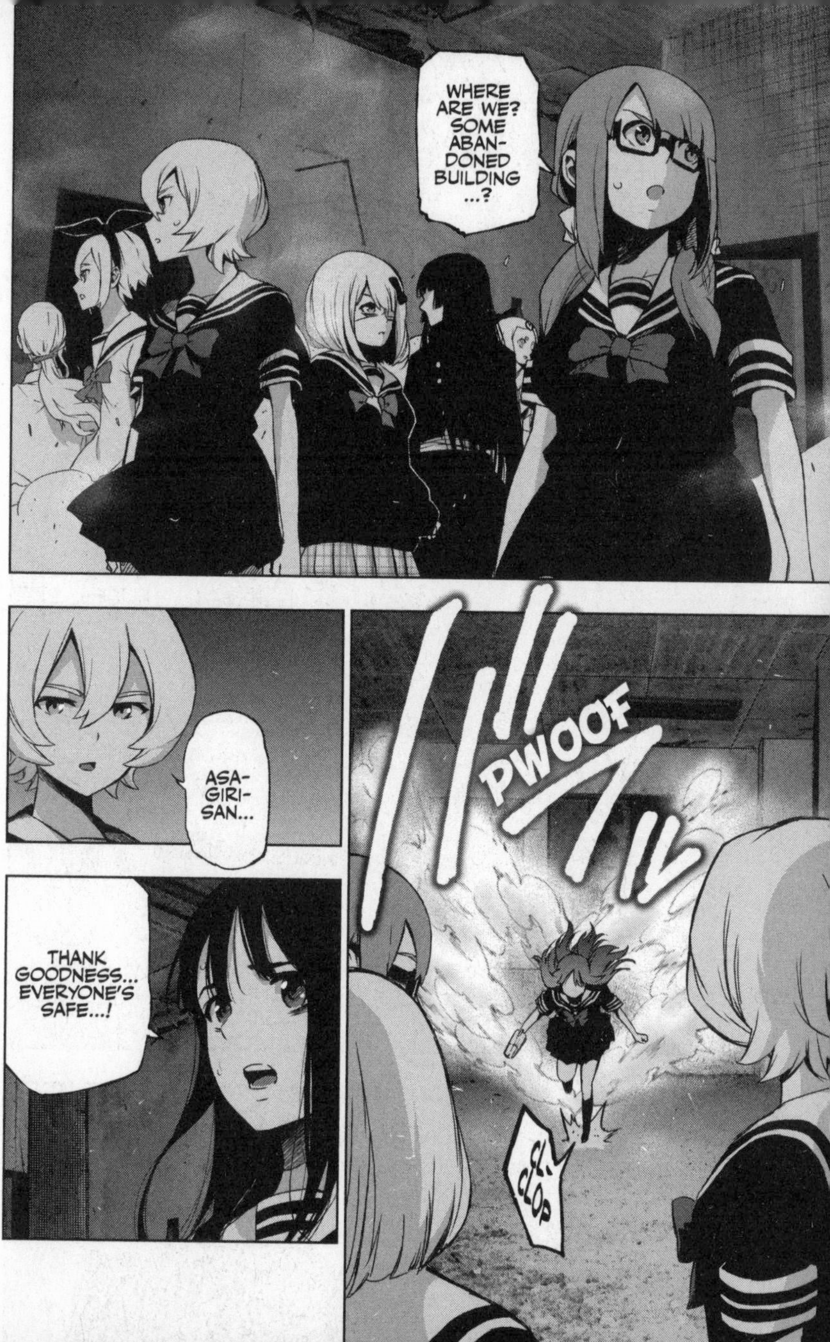
WHERE ARE WE? SOME ABAN-DONED BUILDING ...?
PWOOF
CL-CLOP
ASA-GIRI-SAN...
THANK GOODNESS... EVERYONE'S SAFE...!

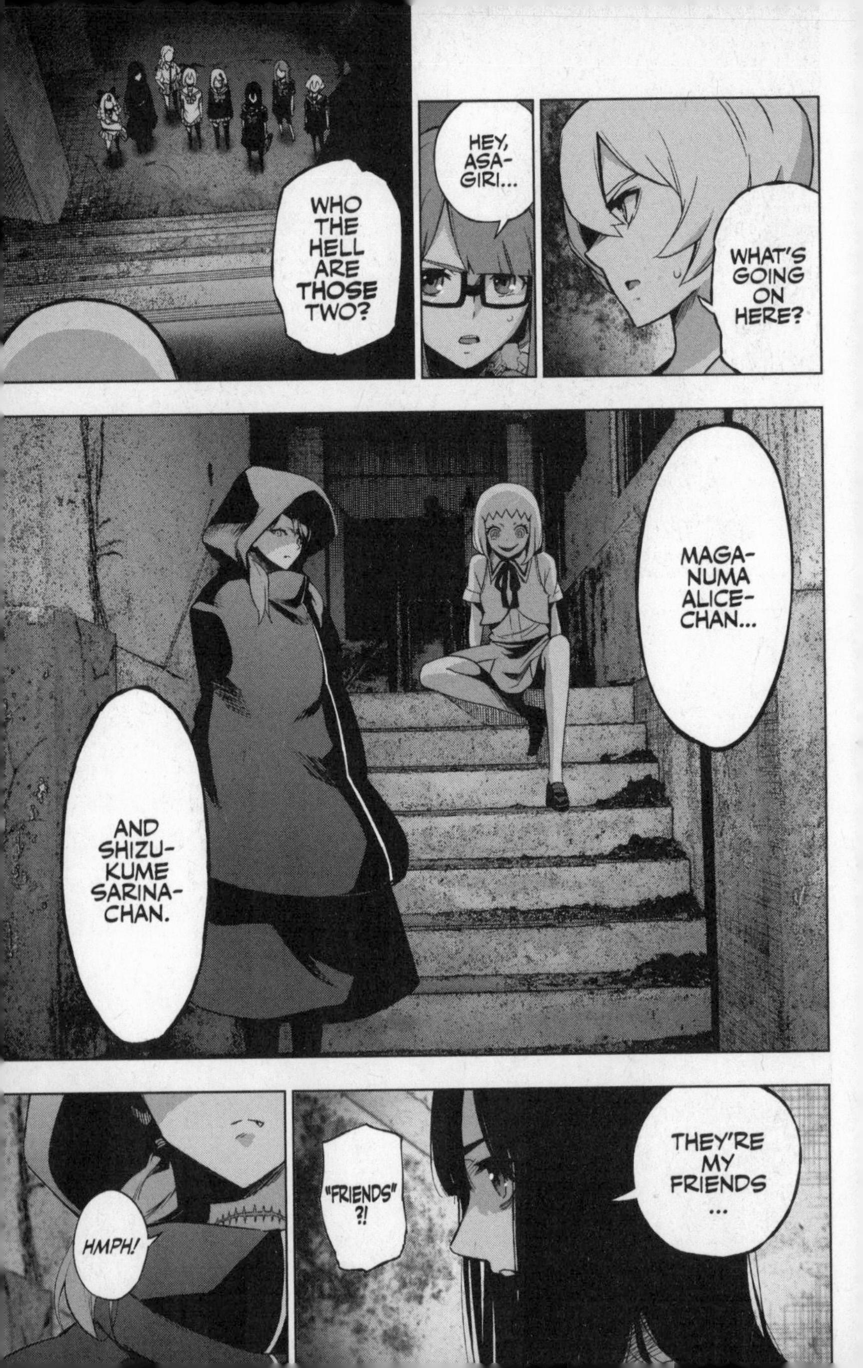
WHAT'S GOING ON HERE?
HEY, ASA-GIRI...
WHO THE HELL ARE THOSE TWO?
MAGA-NUMA ALICE-CHAN...
AND SHIZU-KUME SARINA-CHAN.
THEY'RE MY FRIENDS ...
"FRIENDS" ?!
HMPH!

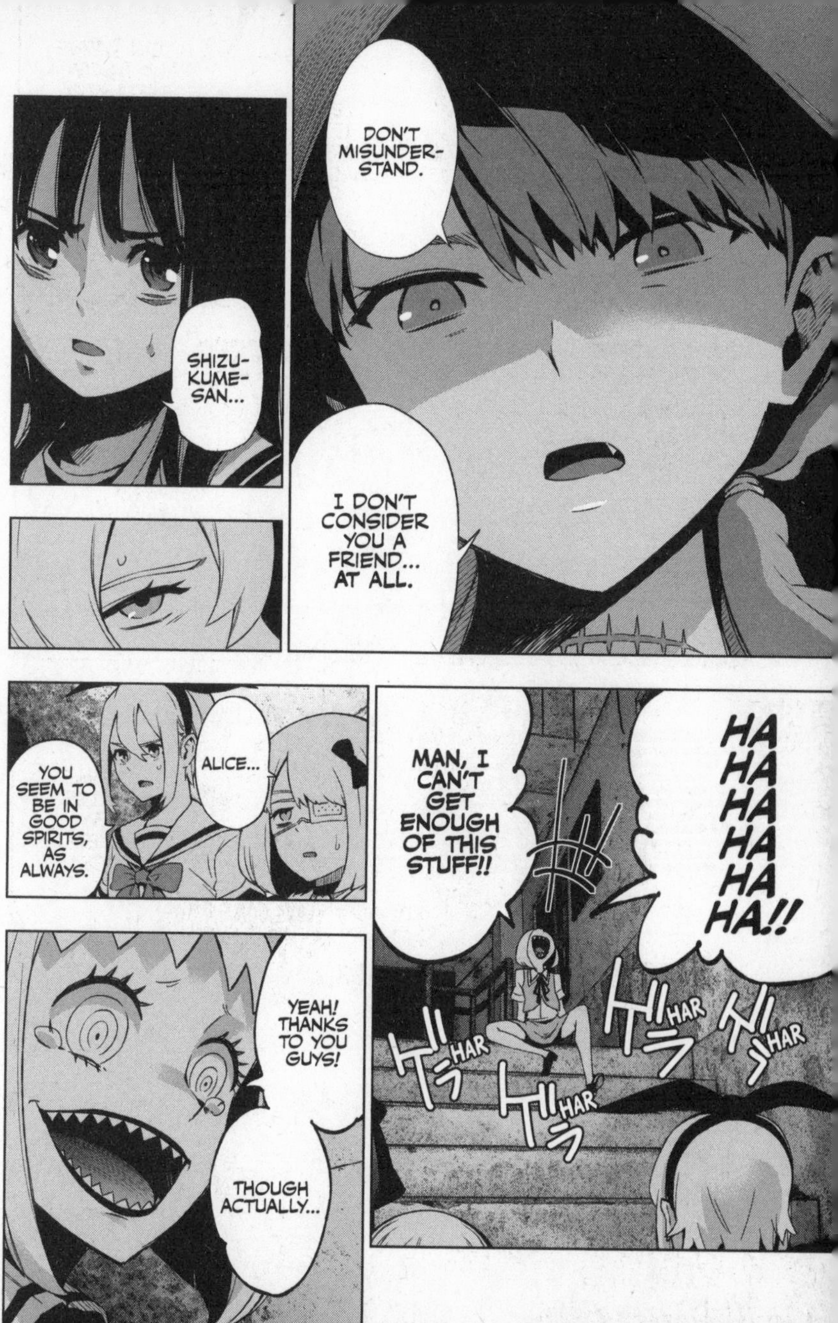
DON'T MISUNDER-STAND.
I DON'T CONSIDER YOU A FRIEND... AT ALL.
SHIZU-KUME-SAN...
HA HA HA HA HA HA HA!!
MAN, I CAN'T GET ENOUGH OF THIS STUFF!!
ゲラ HAR
ゲラ HAR
ゲラ HAR
ゲラ HAR
ALICE...
YOU SEEM TO BE IN GOOD SPIRITS, AS ALWAYS.
YEAH! THANKS TO YOU GUYS!
THOUGH ACTUALLY...

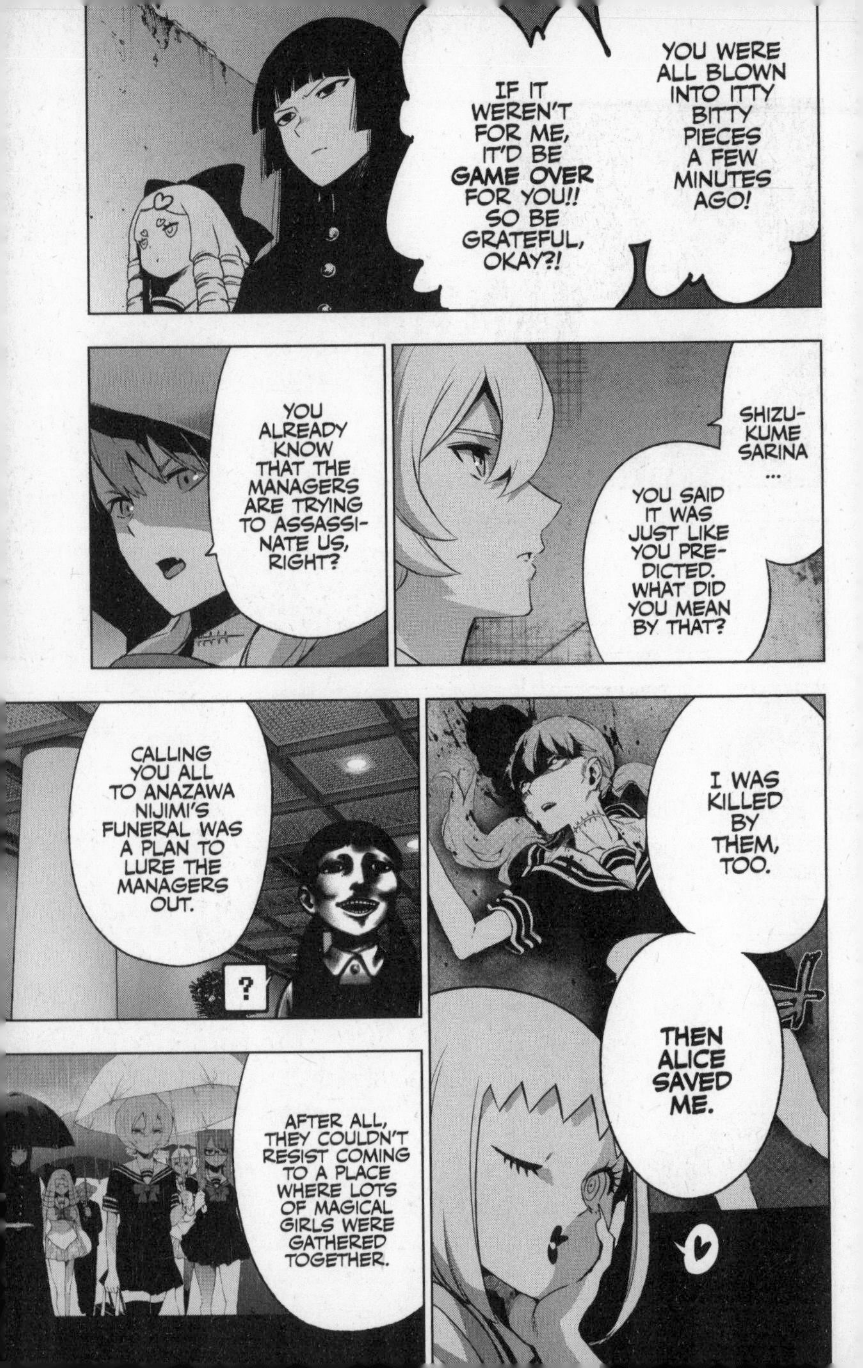
YOU WERE ALL BLOWN INTO ITTY BITTY PIECES A FEW MINUTES AGO!
IF IT WEREN'T FOR ME, IT'D BE GAME OVER FOR YOU!! SO BE GRATEFUL, OKAY?!
SHIZUKUME SARINA ...
YOU SAID IT WAS JUST LIKE YOU PREDICTED. WHAT DID YOU MEAN BY THAT?
YOU ALREADY KNOW THAT THE MANAGERS ARE TRYING TO ASSASSINATE US, RIGHT?
I WAS KILLED BY THEM, TOO.
THEN ALICE SAVED ME.
♥
CALLING YOU ALL TO ANAZAWA NIJIMI'S FUNERAL WAS A PLAN TO LURE THE MANAGERS OUT.
?
AFTER ALL, THEY COULDN'T RESIST COMING TO A PLACE WHERE LOTS OF MAGICAL GIRLS WERE GATHERED TOGETHER.

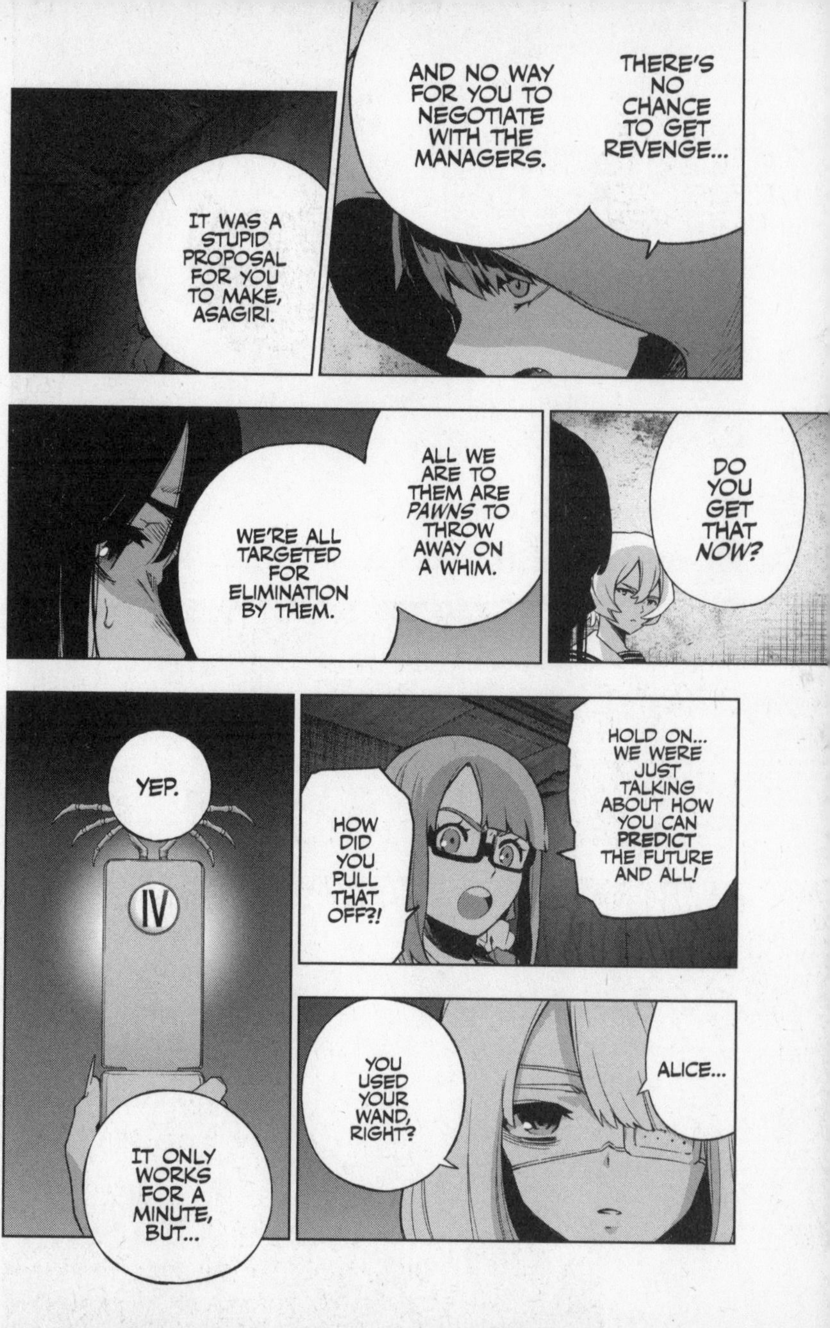
THERE'S NO CHANCE TO GET REVENGE...
AND NO WAY FOR YOU TO NEGOTIATE WITH THE MANAGERS.
IT WAS A STUPID PROPOSAL FOR YOU TO MAKE, ASAGIRI.
DO YOU GET THAT *NOW?*
ALL WE ARE TO THEM ARE *PAWNS* TO THROW AWAY ON A WHIM.
WE'RE ALL TARGETED FOR ELIMINATION BY THEM.
HOLD ON... WE WERE JUST TALKING ABOUT HOW YOU CAN PREDICT THE FUTURE AND ALL!
HOW DID YOU PULL THAT OFF?!
ALICE...
YOU USED YOUR WAND, RIGHT?
YEP.
IV
IT ONLY WORKS FOR A MINUTE, BUT...

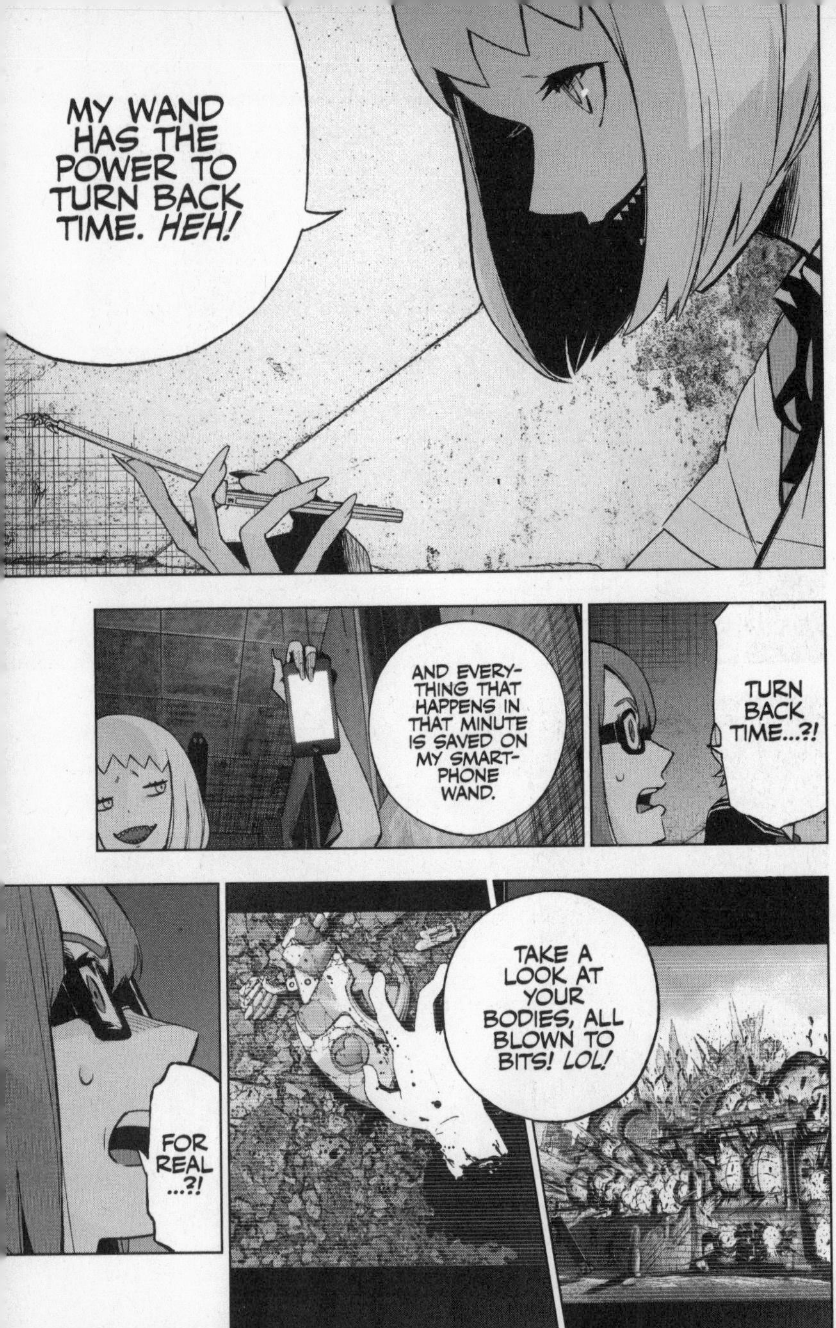
MY WAND HAS THE POWER TO TURN BACK TIME. *HEH!*
TURN BACK TIME...?!
AND EVERYTHING THAT HAPPENS IN THAT MINUTE IS SAVED ON MY SMARTPHONE WAND.
TAKE A LOOK AT YOUR BODIES, ALL BLOWN TO BITS! *LOL!*
FOR REAL ...?!

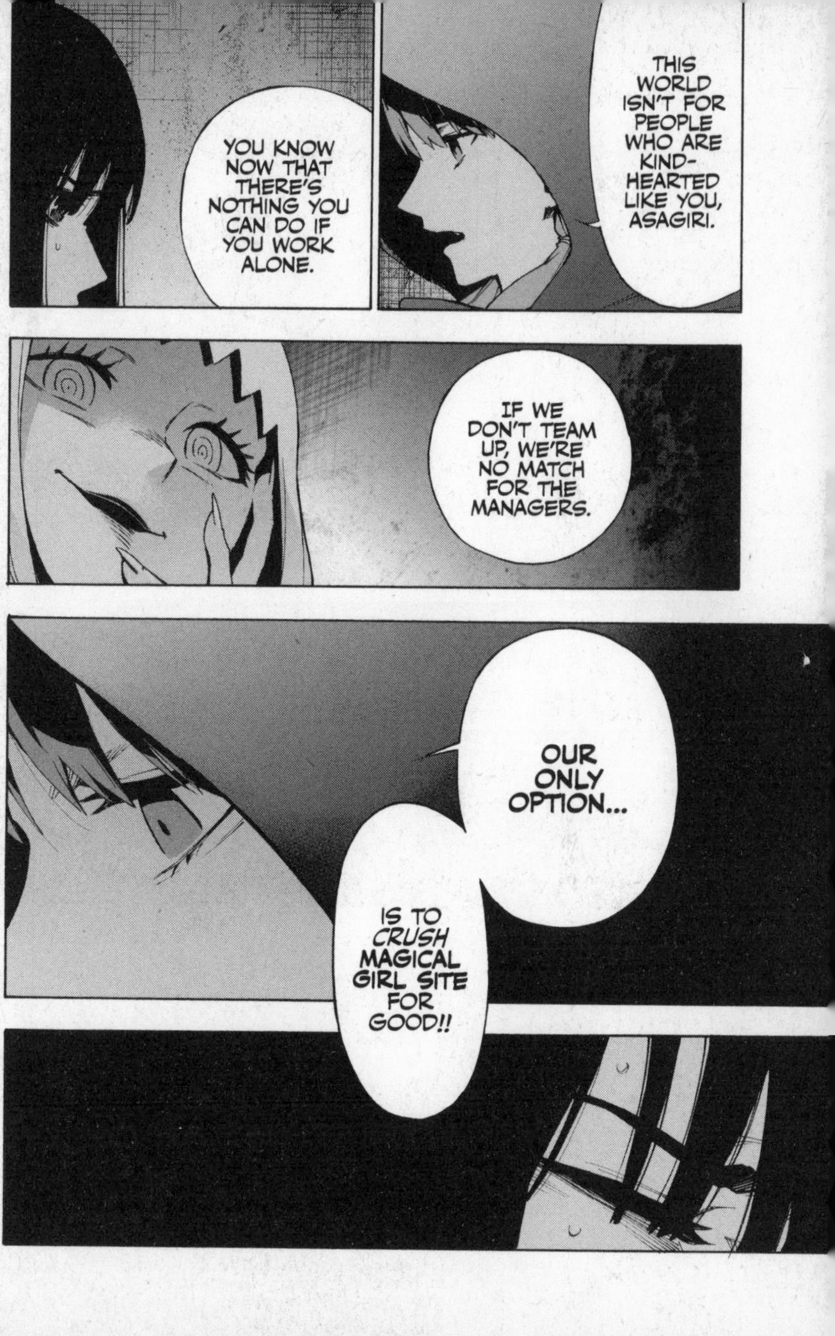
THIS WORLD ISN'T FOR PEOPLE WHO ARE KIND-HEARTED LIKE YOU, ASAGIRI.
YOU KNOW NOW THAT THERE'S NOTHING YOU CAN DO IF YOU WORK ALONE.
IF WE DON'T TEAM UP, WE'RE NO MATCH FOR THE MANAGERS.
OUR ONLY OPTION...
IS TO *CRUSH* MAGICAL GIRL SITE FOR GOOD!!

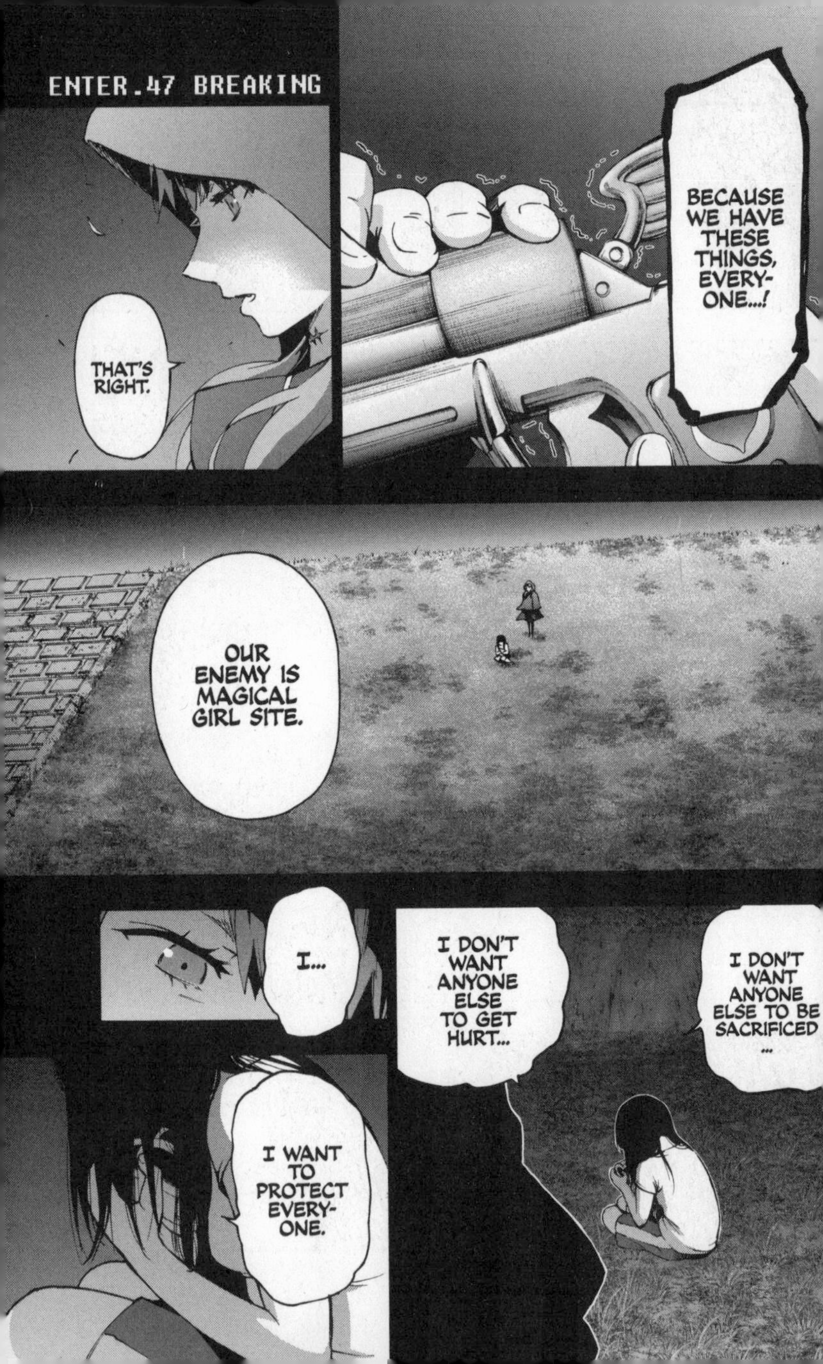
ENTER.47 BREAKING
BECAUSE WE HAVE THESE THINGS, EVERYONE...!
THAT'S RIGHT.
OUR ENEMY IS MAGICAL GIRL SITE.
I DON'T WANT ANYONE ELSE TO BE SACRIFICED...
I DON'T WANT ANYONE ELSE TO GET HURT...
I...
I WANT TO PROTECT EVERYONE.

ENTER.47 BREAKING

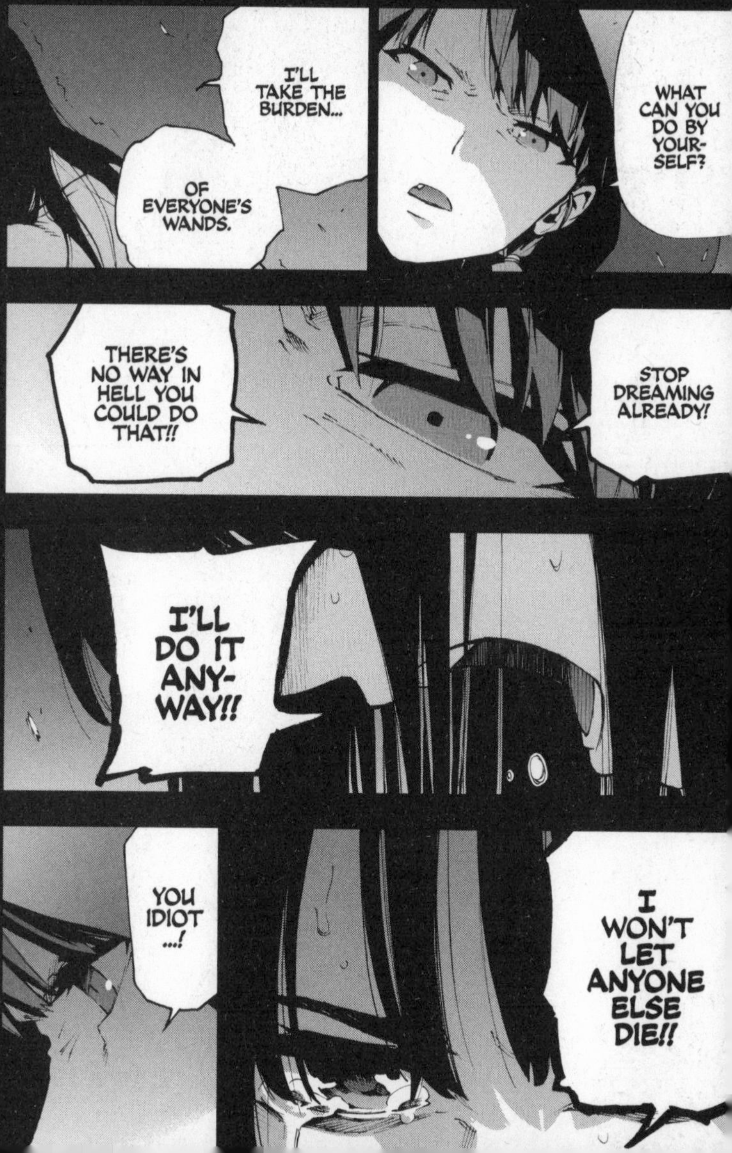
WHAT CAN YOU DO BY YOURSELF?
I'LL TAKE THE BURDEN...
OF EVERYONE'S WANDS.
STOP DREAMING ALREADY!
THERE'S NO WAY IN HELL YOU COULD DO THAT!!
I'LL DO IT ANY-WAY!!
I WON'T LET ANYONE ELSE DIE!!
YOU IDIOT ...!

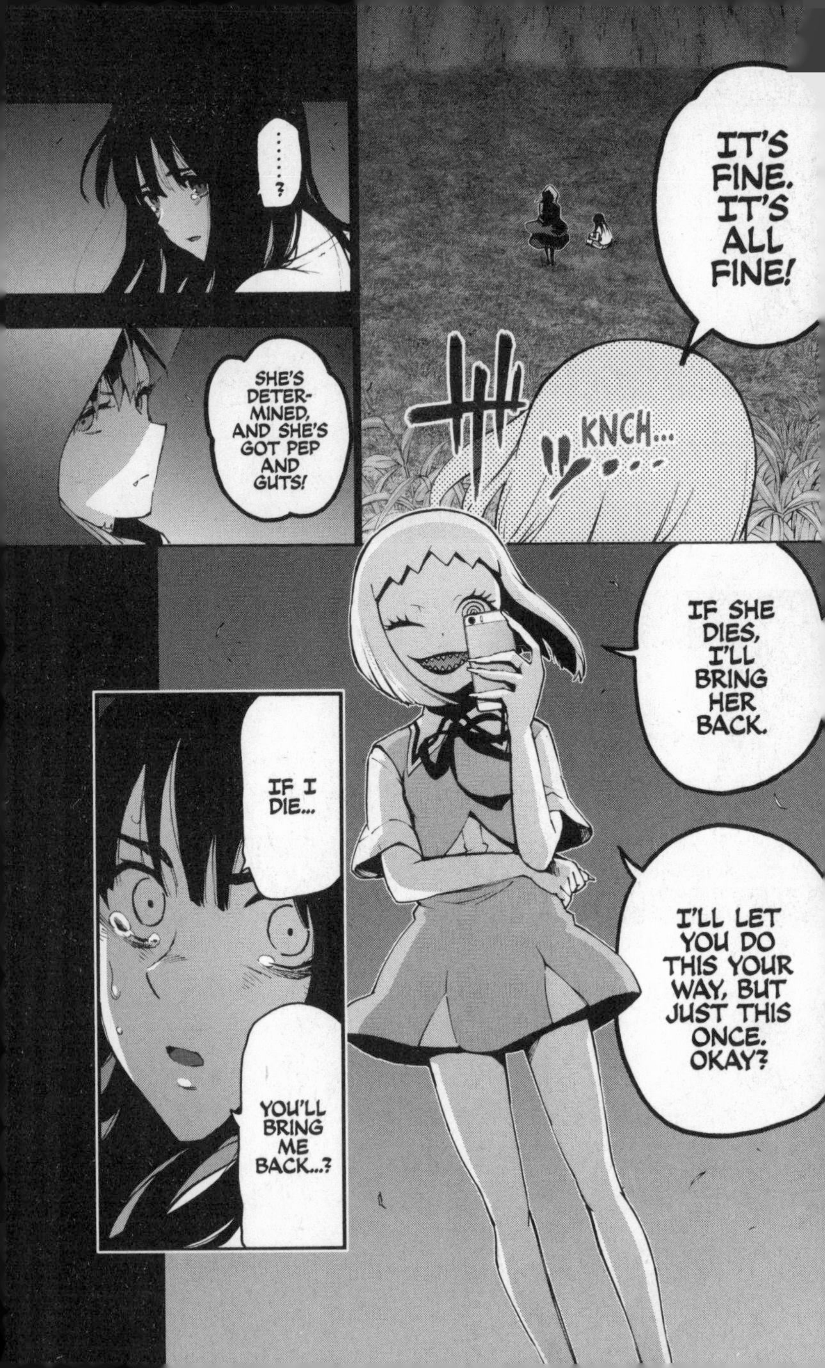
IT'S FINE. IT'S ALL FINE!
KNCH...
......?
SHE'S DETER-MINED, AND SHE'S GOT PEP AND GUTS!
IF SHE DIES, I'LL BRING HER BACK.
I'LL LET YOU DO THIS YOUR WAY, BUT JUST THIS ONCE. OKAY?
IF I DIE...
YOU'LL BRING ME BACK...?

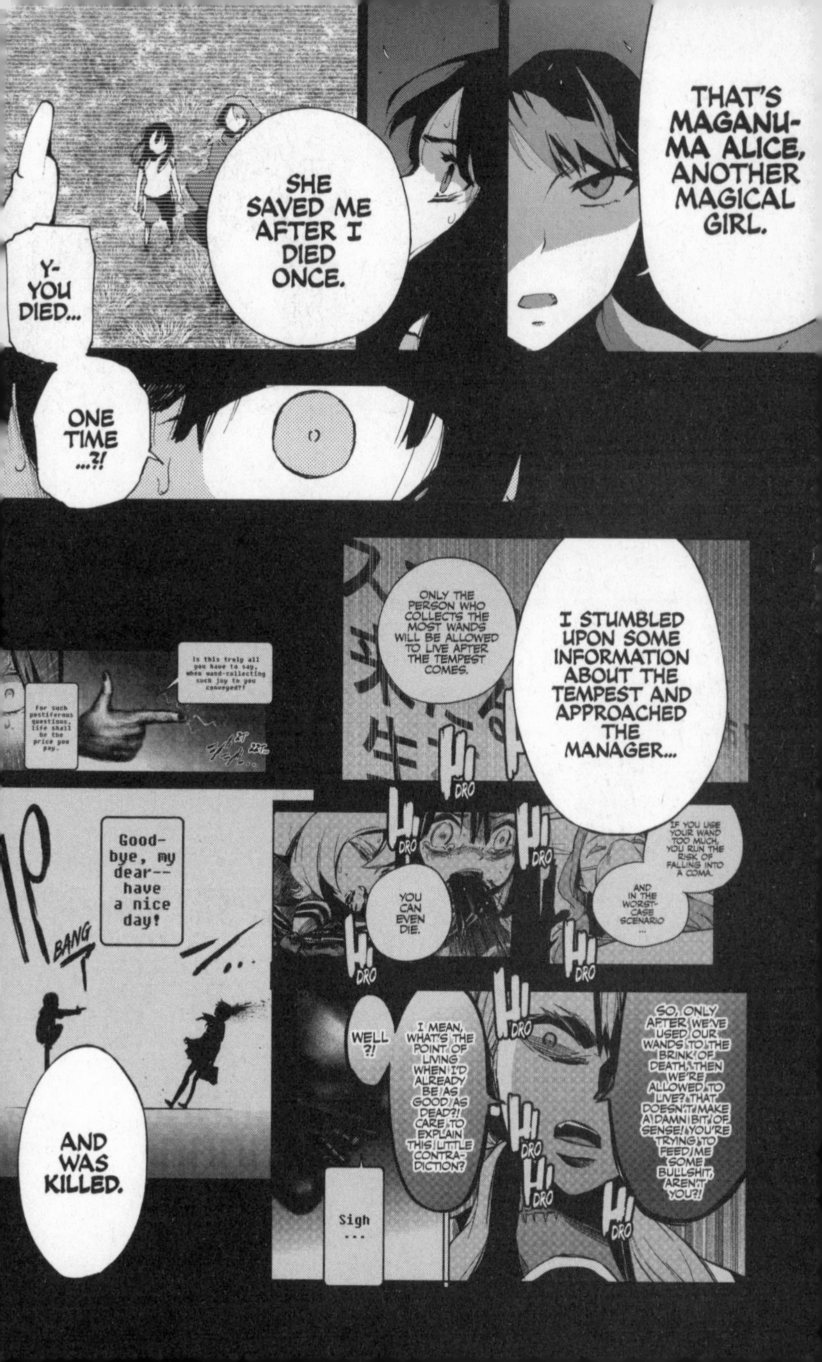
THAT'S MAGANUMA ALICE, ANOTHER MAGICAL GIRL.
SHE SAVED ME AFTER I DIED ONCE.
Y-YOU DIED...
ONE TIME ...?!
I STUMBLED UPON SOME INFORMATION ABOUT THE TEMPEST AND APPROACHED THE MANAGER...
ONLY THE PERSON WHO COLLECTS THE MOST WANDS WILL BE ALLOWED TO LIVE AFTER THE TEMPEST COMES.
DRO
Is this truly all you have to say, when wand-collecting such joy to you conveyed?!
For such pestiferous questions, life shall be the price you pay.
IF YOU USE YOUR WAND TOO MUCH, YOU RUN THE RISK OF FALLING INTO A COMA.
AND IN THE WORST-CASE SCENARIO...
DRO
DRO
YOU CAN EVEN DIE.
DRO
DRO
SO, ONLY AFTER WE'VE USED OUR WANDS TO THE BRINK OF DEATH, THEN WE'RE ALLOWED TO LIVE? THAT DOESN'T MAKE A DAMN BIT OF SENSE! YOU'RE TRYING TO FEED ME SOME BULLSHIT, AREN'T YOU?!
DRO
I MEAN, WHAT'S THE POINT OF LIVING WHEN I'D ALREADY BE AS GOOD AS DEAD?! CARE TO EXPLAIN THIS LITTLE CONTRADICTION?
WELL ?!
DRO
DRO
DRO
Sigh ...
Good-bye, my dear--have a nice day!
BANG
AND WAS KILLED.

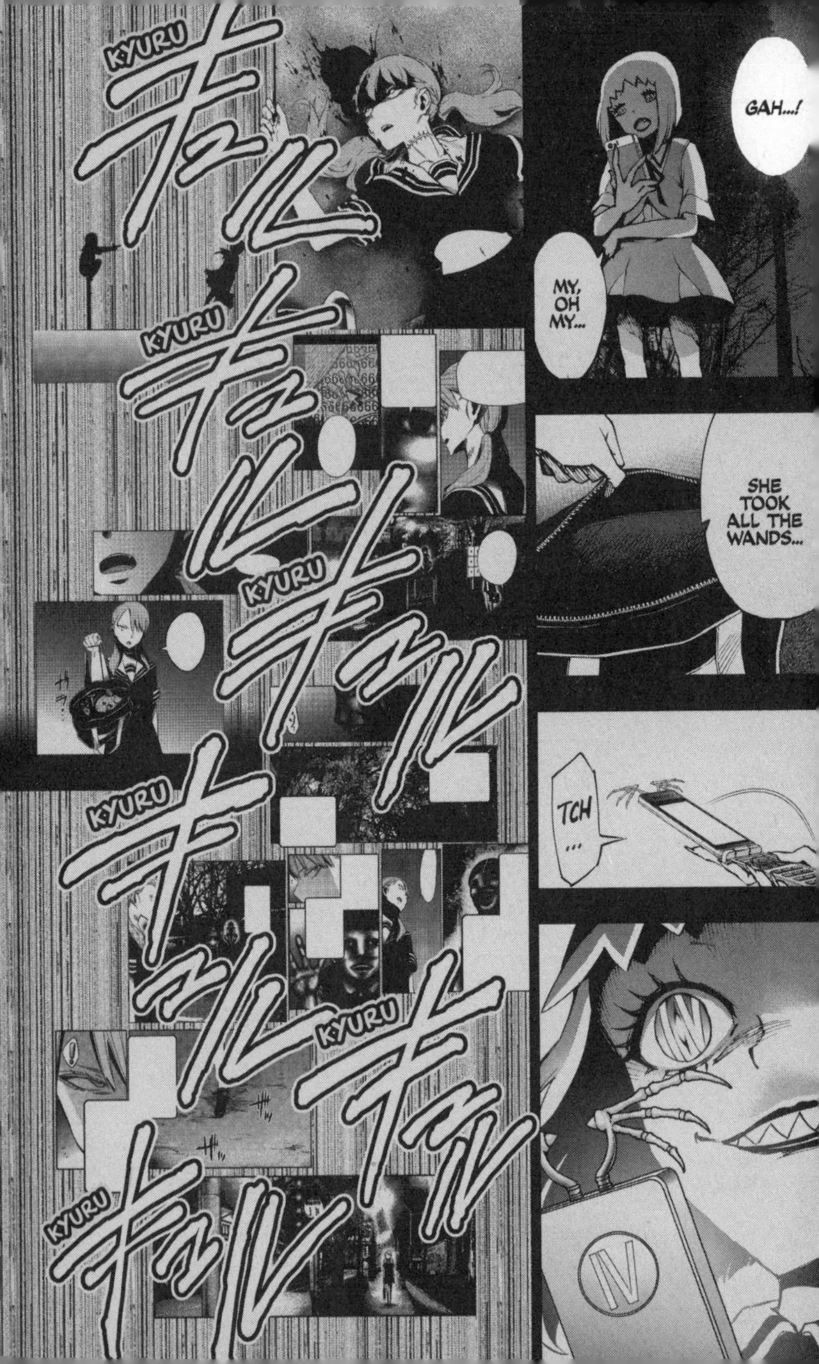
GAH...!
MY, OH MY...
SHE TOOK ALL THE WANDS...
TCH ...
KYURU
KYURU
KYURU
KYURU
KYURU
KYURU

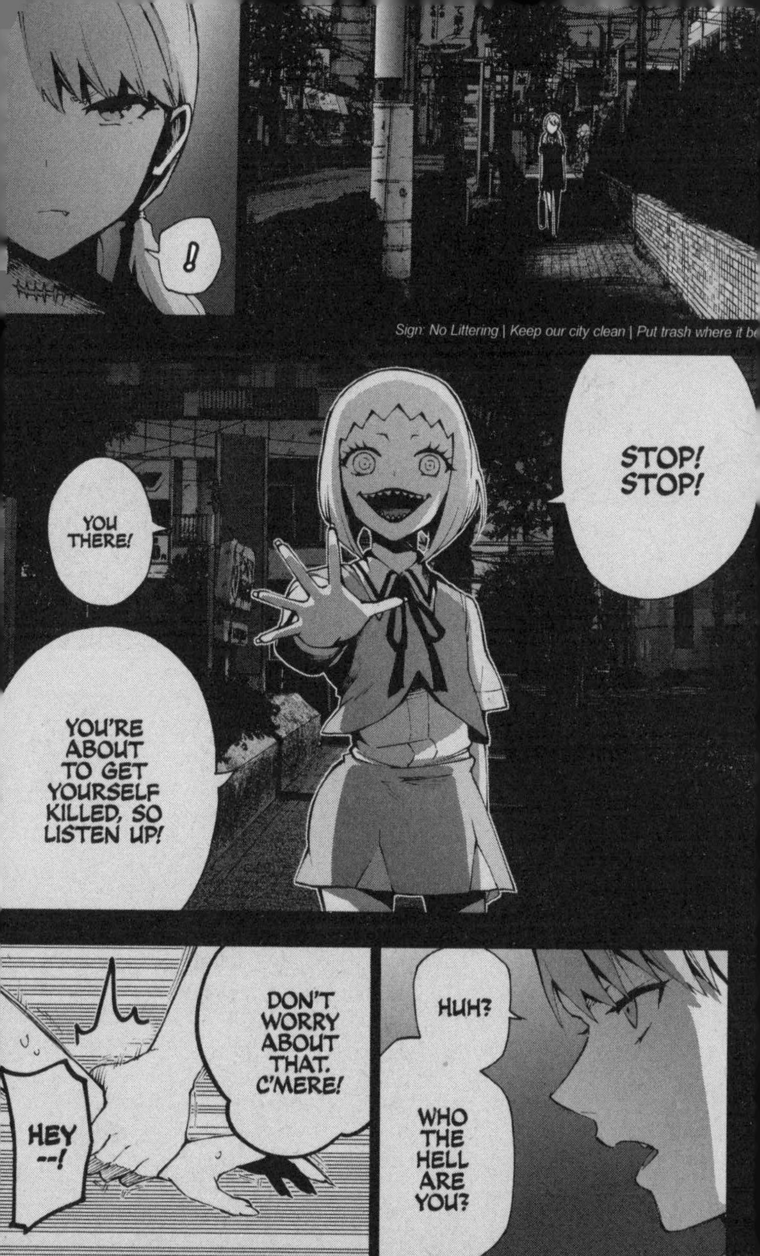
Sign: No Littering | Keep our city clean | Put trash where it be
!
STOP! STOP!
YOU THERE!
YOU'RE ABOUT TO GET YOURSELF KILLED, SO LISTEN UP!
HUH?
WHO THE HELL ARE YOU?
DON'T WORRY ABOUT THAT. C'MERE!
HEY --!

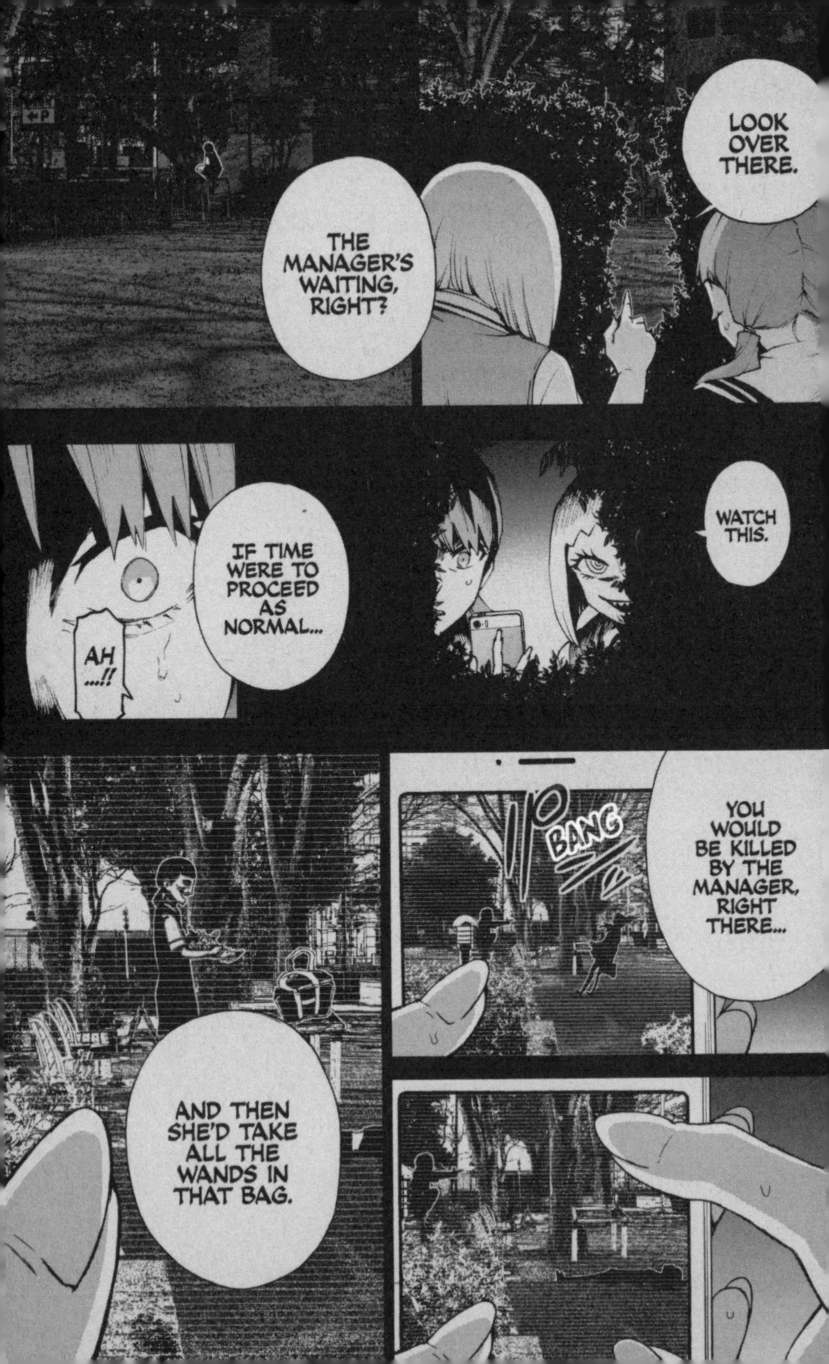
LOOK OVER THERE.
THE MANAGER'S WAITING, RIGHT?
WATCH THIS.
IF TIME WERE TO PROCEED AS NORMAL...
AH ...!!
BANG
YOU WOULD BE KILLED BY THE MANAGER, RIGHT THERE...
AND THEN SHE'D TAKE ALL THE WANDS IN THAT BAG.

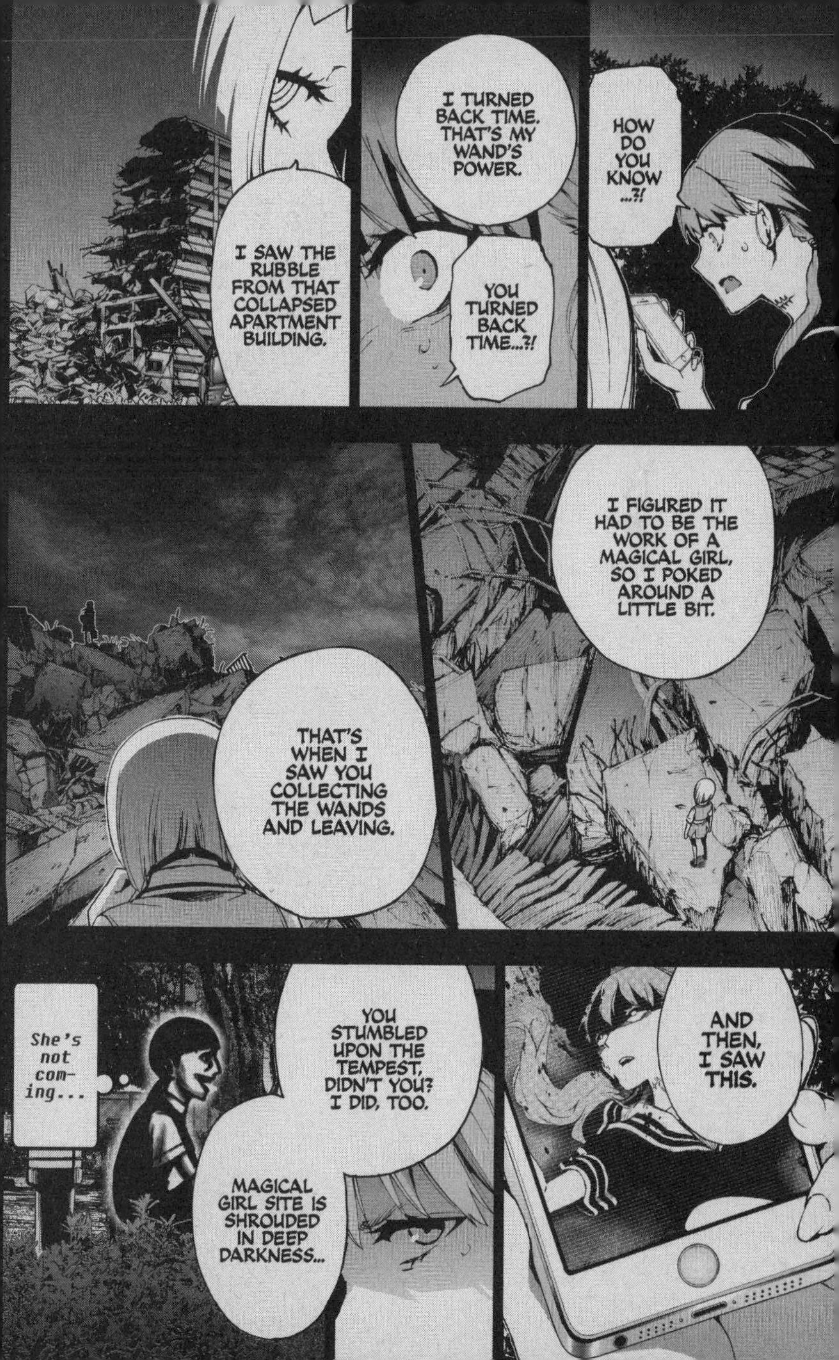
HOW DO YOU KNOW ...?!
I TURNED BACK TIME. THAT'S MY WAND'S POWER.
YOU TURNED BACK TIME...?!
I SAW THE RUBBLE FROM THAT COLLAPSED APARTMENT BUILDING.
I FIGURED IT HAD TO BE THE WORK OF A MAGICAL GIRL, SO I POKED AROUND A LITTLE BIT.
THAT'S WHEN I SAW YOU COLLECTING THE WANDS AND LEAVING.
AND THEN, I SAW THIS.
YOU STUMBLED UPON THE TEMPEST, DIDN'T YOU? I DID, TOO.
MAGICAL GIRL SITE IS SHROUDED IN DEEP DARKNESS...
She's not com-ing...

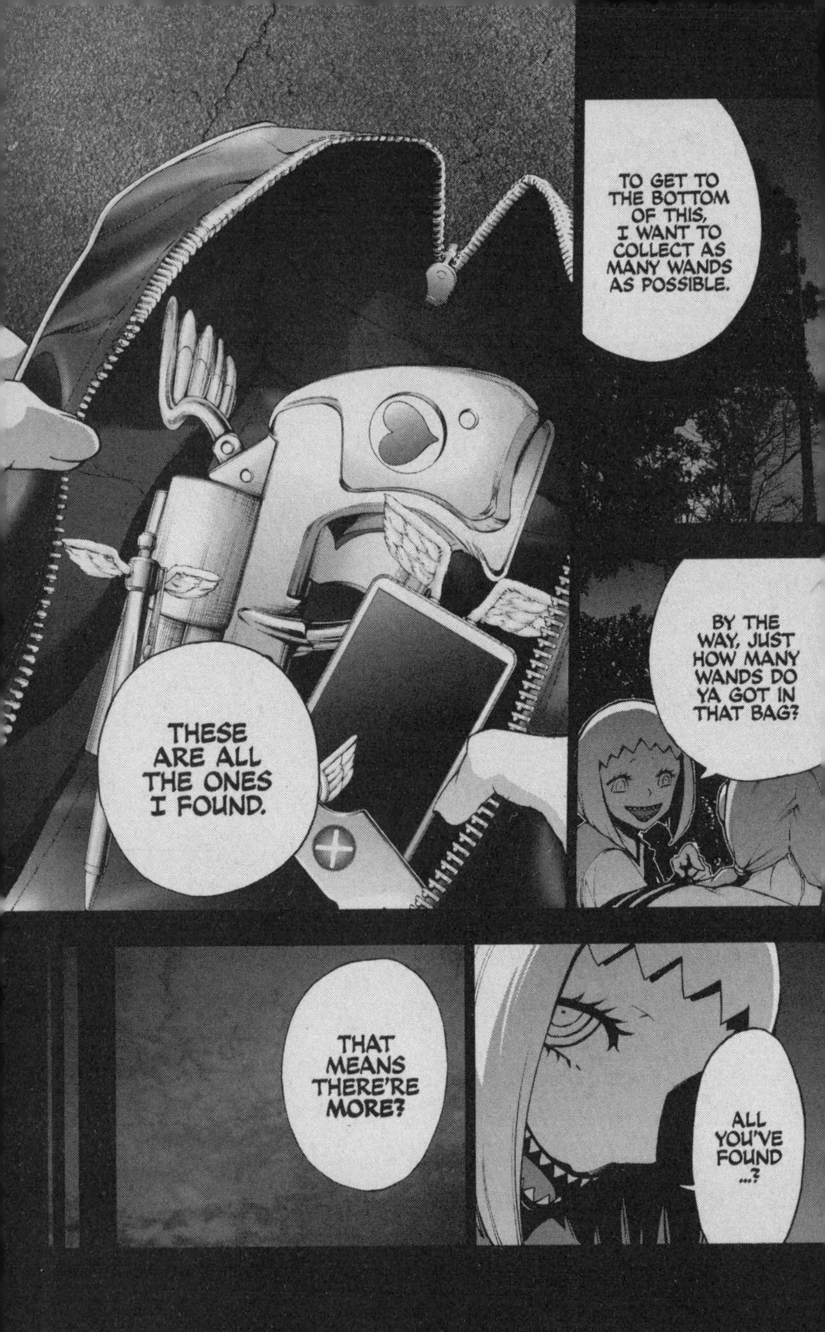
TO GET TO THE BOTTOM OF THIS, I WANT TO COLLECT AS MANY WANDS AS POSSIBLE.
BY THE WAY, JUST HOW MANY WANDS DO YA GOT IN THAT BAG?
THESE ARE ALL THE ONES I FOUND.
ALL YOU'VE FOUND ...?
THAT MEANS THERE'RE MORE?

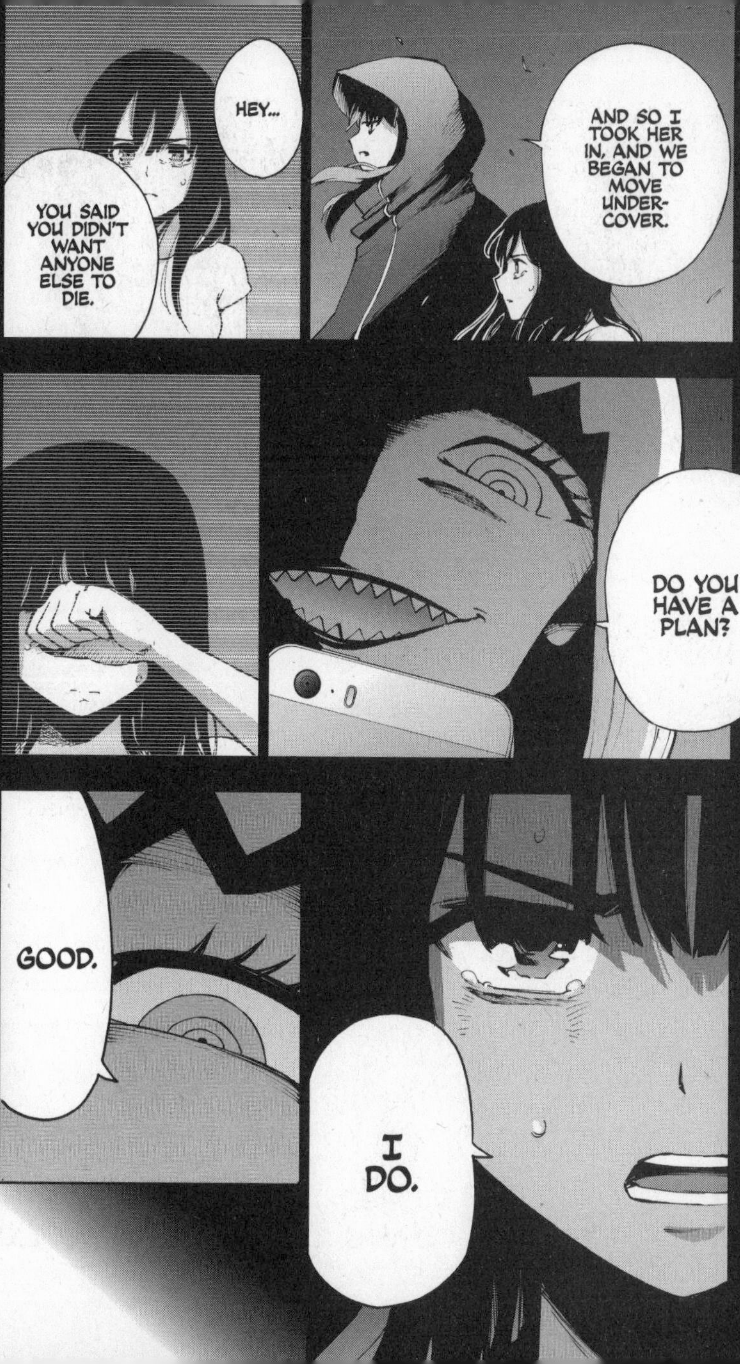
AND SO I TOOK HER IN, AND WE BEGAN TO MOVE UNDER-COVER.
HEY...
YOU SAID YOU DIDN'T WANT ANYONE ELSE TO DIE.
DO YOU HAVE A PLAN?
I DO.
GOOD.

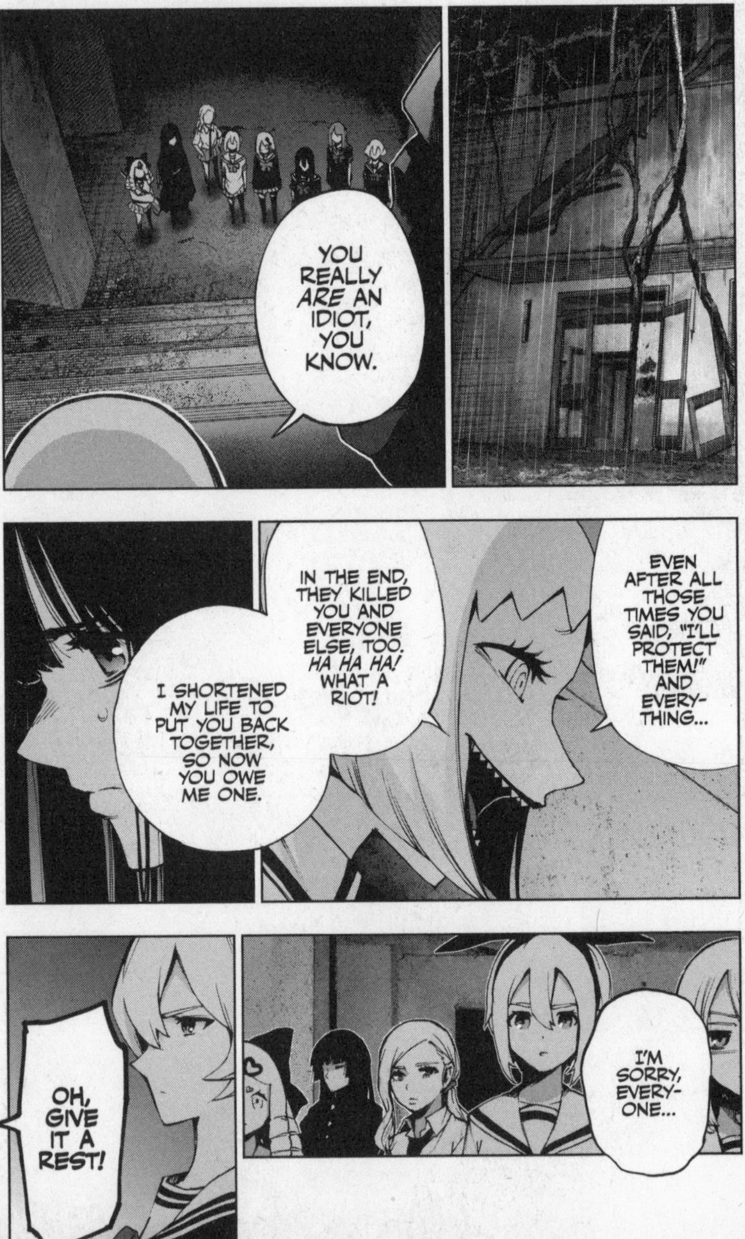
YOU REALLY ARE AN IDIOT, YOU KNOW.
EVEN AFTER ALL THOSE TIMES YOU SAID, "I'LL PROTECT THEM!" AND EVERYTHING...
IN THE END, THEY KILLED YOU AND EVERYONE ELSE, TOO. HA HA HA! WHAT A RIOT!
I SHORTENED MY LIFE TO PUT YOU BACK TOGETHER, SO NOW YOU OWE ME ONE.
I'M SORRY, EVERYONE...
OH, GIVE IT A REST!

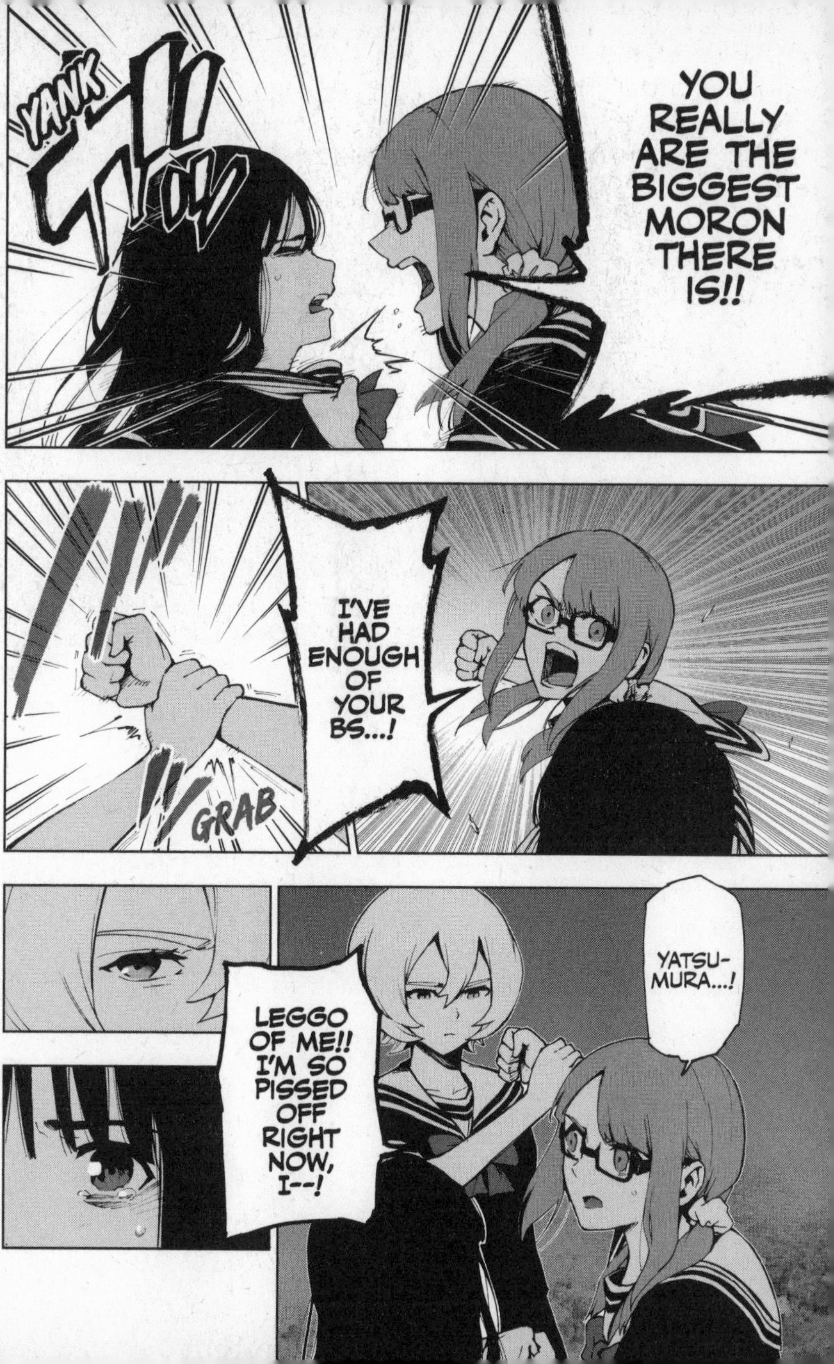
YOU REALLY ARE THE BIGGEST MORON THERE IS!!
YANK
I'VE HAD ENOUGH OF YOUR BS...!
GRAB
YATSU-MURA...!
LEGGO OF ME!! I'M SO PISSED OFF RIGHT NOW, I--!

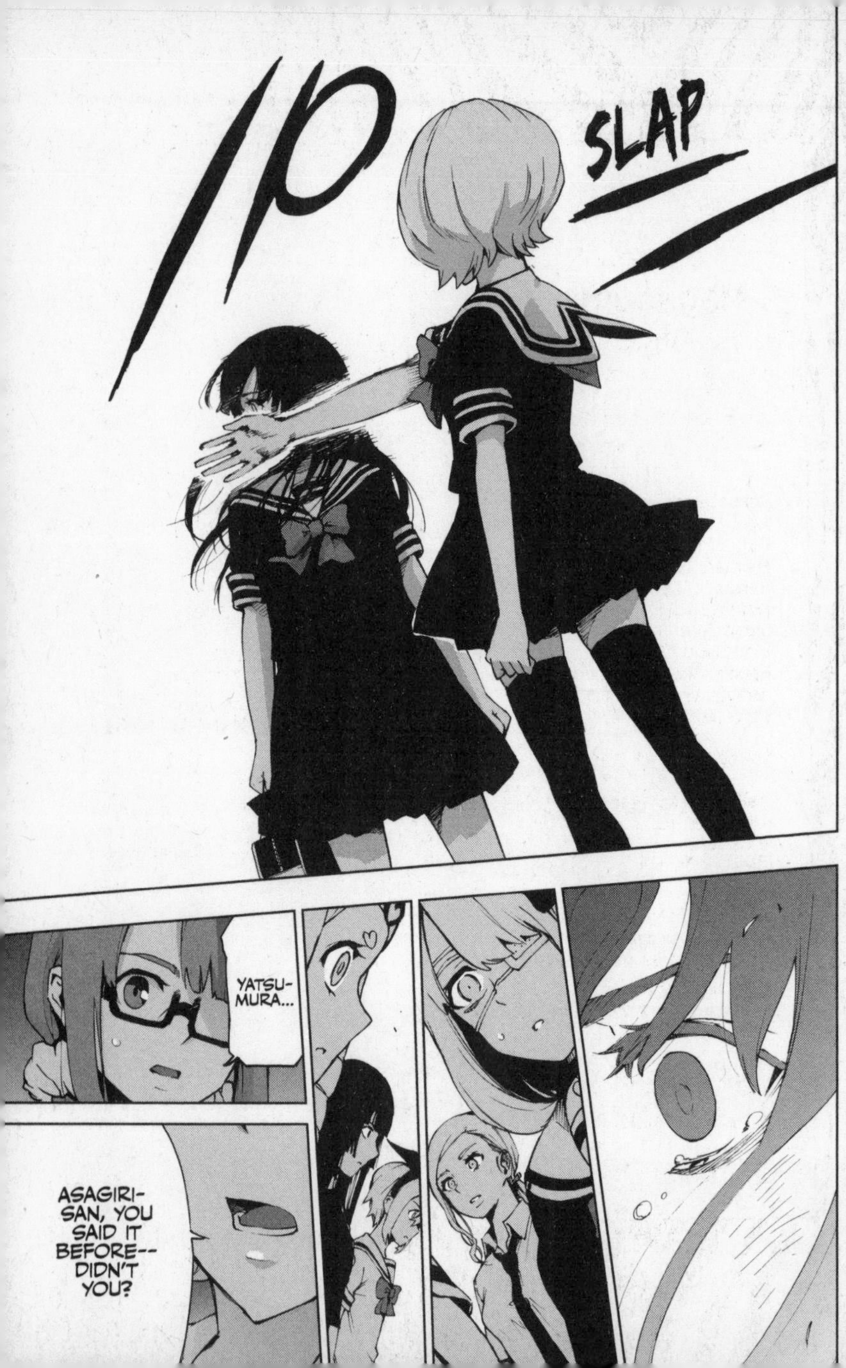
SLAP
YATSUMURA...
ASAGIRI-SAN, YOU SAID IT BEFORE--DIDN'T YOU?

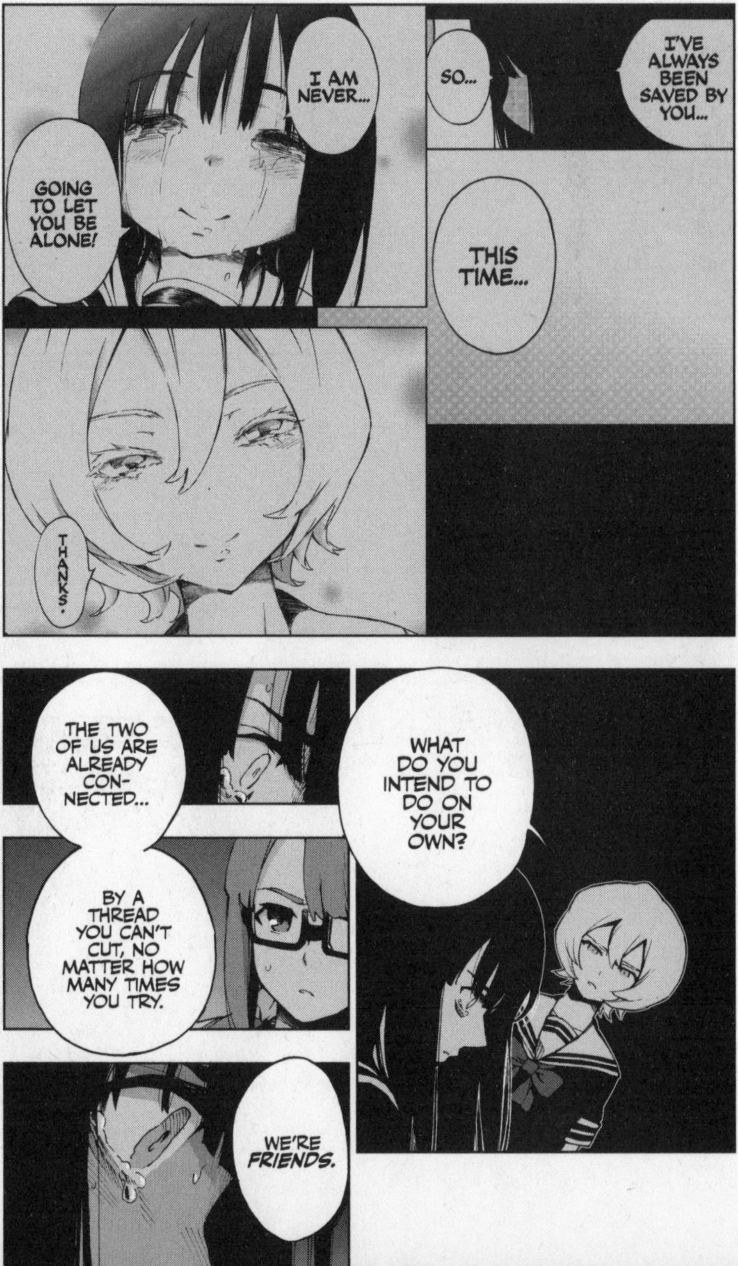
I'VE ALWAYS BEEN SAVED BY YOU...
SO...
THIS TIME...
I AM NEVER...
GOING TO LET YOU BE ALONE!
THANKS.
WHAT DO YOU INTEND TO DO ON YOUR OWN?
THE TWO OF US ARE ALREADY CON-NECTED...
BY A THREAD YOU CAN'T CUT, NO MATTER HOW MANY TIMES YOU TRY.
WE'RE *FRIENDS.*

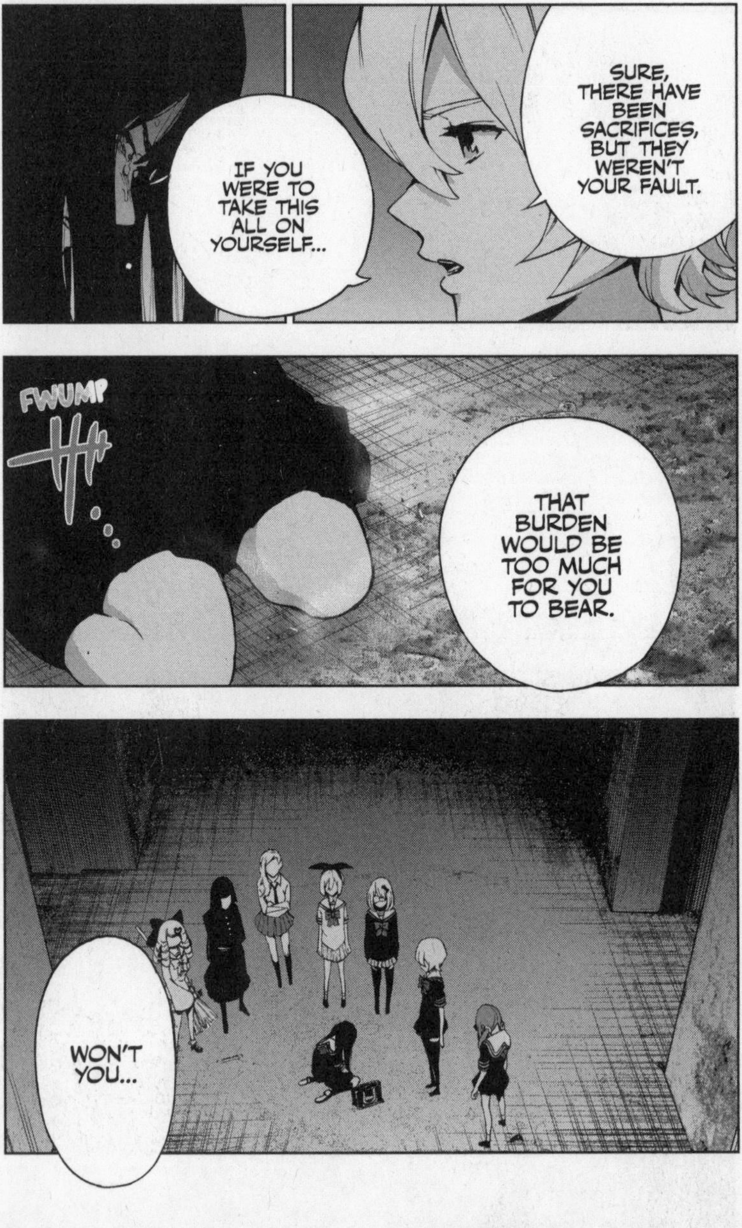
SURE, THERE HAVE BEEN SACRIFICES, BUT THEY WEREN'T YOUR FAULT.
IF YOU WERE TO TAKE THIS ALL ON YOURSELF...
THAT BURDEN WOULD BE TOO MUCH FOR YOU TO BEAR.
FWUMP
WON'T YOU...

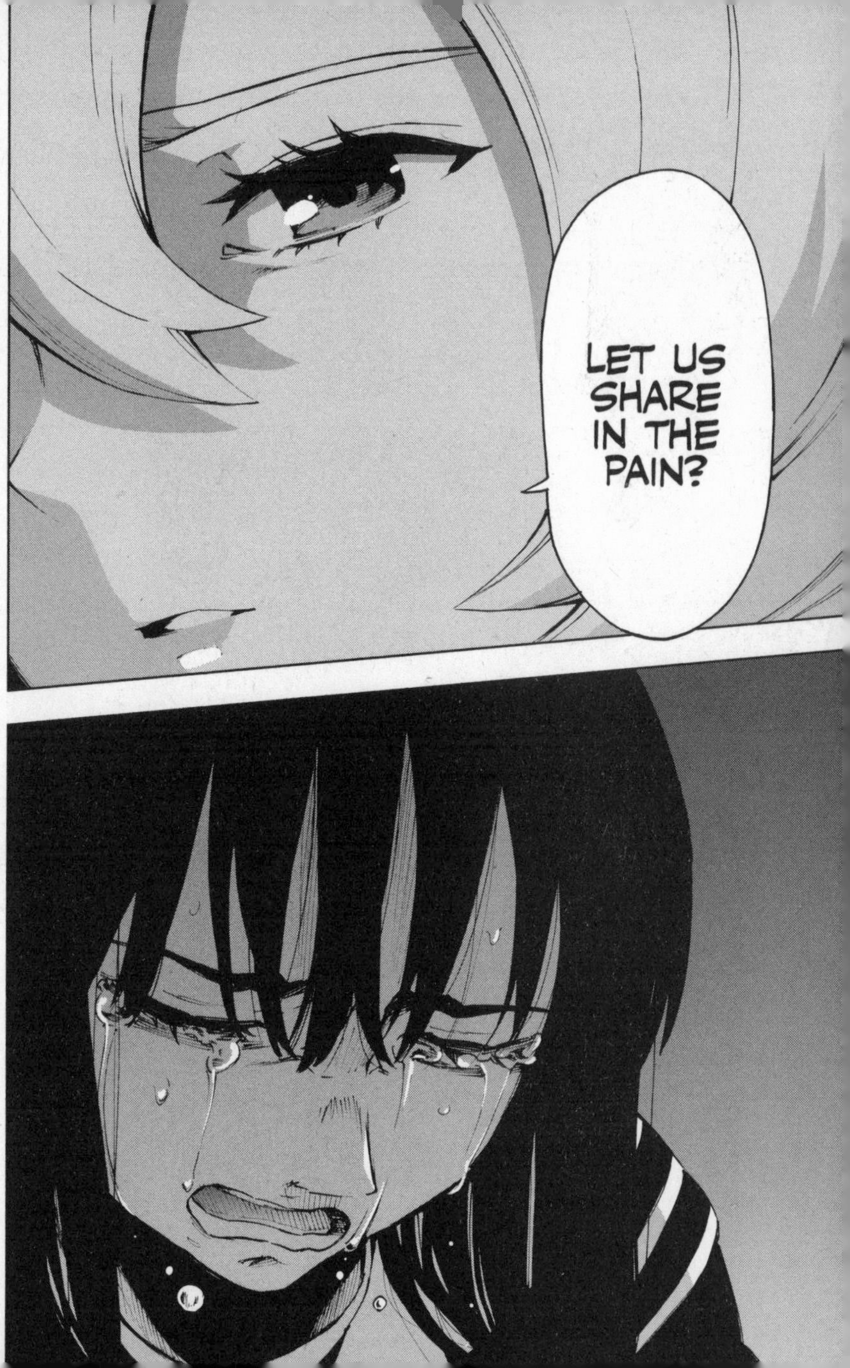
LET US SHARE IN THE PAIN?

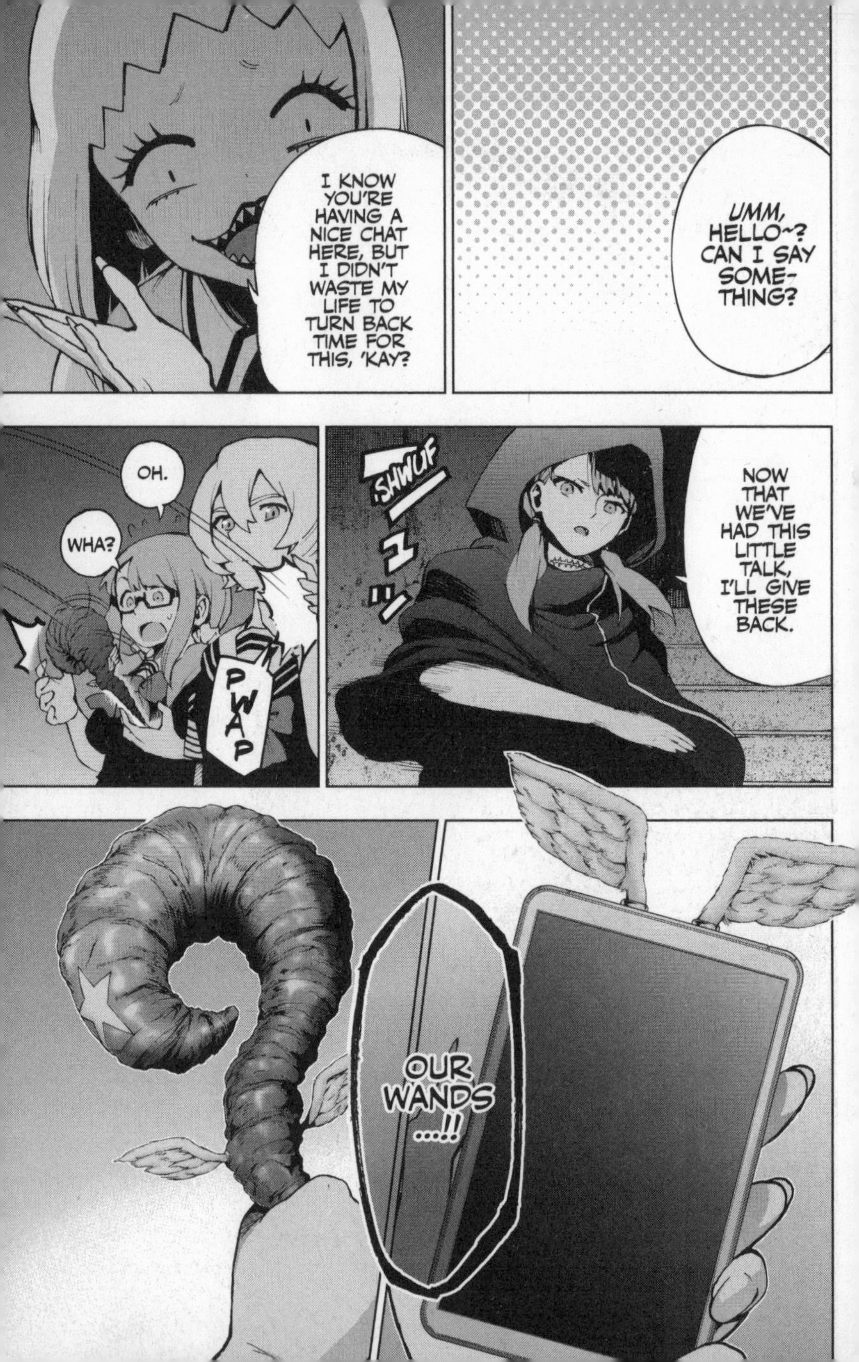
UMM, HELLO~? CAN I SAY SOME-THING?
I KNOW YOU'RE HAVING A NICE CHAT HERE, BUT I DIDN'T WASTE MY LIFE TO TURN BACK TIME FOR THIS, 'KAY?
NOW THAT WE'VE HAD THIS LITTLE TALK, I'LL GIVE THESE BACK.
SHWUF
OH.
WHA?
PWAP
OUR WANDS ...!!

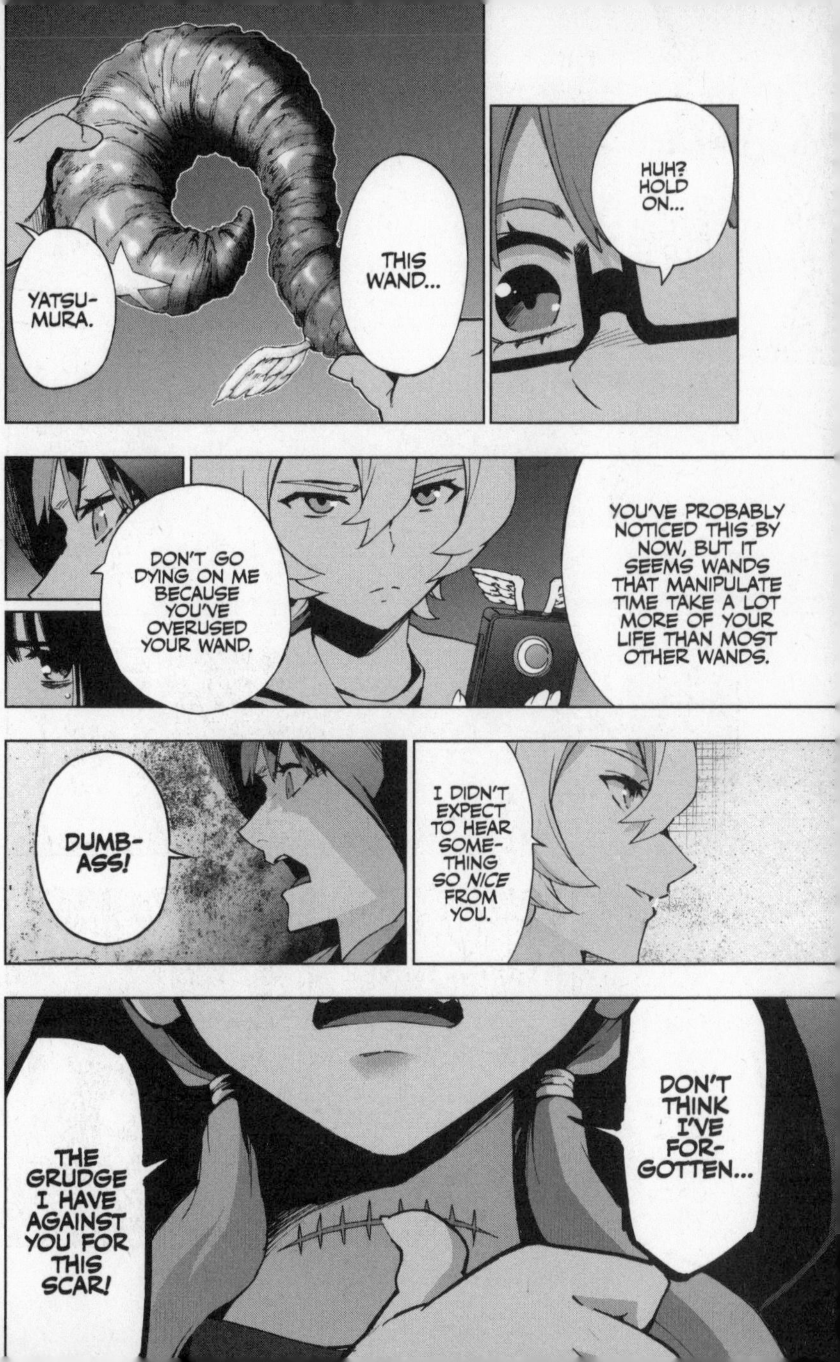
HUH? HOLD ON...
THIS WAND...
YATSU-MURA.
YOU'VE PROBABLY NOTICED THIS BY NOW, BUT IT SEEMS WANDS THAT MANIPULATE TIME TAKE A LOT MORE OF YOUR LIFE THAN MOST OTHER WANDS.
DON'T GO DYING ON ME BECAUSE YOU'VE OVERUSED YOUR WAND.
I DIDN'T EXPECT TO HEAR SOME-THING SO *NICE* FROM YOU.
DUMB-ASS!
DON'T THINK I'VE FOR-GOTTEN...
THE GRUDGE I HAVE AGAINST YOU FOR THIS SCAR!

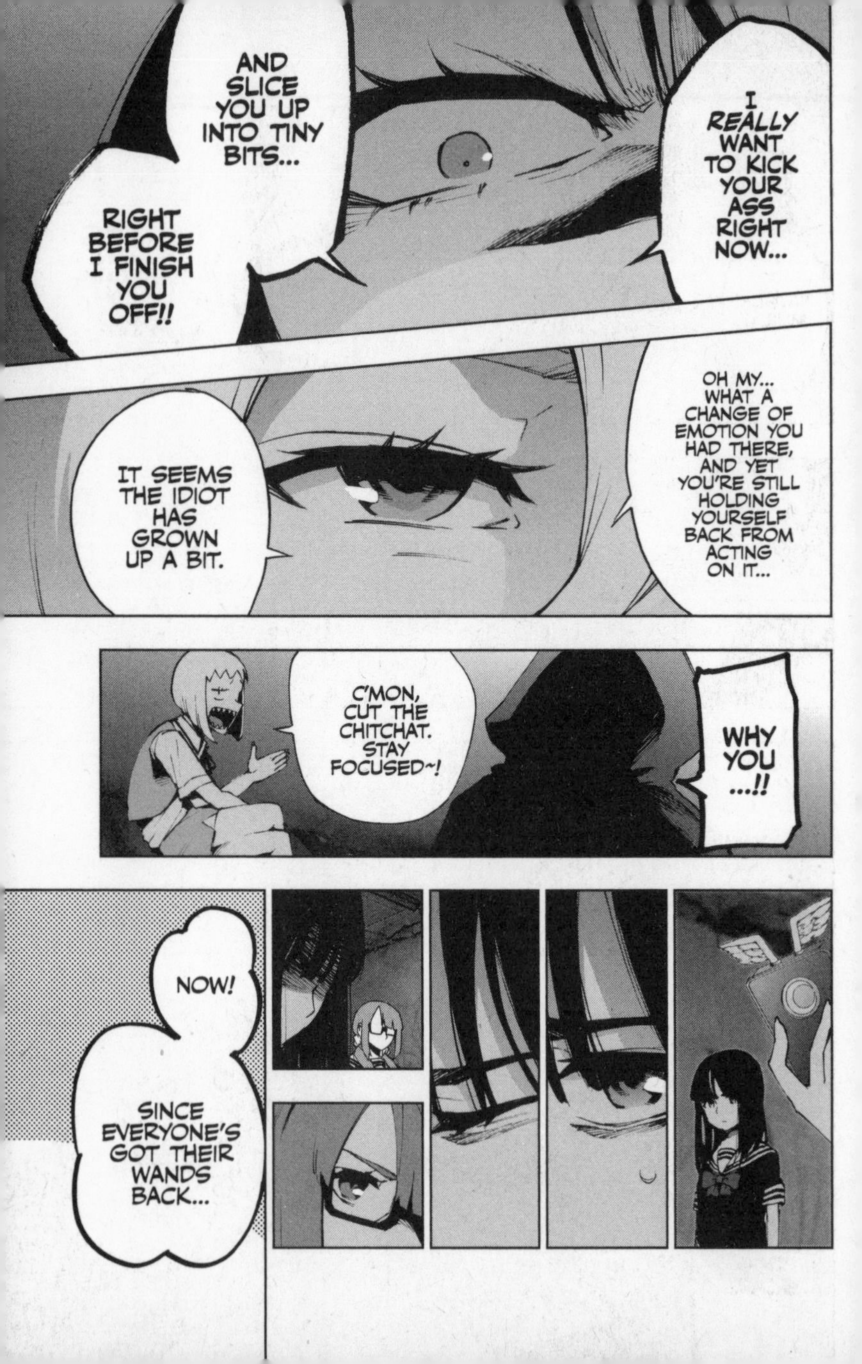
I REALLY WANT TO KICK YOUR ASS RIGHT NOW...
AND SLICE YOU UP INTO TINY BITS...
RIGHT BEFORE I FINISH YOU OFF!!
OH MY... WHAT A CHANGE OF EMOTION YOU HAD THERE, AND YET YOU'RE STILL HOLDING YOURSELF BACK FROM ACTING ON IT...
IT SEEMS THE IDIOT HAS GROWN UP A BIT.
WHY YOU ...!!
C'MON, CUT THE CHITCHAT. STAY FOCUSED~!
NOW!
SINCE EVERYONE'S GOT THEIR WANDS BACK...

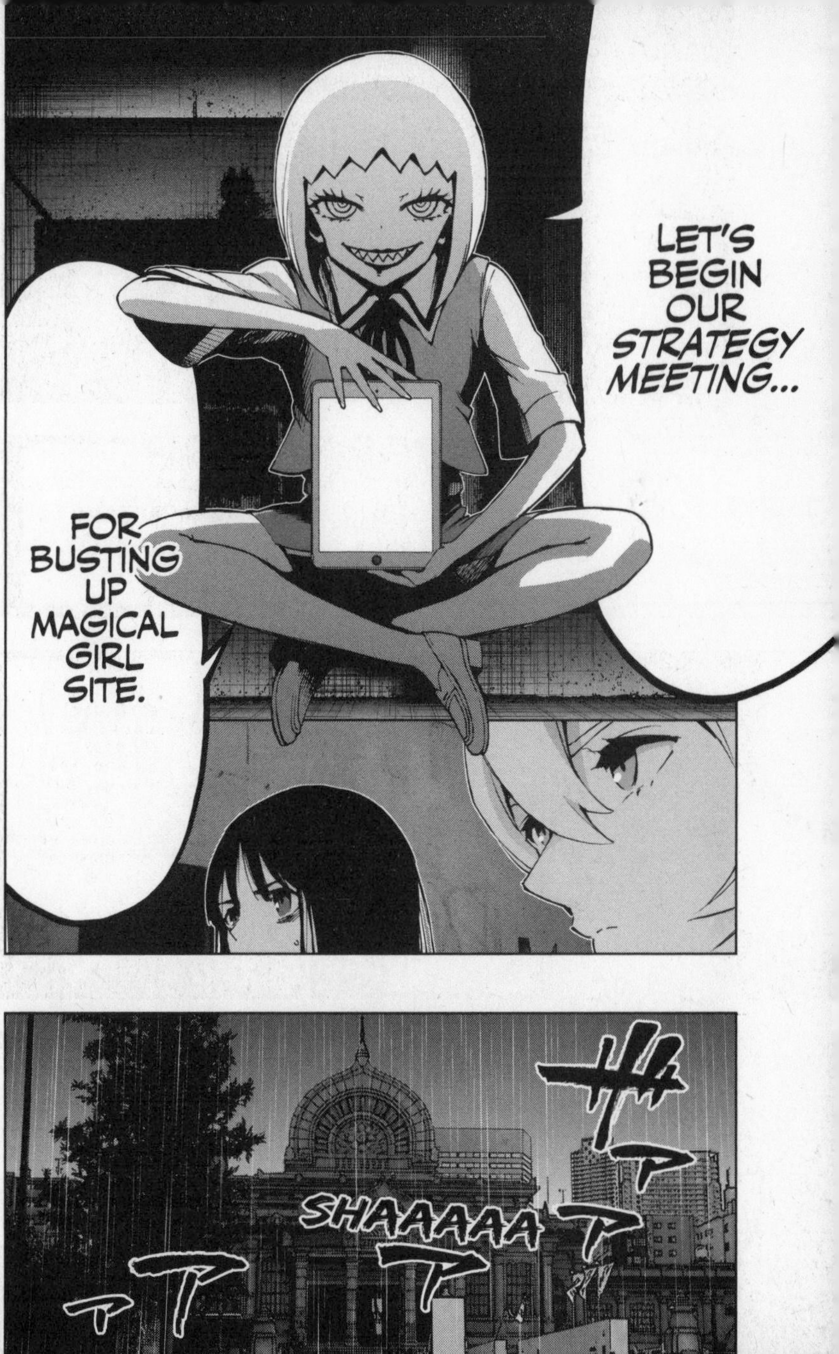
LET'S BEGIN OUR STRATEGY MEETING...
FOR BUSTING UP MAGICAL GIRL SITE.
SHAAAAAA

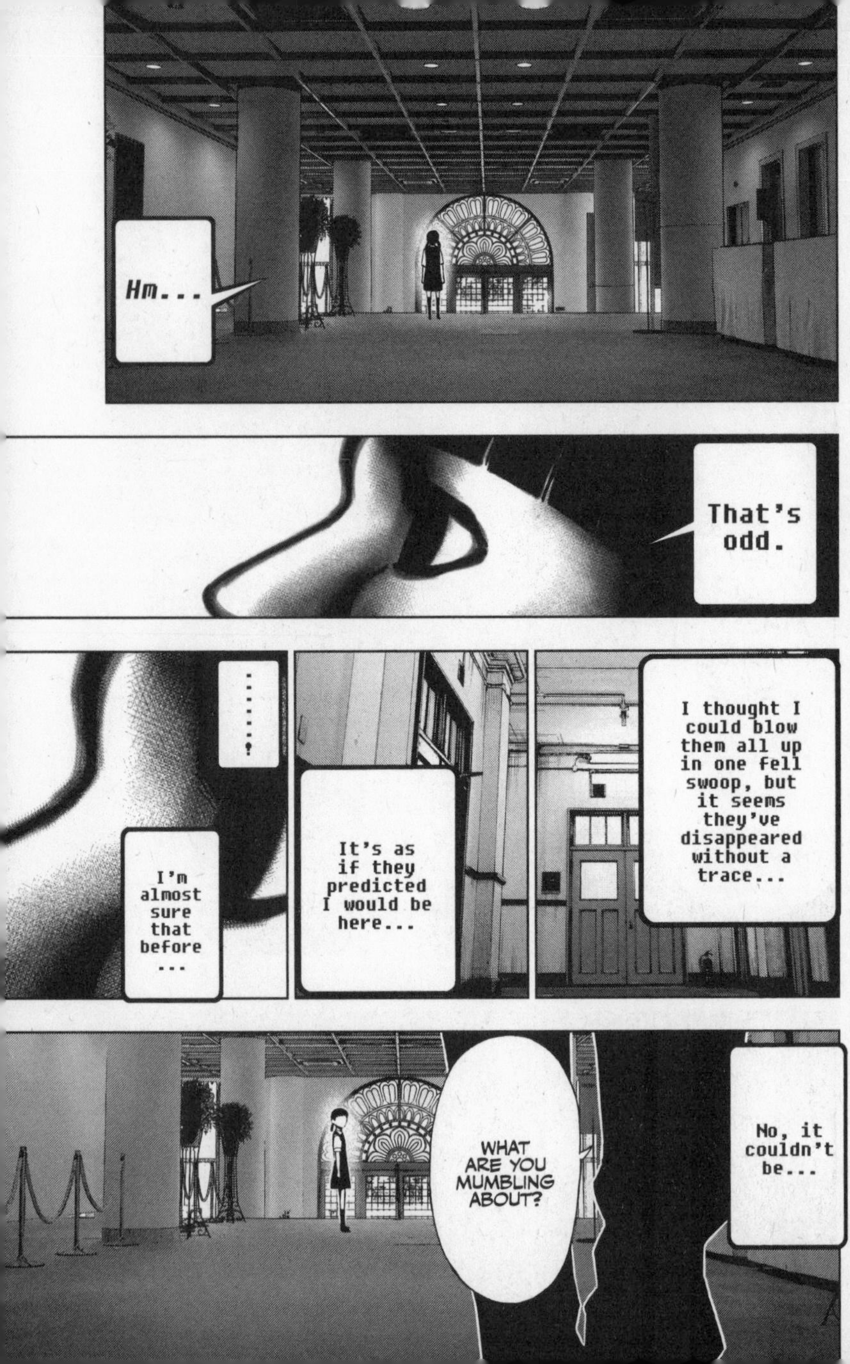

Hm...
That's odd.
I thought I could blow them all up in one fell swoop, but it seems they've disappeared without a trace...
It's as if they predicted I would be here...
......!
I'm almost sure that before ...
No, it couldn't be...
WHAT ARE YOU MUMBLING ABOUT?

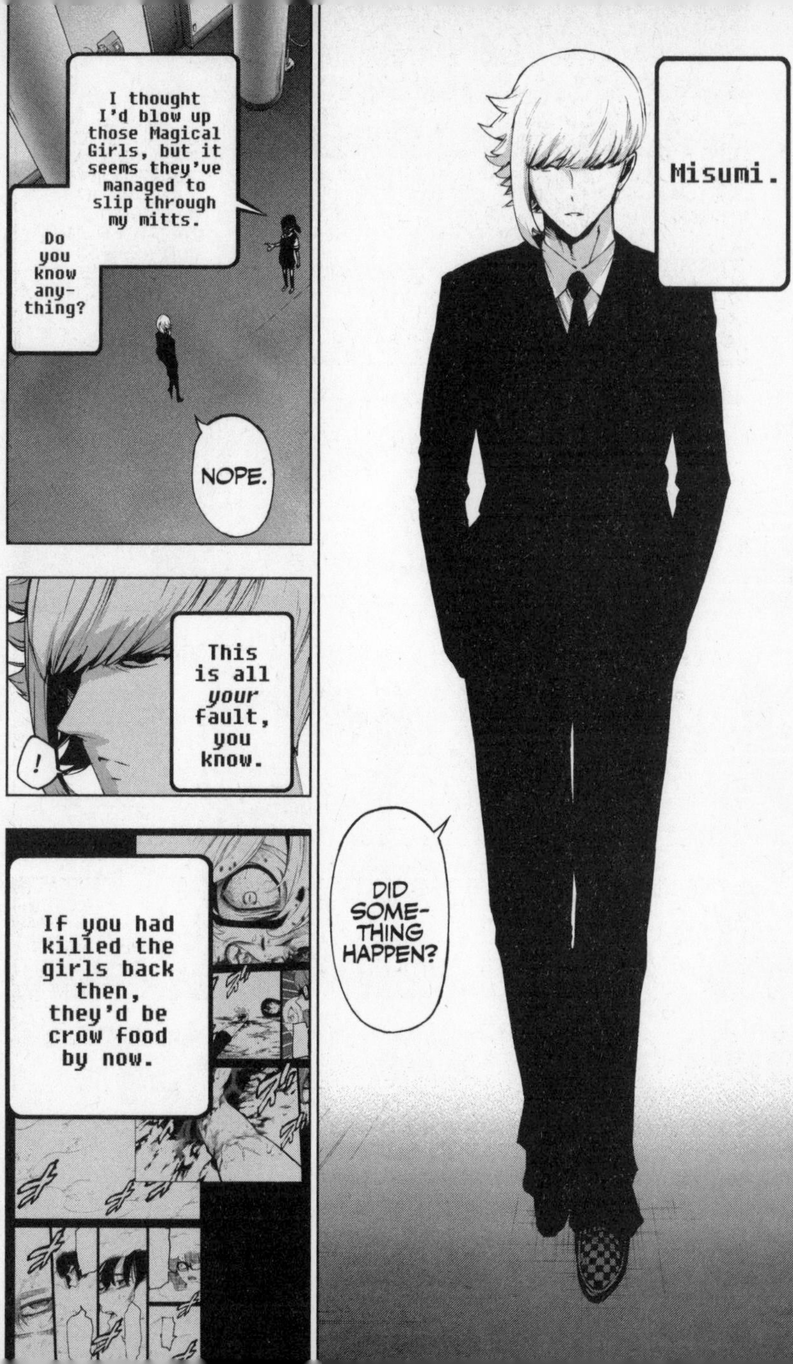
Misumi.
DID SOMETHING HAPPEN?
I thought I'd blow up those Magical Girls, but it seems they've managed to slip through my mitts.
Do you know any-thing?
NOPE.
This is all *your* fault, you know.
!
If you had killed the girls back then, they'd be crow food by now.

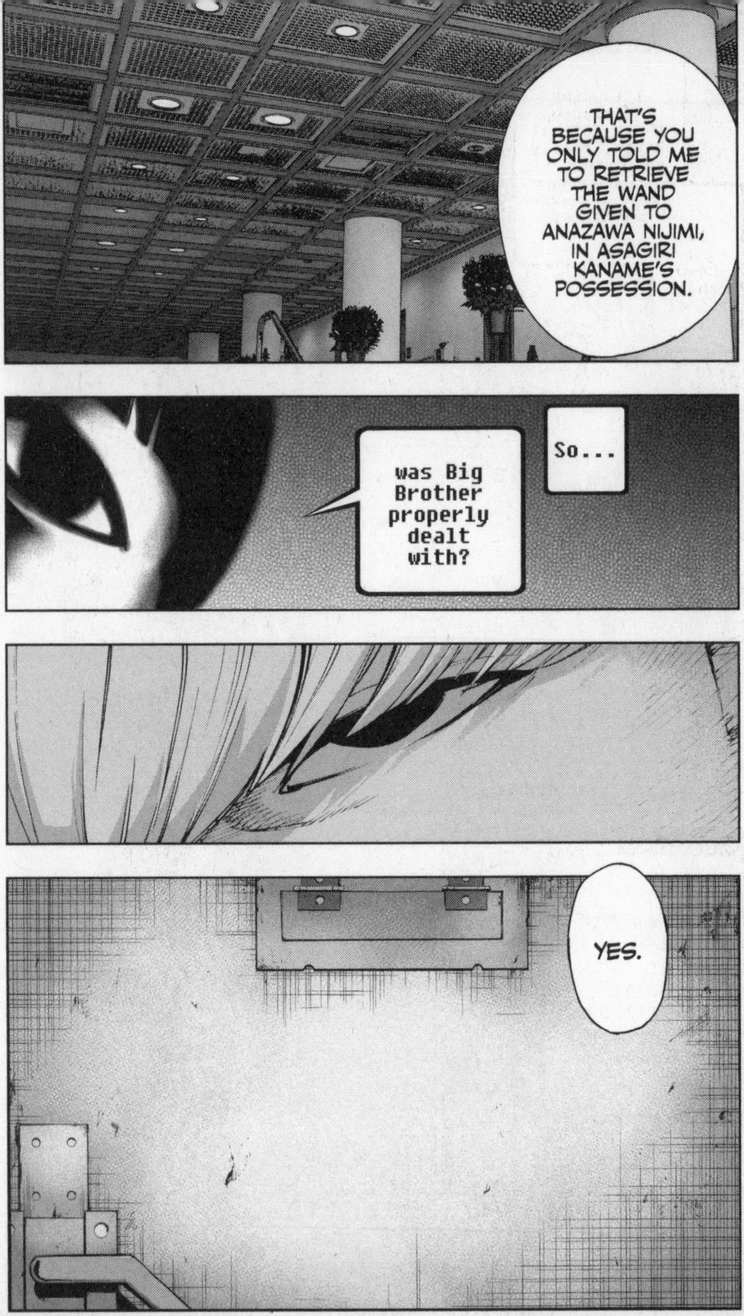
THAT'S BECAUSE YOU ONLY TOLD ME TO RETRIEVE THE WAND GIVEN TO ANAZAWA NIJIMI, IN ASAGIRI KANAME'S POSSESSION.
So...
was Big Brother properly dealt with?
YES.

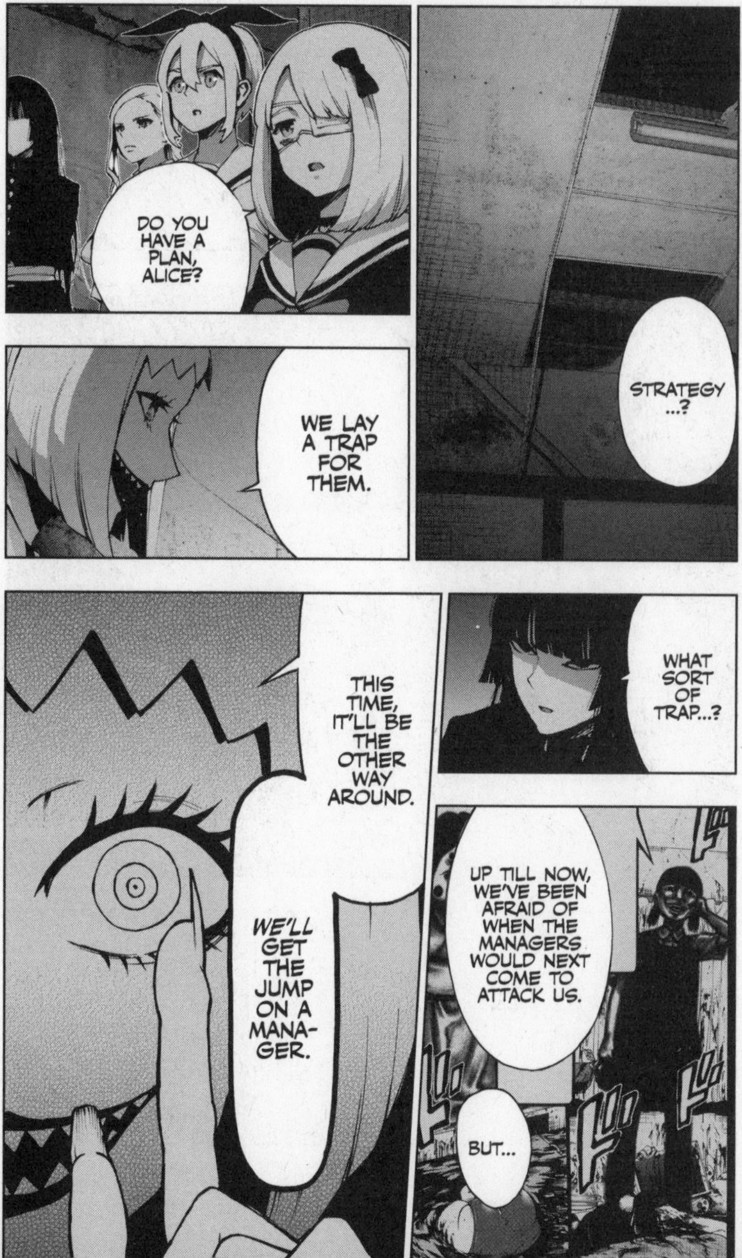
STRATEGY ...?
DO YOU HAVE A PLAN, ALICE?
WE LAY A TRAP FOR THEM.
WHAT SORT OF TRAP...?
UP TILL NOW, WE'VE BEEN AFRAID OF WHEN THE MANAGERS WOULD NEXT COME TO ATTACK US.
BUT...
THIS TIME, IT'LL BE THE OTHER WAY AROUND.
WE'LL GET THE JUMP ON A MANA-GER.

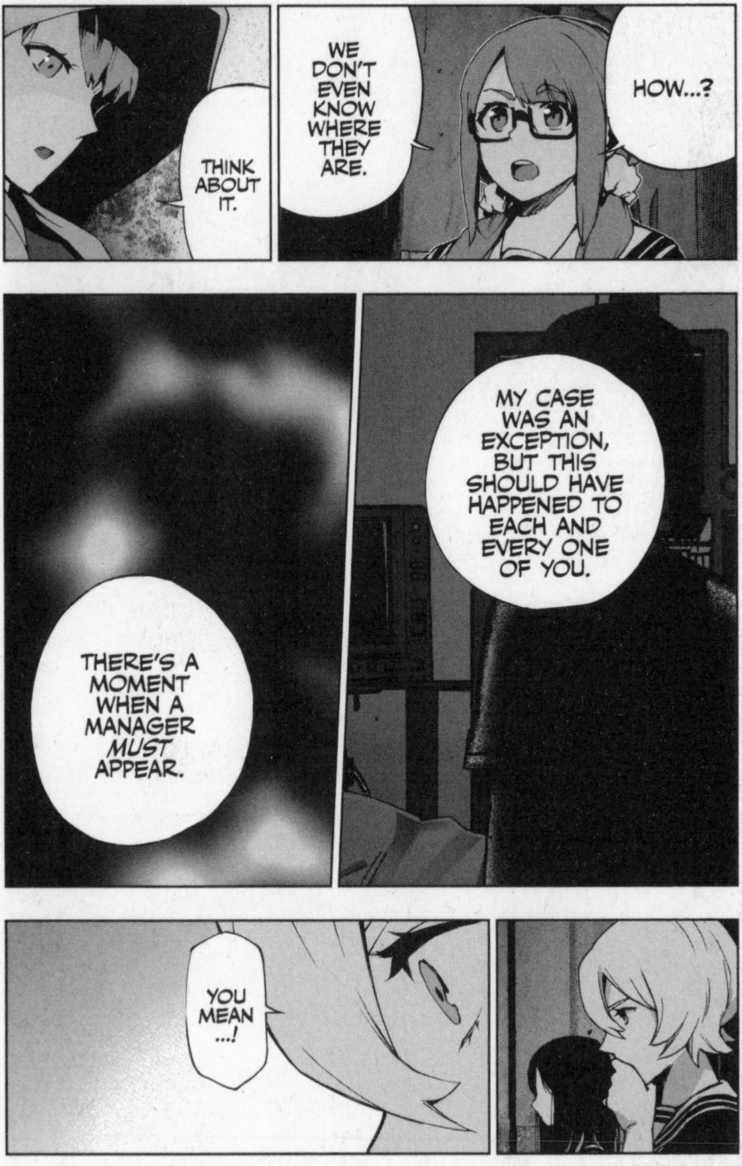
HOW...?
WE DON'T EVEN KNOW WHERE THEY ARE.
THINK ABOUT IT.
MY CASE WAS AN EXCEPTION, BUT THIS SHOULD HAVE HAPPENED TO EACH AND EVERY ONE OF YOU.
THERE'S A MOMENT WHEN A MANAGER *MUST* APPEAR.
YOU MEAN ...!

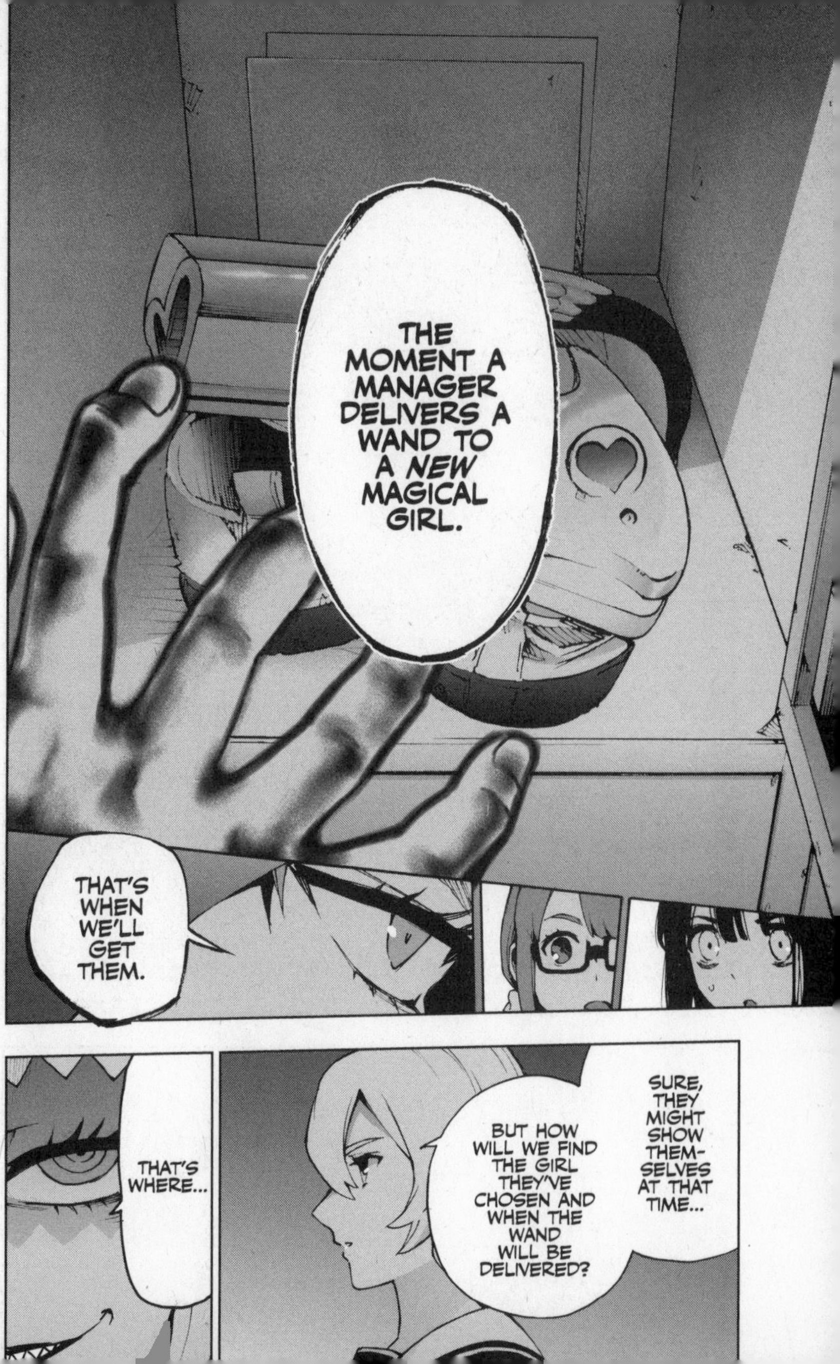
THE MOMENT A MANAGER DELIVERS A WAND TO A *NEW* MAGICAL GIRL.
THAT'S WHEN WE'LL GET THEM.
SURE, THEY MIGHT SHOW THEM-SELVES AT THAT TIME...
BUT HOW WILL WE FIND THE GIRL THEY'VE CHOSEN AND WHEN THE WAND WILL BE DELIVERED?
THAT'S WHERE...

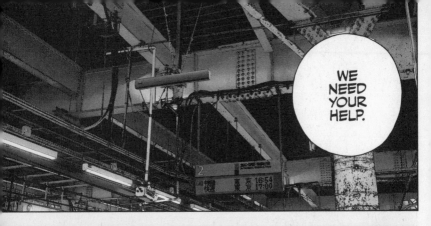

WE
NEED
YOUR
HELP.

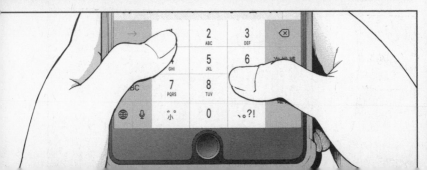

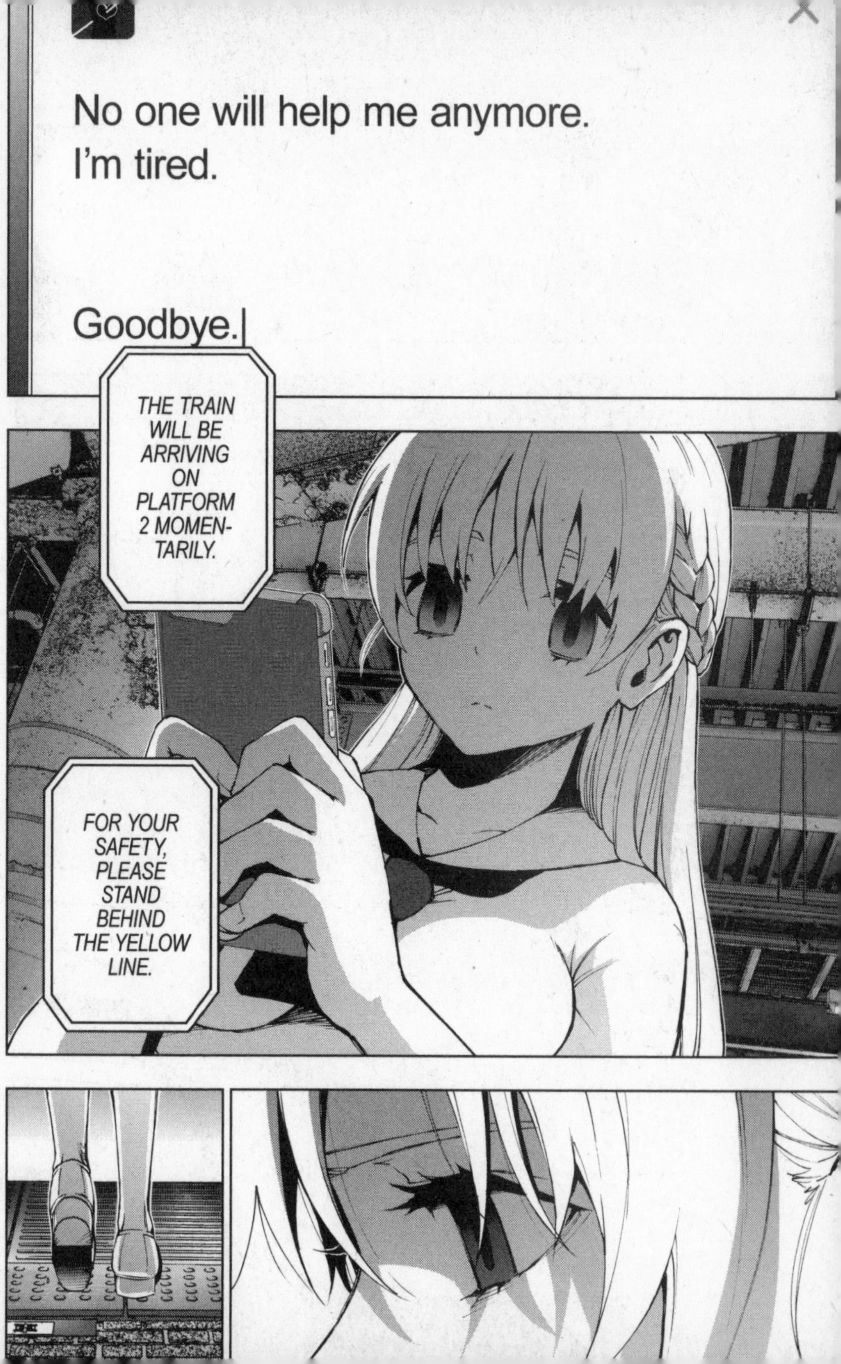
No one will help me anymore.
I'm tired.
Goodbye.
THE TRAIN WILL BE ARRIVING ON PLATFORM 2 MOMEN-TARILY.
FOR YOUR SAFETY, PLEASE STAND BEHIND THE YELLOW LINE.

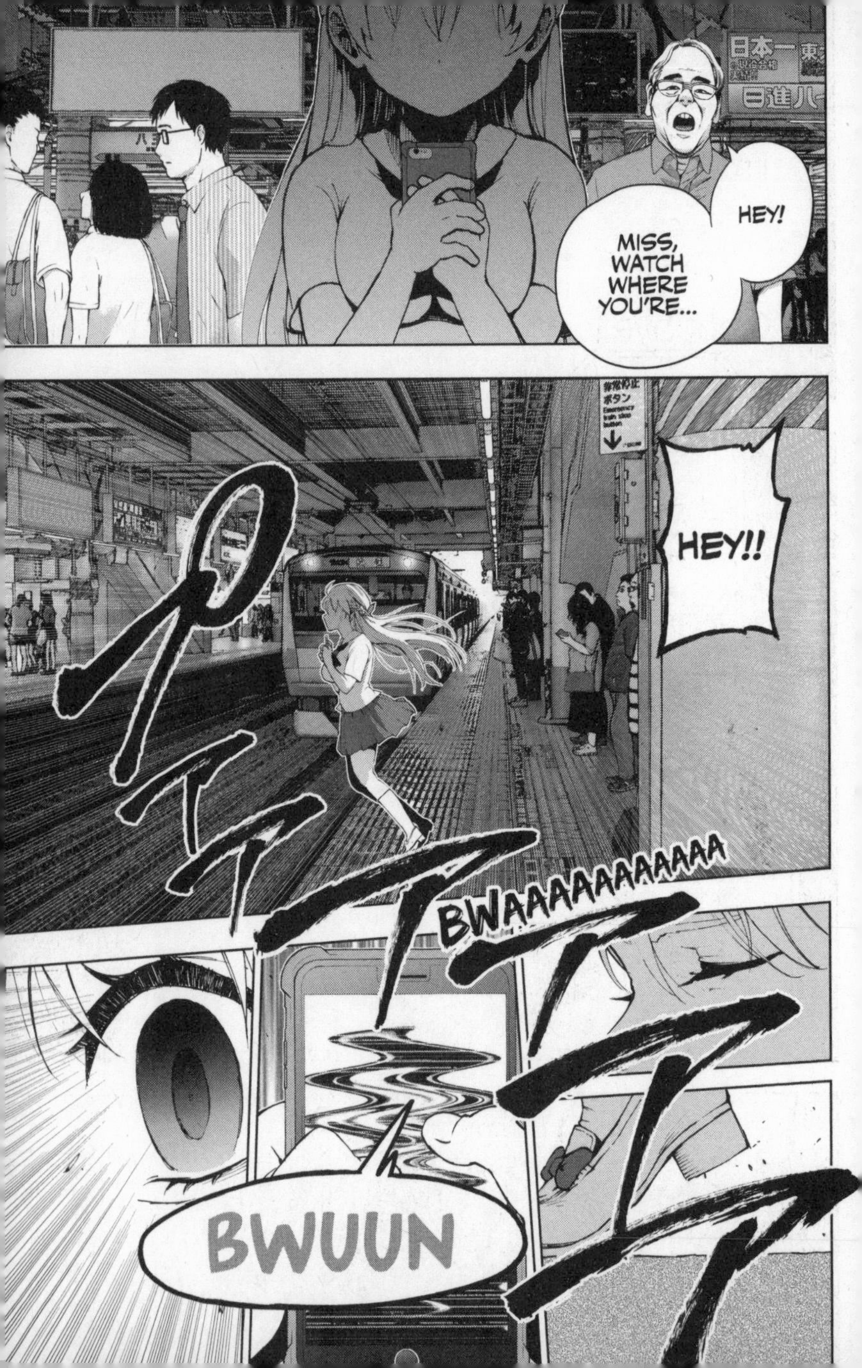
HEY!
MISS, WATCH WHERE YOU'RE...
HEY!!
BWAAAAAAAAAAA
BWUUN

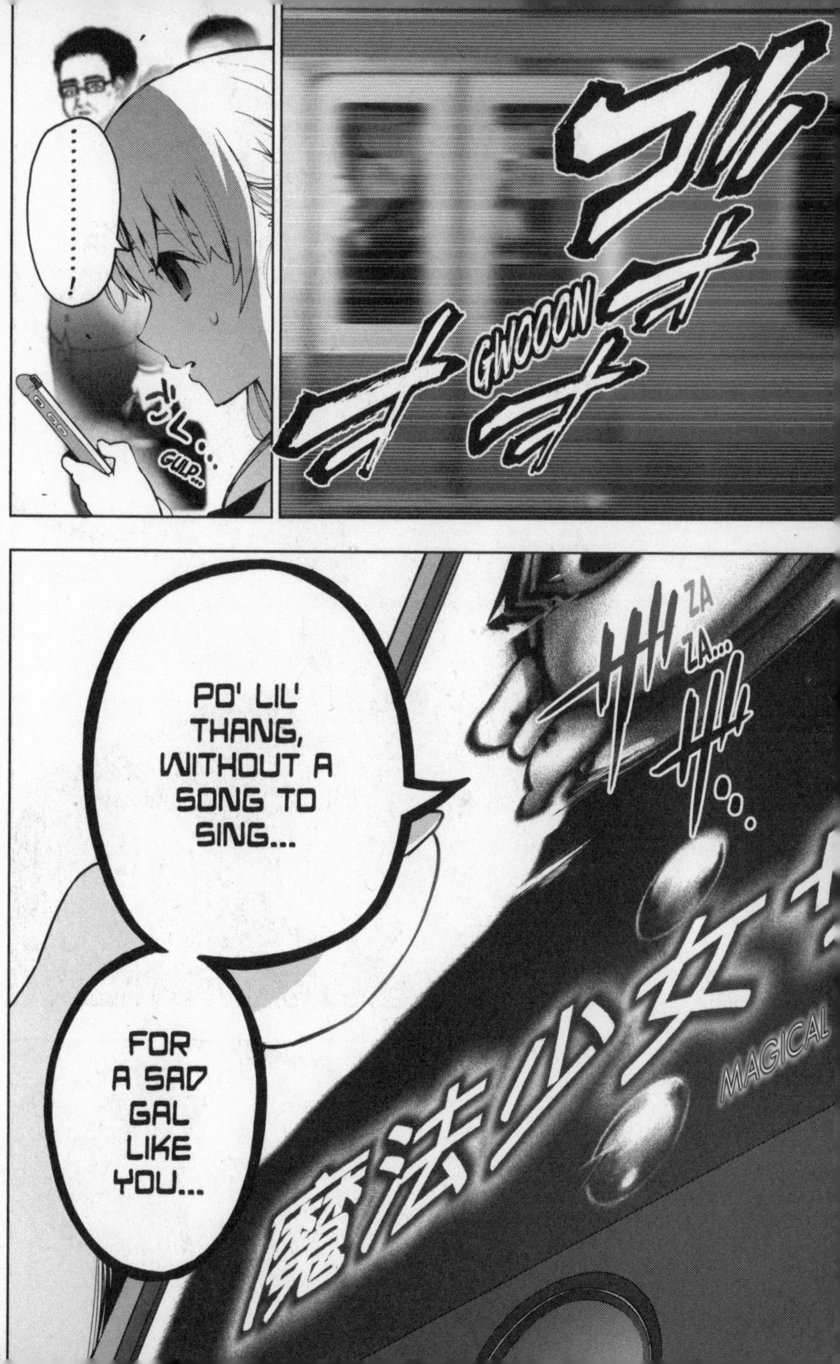
GWOOON
......!
GULP...
ZA ZA...
PO' LIL' THANG, WITHOUT A SONG TO SING...
FOR A SAD GAL LIKE YOU...
魔法少女
MAGICAL

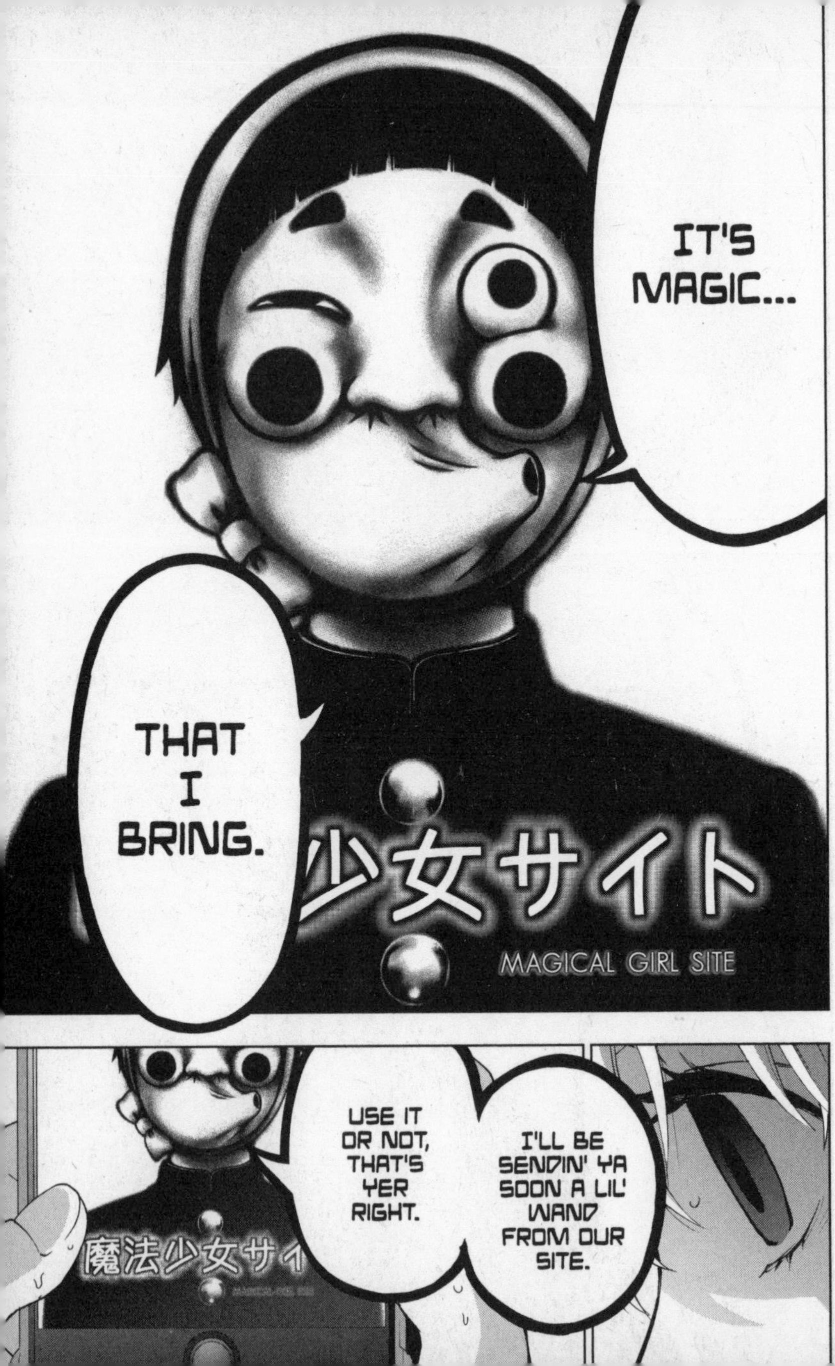
IT'S MAGIC...
THAT I BRING.
少女サイト
MAGICAL GIRL SITE
I'LL BE SENDIN' YA SOON A LIL' WAND FROM OUR SITE.
USE IT OR NOT, THAT'S YER RIGHT.
魔法少女サイ

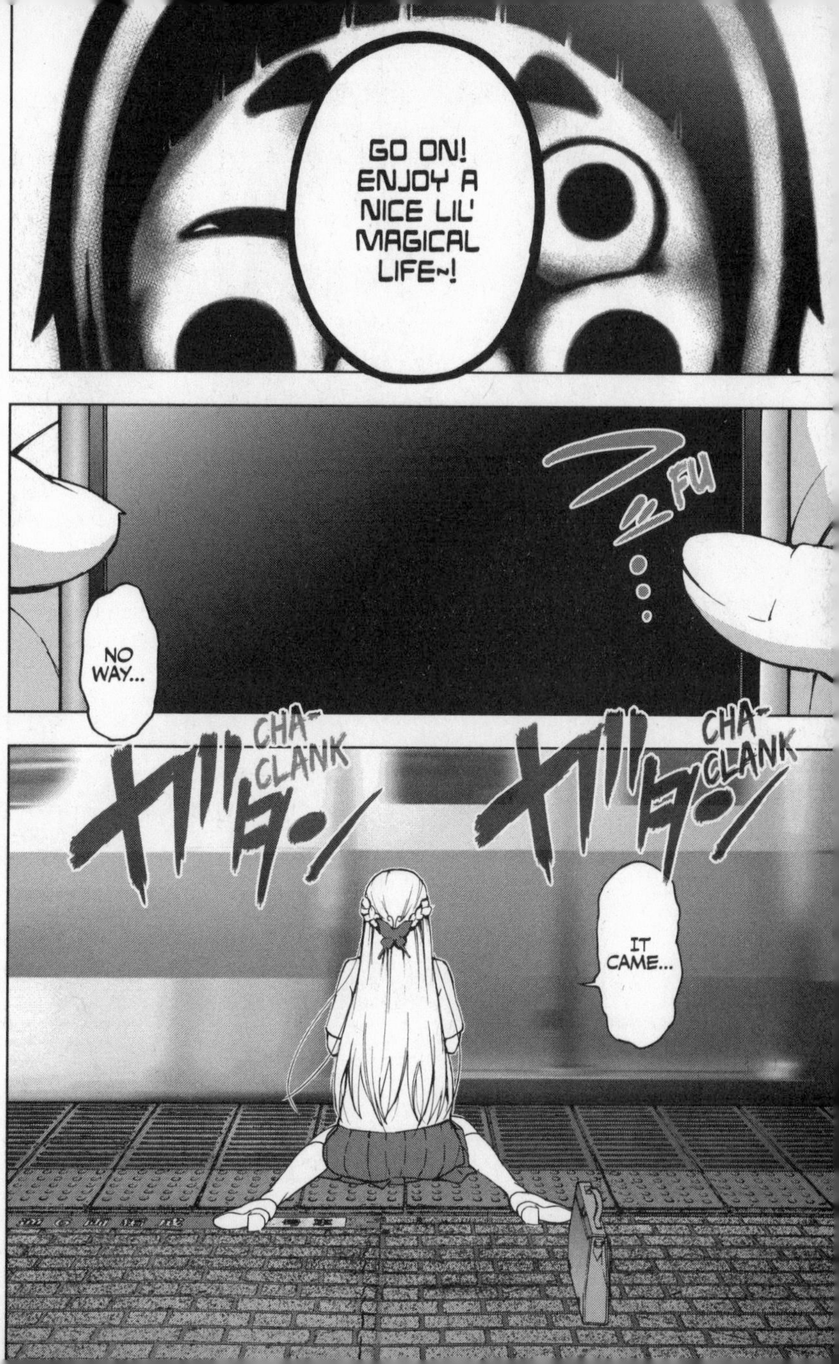
GO ON! ENJOY A NICE LIL' MAGICAL LIFE~!
FU
...
NO WAY...
CHA-CLANK
CHA-CLANK
IT CAME...

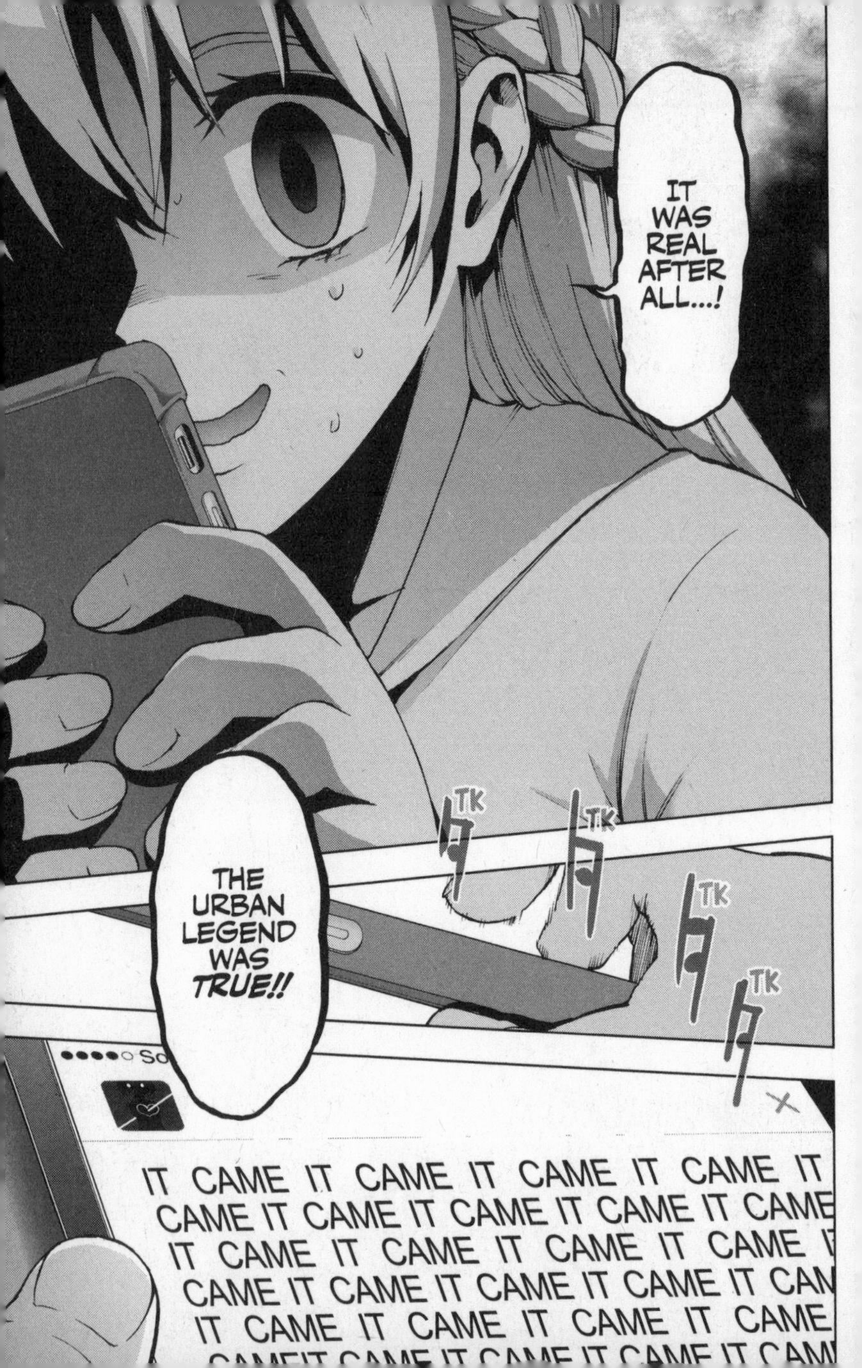
IT WAS REAL AFTER ALL...!
THE URBAN LEGEND WAS TRUE!!
TK
TK
TK
TK
IT CAME IT CAME

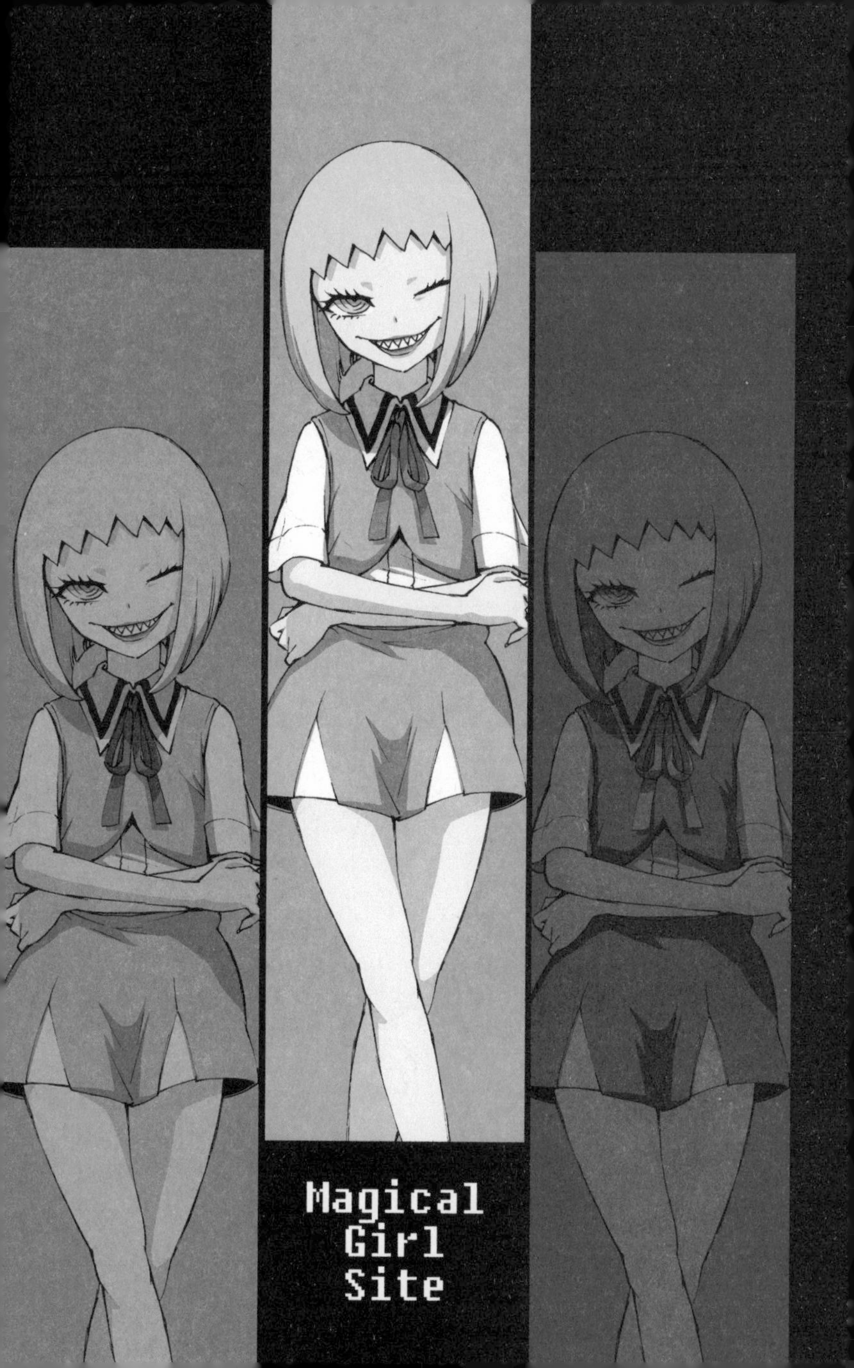
Magical
Girl
Site

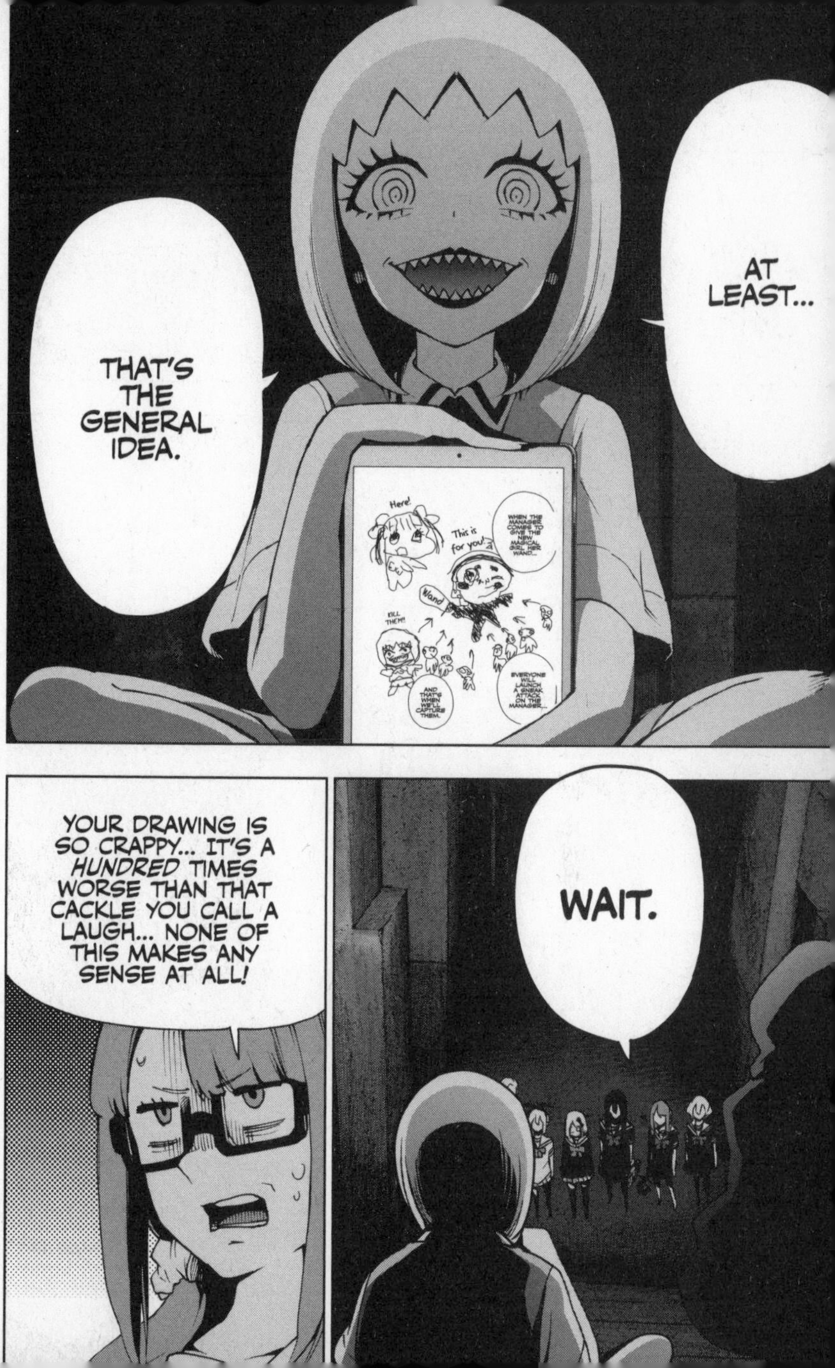
AT LEAST...
THAT'S THE GENERAL IDEA.
WHEN THE MANAGER COMES TO GIVE THE NEW MAGICAL GIRL HER WAND...
This is for you!
Here!
Wand
EVERYONE WILL LAUNCH A SNEAK ATTACK ON THE MANAGER...
KILL THEM!!
AND THAT'S WHEN WE'LL CAPTURE THEM.
WAIT.
YOUR DRAWING IS SO CRAPPY... IT'S A *HUNDRED* TIMES WORSE THAN THAT CACKLE YOU CALL A LAUGH... NONE OF THIS MAKES ANY SENSE AT ALL!

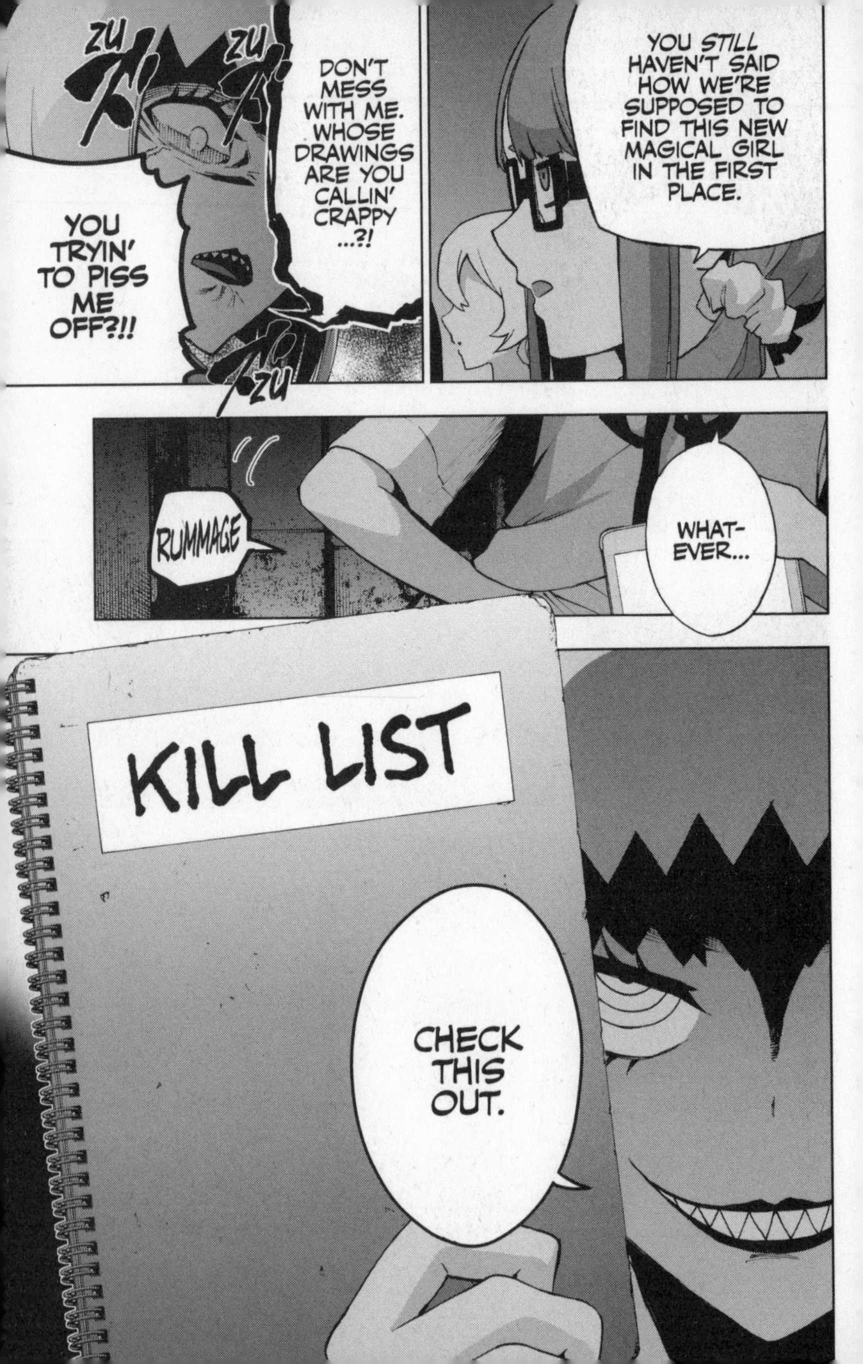
YOU STILL HAVEN'T SAID HOW WE'RE SUPPOSED TO FIND THIS NEW MAGICAL GIRL IN THE FIRST PLACE.
ZU
ZU
DON'T MESS WITH ME. WHOSE DRAWINGS ARE YOU CALLIN' CRAPPY ...?!
YOU TRYIN' TO PISS ME OFF?!!
ZU
WHAT-EVER...
RUMMAGE
KILL LIST
CHECK THIS OUT.

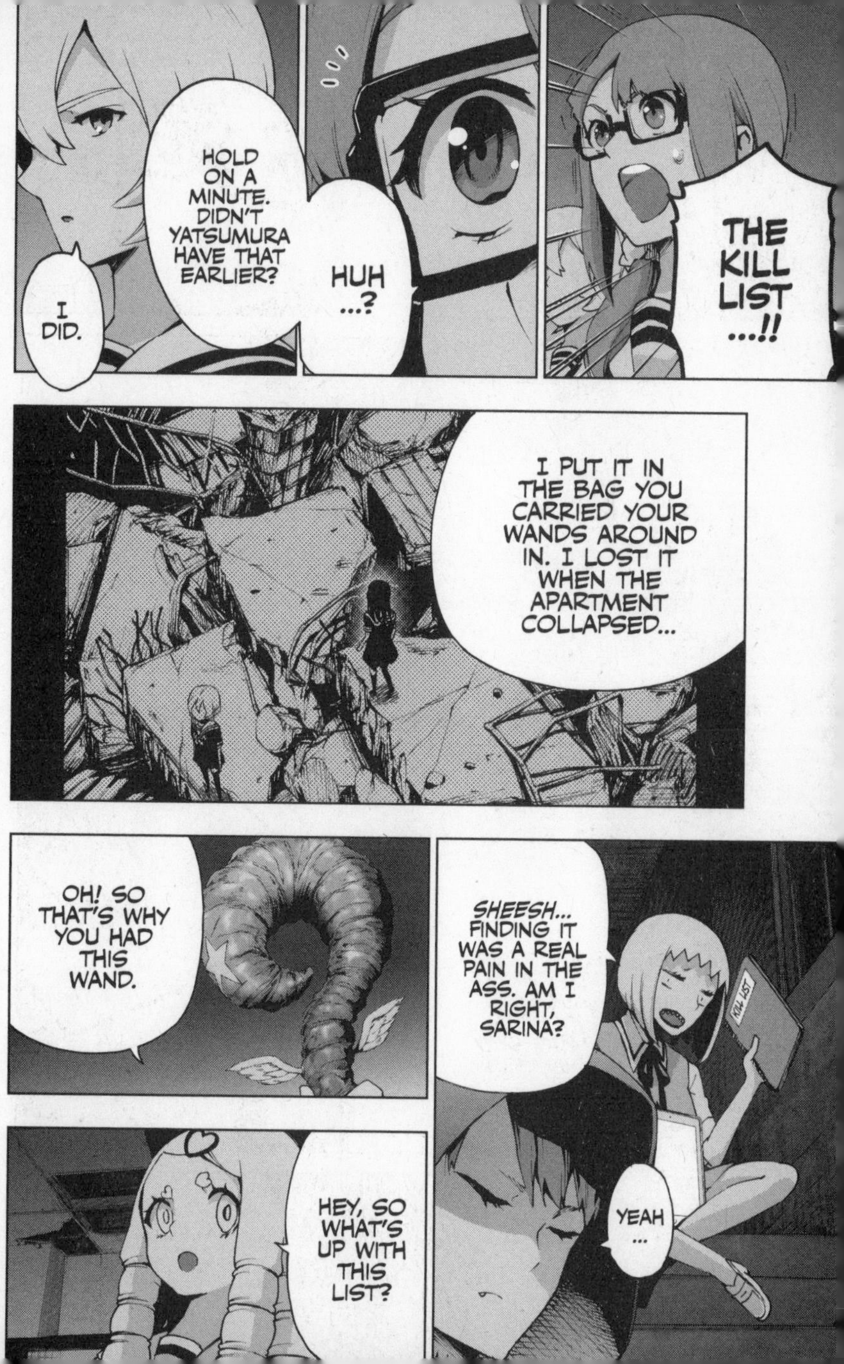
THE KILL LIST ...!!
HUH ...?
HOLD ON A MINUTE. DIDN'T YATSUMURA HAVE THAT EARLIER?
I DID.
I PUT IT IN THE BAG YOU CARRIED YOUR WANDS AROUND IN. I LOST IT WHEN THE APARTMENT COLLAPSED...
SHEESH... FINDING IT WAS A REAL PAIN IN THE ASS. AM I RIGHT, SARINA?
KILL LIST
YEAH ...
OH! SO THAT'S WHY YOU HAD THIS WAND.
HEY, SO WHAT'S UP WITH THIS LIST?

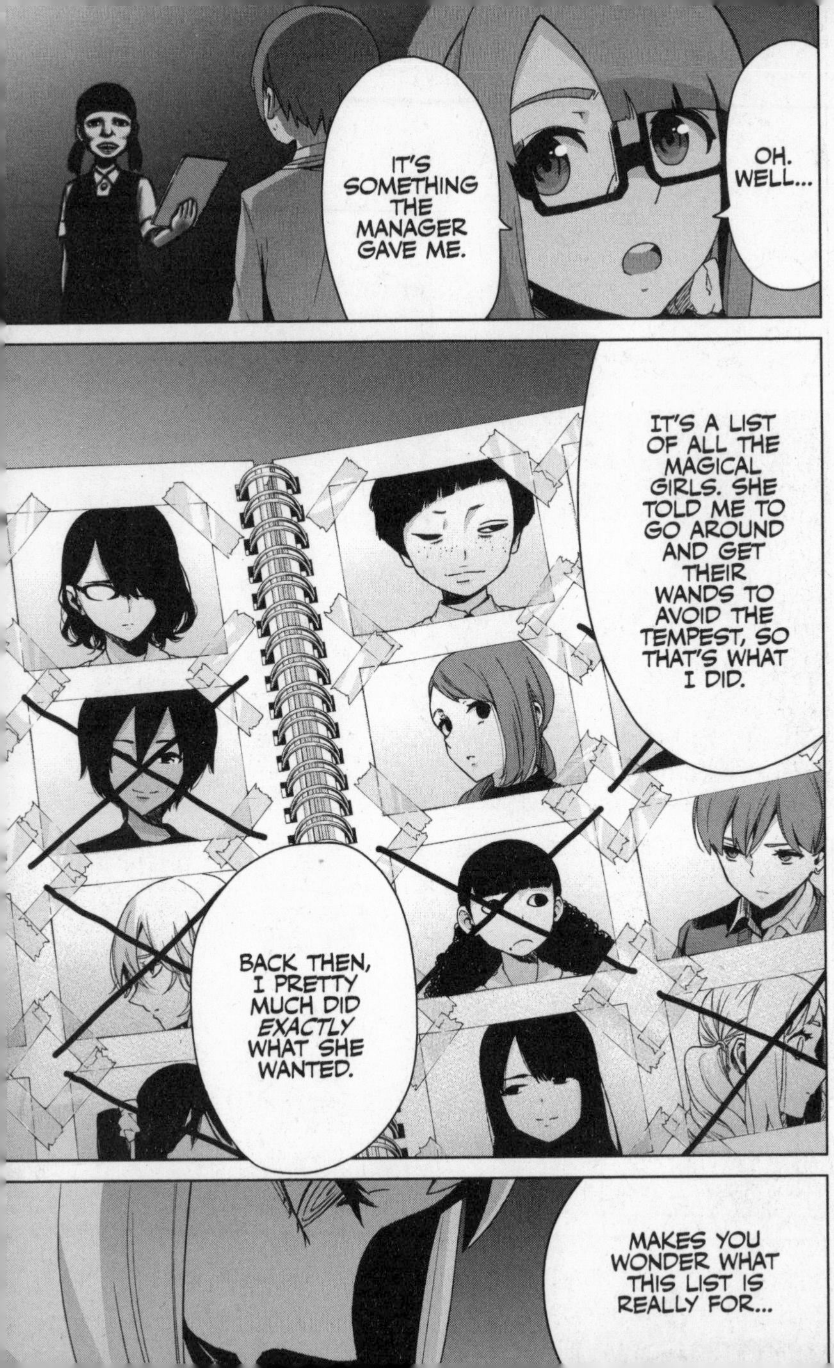
OH. WELL...
IT'S SOMETHING THE MANAGER GAVE ME.
IT'S A LIST OF ALL THE MAGICAL GIRLS. SHE TOLD ME TO GO AROUND AND GET THEIR WANDS TO AVOID THE TEMPEST, SO THAT'S WHAT I DID.
BACK THEN, I PRETTY MUCH DID *EXACTLY* WHAT SHE WANTED.
MAKES YOU WONDER WHAT THIS LIST IS REALLY FOR...

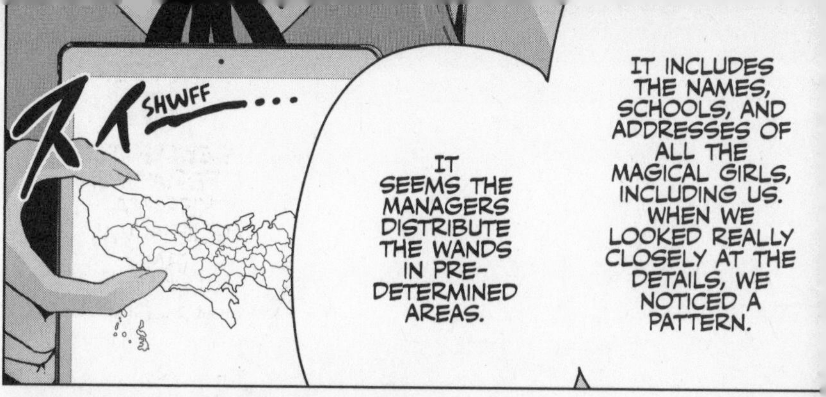
IT INCLUDES THE NAMES, SCHOOLS, AND ADDRESSES OF ALL THE MAGICAL GIRLS, INCLUDING US. WHEN WE LOOKED REALLY CLOSELY AT THE DETAILS, WE NOTICED A PATTERN.
IT SEEMS THE MANAGERS DISTRIBUTE THE WANDS IN PRE-DETERMINED AREAS.
SHWFF...

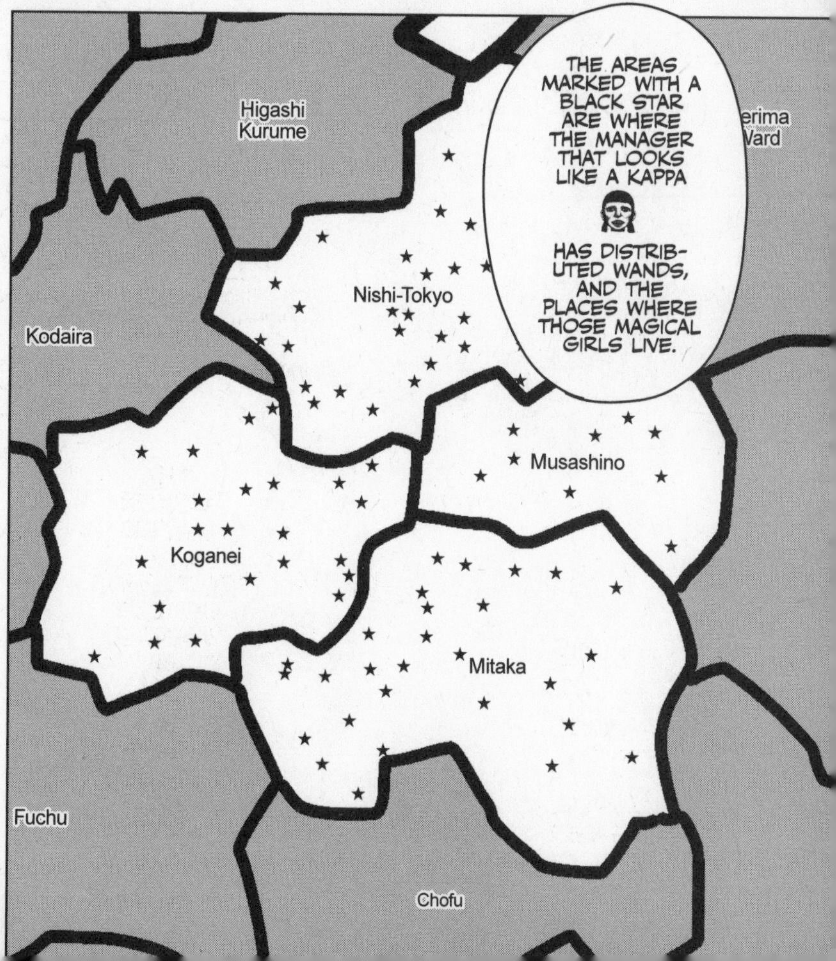
THE AREAS MARKED WITH A BLACK STAR ARE WHERE THE MANAGER THAT LOOKS LIKE A KAPPA
HAS DISTRIB-UTED WANDS, AND THE PLACES WHERE THOSE MAGICAL GIRLS LIVE.
erima Ward
Higashi Kurume
Nishi-Tokyo
Kodaira
Musashino
Koganei
Mitaka
Fuchu
Chofu

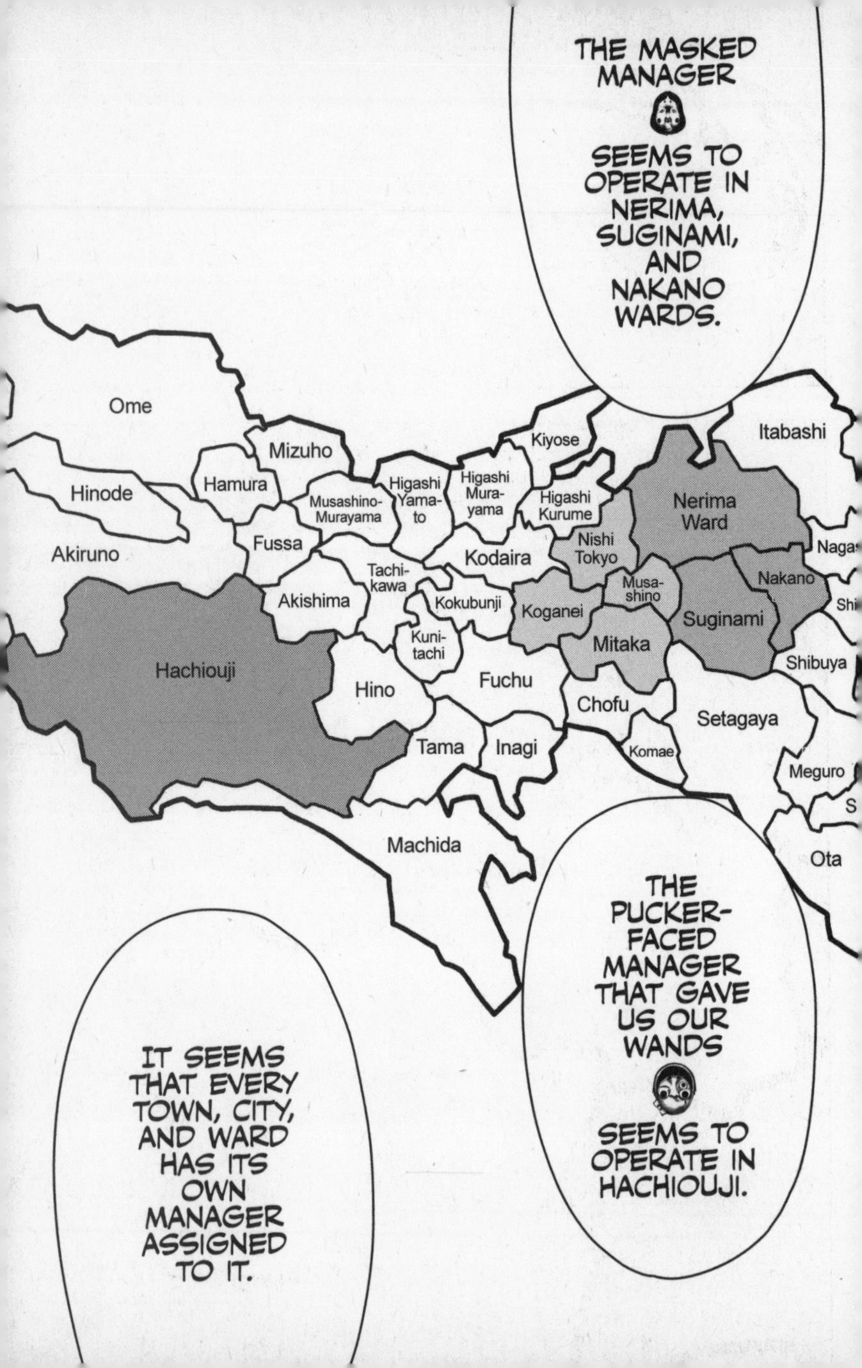
THE MASKED MANAGER SEEMS TO OPERATE IN NERIMA, SUGINAMI, AND NAKANO WARDS.
Ome
Mizuho
Hamura
Hinode
Akiruno
Fussa
Musashino-Murayama
Higashi Yama-to
Higashi Mura-yama
Kiyose
Higashi Kurume
Itabashi
Nerima Ward
Nishi Tokyo
Kodaira
Tachi-kawa
Akishima
Kokubunji
Koganei
Musa-shino
Nakano
Suginami
Mitaka
Kuni-tachi
Hachiouji
Hino
Fuchu
Chofu
Shibuya
Setagaya
Tama
Inagi
Komae
Meguro
Machida
Ota
THE PUCKER-FACED MANAGER THAT GAVE US OUR WANDS SEEMS TO OPERATE IN HACHIOUJI.
IT SEEMS THAT EVERY TOWN, CITY, AND WARD HAS ITS OWN MANAGER ASSIGNED TO IT.

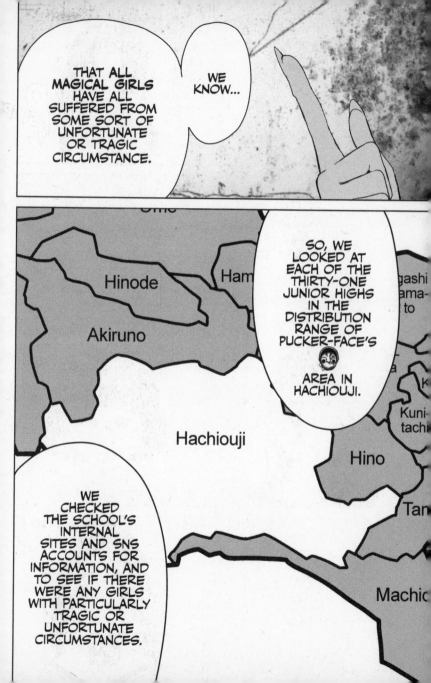

THAT ALL MAGICAL GIRLS HAVE ALL SUFFERED FROM SOME SORT OF UNFORTUNATE OR TRAGIC CIRCUMSTANCE.

WE KNOW...

SO, WE LOOKED AT EACH OF THE THIRTY-ONE JUNIOR HIGHS IN THE DISTRIBUTION RANGE OF PUCKER-FACE'S AREA IN HACHIOUJI.

WE CHECKED THE SCHOOL'S INTERNAL SITES AND SNS ACCOUNTS FOR INFORMATION, AND TO SEE IF THERE WERE ANY GIRLS WITH PARTICULARLY TRAGIC OR UNFORTUNATE CIRCUMSTANCES.

Hinode

Akiruno

Ham

Hachiouji

Hino

Kuni-tachi

Tan

Machi

gashi ama- to

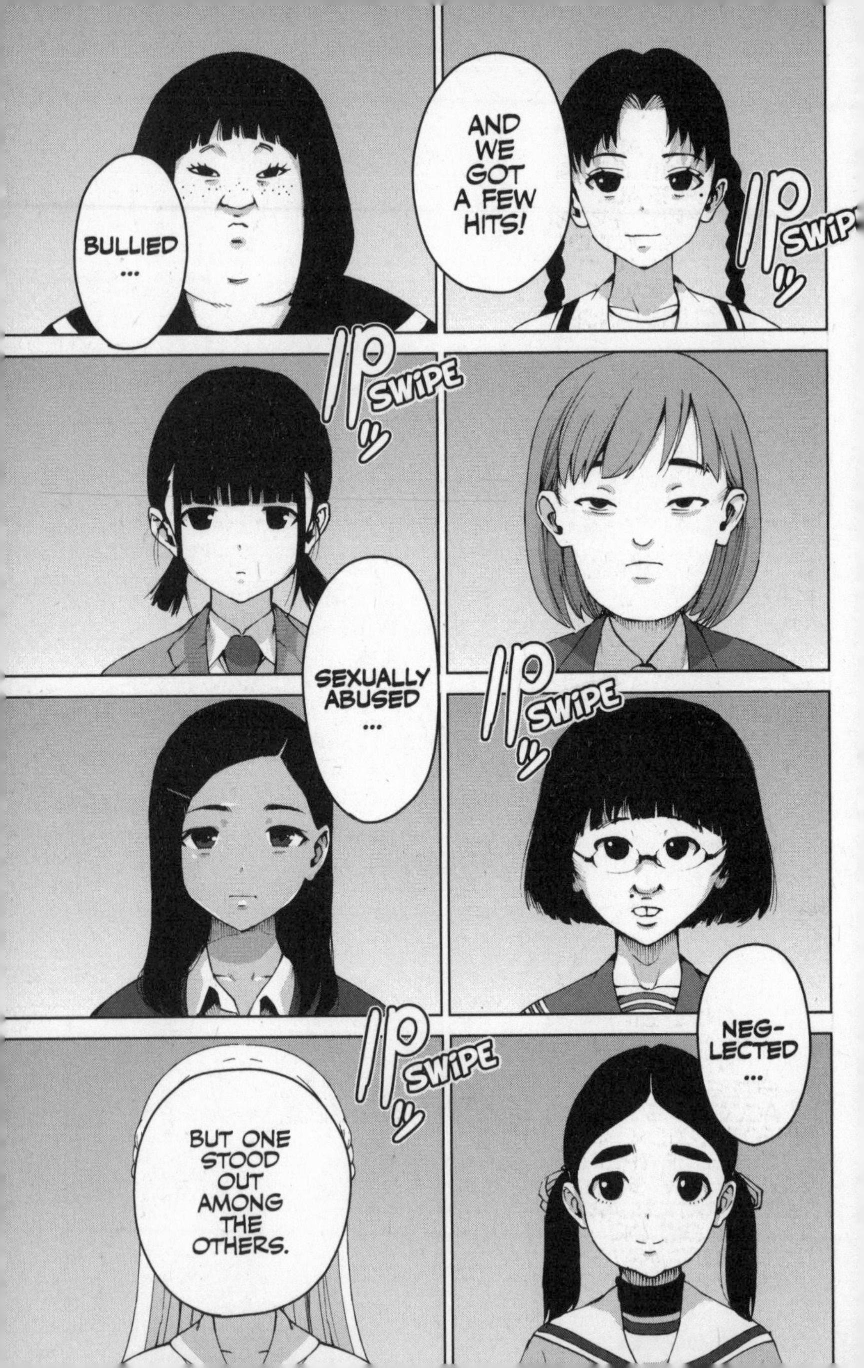
AND WE GOT A FEW HITS!
SWIP
BULLIED ...
SWIPE
SWIPE
SEXUALLY ABUSED ...
NEG-LECTED ...
SWIPE
BUT ONE STOOD OUT AMONG THE OTHERS.

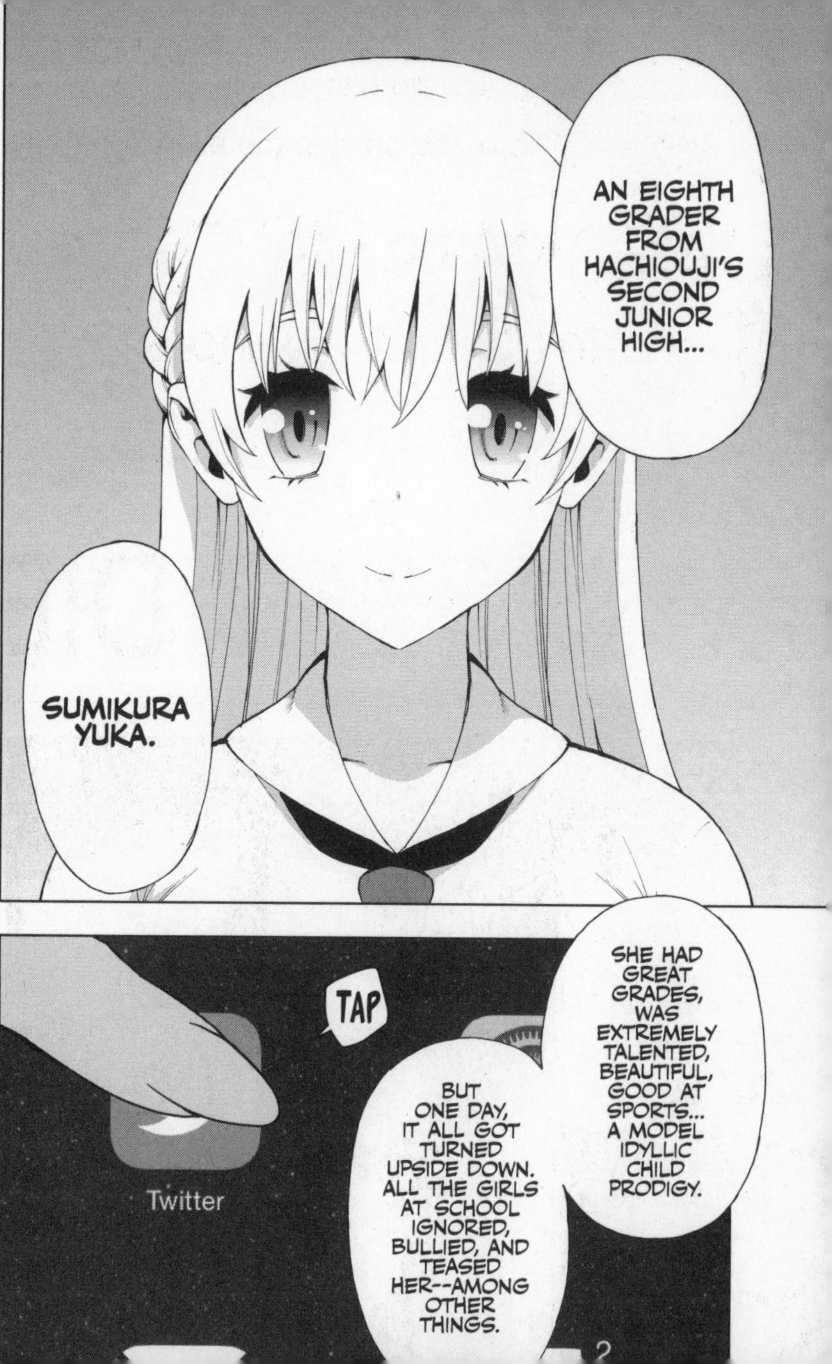
AN EIGHTH GRADER FROM HACHIOUJI'S SECOND JUNIOR HIGH...
SUMIKURA YUKA.
SHE HAD GREAT GRADES, WAS EXTREMELY TALENTED, BEAUTIFUL, GOOD AT SPORTS... A MODEL IDYLLIC CHILD PRODIGY.
TAP
BUT ONE DAY, IT ALL GOT TURNED UPSIDE DOWN. ALL THE GIRLS AT SCHOOL IGNORED, BULLIED, AND TEASED HER--AMONG OTHER THINGS.
Twitter

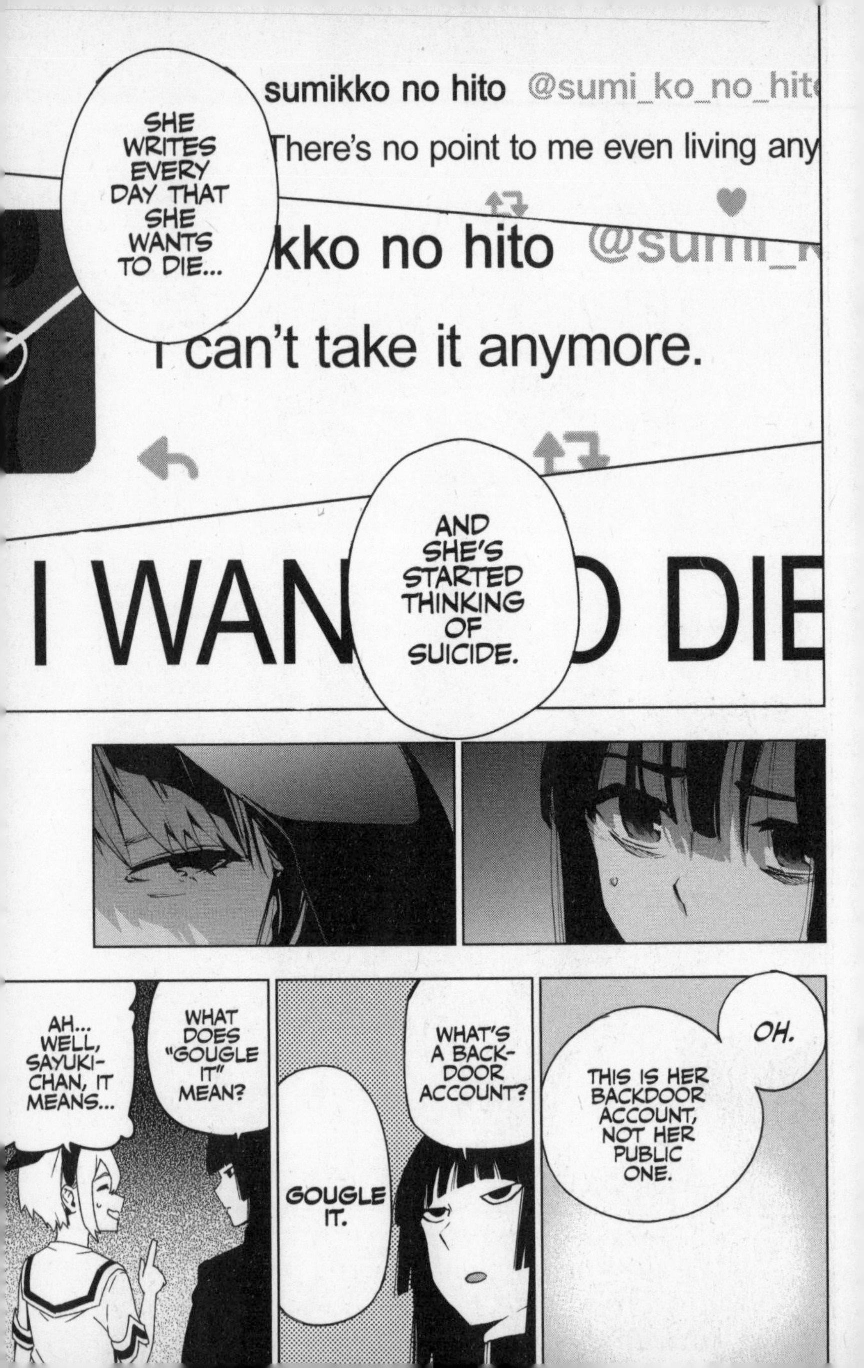
sumikko no hito @sumi_ko_no_hit
There's no point to me even living any
SHE WRITES EVERY DAY THAT SHE WANTS TO DIE...
kko no hito @sumi_
I can't take it anymore.
AND SHE'S STARTED THINKING OF SUICIDE.
I WAN
O DIE
OH.
THIS IS HER BACKDOOR ACCOUNT, NOT HER PUBLIC ONE.
WHAT'S A BACK-DOOR ACCOUNT?
GOUGLE IT.
WHAT DOES "GOUGLE IT" MEAN?
AH... WELL, SAYUKI-CHAN, IT MEANS...

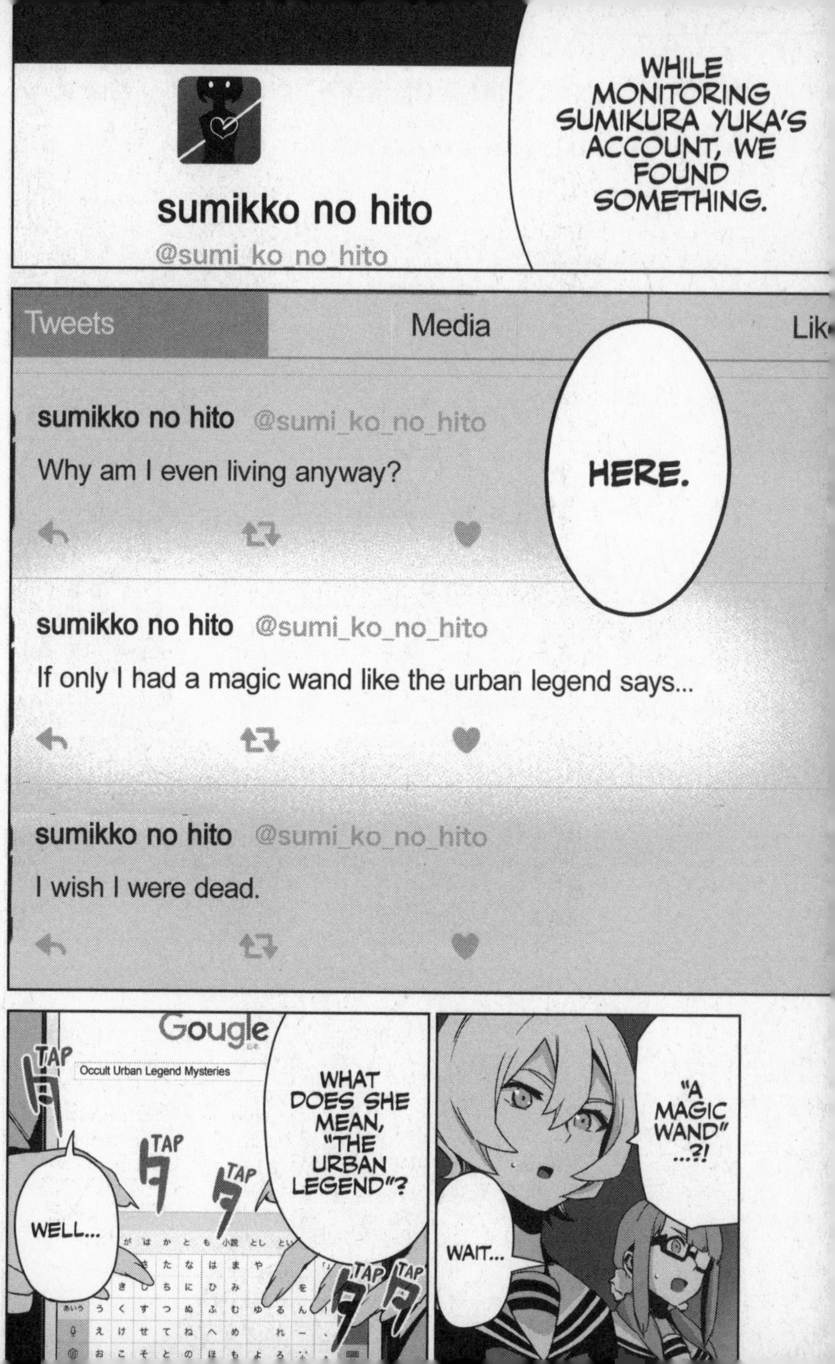
WHILE MONITORING SUMIKURA YUKA'S ACCOUNT, WE FOUND SOMETHING.
sumikko no hito
@sumi_ko_no_hito
HERE.
Tweets
Media
Lik
sumikko no hito @sumi_ko_no_hito
Why am I even living anyway?
sumikko no hito @sumi_ko_no_hito
If only I had a magic wand like the urban legend says...
sumikko no hito @sumi_ko_no_hito
I wish I were dead.
"A MAGIC WAND" ...?!
WAIT...
WHAT DOES SHE MEAN, "THE URBAN LEGEND"?
Gougle
Occult Urban Legend Mysteries
TAP
TAP
TAP
TAP
TAP
WELL...

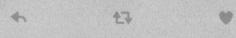

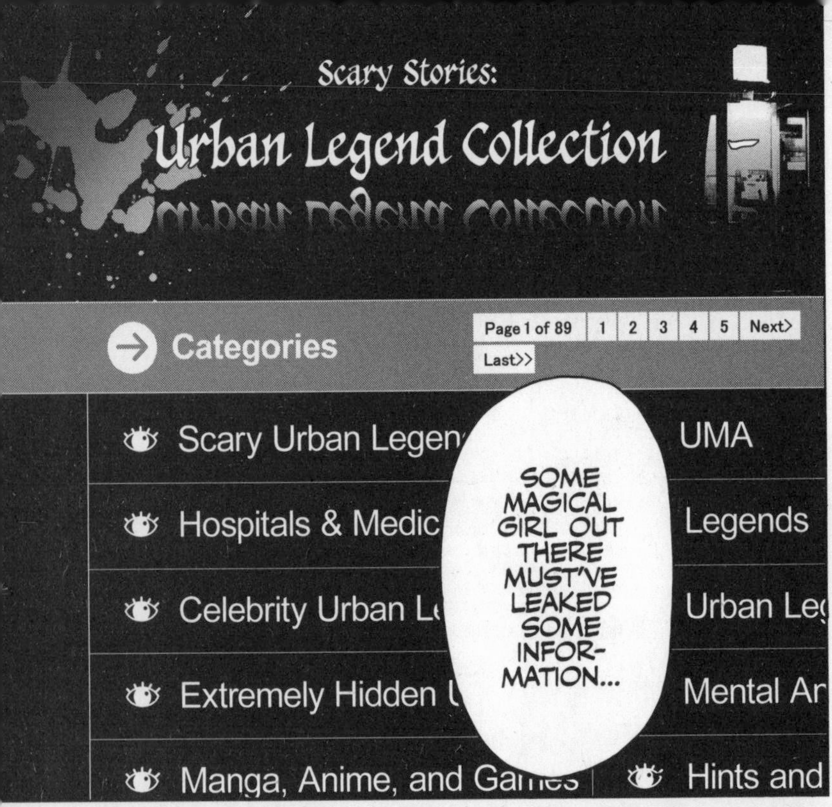
Scary Stories:
Urban Legend Collection
Categories
Page 1 of 89 1 2 3 4 5 Next>
Last>>
Scary Urban Legen
UMA
Hospitals & Medic
Legends
Celebrity Urban Le
Urban Leg
Extremely Hidden U
Mental Ar
Manga, Anime, and Ga
Hints and
SOME MAGICAL GIRL OUT THERE MUST'VE LEAKED SOME INFOR-MATION...

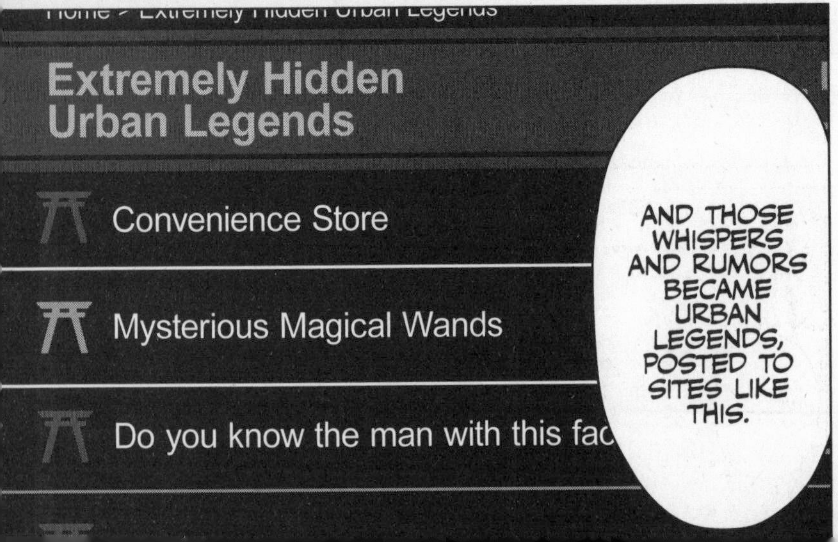
Extremely Hidden Urban Legends
Convenience Store
Mysterious Magical Wands
Do you know the man with this fac
AND THOSE WHISPERS AND RUMORS BECAME URBAN LEGENDS, POSTED TO SITES LIKE THIS.

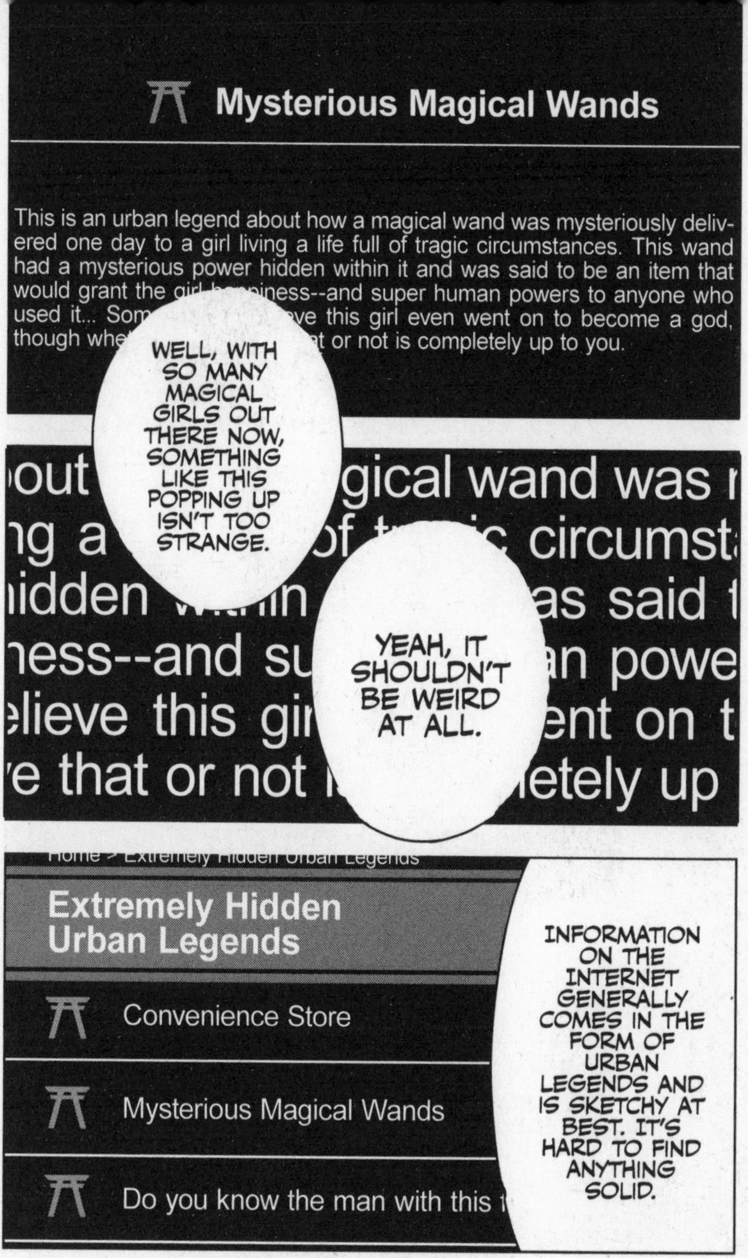
Mysterious Magical Wands
This is an urban legend about how a magical wand was mysteriously delivered one day to a girl living a life full of tragic circumstances. This wand had a mysterious power hidden within it and was said to be an item that would grant the girl h...piness--and super human powers to anyone who used it... Som... ...ve this girl even went on to become a god, though whe... ...t or not is completely up to you.
WELL, WITH SO MANY MAGICAL GIRLS OUT THERE NOW, SOMETHING LIKE THIS POPPING UP ISN'T TOO STRANGE.
YEAH, IT SHOULDN'T BE WEIRD AT ALL.
Extremely Hidden Urban Legends
Convenience Store
Mysterious Magical Wands
Do you know the man with this
INFORMATION ON THE INTERNET GENERALLY COMES IN THE FORM OF URBAN LEGENDS AND IS SKETCHY AT BEST. IT'S HARD TO FIND ANYTHING SOLID.

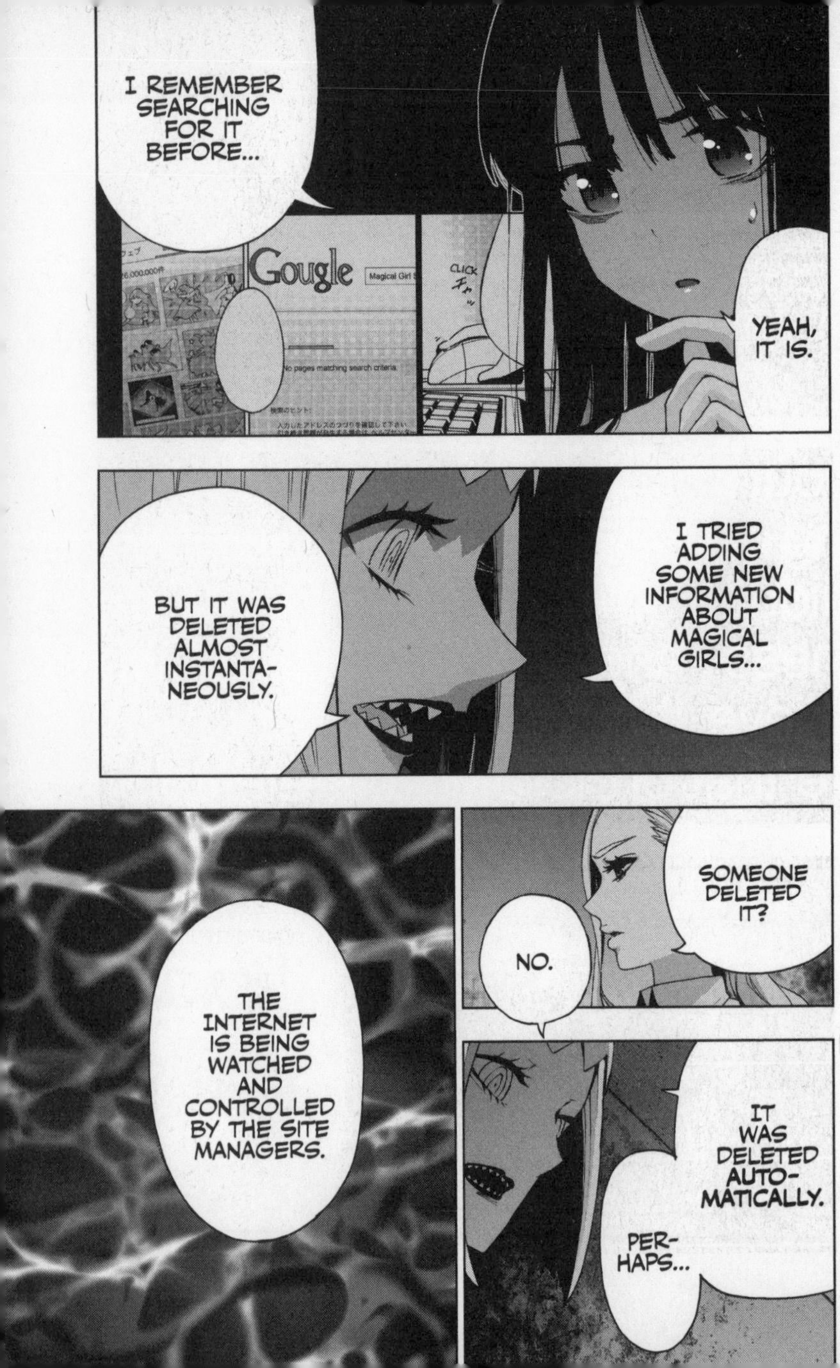
YEAH, IT IS.
I REMEMBER SEARCHING FOR IT BEFORE...
Gougle
Magical Girl S
CLICK
No pages matching search criteria
I TRIED ADDING SOME NEW INFORMATION ABOUT MAGICAL GIRLS...
BUT IT WAS DELETED ALMOST INSTANTA-NEOUSLY.
SOMEONE DELETED IT?
NO.
IT WAS DELETED AUTO-MATICALLY.
PER-HAPS...
THE INTERNET IS BEING WATCHED AND CONTROLLED BY THE SITE MANAGERS.

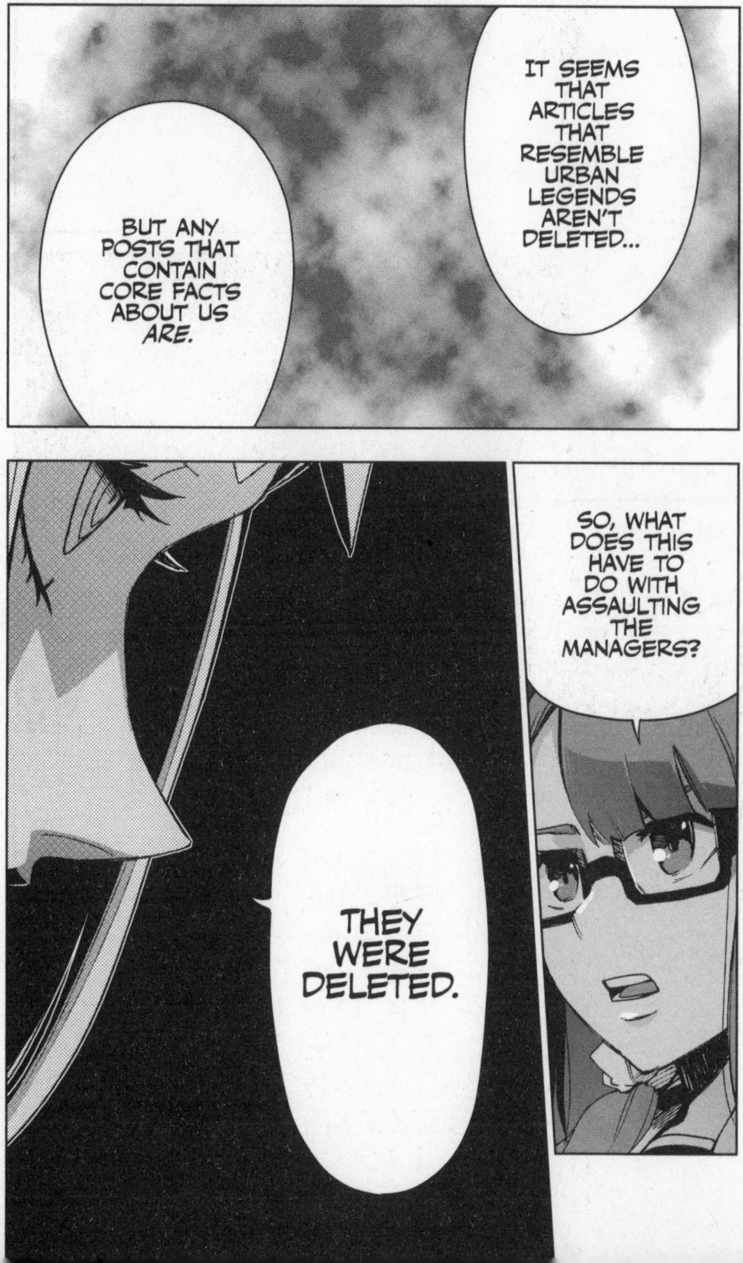
IT SEEMS THAT ARTICLES THAT RESEMBLE URBAN LEGENDS AREN'T DELETED...
BUT ANY POSTS THAT CONTAIN CORE FACTS ABOUT US ARE.
SO, WHAT DOES THIS HAVE TO DO WITH ASSAULTING THE MANAGERS?
THEY WERE DELETED.

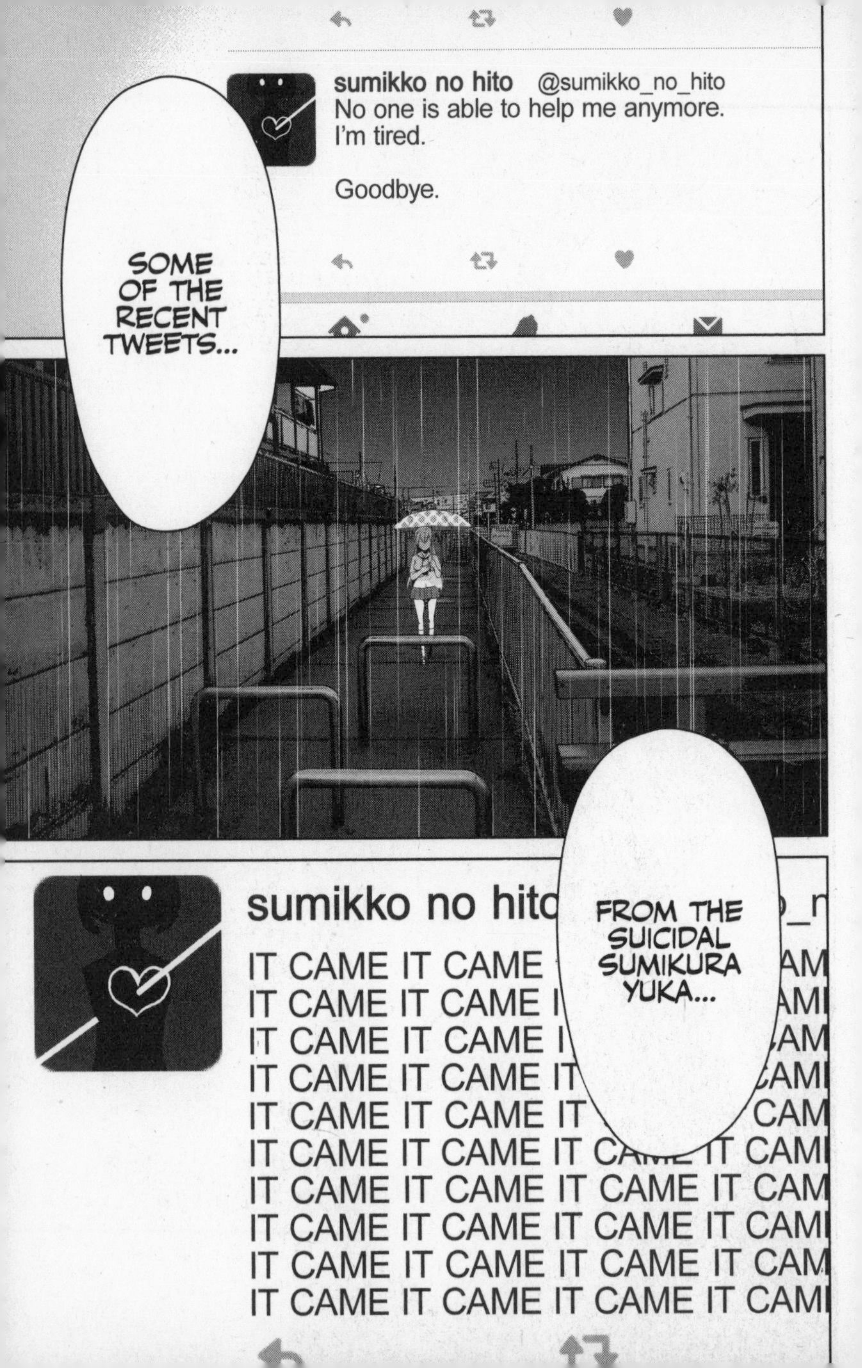
sumikko no hito @sumikko_no_hito
No one is able to help me anymore.
I'm tired.
Goodbye.
SOME OF THE RECENT TWEETS...
sumikko no hito
IT CAME IT CAME
IT CAME IT CAME
IT CAME IT CAME
IT CAME IT CAME IT
IT CAME IT CAME IT
IT CAME IT CAME IT
IT CAME IT CAME IT CAME IT
IT CAME IT CAME IT CAME IT
IT CAME IT CAME IT CAME IT
IT CAME IT CAME IT CAME IT
FROM THE SUICIDAL SUMIKURA YUKA...

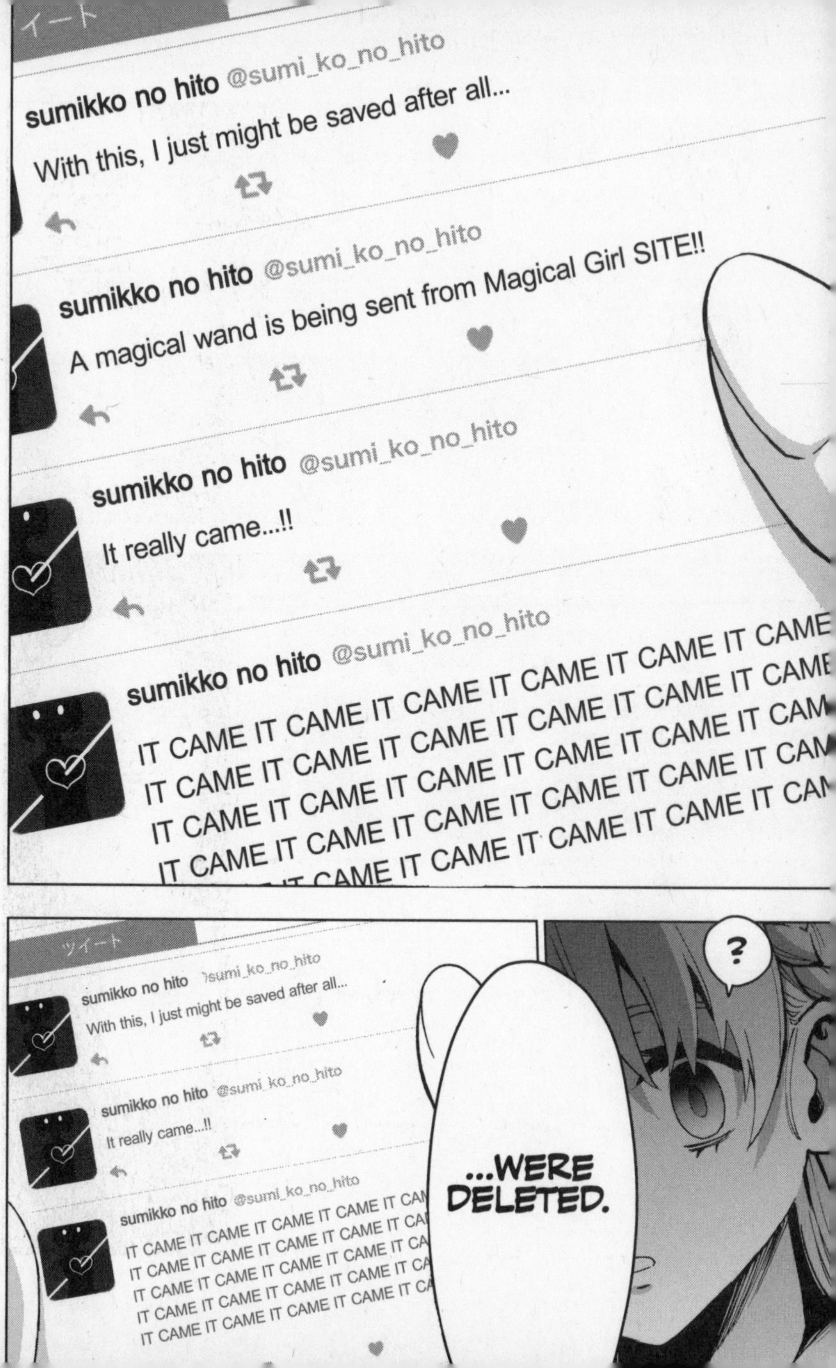
イート
sumikko no hito @sumi_ko_no_hito
With this, I just might be saved after all...
sumikko no hito @sumi_ko_no_hito
A magical wand is being sent from Magical Girl SITE!!
sumikko no hito @sumi_ko_no_hito
It really came...!!
sumikko no hito @sumi_ko_no_hito
IT CAME IT CAME IT CAME IT CAME IT CAME IT CAME
IT CAME IT CAME IT CAME IT CAME IT CAME IT CAME
IT CAME IT CAME IT CAME IT CAME IT CAME IT CAM
IT CAME IT CAME IT CAME IT CAME IT CAME IT CAM
IT CAME IT CAME IT CAME IT CAME IT CAME IT CAN
?
...WERE DELETED.
ツイート
sumikko no hito @sumi_ko_no_hito
With this, I just might be saved after all...
sumikko no hito @sumi_ko_no_hito
It really came...!!
sumikko no hito @sumi_ko_no_hito
IT CAME IT CAME IT CAME IT CAME IT CAN
IT CAME IT CAME IT CAME IT CAME IT CA
IT CAME IT CAME IT CAME IT CAME IT CA
IT CAME IT CAME IT CAME IT CAME IT CA
IT CAME IT CAME IT CAME IT CAME IT CA
IT CAME IT CAME IT CAME IT CAME

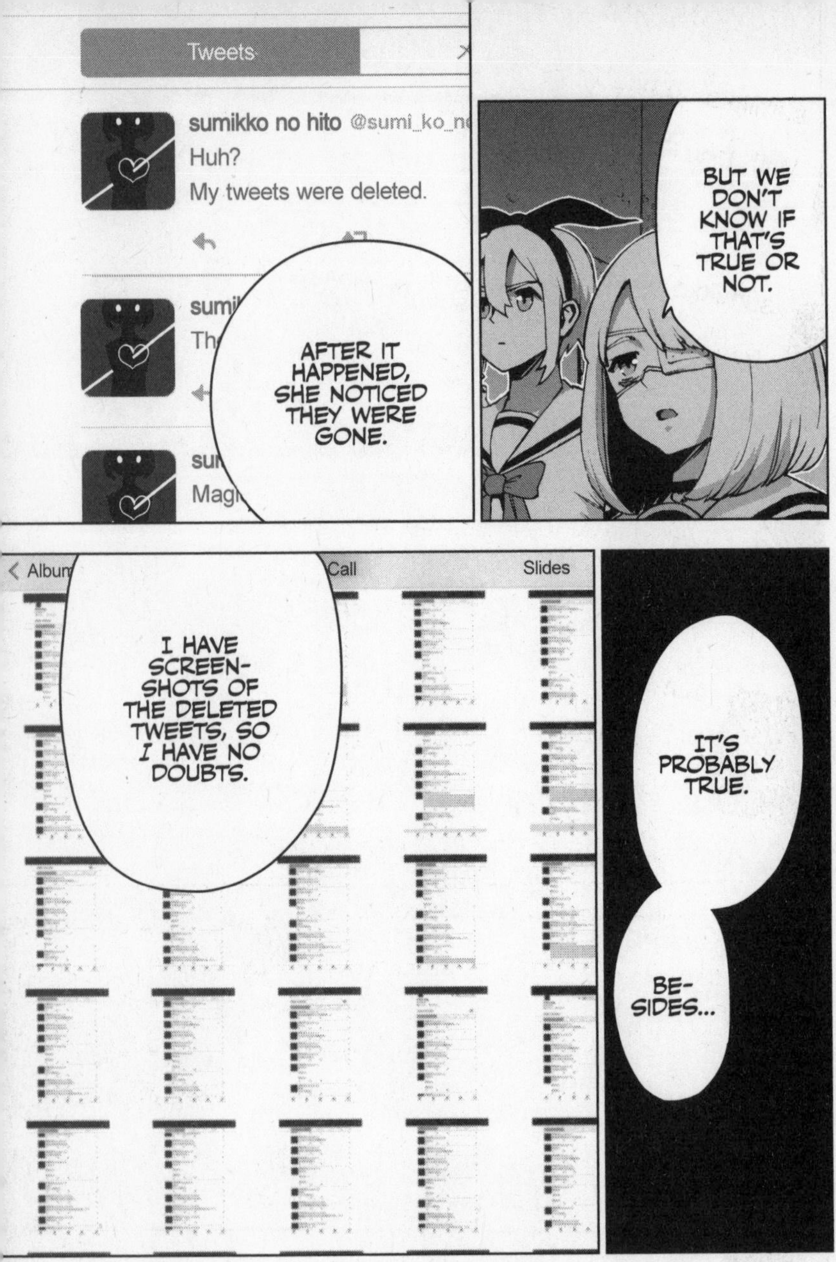
BUT WE DON'T KNOW IF THAT'S TRUE OR NOT.
Tweets
sumikko no hito @sumi_ko_ne
Huh?
My tweets were deleted.
AFTER IT HAPPENED, SHE NOTICED THEY WERE GONE.
IT'S PROBABLY TRUE.
BE-SIDES...
Call
Slides
I HAVE SCREEN-SHOTS OF THE DELETED TWEETS, SO *I* HAVE NO DOUBTS.

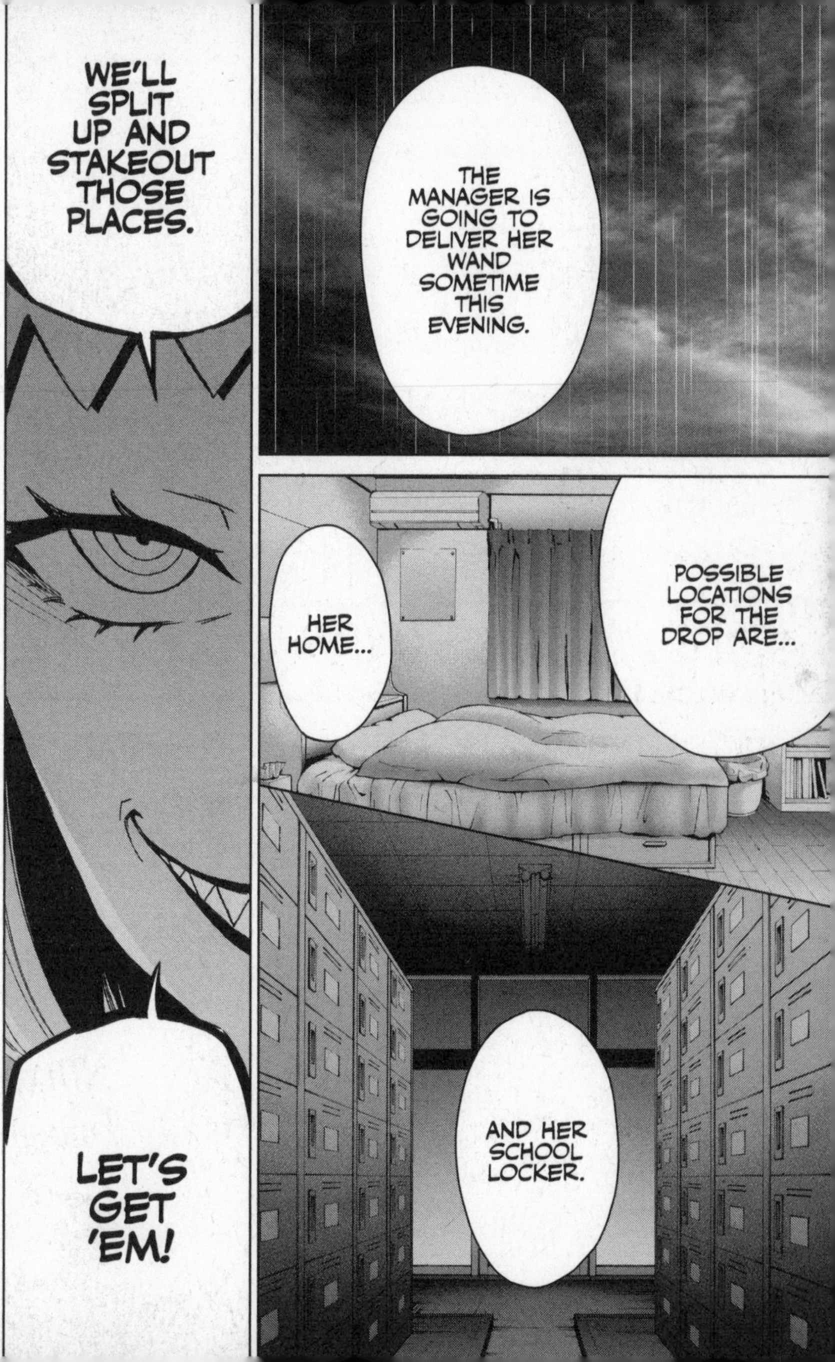
THE MANAGER IS GOING TO DELIVER HER WAND SOMETIME THIS EVENING.
POSSIBLE LOCATIONS FOR THE DROP ARE...
HER HOME...
AND HER SCHOOL LOCKER.
WE'LL SPLIT UP AND STAKEOUT THOSE PLACES.
LET'S GET 'EM!

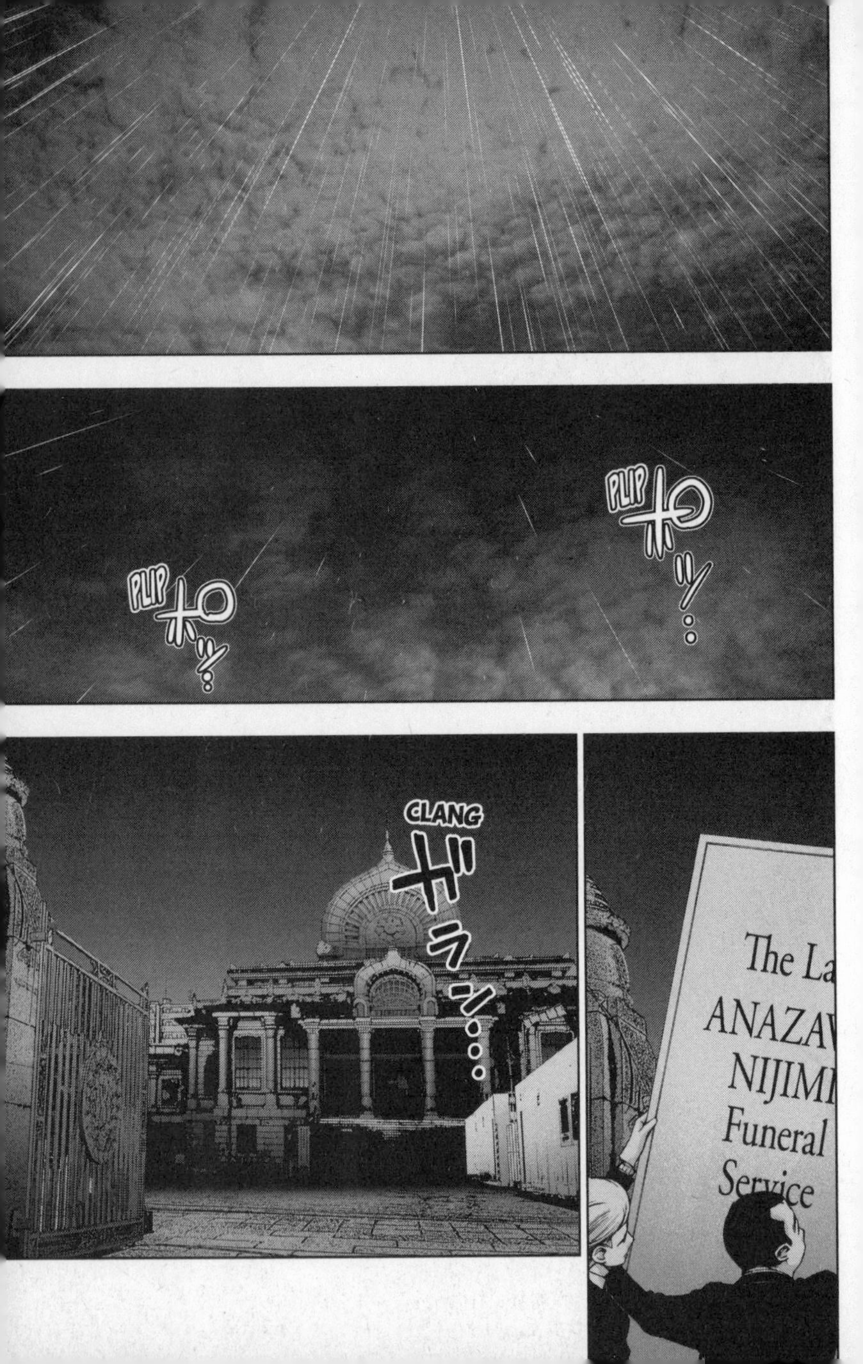
PLIP
ポツ..
PLIP
ポツ..
The La
ANAZA
NIJIM
Funeral
Service
CLANG
ガラーン...

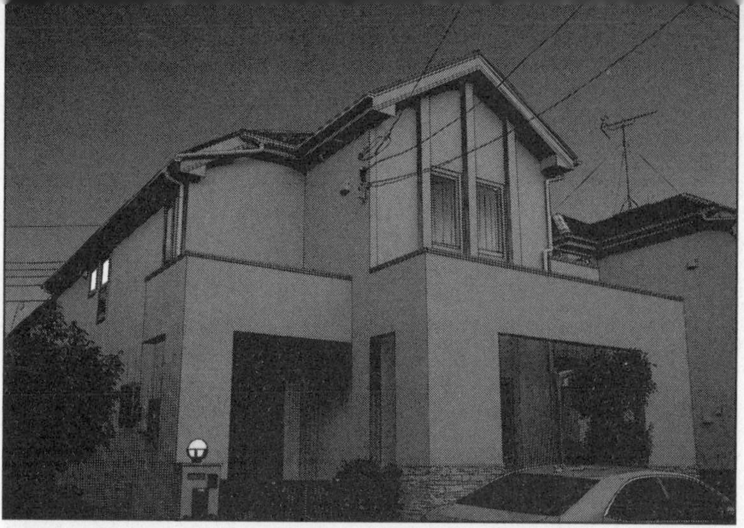
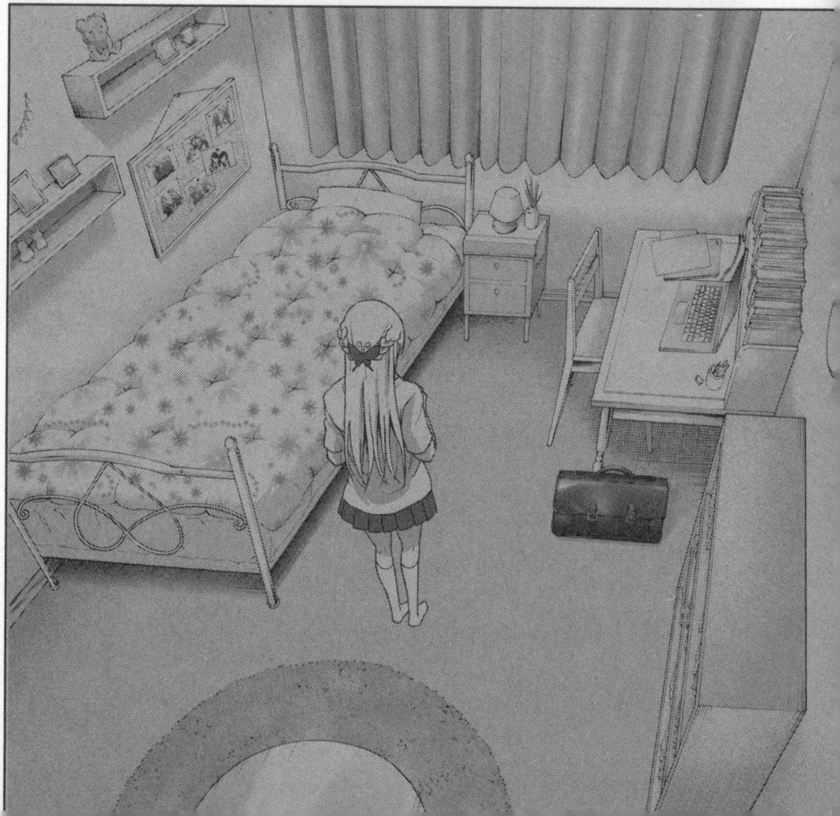

SHFF ず ぎ...

MAGICAL GIRL SITE...

I WONDER WHAT KIND OF WAND WILL COME...

FWUMP

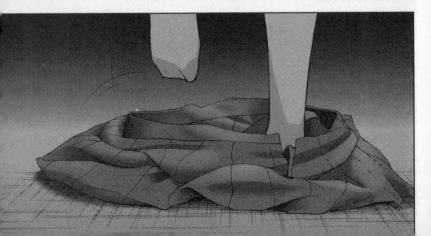

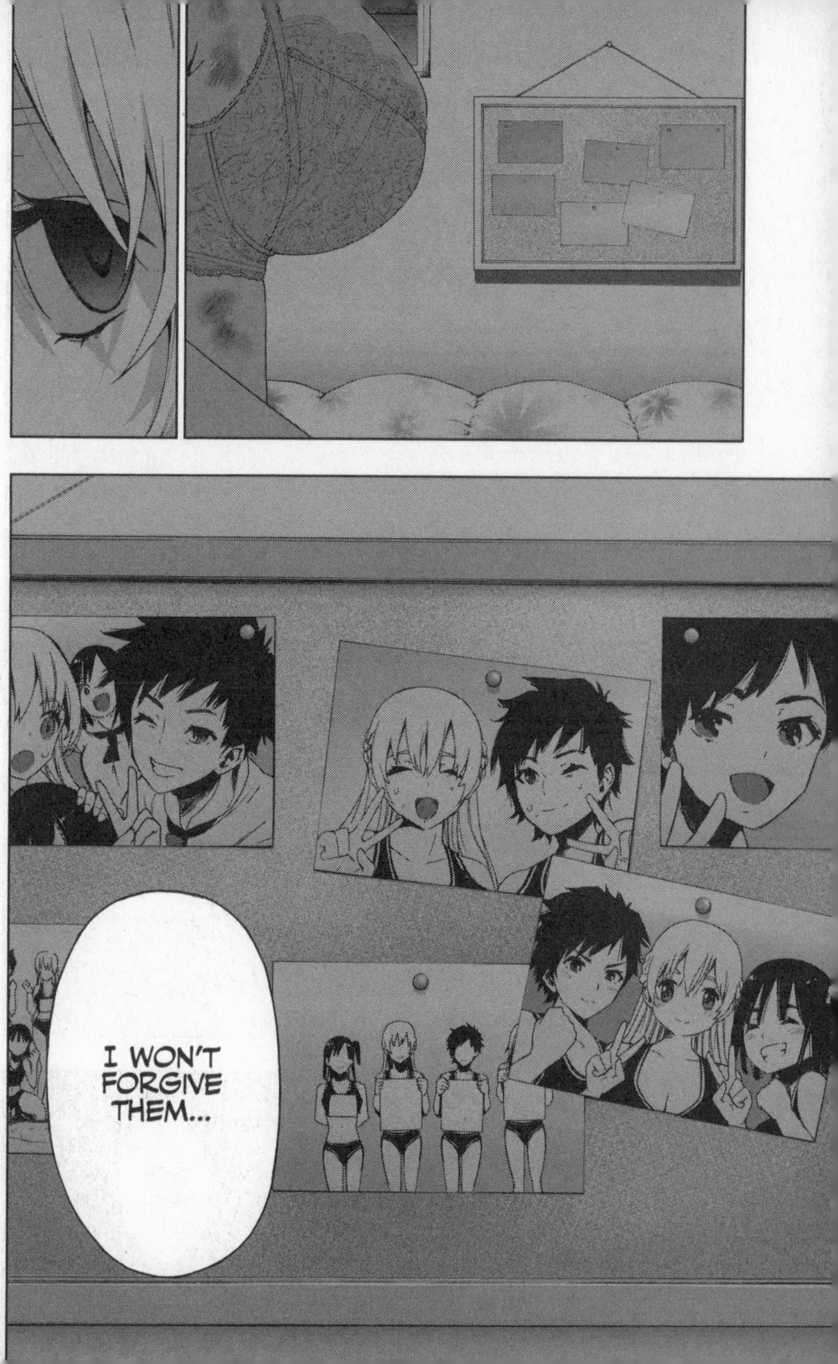
I WON'T FORGIVE THEM...

I HOPE THAT MY WAND...
WILL LET ME GET REVENGE ON EVERYONE WHO WAS MEAN TO ME...
HEH HEH...

IV

Maganuma Alice

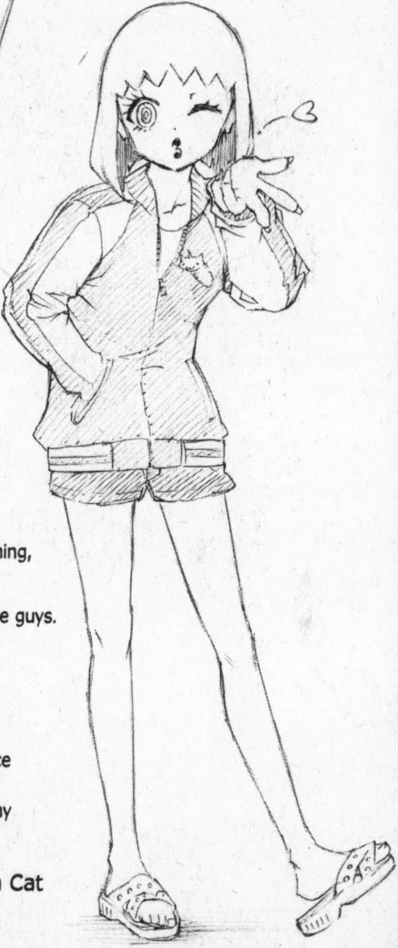

Sex: Female
Age: 14
Date of Birth:
February 20 (Pisces)
Height: 145cm
Weight: 42kg
Blood Type: A
Birthplace: Tokyo
Hobbies/Interests: Games, hacking, speed reading, shogi (Japanese chess).

Strengths: Quick thinking

Dislikes/Weaknesses: Swimming, ball games, singing.

Likes: Sweet things, handsome guys.

- 9th grader.
- Likes seeing disgusted or troubled faces on strangers.
- She has a strange level of confidence in her appearance and figure.
- Her skin is a rather unhealthy color.

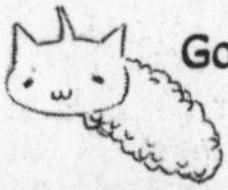

Goya Cat

ENTER.49 MIDNIGHT WATCH

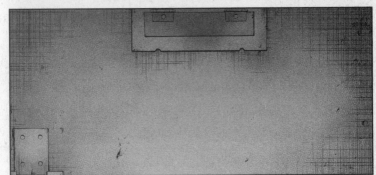

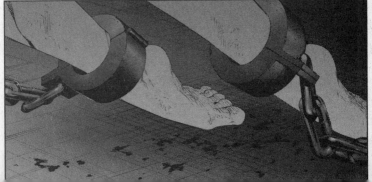

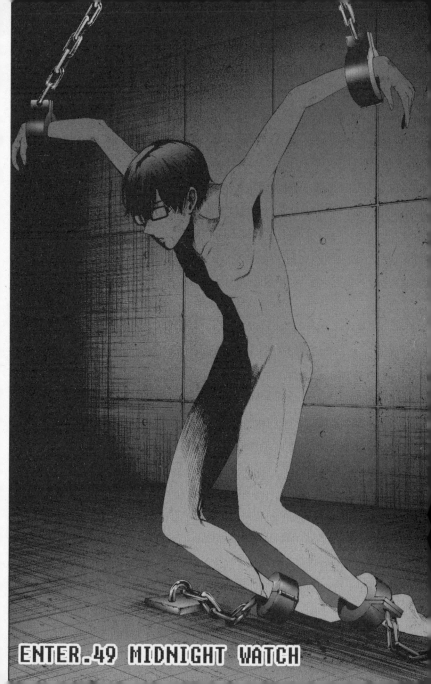

ENTER.49 MIDNIGHT WATCH

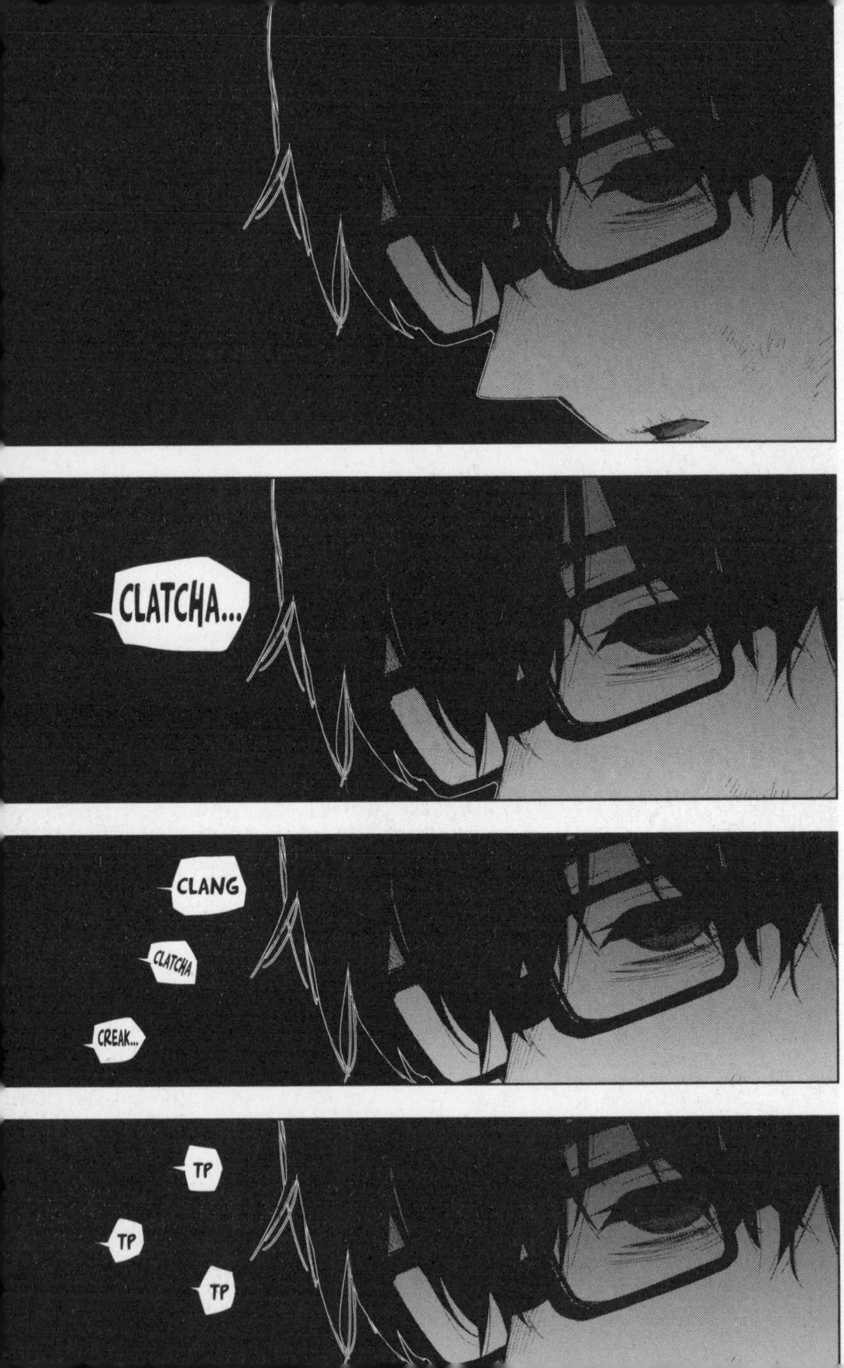
CLATCHA...
CLANG
CLATCHA
CREAK...
TP
TP
TP

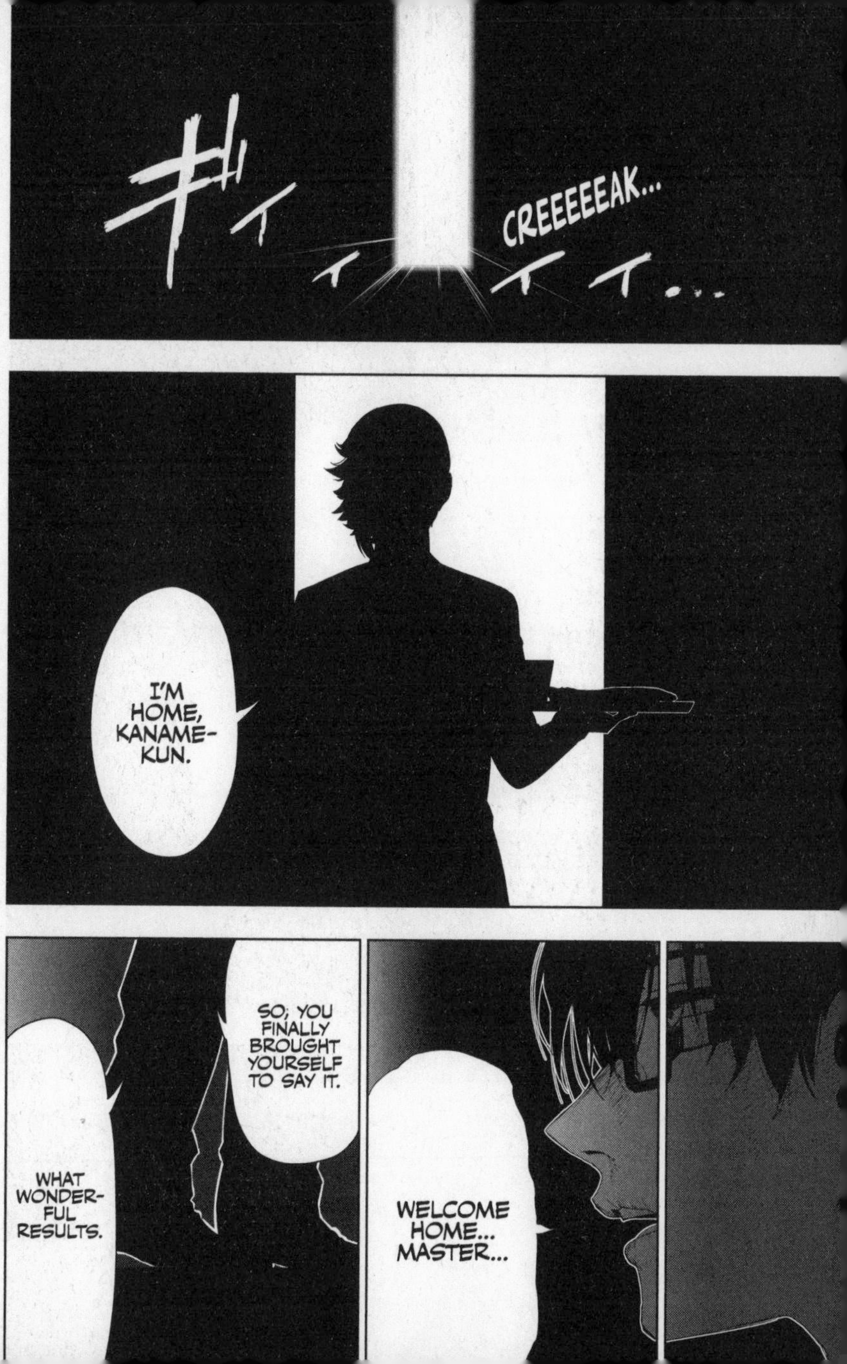
CREEEEEAK...
I'M HOME, KANAME-KUN.
WELCOME HOME... MASTER...
SO; YOU FINALLY BROUGHT YOURSELF TO SAY IT.
WHAT WONDERFUL RESULTS.

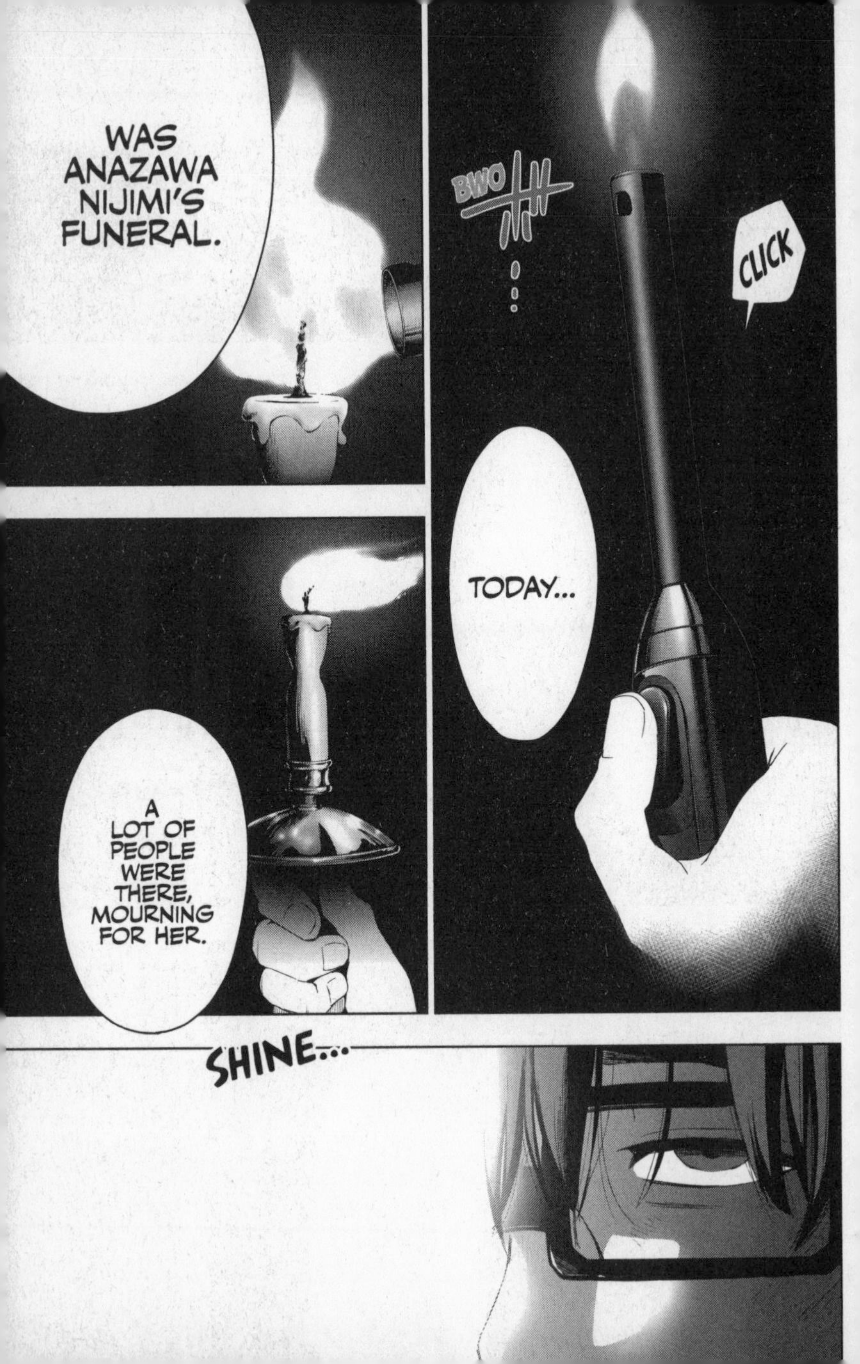
CLICK
BWO
...
TODAY...
WAS ANAZAWA NIJIMI'S FUNERAL.
A LOT OF PEOPLE WERE THERE, MOURNING FOR HER.
SHINE...

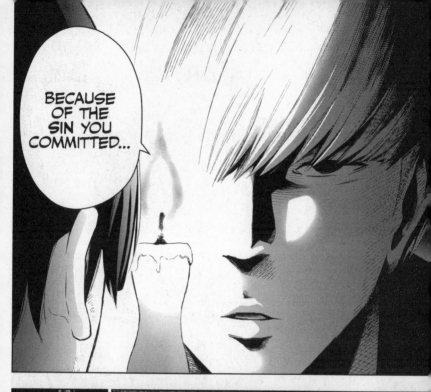

BECAUSE OF THE SIN YOU COMMITTED...

JANGLE

JANGLE

JANGLE

JANGLE

KLAK...

NOW, TIME TO EAT.

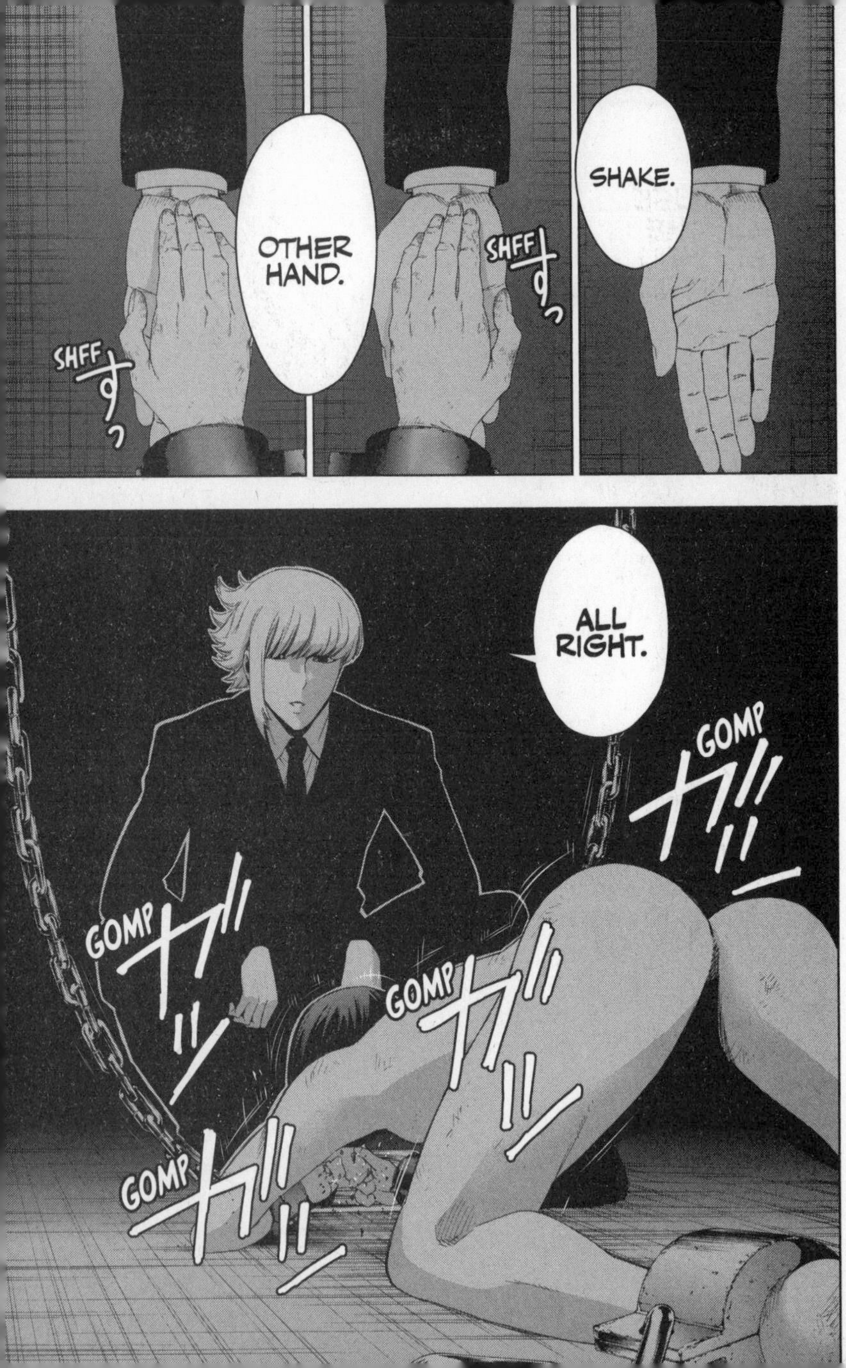
SHAKE.
SHFF すっ
OTHER HAND.
SHFF すっ
ALL RIGHT.
GOMP ガッ
GOMP ガッ
GOMP ガッ
GOMP ガッ

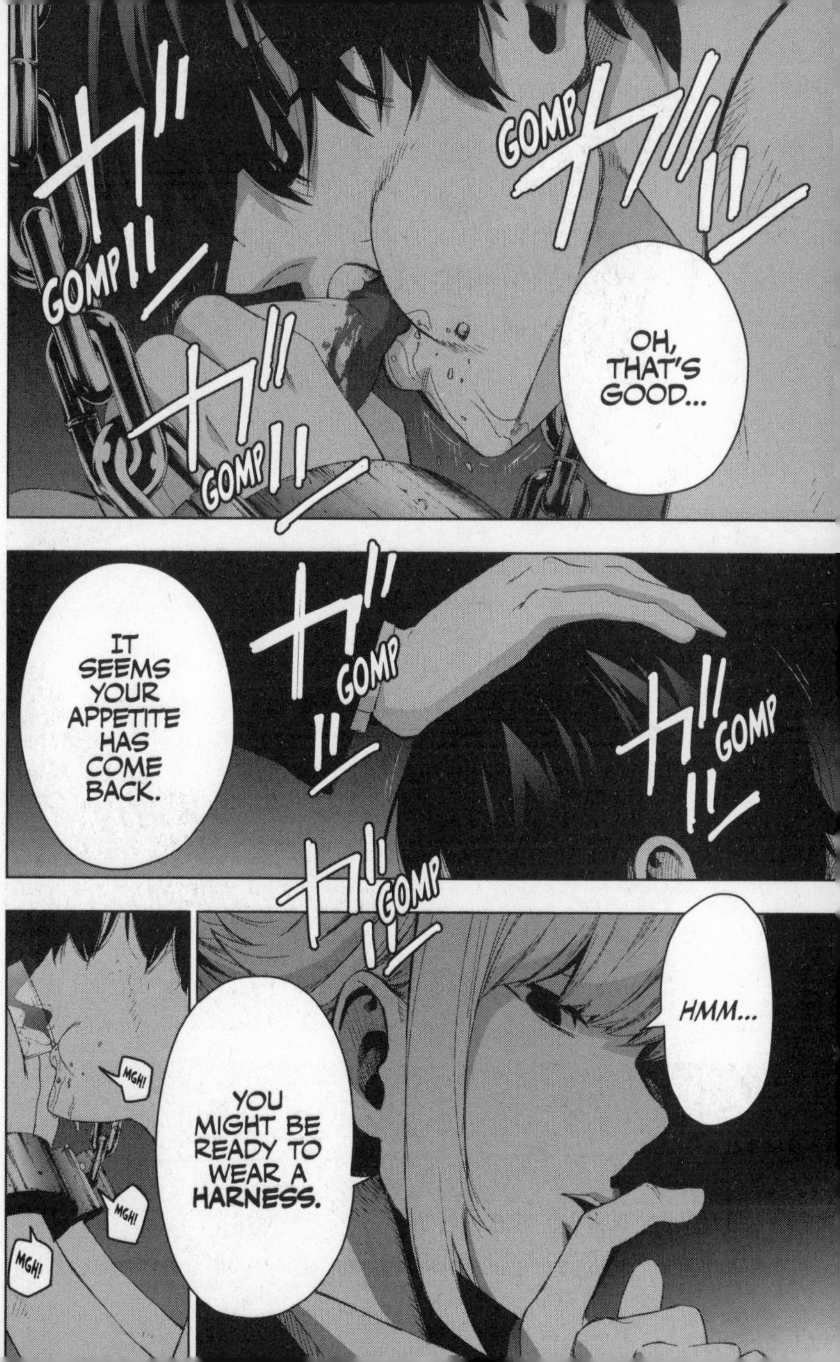
GOMP
OH, THAT'S GOOD...
GOMP!!
GOMP!!
GOMP!!
GOMP!!
IT SEEMS YOUR APPETITE HAS COME BACK.
GOMP!!
HMM...
YOU MIGHT BE READY TO WEAR A HARNESS.
MGH!
MGH!
MGH!

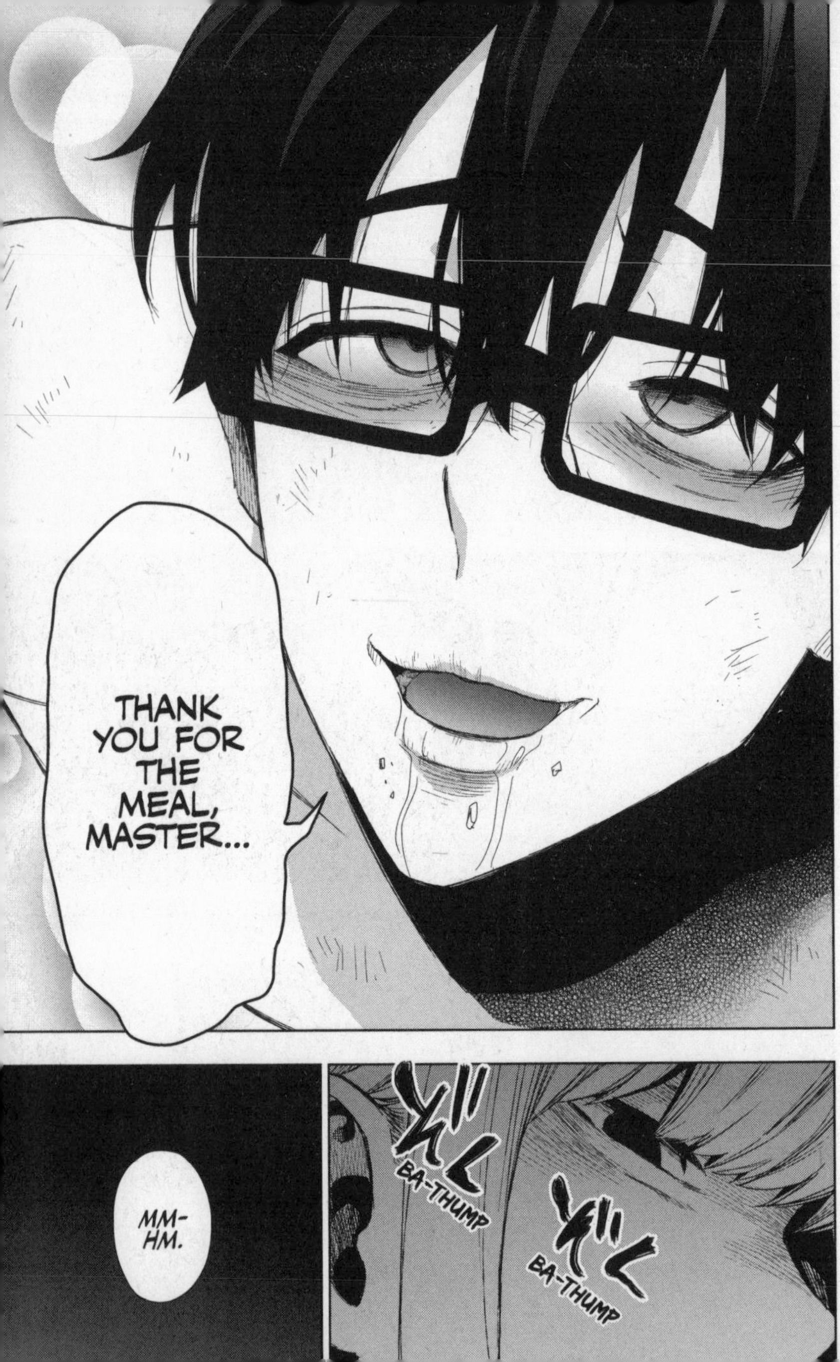
THANK YOU FOR THE MEAL, MASTER...
BA-THUMP
BA-THUMP
MM-HM.

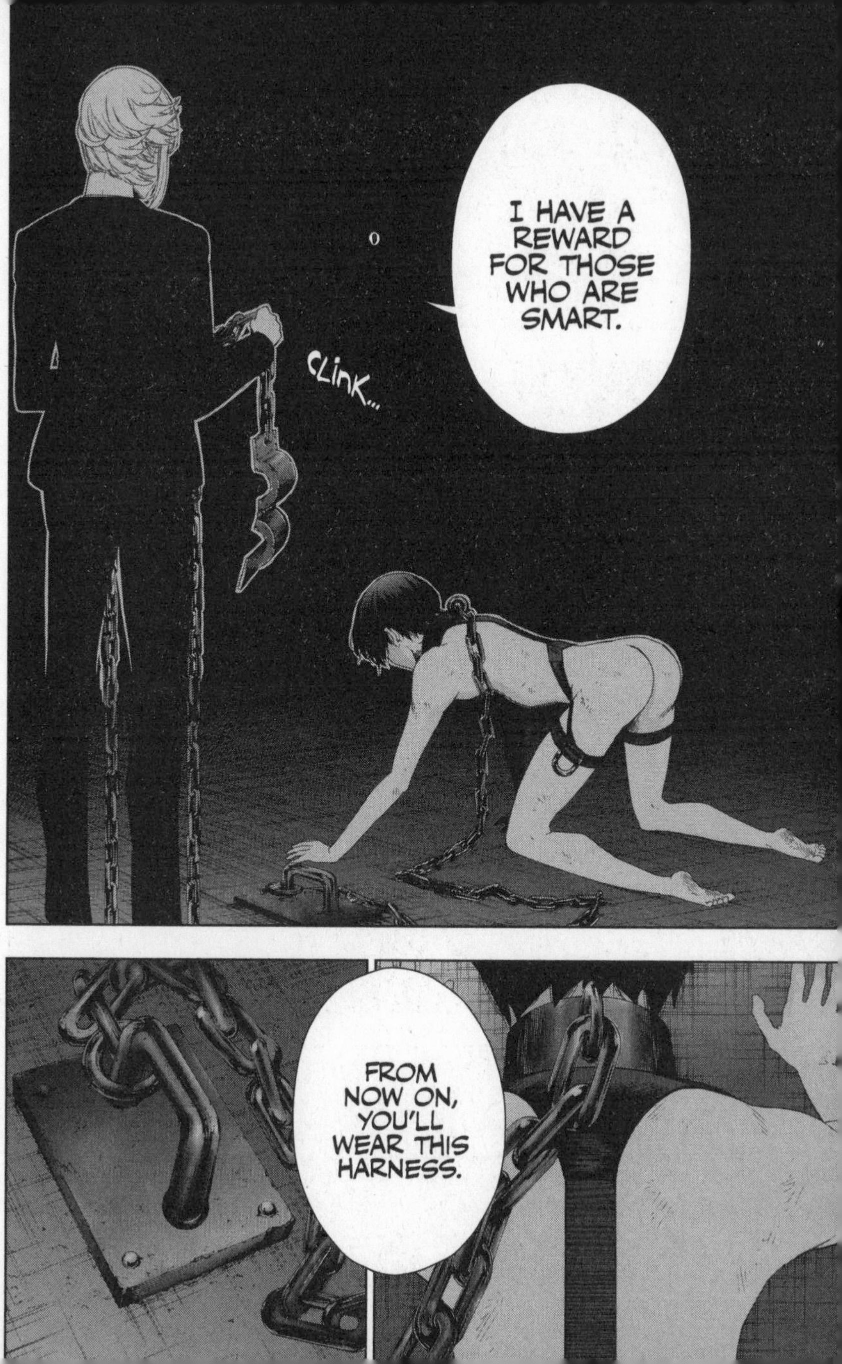
I HAVE A REWARD FOR THOSE WHO ARE SMART.
CLINK...
FROM NOW ON, YOU'LL WEAR THIS HARNESS.

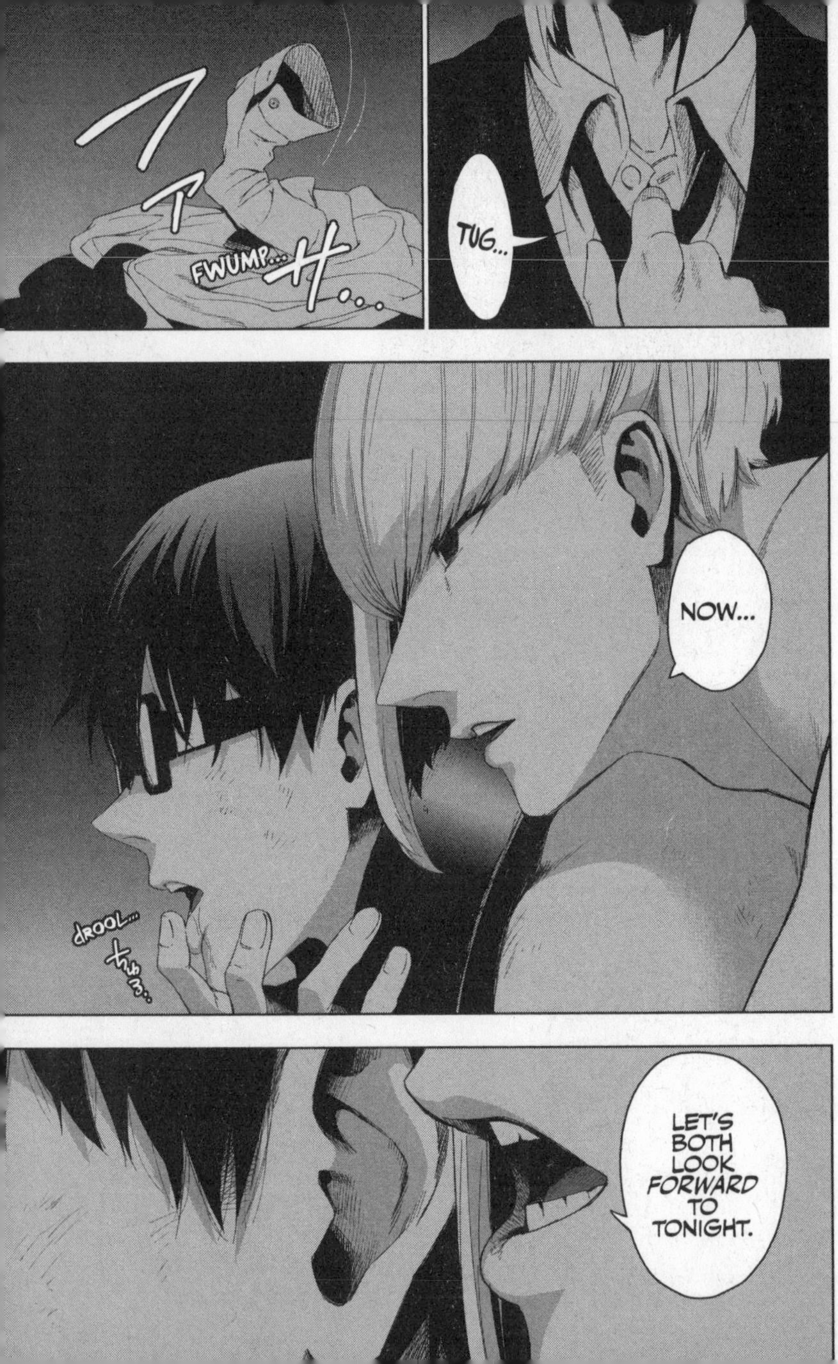
TUG...
FWUMP...
NOW...
drool...
LET'S BOTH LOOK FORWARD TO TONIGHT.

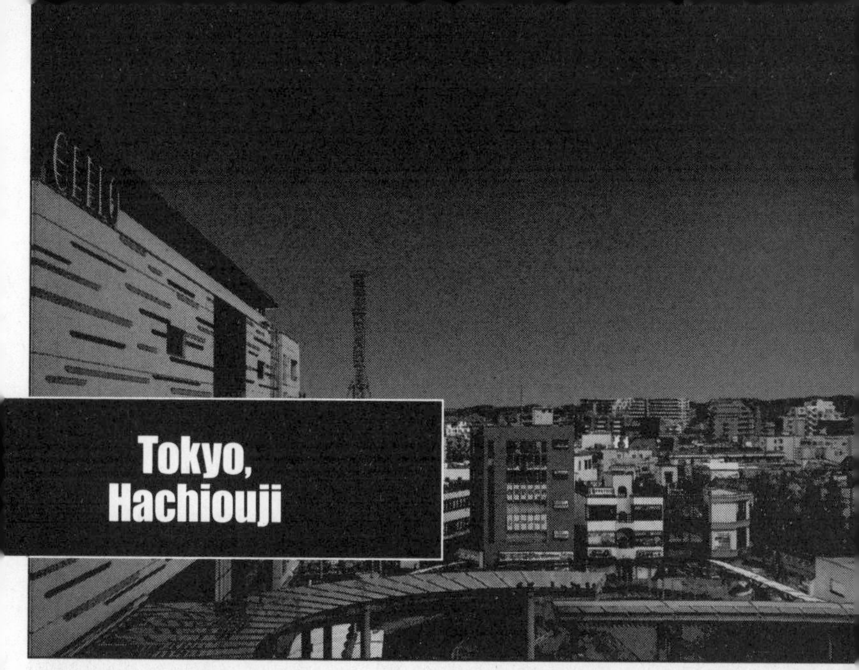
Tokyo,
Hachiouji
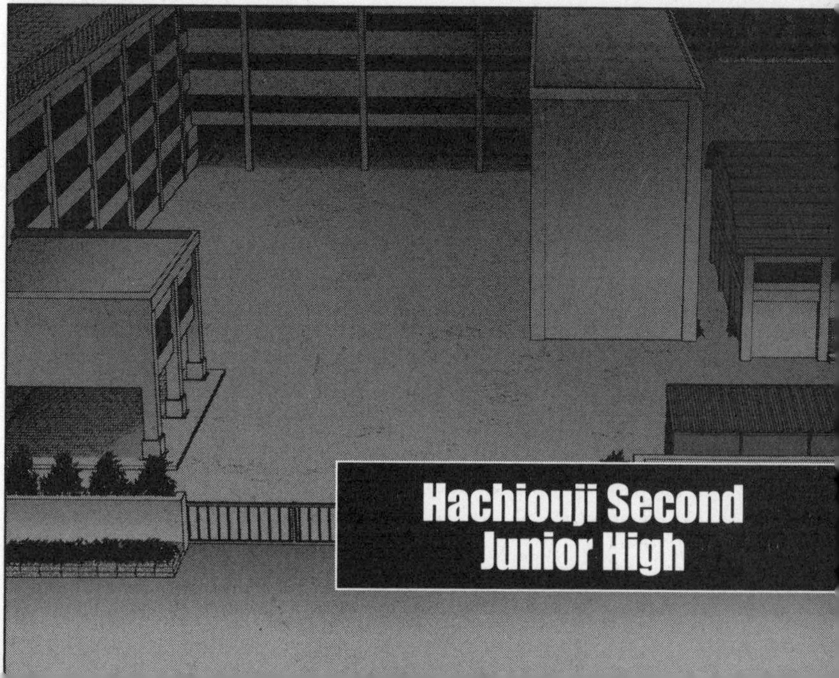
Hachiouji Second
Junior High

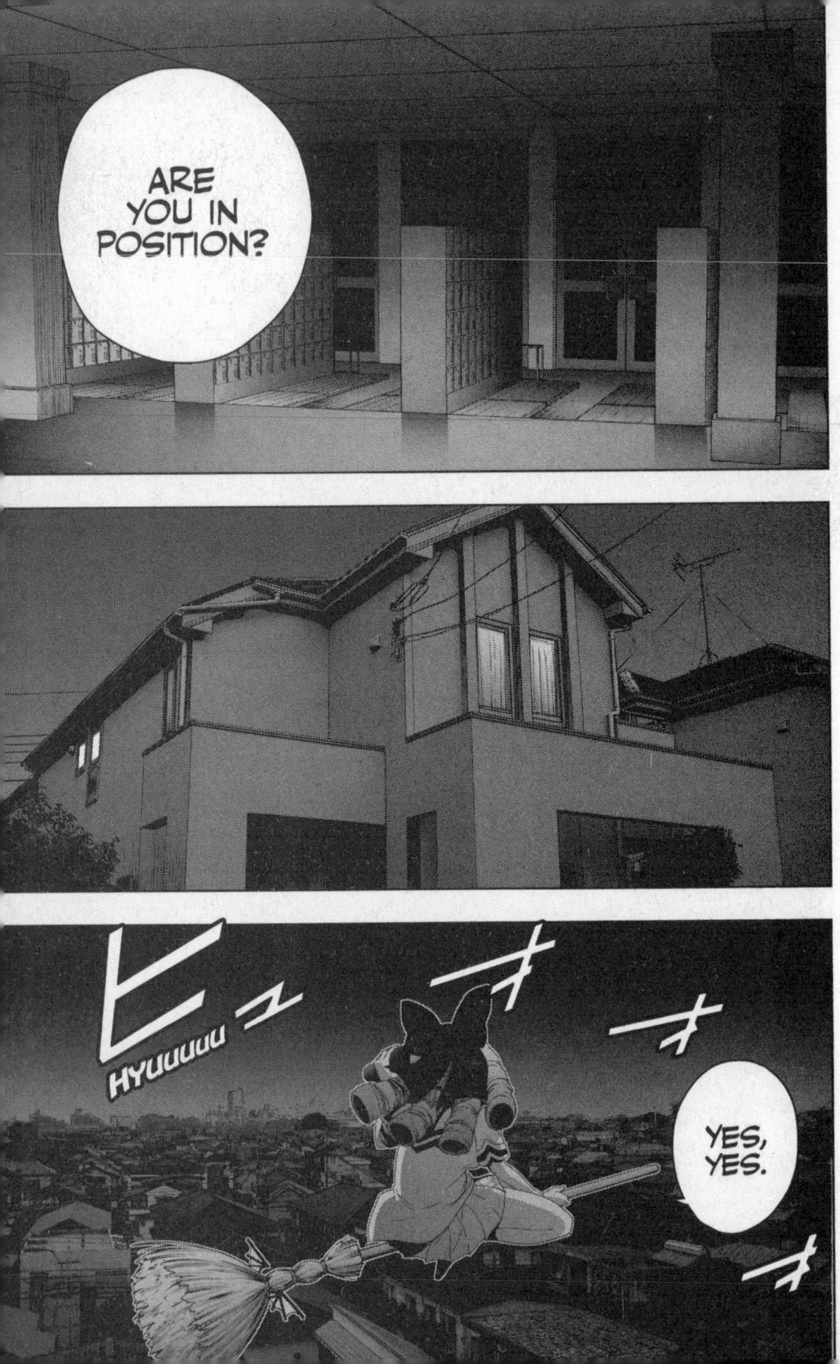
ARE YOU IN POSITION?
ヒューォーォーォ
HYUUUUU
YES, YES.

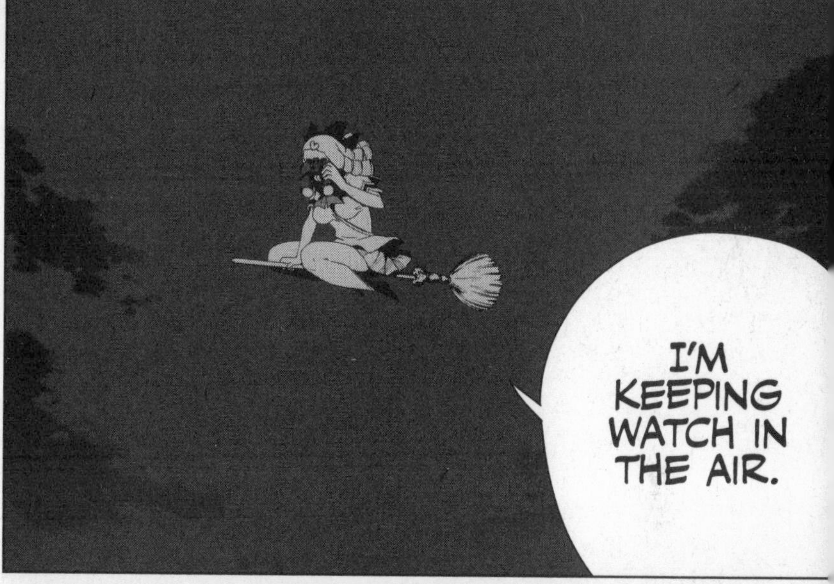
I'M KEEPING WATCH IN THE AIR.
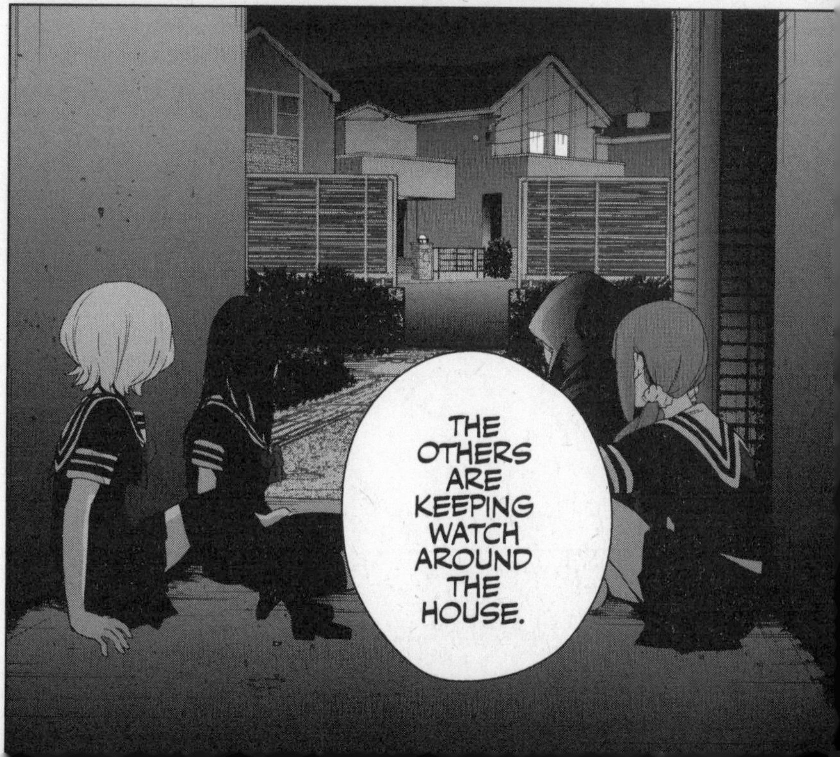
THE OTHERS ARE KEEPING WATCH AROUND THE HOUSE.

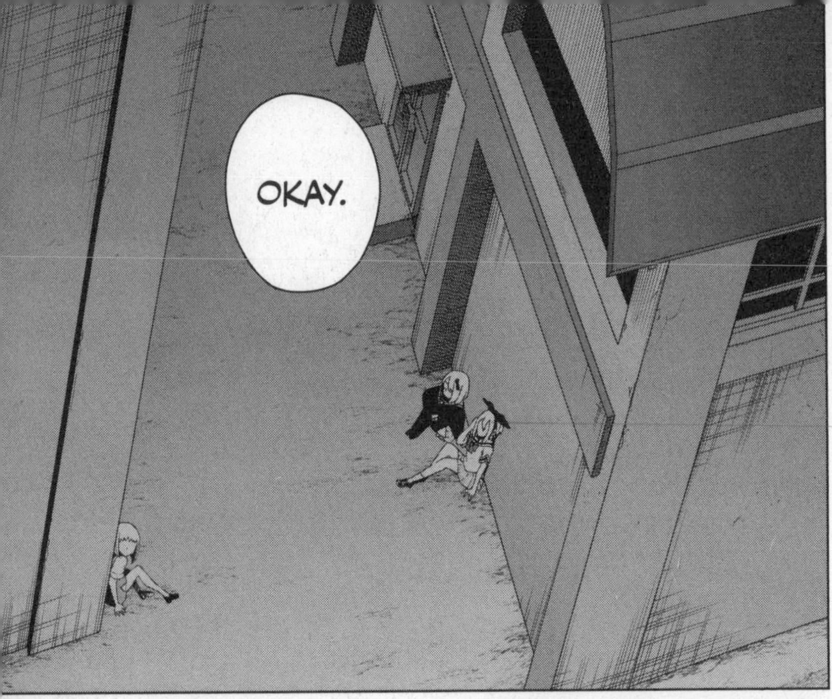
OKAY.
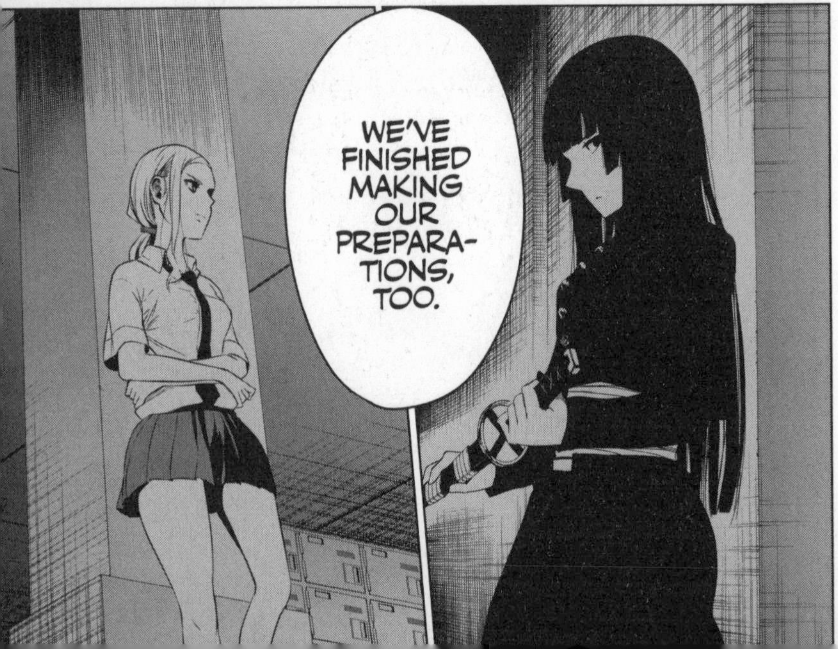
WE'VE FINISHED MAKING OUR PREPARA-TIONS, TOO.

WE DON'T KNOW WHETHER THE MANAGER IS GOING TO COME TO THE SCHOOL OR THE HOUSE.

LISTEN UP.

HOWEVER, NO MATTER WHERE THEY SHOW UP, KIYOHARU'S WAND WILL LET US ALL KNOW.

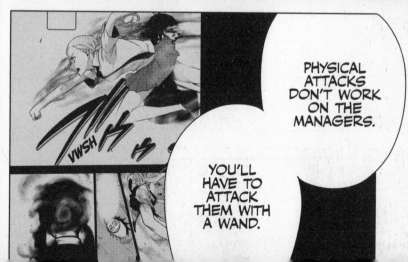

PHYSICAL ATTACKS DON'T WORK ON THE MANAGERS.

YOU'LL HAVE TO ATTACK THEM WITH A WAND.

VWSH

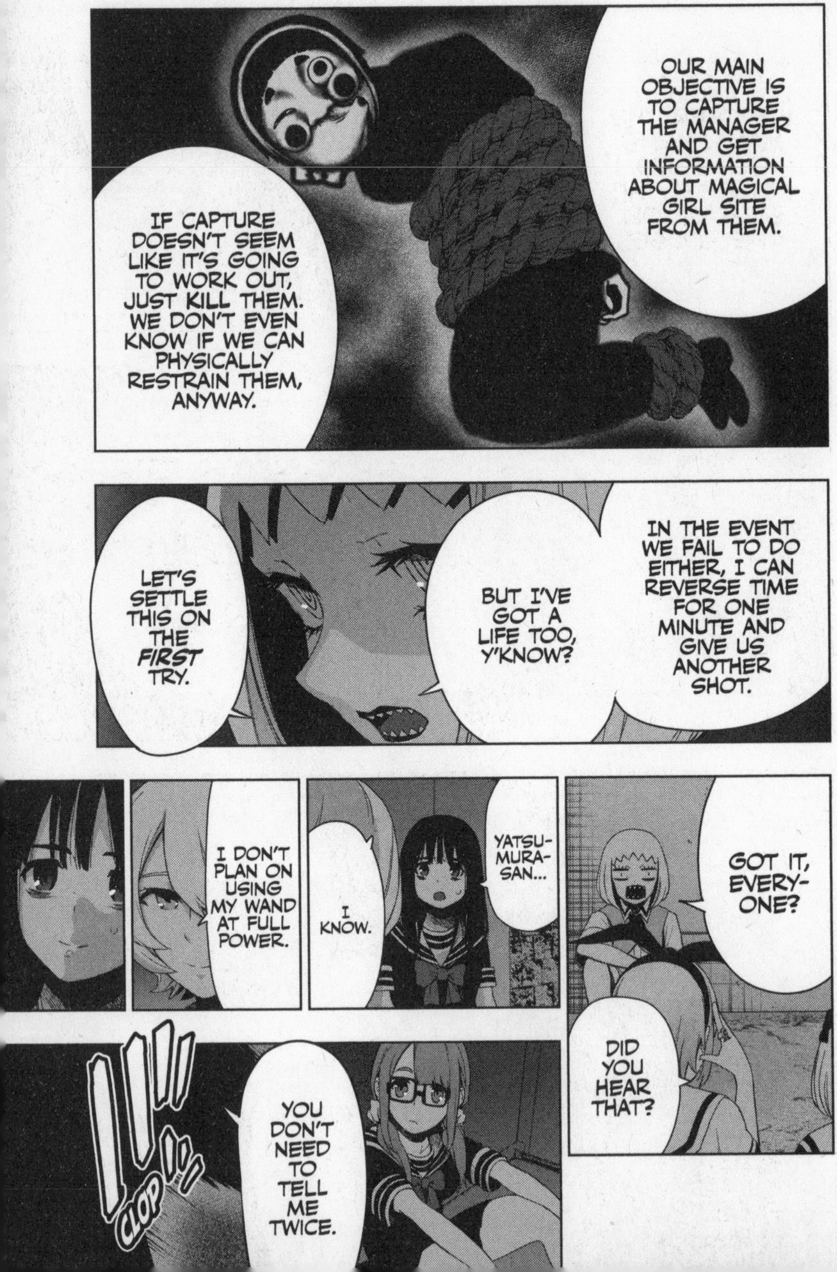
OUR MAIN OBJECTIVE IS TO CAPTURE THE MANAGER AND GET INFORMATION ABOUT MAGICAL GIRL SITE FROM THEM.
IF CAPTURE DOESN'T SEEM LIKE IT'S GOING TO WORK OUT, JUST KILL THEM. WE DON'T EVEN KNOW IF WE CAN PHYSICALLY RESTRAIN THEM, ANYWAY.
IN THE EVENT WE FAIL TO DO EITHER, I CAN REVERSE TIME FOR ONE MINUTE AND GIVE US ANOTHER SHOT.
BUT I'VE GOT A LIFE TOO, Y'KNOW?
LET'S SETTLE THIS ON THE *FIRST* TRY.
GOT IT, EVERY-ONE?
DID YOU HEAR THAT?
YATSU-MURA-SAN...
I KNOW.
I DON'T PLAN ON USING MY WAND AT FULL POWER.
YOU DON'T NEED TO TELL ME TWICE.
CLOP

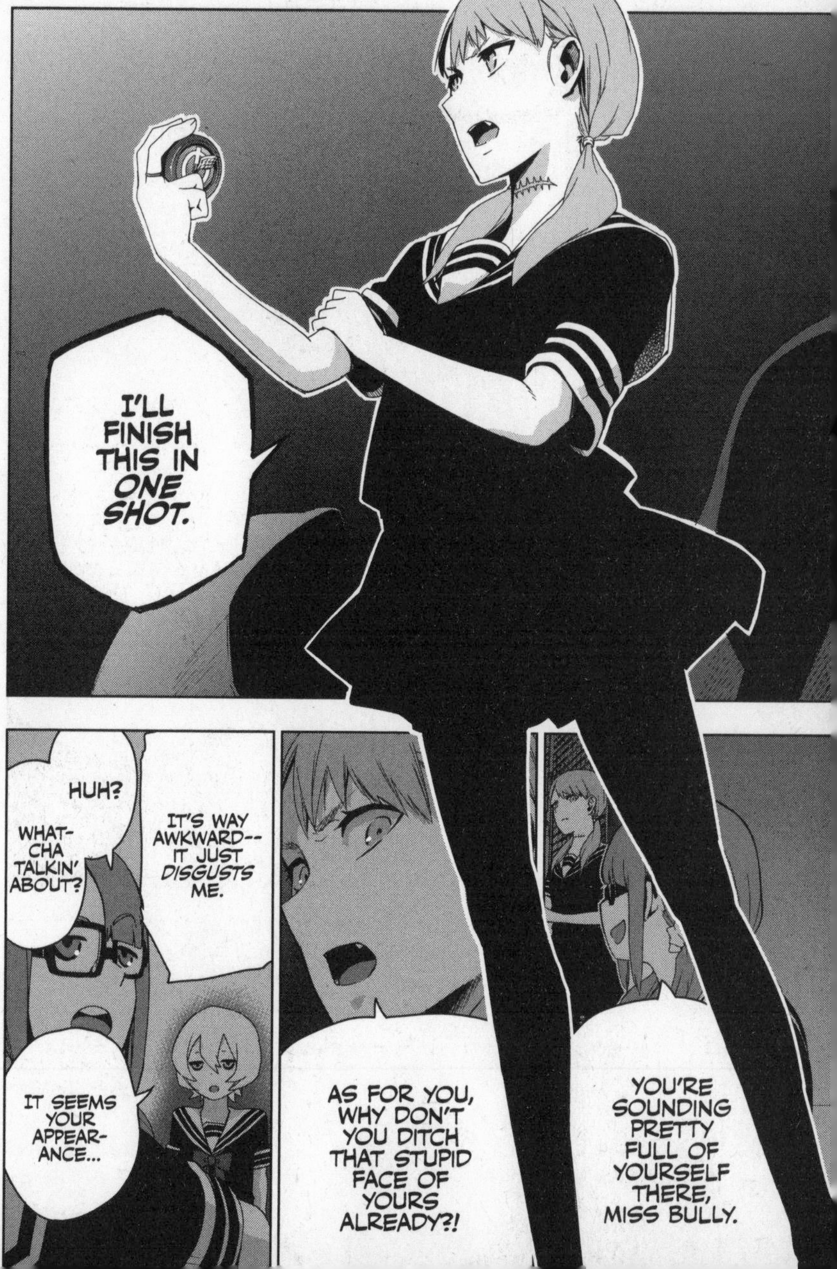
I'LL FINISH THIS IN *ONE SHOT.*
YOU'RE SOUNDING PRETTY FULL OF YOURSELF THERE, MISS BULLY.
AS FOR YOU, WHY DON'T YOU DITCH THAT STUPID FACE OF YOURS ALREADY?!
IT'S WAY AWKWARD-- IT JUST *DISGUSTS* ME.
HUH?
WHAT-CHA TALKIN' ABOUT?
IT SEEMS YOUR APPEAR-ANCE...

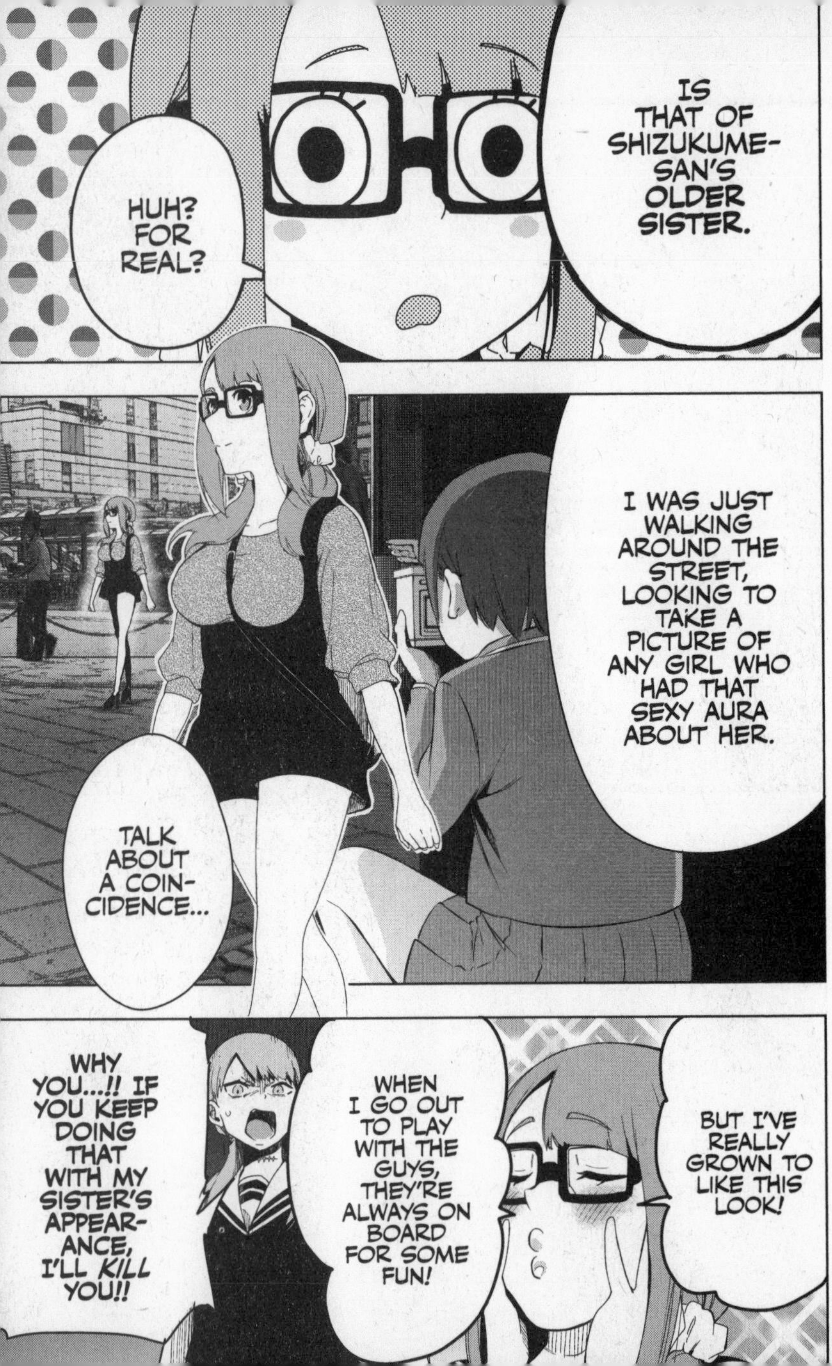
IS THAT OF SHIZUKUME-SAN'S OLDER SISTER.
HUH? FOR REAL?
I WAS JUST WALKING AROUND THE STREET, LOOKING TO TAKE A PICTURE OF ANY GIRL WHO HAD THAT SEXY AURA ABOUT HER.
TALK ABOUT A COINCIDENCE...
BUT I'VE REALLY GROWN TO LIKE THIS LOOK!
WHEN I GO OUT TO PLAY WITH THE GUYS, THEY'RE ALWAYS ON BOARD FOR SOME FUN!
WHY YOU...!! IF YOU KEEP DOING THAT WITH MY SISTER'S APPEARANCE, I'LL *KILL* YOU!!

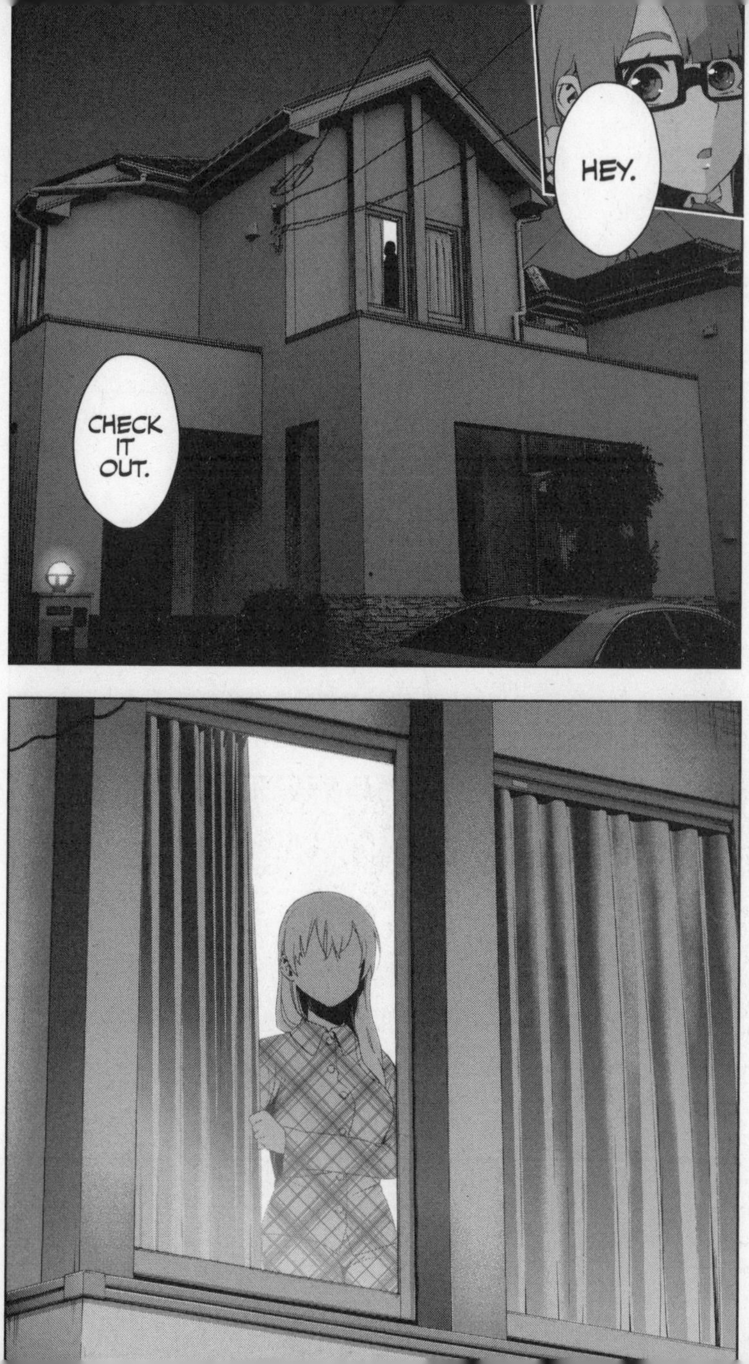
HEY.
CHECK IT OUT.

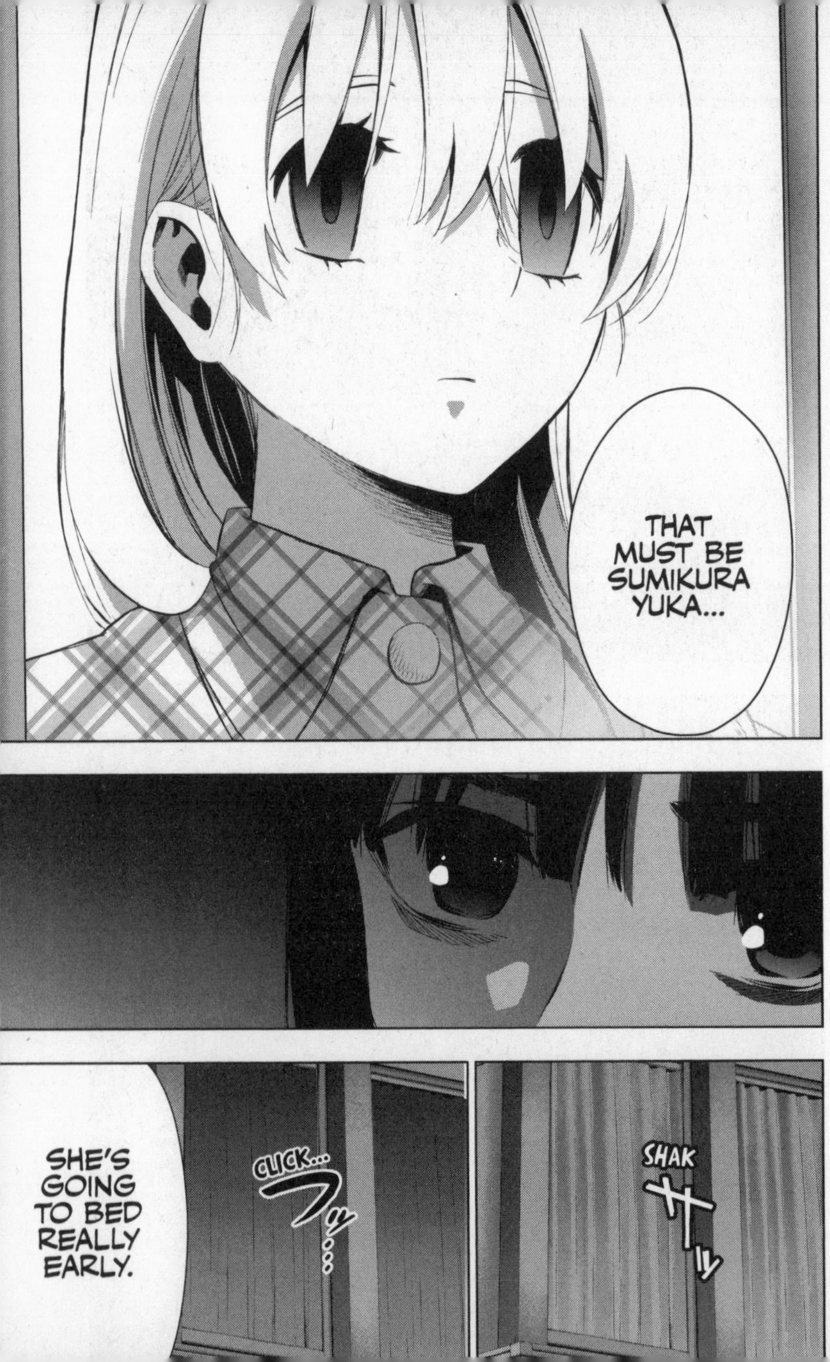
THAT MUST BE SUMIKURA YUKA...
SHAK
CLICK...
SHE'S GOING TO BED REALLY EARLY.

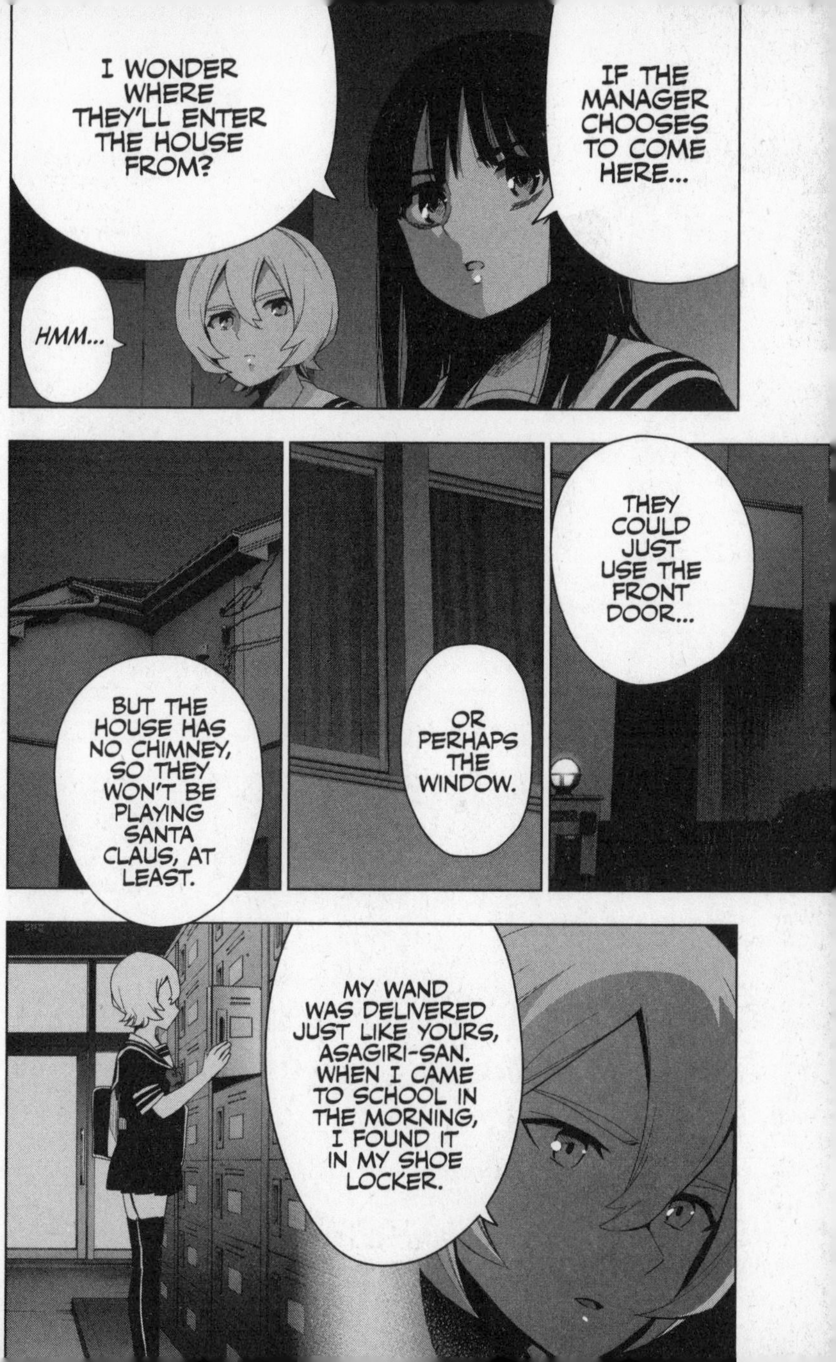
IF THE MANAGER CHOOSES TO COME HERE...
I WONDER WHERE THEY'LL ENTER THE HOUSE FROM?
HMM...
THEY COULD JUST USE THE FRONT DOOR...
OR PERHAPS THE WINDOW.
BUT THE HOUSE HAS NO CHIMNEY, SO THEY WON'T BE PLAYING SANTA CLAUS, AT LEAST.
MY WAND WAS DELIVERED JUST LIKE YOURS, ASAGIRI-SAN. WHEN I CAME TO SCHOOL IN THE MORNING, I FOUND IT IN MY SHOE LOCKER.

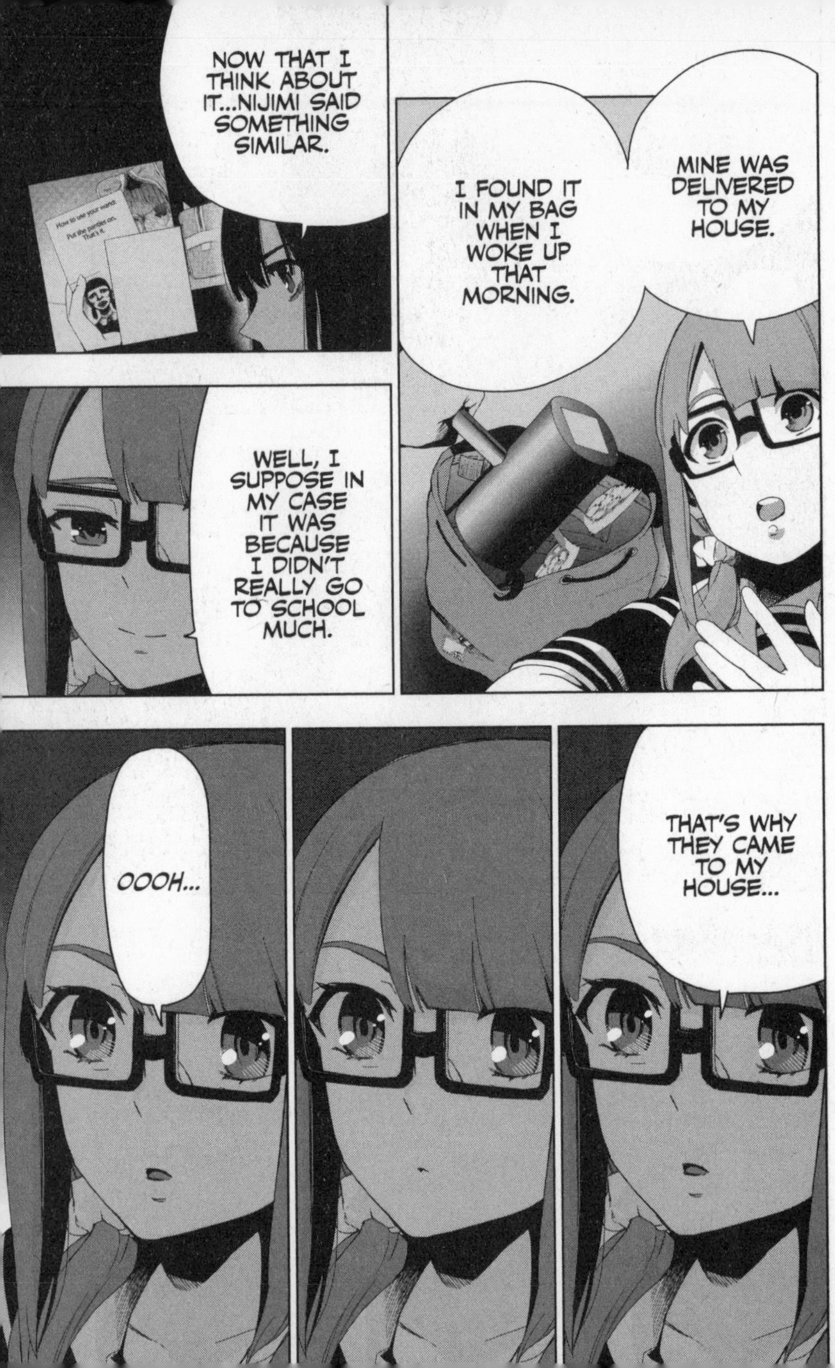
MINE WAS DELIVERED TO MY HOUSE.
I FOUND IT IN MY BAG WHEN I WOKE UP THAT MORNING.
NOW THAT I THINK ABOUT IT...NIJIMI SAID SOMETHING SIMILAR.
WELL, I SUPPOSE IN MY CASE IT WAS BECAUSE I DIDN'T REALLY GO TO SCHOOL MUCH.
THAT'S WHY THEY CAME TO MY HOUSE...
OOOH...

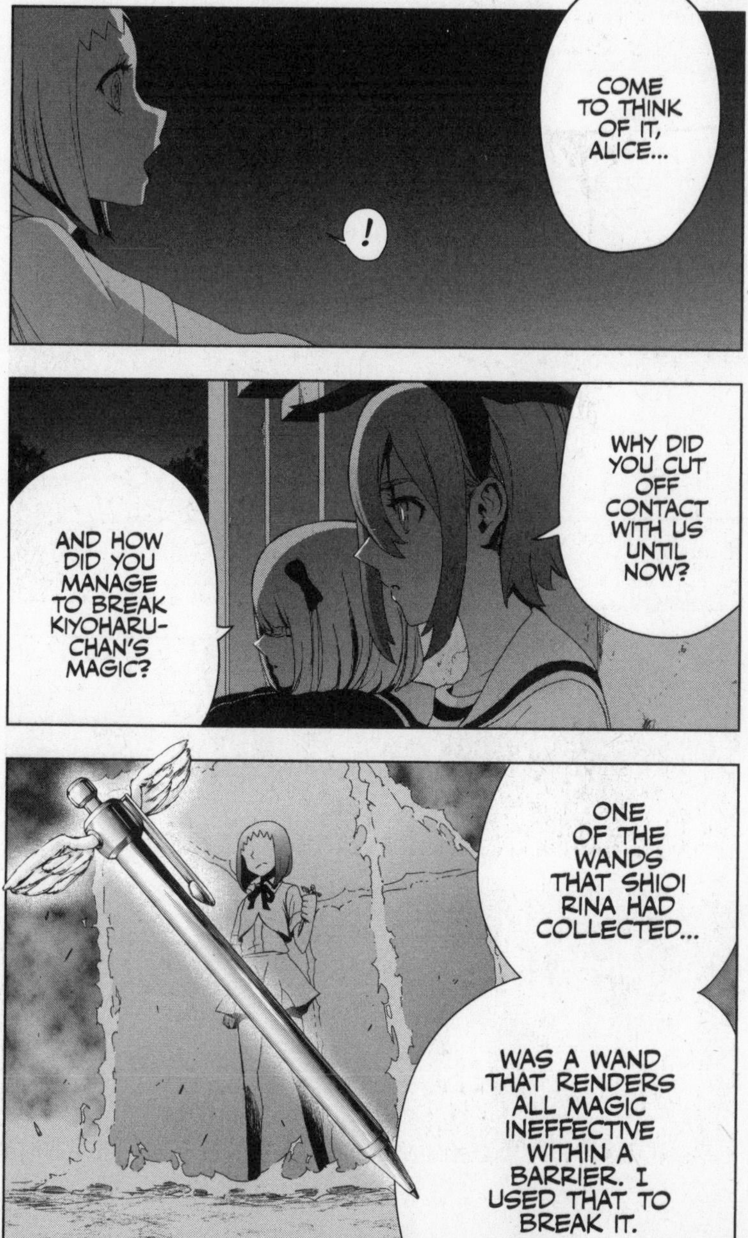
COME TO THINK OF IT, ALICE...
!
WHY DID YOU CUT OFF CONTACT WITH US UNTIL NOW?
AND HOW DID YOU MANAGE TO BREAK KIYOHARU-CHAN'S MAGIC?
ONE OF THE WANDS THAT SHIOI RINA HAD COLLECTED...
WAS A WAND THAT RENDERS ALL MAGIC INEFFECTIVE WITHIN A BARRIER. I USED THAT TO BREAK IT.

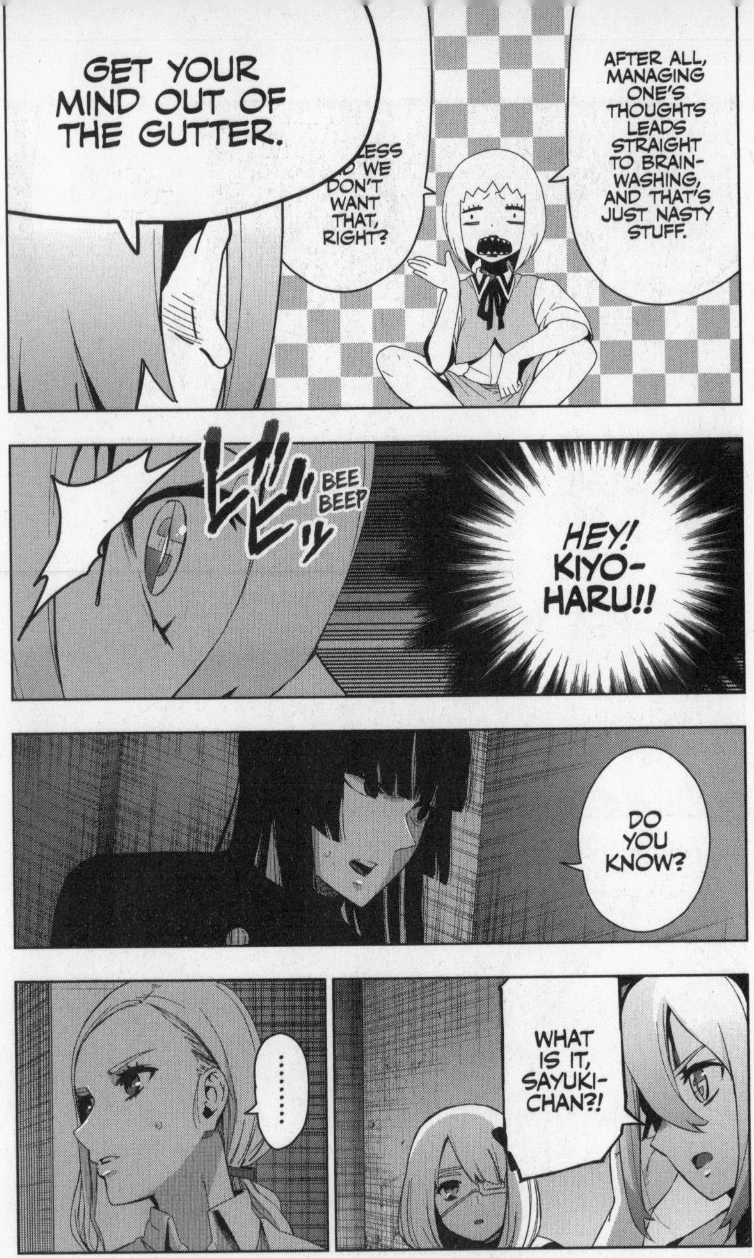
AFTER ALL, MANAGING ONE'S THOUGHTS LEADS STRAIGHT TO BRAIN-WASHING, AND THAT'S JUST NASTY STUFF.
LESS D WE DON'T WANT THAT, RIGHT?
GET YOUR MIND OUT OF THE GUTTER.
HEY! KIYO-HARU!!
ビビッ
BEE BEEP
DO YOU KNOW?
WHAT IS IT, SAYUKI-CHAN?!
....

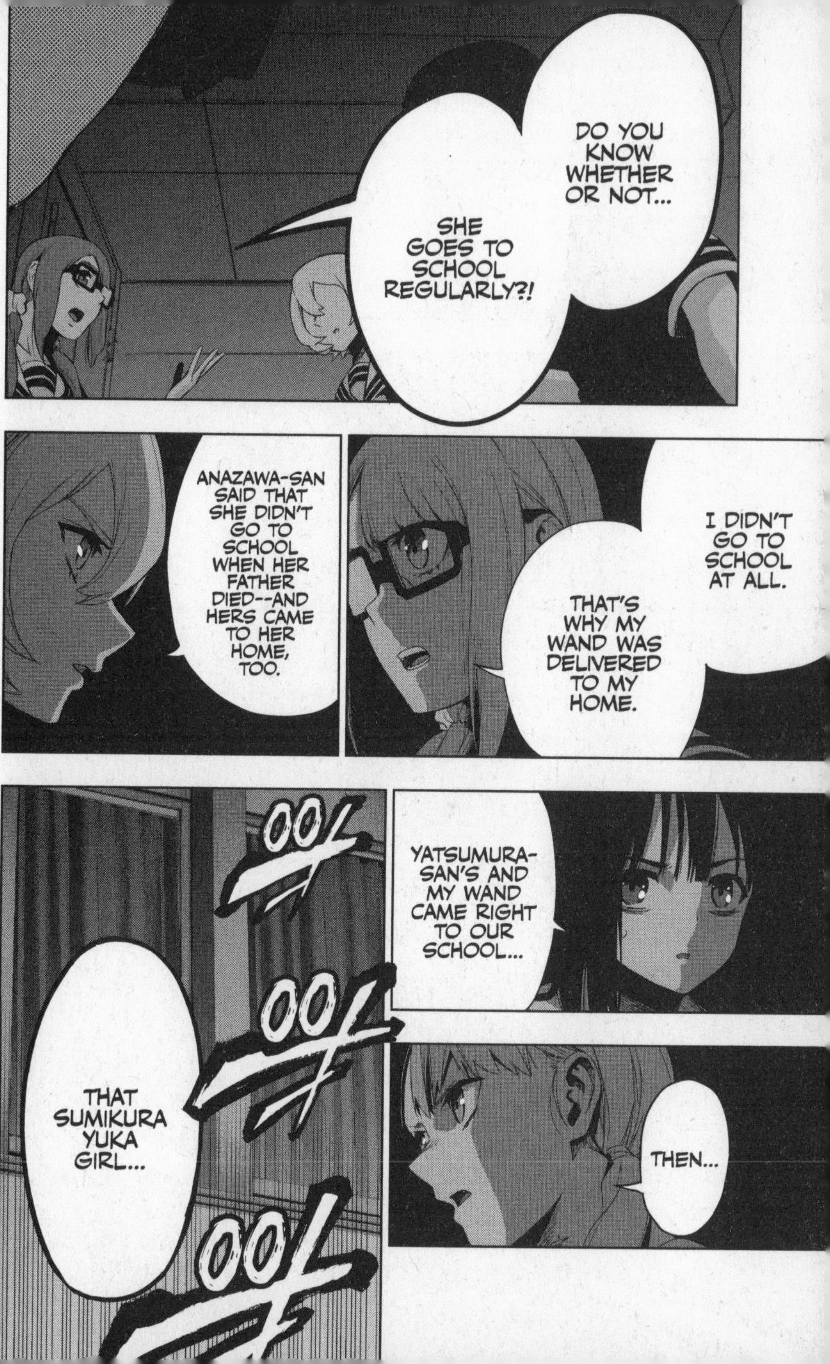
DO YOU KNOW WHETHER OR NOT...
SHE GOES TO SCHOOL REGULARLY?!
I DIDN'T GO TO SCHOOL AT ALL.
THAT'S WHY MY WAND WAS DELIVERED TO MY HOME.
ANAZAWA-SAN SAID THAT SHE DIDN'T GO TO SCHOOL WHEN HER FATHER DIED--AND HERS CAME TO HER HOME, TOO.
YATSUMURA-SAN'S AND MY WAND CAME RIGHT TO OUR SCHOOL...
THEN...
THAT SUMIKURA YUKA GIRL...

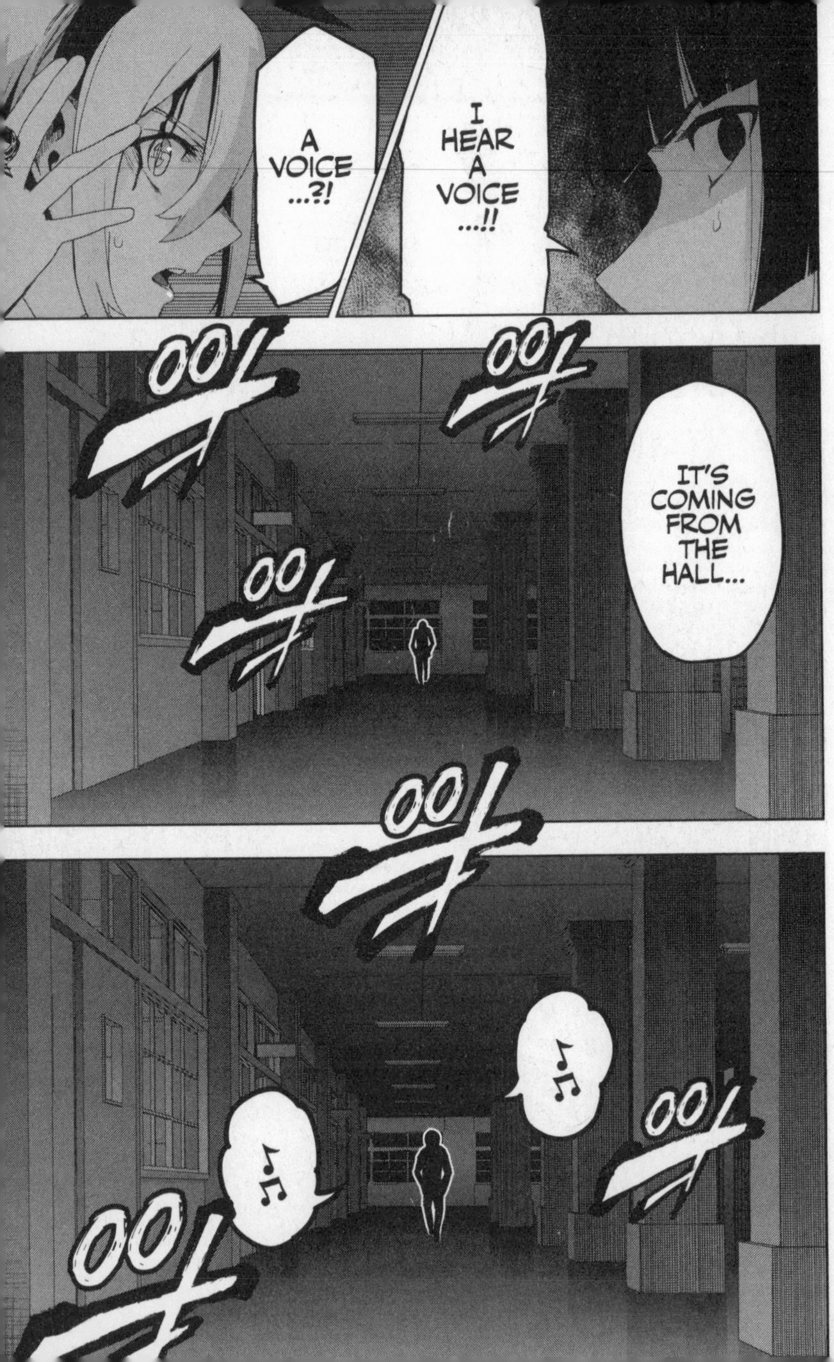
I HEAR A VOICE ...!!
A VOICE ...?!
IT'S COMING FROM THE HALL...

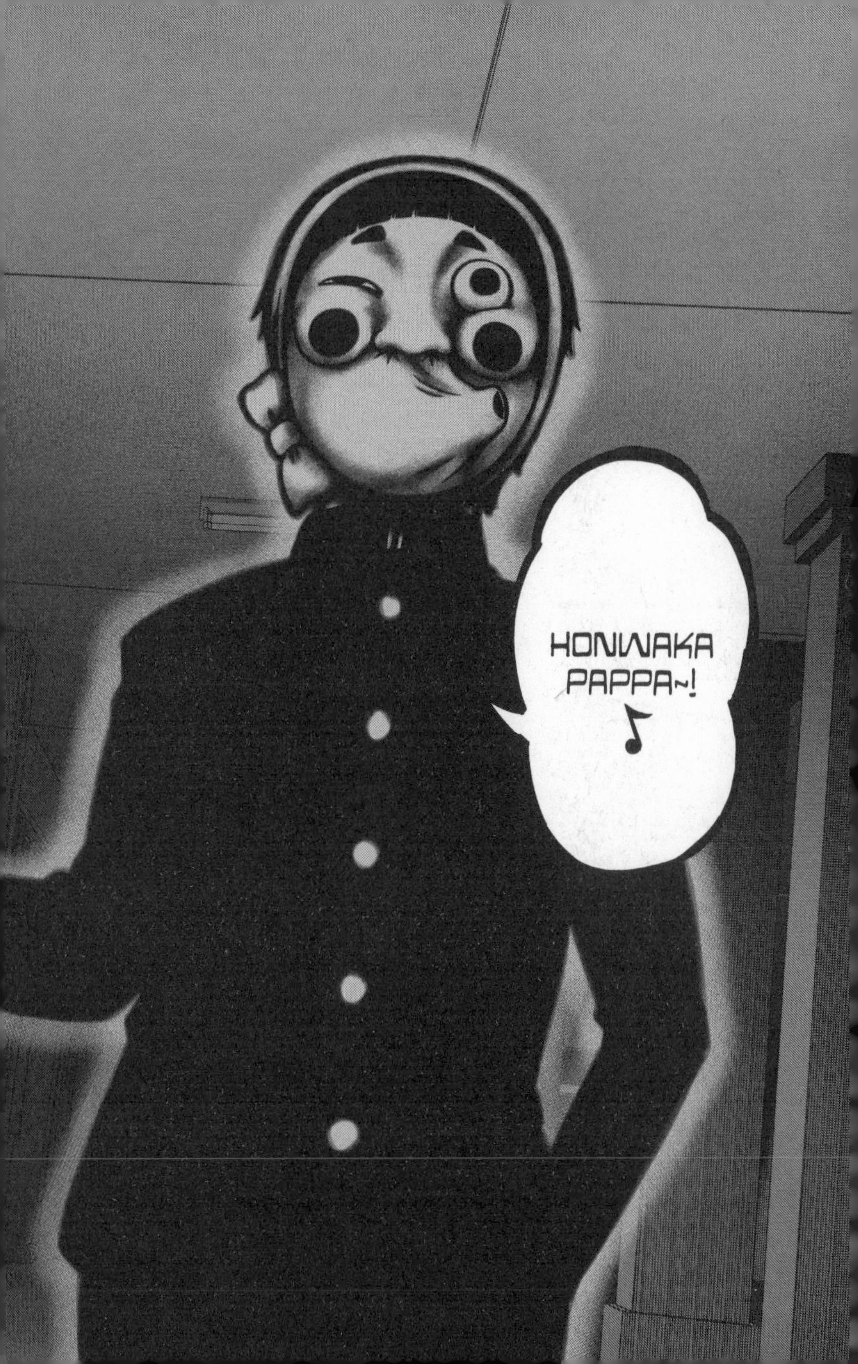
HONWAKA PAPPA~! ♪

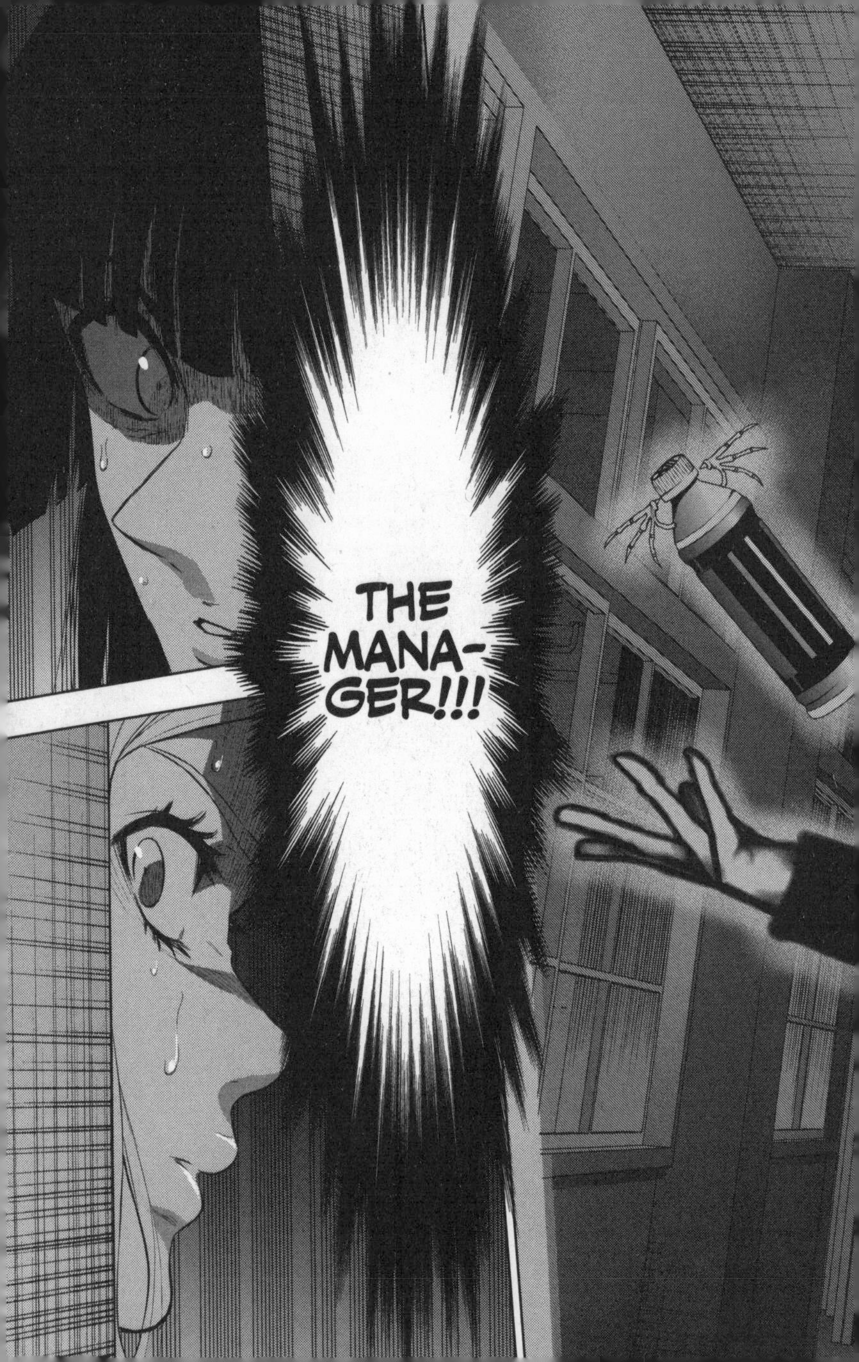
THE MANA-GER!!!

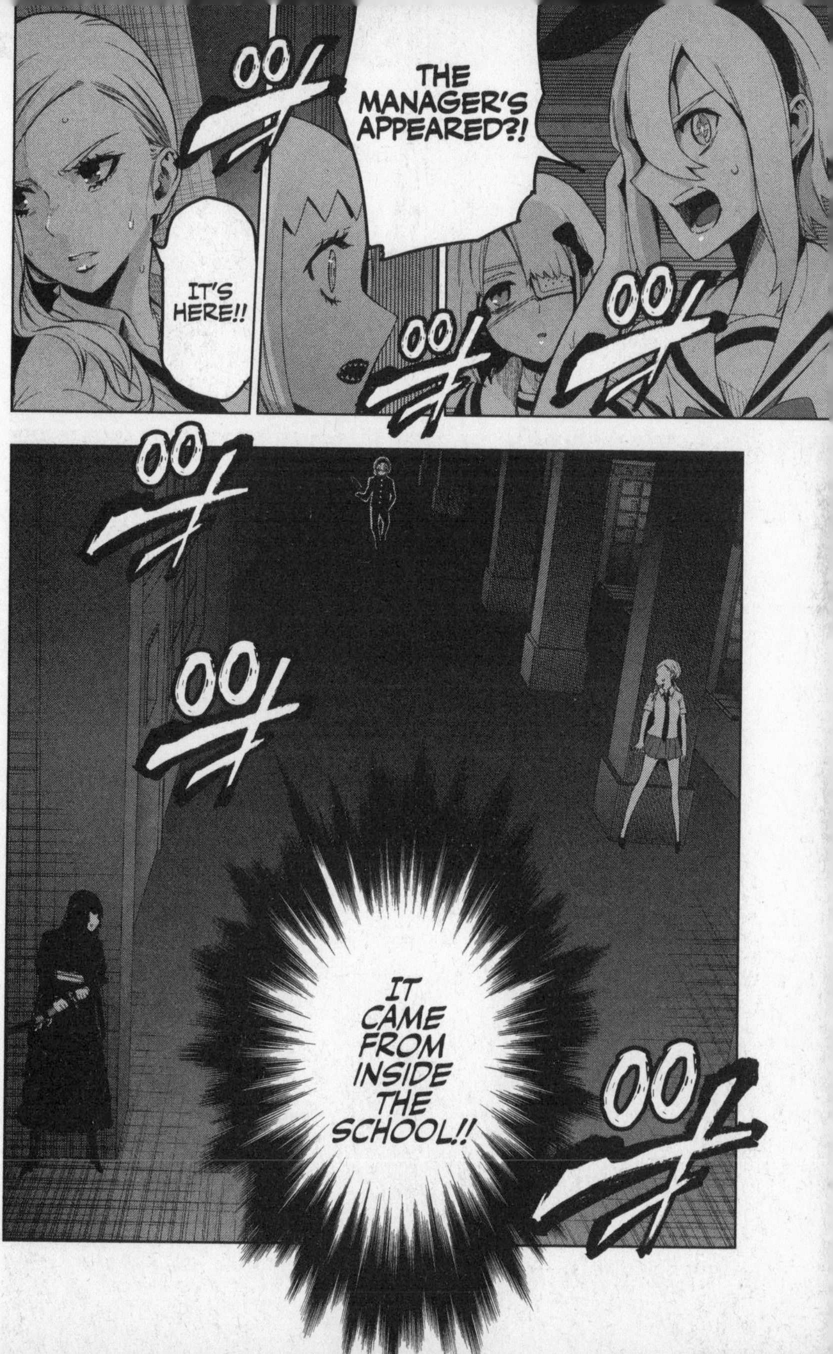
THE MANAGER'S APPEARED?!
IT'S HERE!!
IT CAME FROM INSIDE THE SCHOOL!!

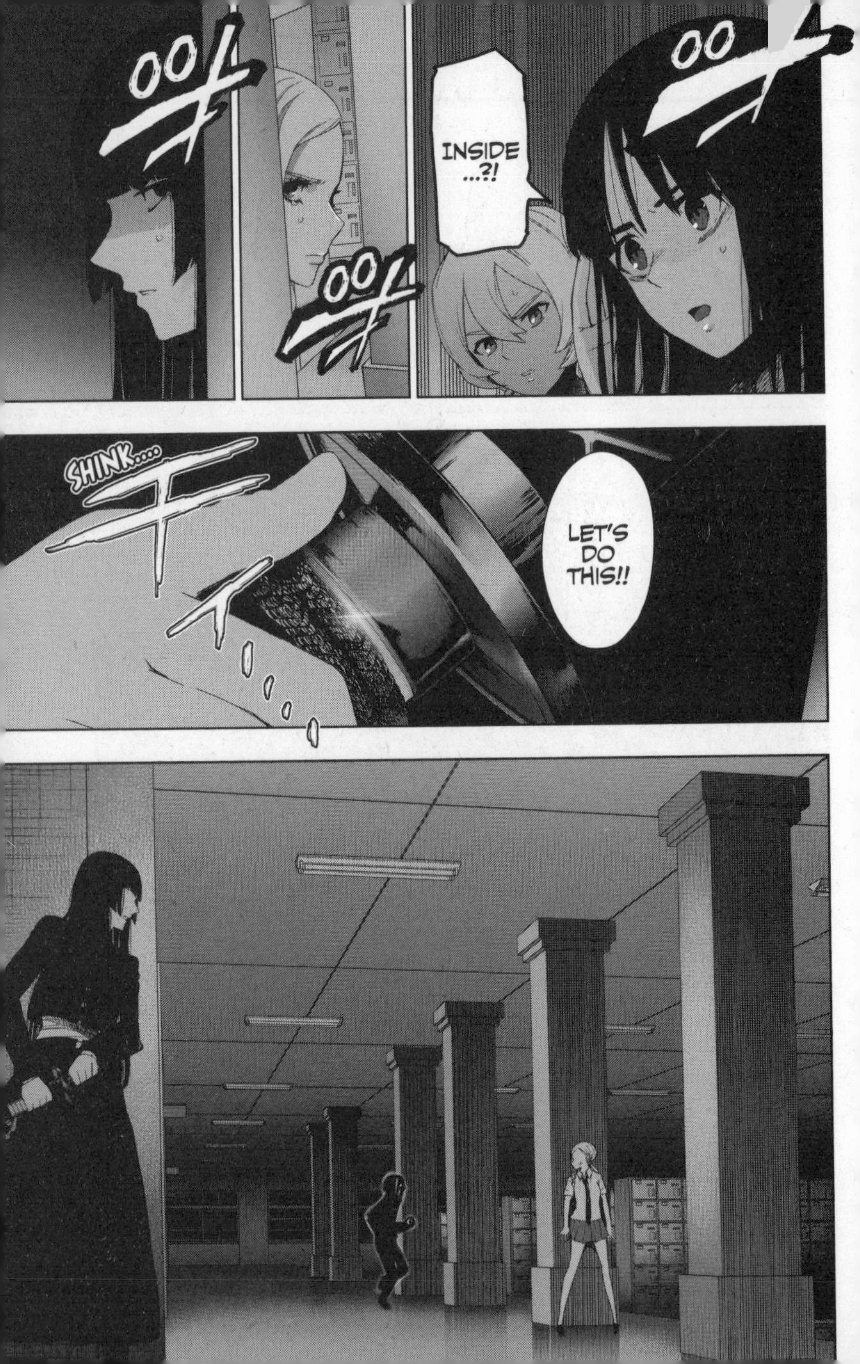
INSIDE ...?!
SHINK....
LET'S DO THIS!!

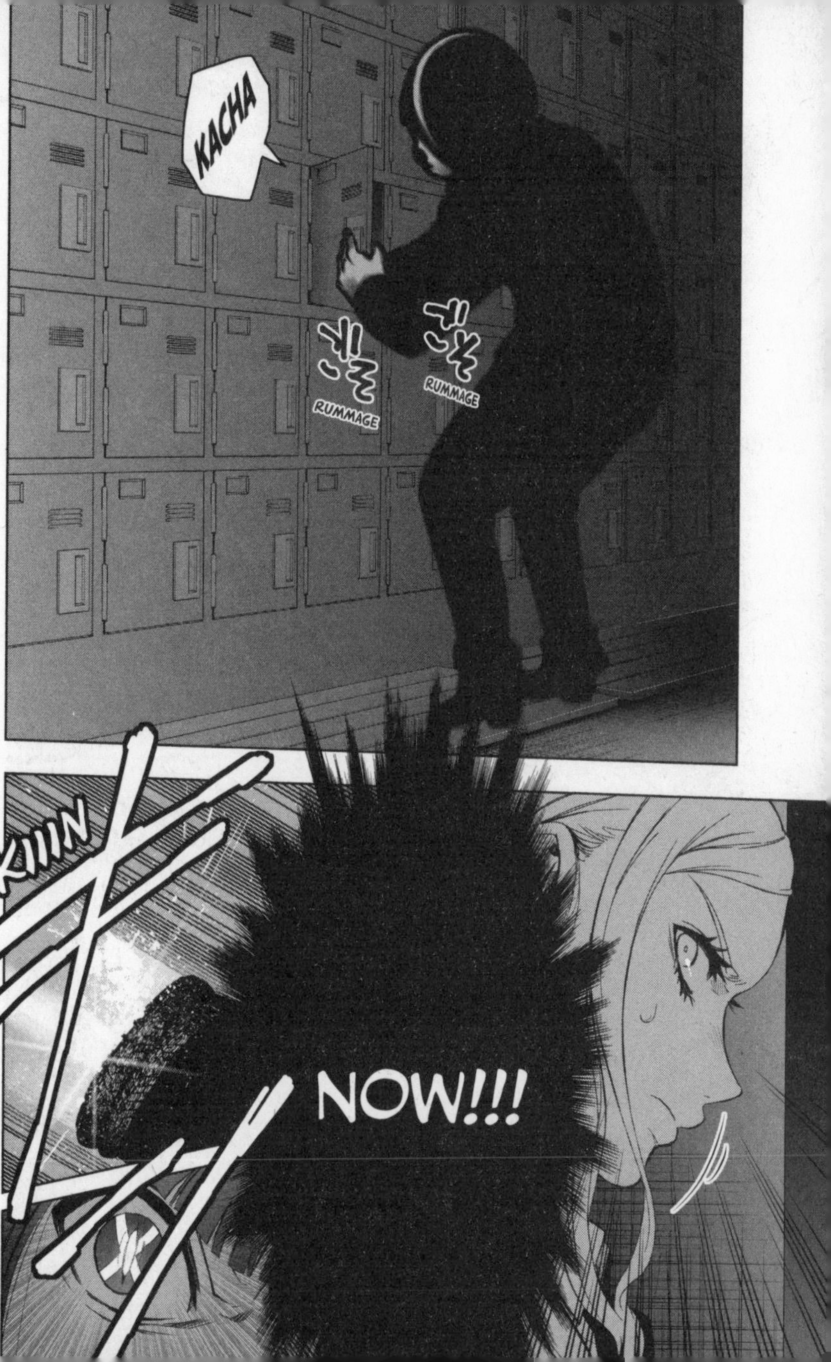
KACHA
RUMMAGE
RUMMAGE
NOW!!!
KIIIN

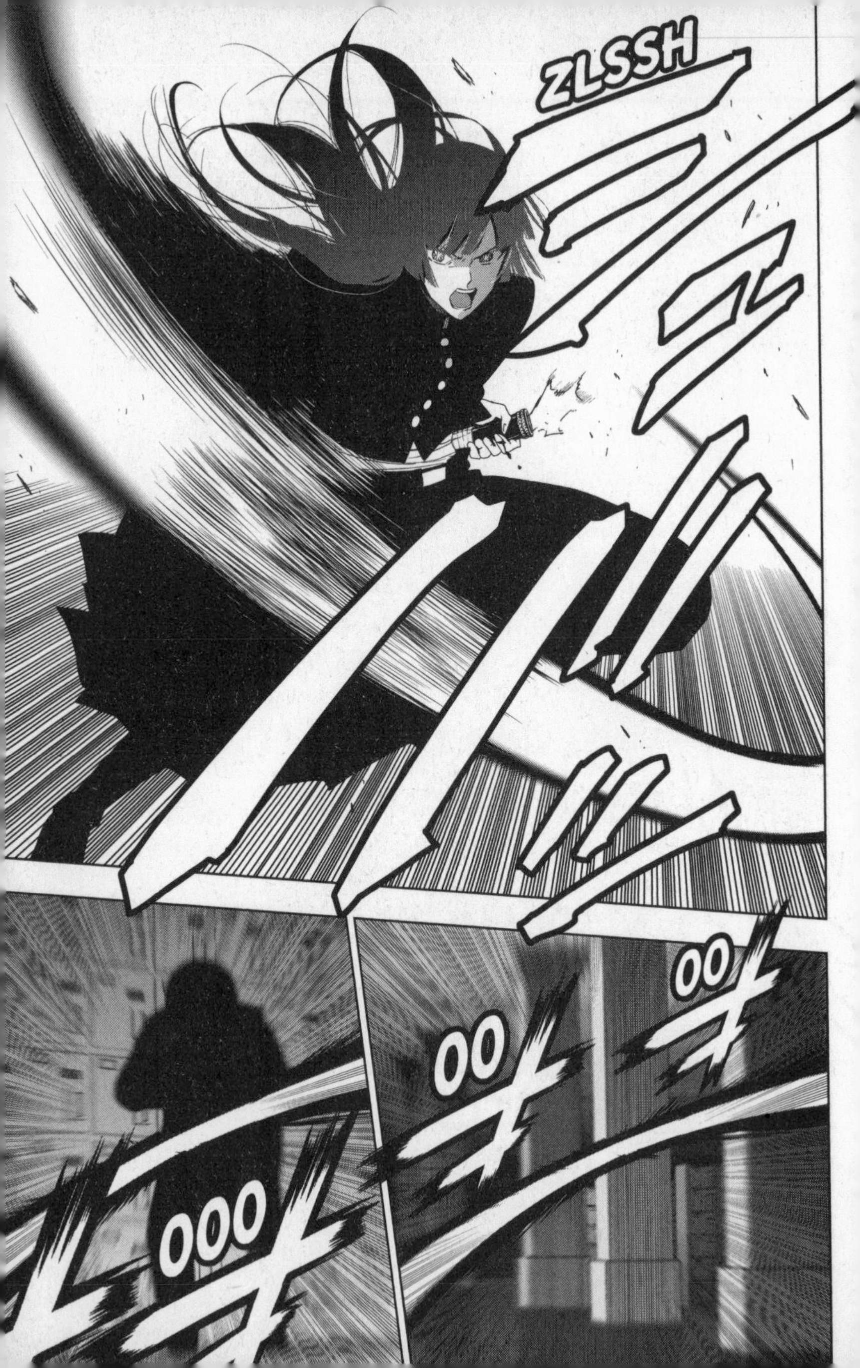
ZLSSH
OO
OO
OOO

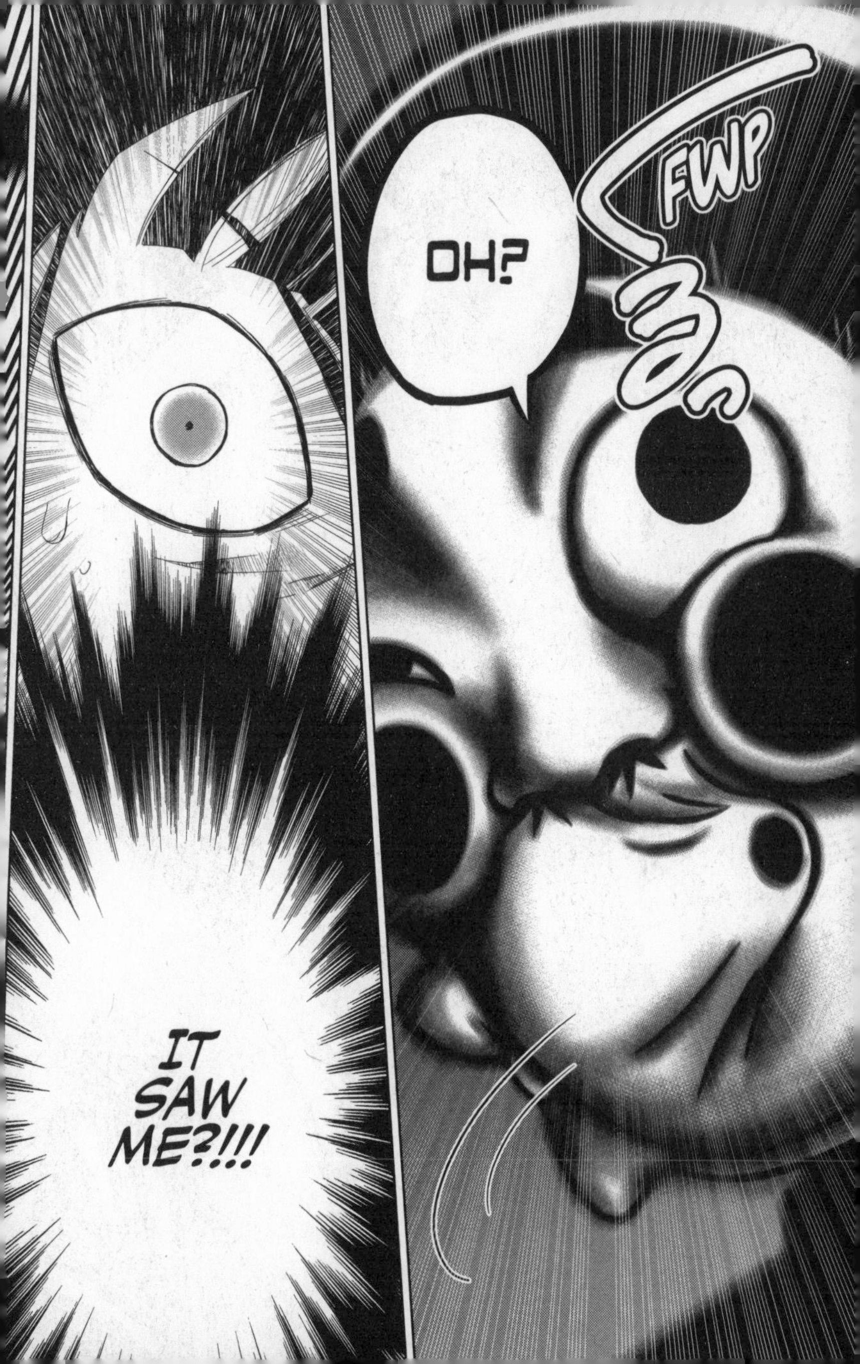
OH?
FWP
IT SAW ME?!!!

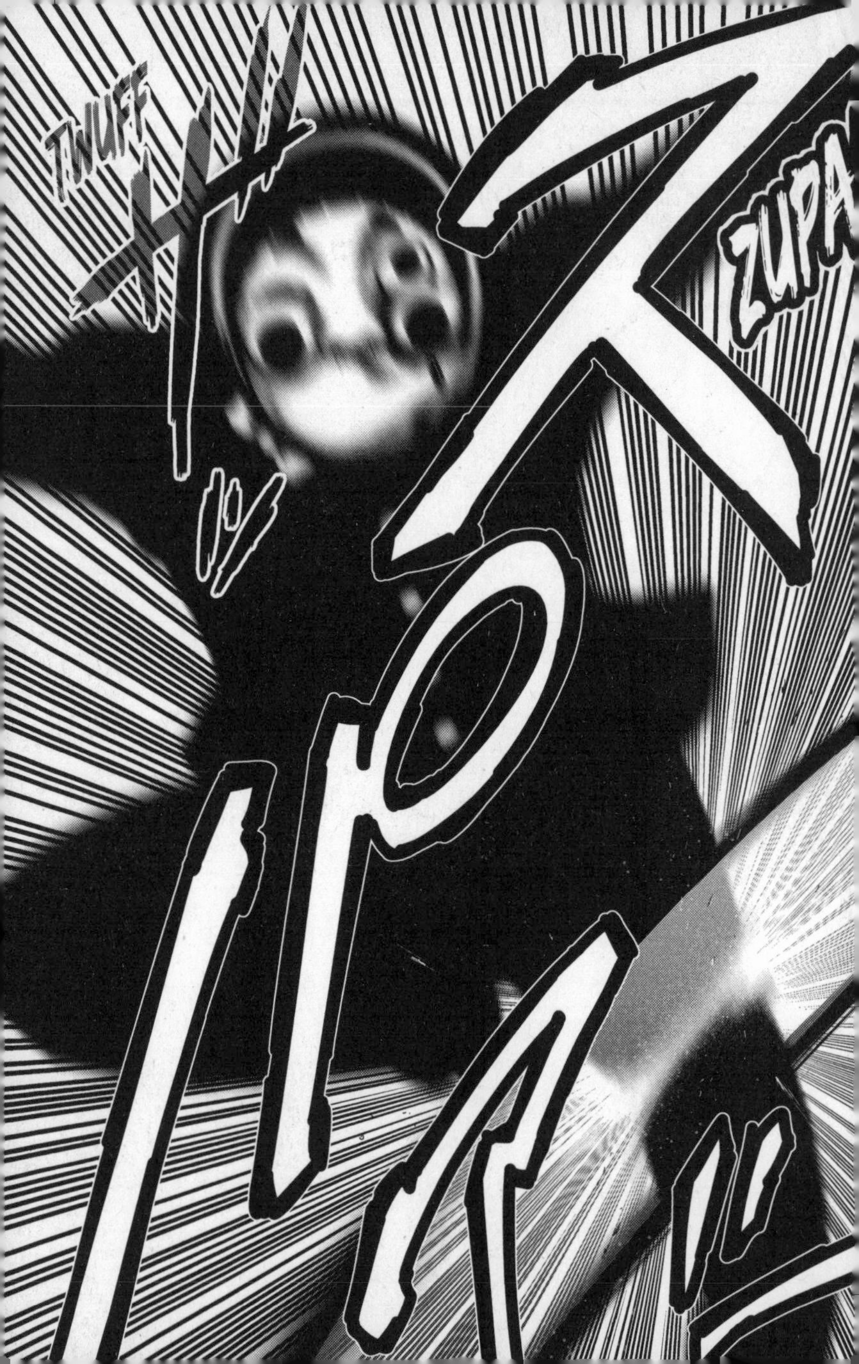
ZUPA
TWUFF

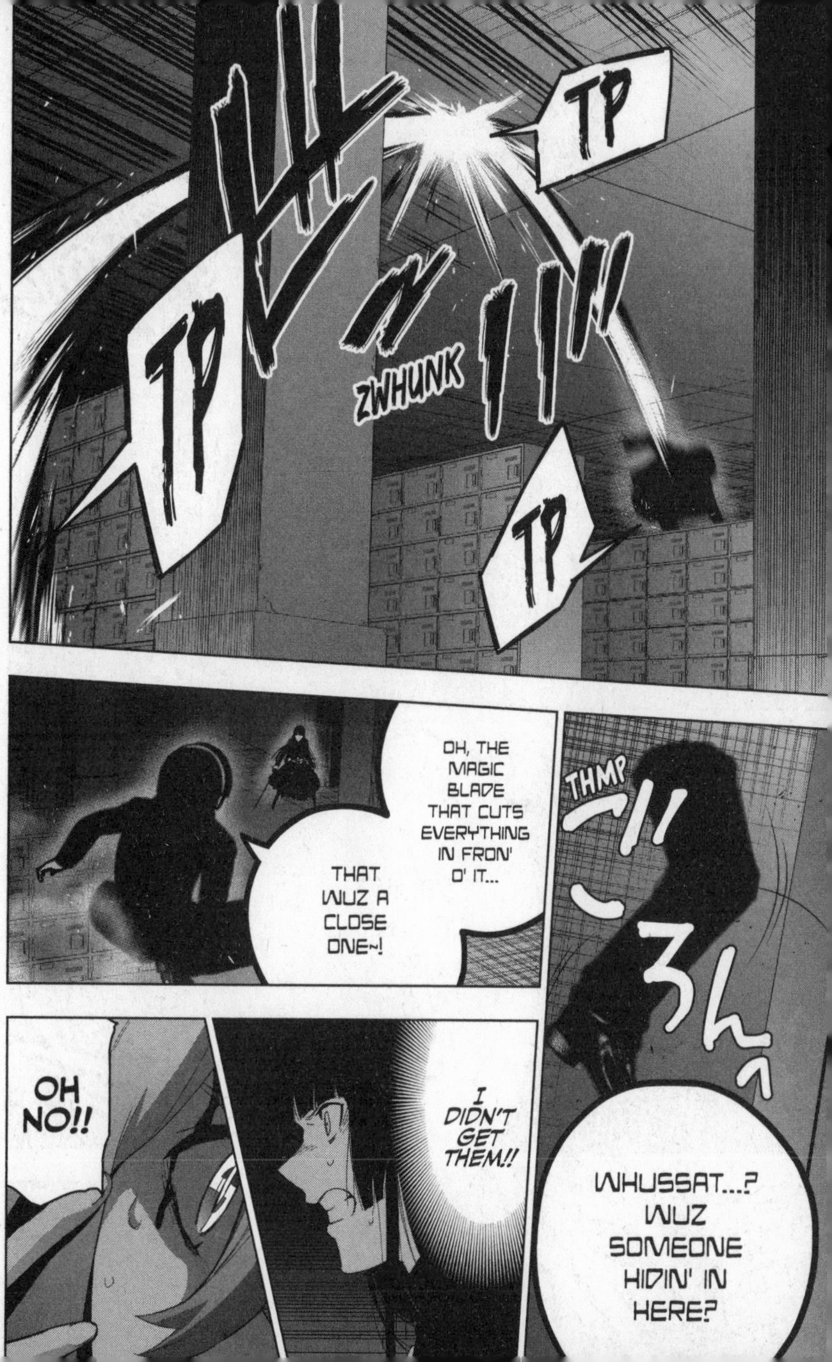
TP
TP
ZWHUNK
TP
THMP
WHUSSAT...? WUZ SOMEONE HIDIN' IN HERE?
OH, THE MAGIC BLADE THAT CUTS EVERYTHING IN FRON' O' IT...
THAT WUZ A CLOSE ONE~!
I DIDN'T GET THEM!!
OH NO!!

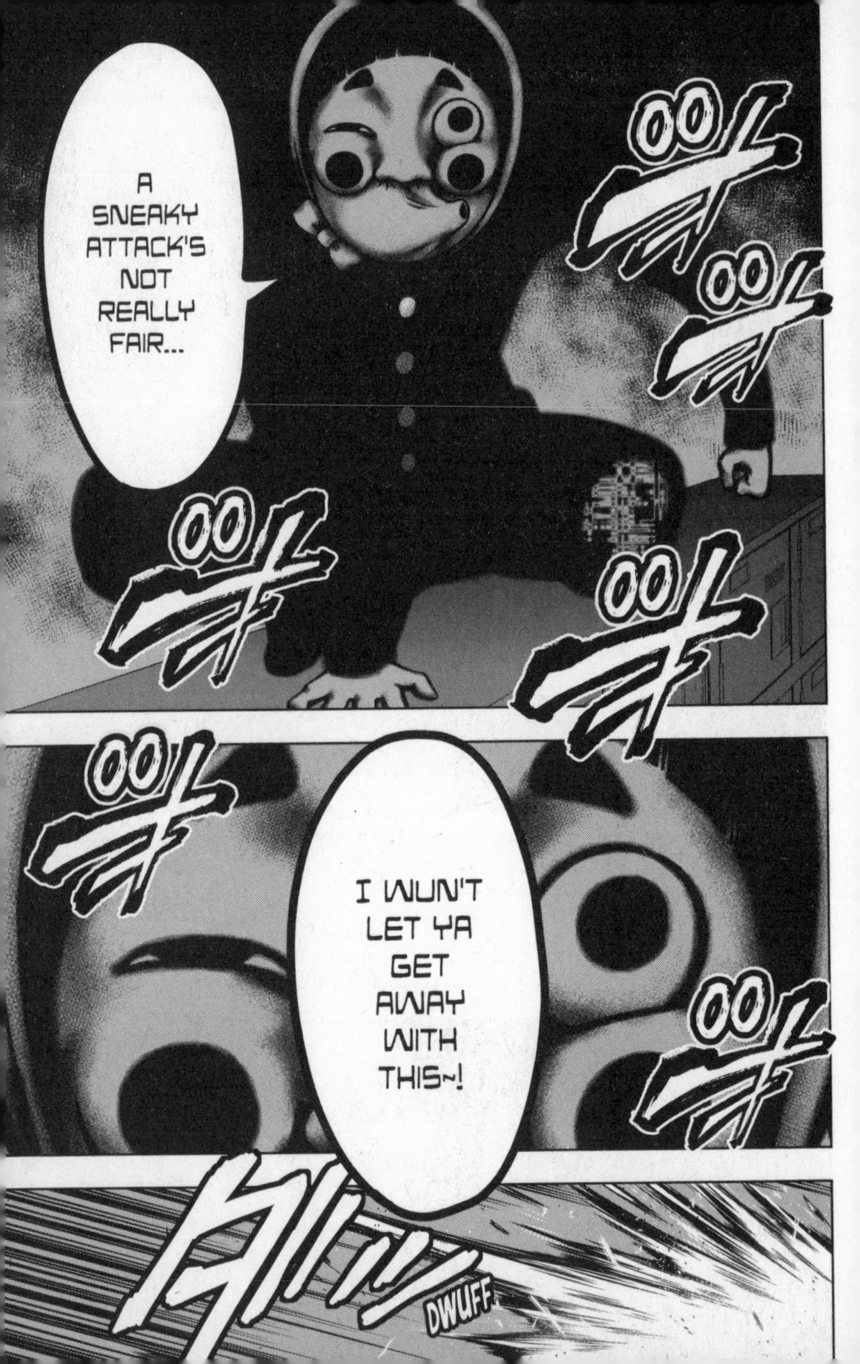
A SNEAKY ATTACK'S NOT REALLY FAIR...
I WUN'T LET YA GET AWAY WITH THIS~!
DWUFF

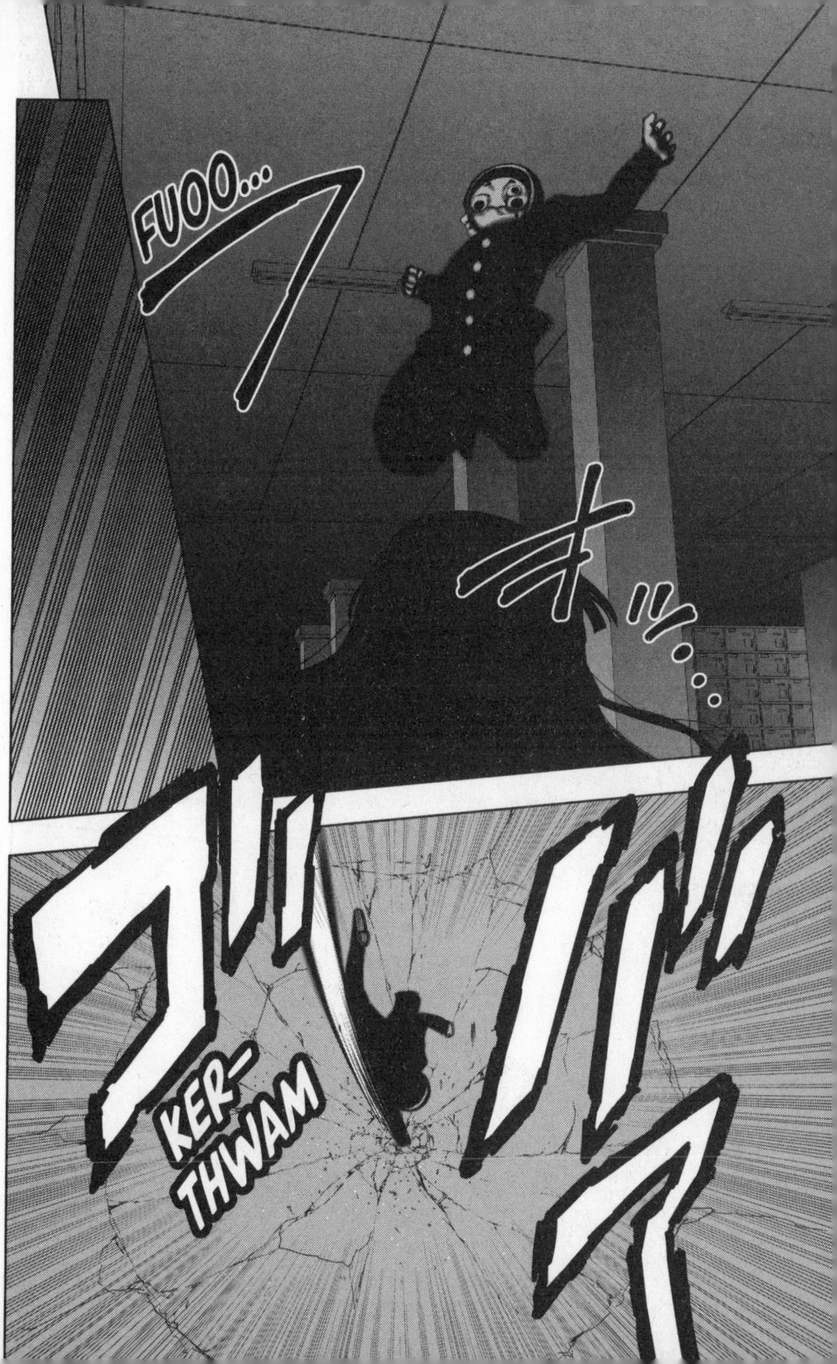
FUOO...
KER-
THWAM

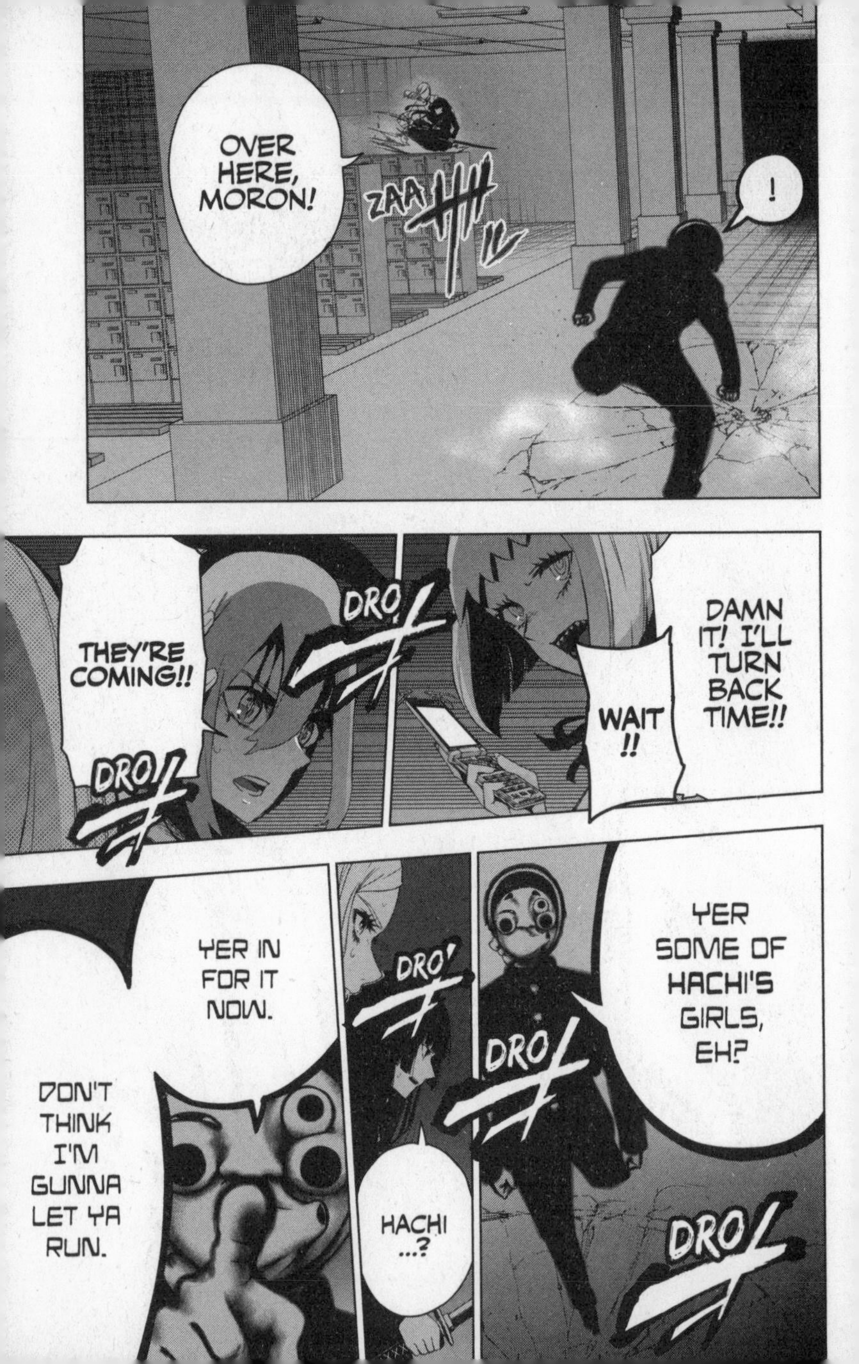
OVER HERE, MORON!
ZAA
!
DAMN IT! I'LL TURN BACK TIME!!
WAIT !!
DRO
THEY'RE COMING!!
DRO
YER SOME OF HACHI'S GIRLS, EH?
DRO
DRO
DRO
HACHI ...?
YER IN FOR IT NOW.
DON'T THINK I'M GUNNA LET YA RUN.

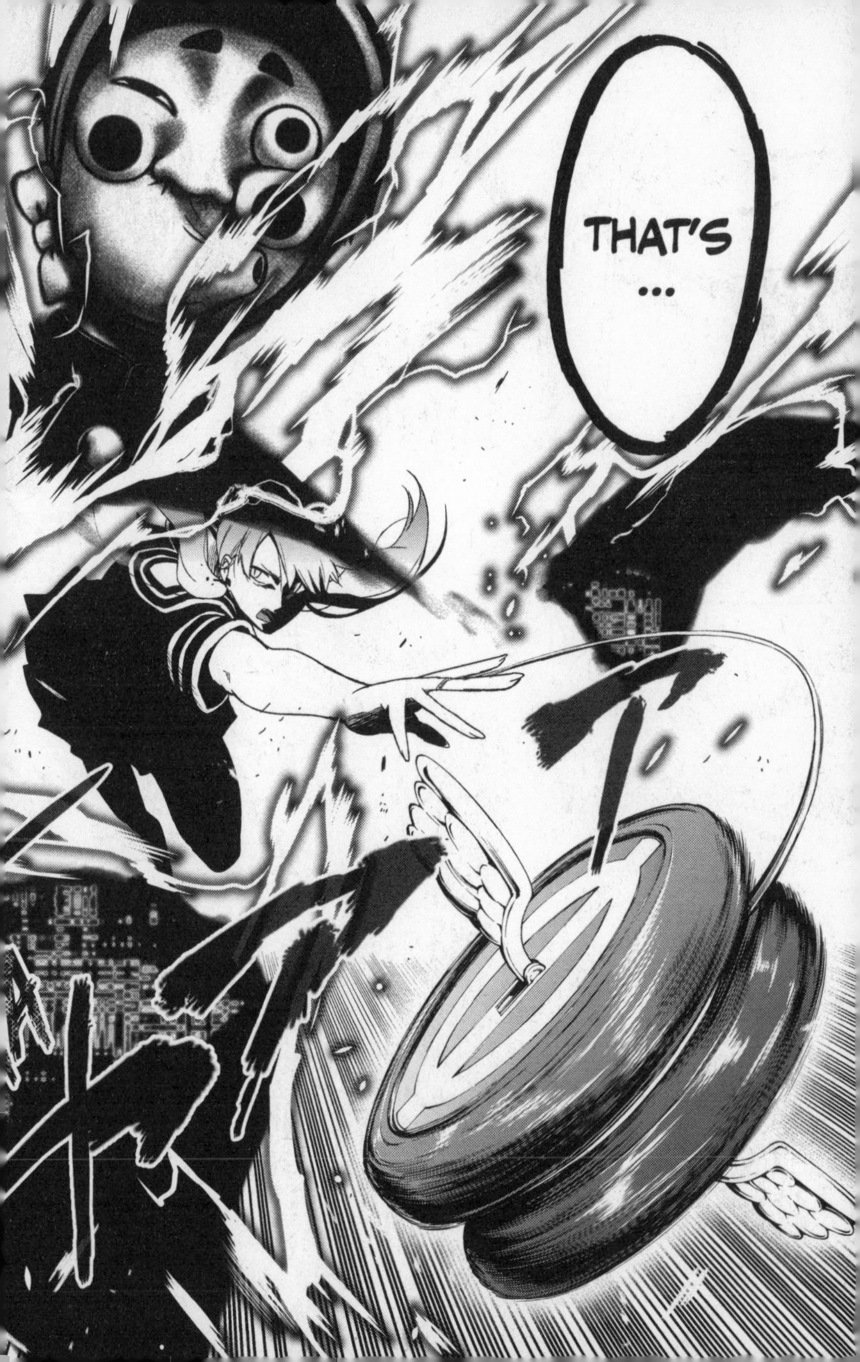
THAT'S ...

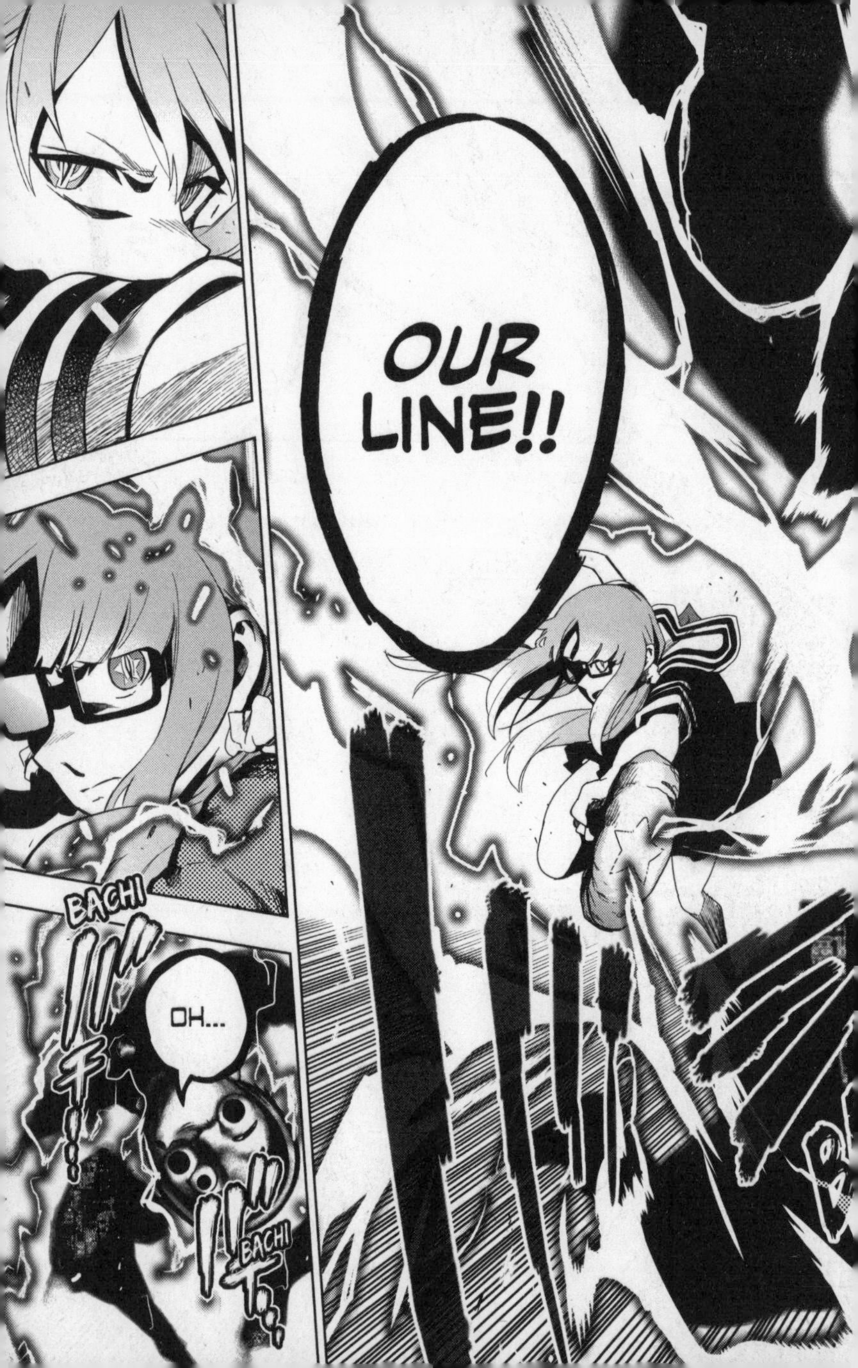
OUR LINE!!
BACHI
OH...
BACHI

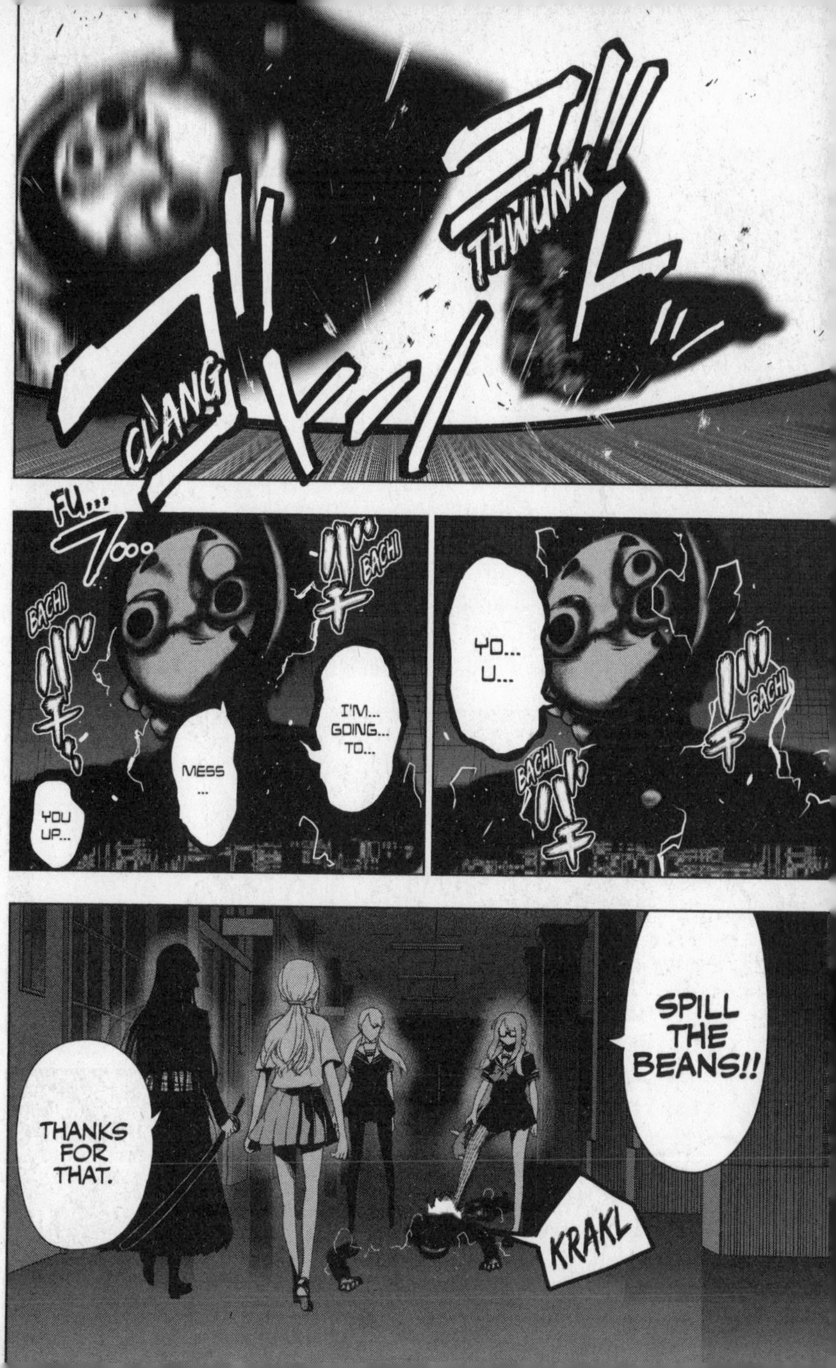
THWUNK
CLANG
BACHI
BACHI
YO... U...
FU...
BACHI
BACHI
I'M... GOING... TO...
MESS ...
YOU UP...
SPILL THE BEANS!!
KRAKL
THANKS FOR THAT.

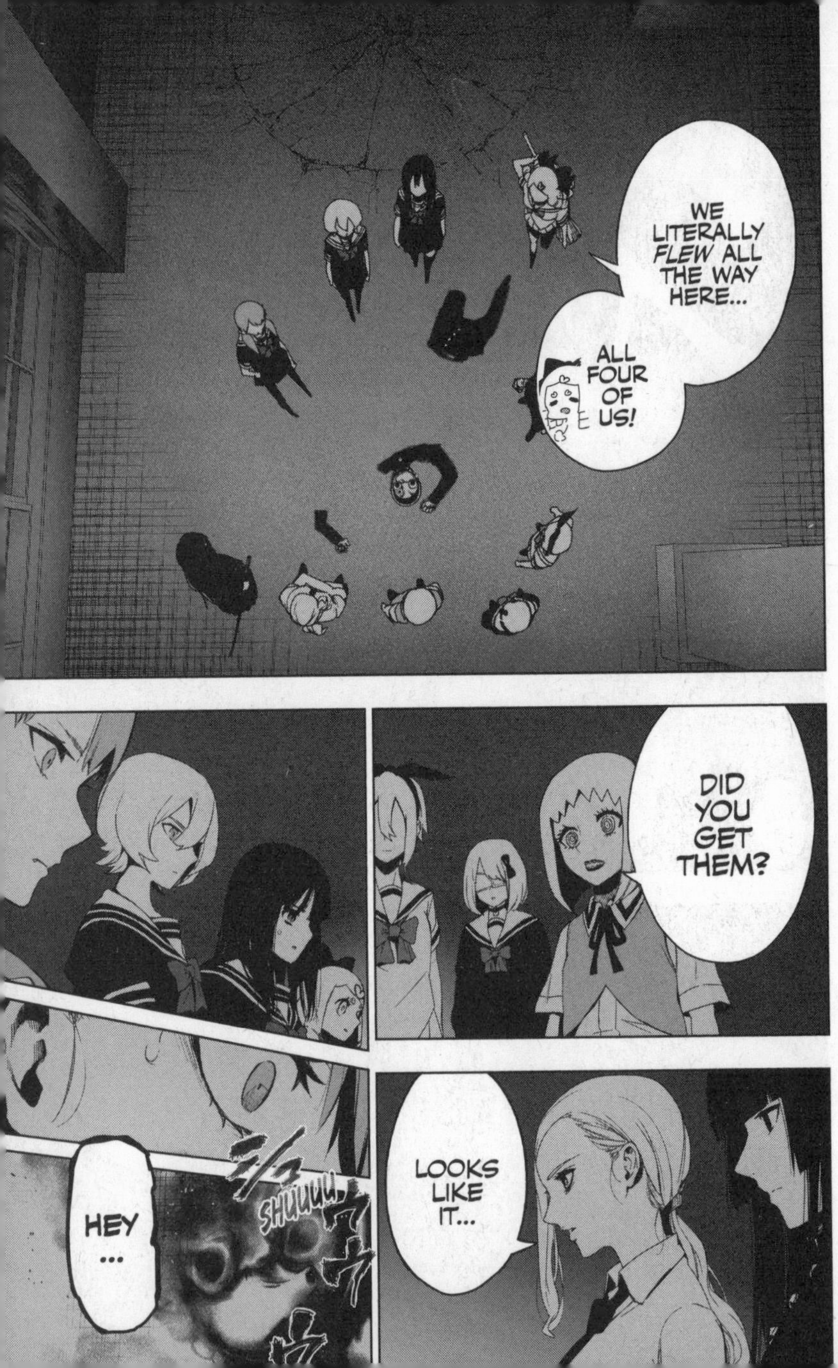
WE LITERALLY FLEW ALL THE WAY HERE...
ALL FOUR OF US!
DID YOU GET THEM?
LOOKS LIKE IT...
SHUUUU
HEY ...

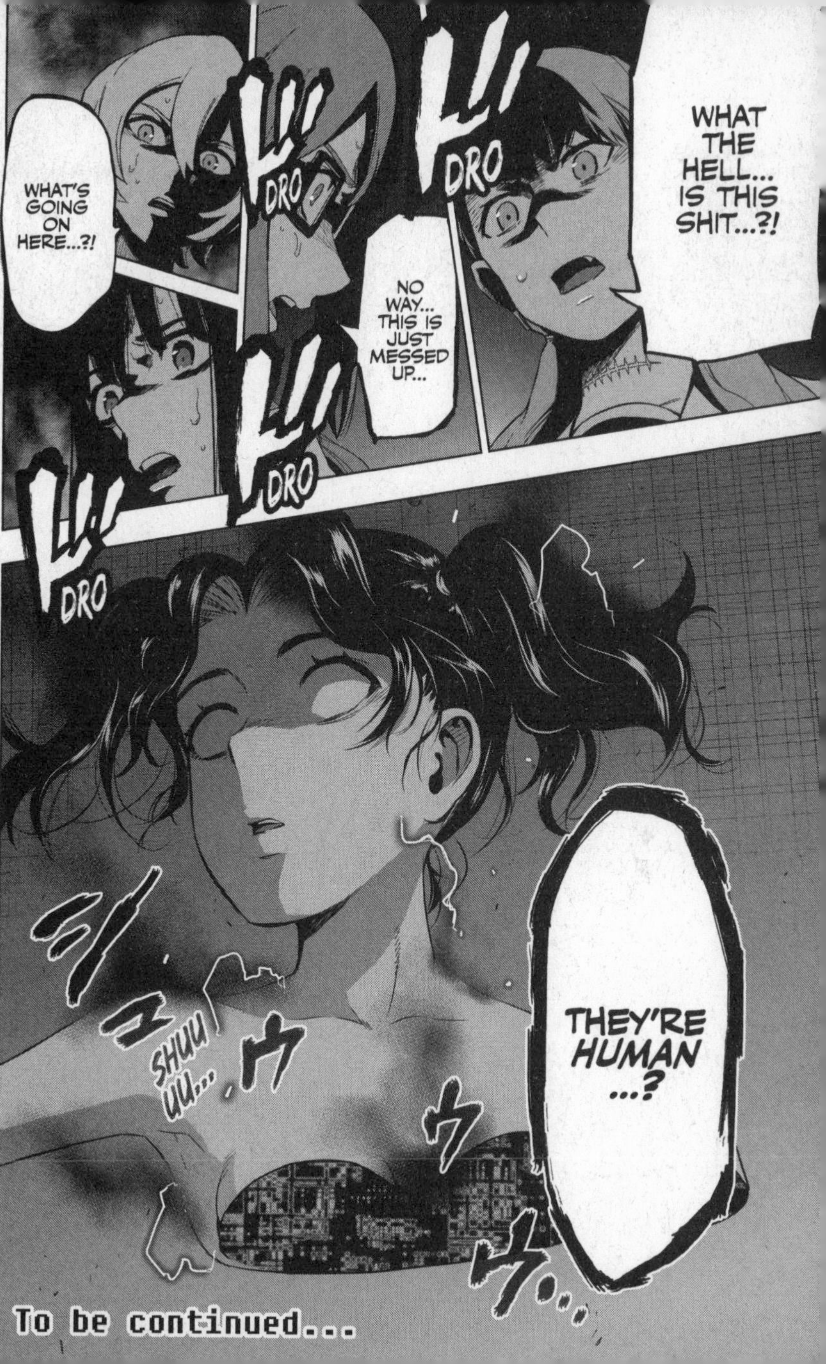

DRO
WHAT THE HELL... IS THIS SHIT...?!
DRO
NO WAY... THIS IS JUST MESSED UP...
DRO
WHAT'S GOING ON HERE...?!
DRO
THEY'RE HUMAN ...?
SHUU UU...
To be continued...

Loading . . . Please Wait

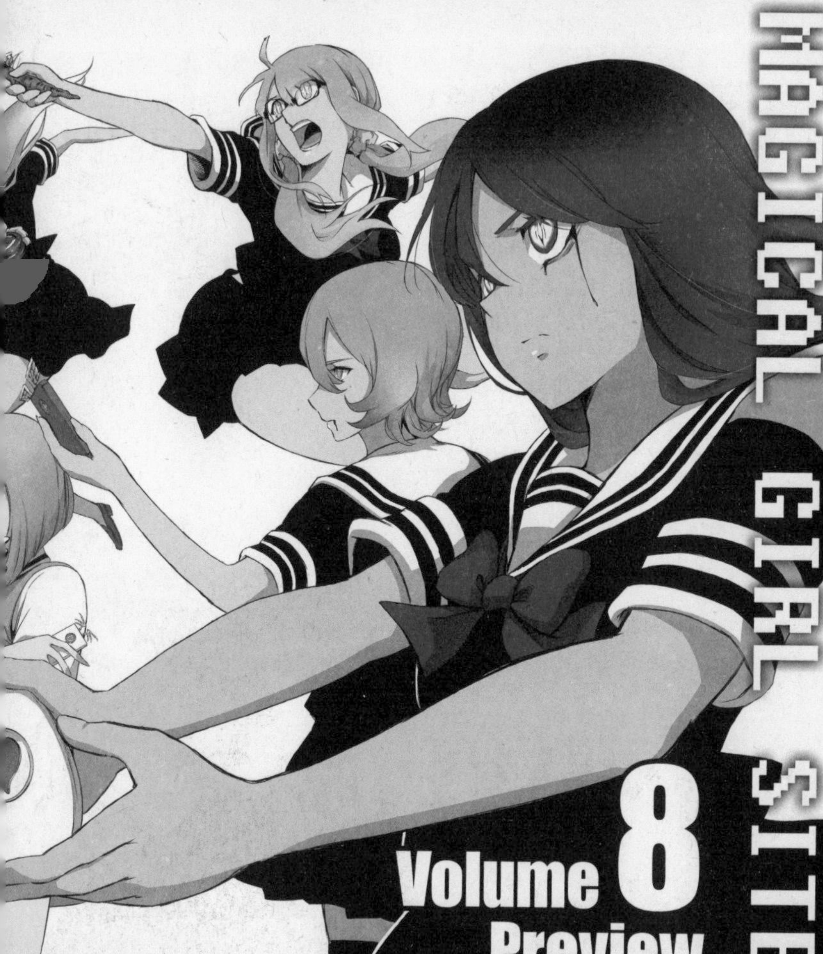
MAGICAL GIRL SITE
Volume 8
Preview

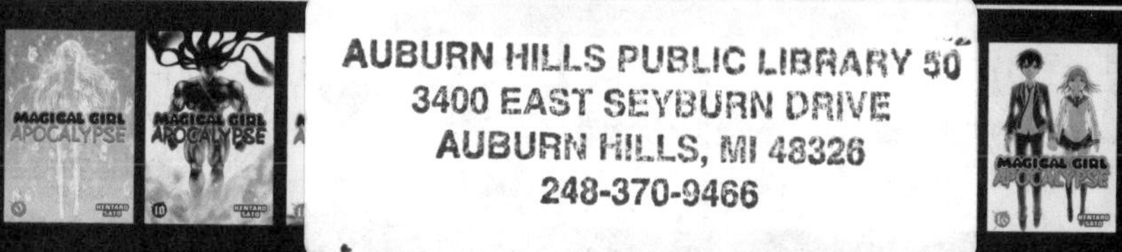
MAGICAL GIRL APOCALYPSE
MAGICAL GIRL APOCALYPSE
MAGICAL GIRL APOCALYPSE

Aya and her friends
manage to launch a
successful sneak attack
versus a manager!
But the defeated
manager's body
suddenly changed?!
Just who or what
are the managers?!
They declare a victory,
but unveil a new
mystery!

COMING SOON!

魔法少女サイト
MAGICAL GIRL SITE